RELIEF. W.ᵐ CASEDY MASTER.

JENNIE CLARK, J. MYRICK, MASTER.

F.S. HOLLAND

T. JOHNSON.

JACOB BOEHM.

J. C. GIBSON.

W.L. ADAMS

LOUIS BEHRENS.

CHARMAN & WARNER.

COURT HOUSE.

E.A. BARNES.

F. WILDE.

The early view of Oregon City on the reverse of this sheet could be dated ca 1850. A drawing of Dr. McLoughlin's home appears in the border on the left side.

Alberta Brooks Fogdall

Seal of the Hudson's Bay Company

ROYAL FAMILY OF THE COLUMBIA

Alberta Brooks Fogdall

End sheets courtesy McLoughlin House, Oregon City

ROYAL FAMILY
OF THE
COLUMBIA

Dr. JOHN McLOUGHLIN AND HIS FAMILY

ALBERTA BROOKS FOGDALL

YE GALLEON PRESS
Fairfield, Washington
1978

Library of Congress Cataloging in Publication Data

Fogdall, Alberta Brooks, 1912-
  Royal family of the Columbia.

  Bibliography: p.
  Includes index.
  1. McLoughin, John, 1784-1857. 2. Pioneers—Northwest, Pacific—Bio-
graphy. 3. Merchants—Northwest, Pacific—Biography. 4. Hudson's Bay
Company. 5. Oregon—History—To 1859. 6. Northwest, Pacific—History.
7. Fur trade—Northwest, Pacific—History. I. Title.
F880.M17F63   1978   979.5'03'0924   [B]   78-17170
ISBN 0-87770-168-7

FOR CAROL

ERRATA

Pages 2 and 190 Photograph of the author by Harrison Hornish
Page 8 Wm Cogswall should be William Cogswell
Page 44 Delete "Oregon Historical Society Archives"
Pages 162, 175 Delete "extra" lines of credit & identification
All pictures on pages 163, 244, 309, courtesy of Oregon Historical Society
All sketches on pages 18, 28, 64, 310, courtesy of *The Beaver*
On page 46 — Courtesy of *The Beaver*, not *The Banner*
On page 7 (Contents): Illustrations appear also on pages 8, 10, 16, 18, 28, 46, 64, 134, 190, 204, 244, 270, 282, 302, 309, 310, 316
Genealogy chart on pages 26-27
Map on pages 44-45

CONTENTS   PAGE

Portrait of John McLoughlin
by Wm. Cogswall
from living room of McLoughlin House.

ACKNOWLEDGEMENTS

I gratefully acknowledge the assistance of the library staff of the Oregon Historical Society, whose personnel has been most helpful; of the California Historical Society, Mr. Jay Williar, reference librarian; also of the staffs of the library of the University of Washington, particularly of the Northwest Collection archives; of the Seattle Public Library; of the central branch of the Multnomah County Public Library, Portland; of the Clackamas County Public Library, Lake Oswego branch; of the Aubrey Watzek Library of Lewis and Clark College, Portland; and, most of all, of the Provincial Archives, Victoria British Columbia.

Most helpful also were (Mrs.) Margaret Keillor, reference archivist of the State of Oregon; the historians, rangers, and other personnel of the Fort Vancouver Visitors Center.

In Oregon City, to past and present curators of McLoughlin House: Mrs. Charles (Nancy) Gildea, Miss Isabel Vanlaningham, Wayne Randolph, and Bill Macrostie; to Wilmer Gardner of the Board of the McLoughlin Memorial Association.

To Mrs. Simeon Reed (Mary Tobin) Winch, to Mrs. Gilbert (Rhoda) McKay, and, especially to Thomas M. Whidden, who were most helpful in giving information about various branches of McLoughlin descendants.

To Glen C. Adams of Ye Galleon Press for his advice and guidance; to Harrison Hornish, photographer and friend.

Most of all to my husband, Vergil S. Fogdall, for his designing the photograph and other special features; whose support and understanding have been all-important, and who might very well have justifiably borrowed the expression "Writing a book excuses everything."

Oldest Apple Tree in the Pacific Northwest.

Royal Family of the Columbia

PREFACE

Countless histories and biographies, even books of "historical" fiction, have been written concerning the greatness of John McLoughlin and his contributions to the Oregon Country, to the United States itself. Some of his partisans go so far as to claim that he, more than any one other individual, "saved the Oregon Country for America." Most historians have written of McLoughlin the Chief Factor, rather than of McLoughlin the husband and father; of McLoughlin the head of a business, not of McLoughlin the head of a family. McLoughlin the man was an extremely human and humane being, a man with faults and virtues, an individual hated by some, loved by many.

One of the many interesting by-products of researching a controversial subject such as John McLoughlin is the realization, already familiar to historiographers, that no two historians interpret a subject or an individual in exactly the same way. This difference, sometimes even polarization, in viewpoint is illustrated repeatedly for the reader. Divergence can be attributed to at least two factors: 1. little or very poor research, *i.e.,* carelessness, and 2. differing social attitudes which combine to form an all-important determinant in making interpretations. By "social attitudes" is meant the period of time in which the author lived, his/her age, political affiliation, sex, socio-economic status, nationality, sectionalism, and profession or occupation. Another determinant is accessibility to archival materials, a condition which is not static, since archives that are closed one year may be open the next, making their materials available for use.

The following examples might be considered illustrative of social attitudes and their effect: An elderly man would conceivably view "women's lib" differently than a young woman would do; a person of wealth and social status would have a different attitude toward strikes than a laborer struggling to make ends meet; a Democrat usually interprets differently than a Republican; a Caucasian plantation owner in 1850 regarded slavery differently than a Negro slave; a pioneer settler in the Northwest c. 1840 and a New Englander of that period saw political and economic issues in opposite lights, and so on, with various combinations of attitudes. Unfortunately, "inconsistencies" are often the result of careless or insufficient research, due to haste to "get the book done."

11

Using John McLoughlin as a relevant subject, an even superficial reading of several texts shows that:

I

A. Dr. McLoughlin's father died when he (the son) was a young boy.

B. The father died in 1813. (The son was at that time twenty-nine years old.)

II

A. John McLoughlin was "banished" to the Columbia District as punishment for taking too strong a stand for increased wages for the Company's "servants" (voyageurs). The London officials wanted him kept at a distance—in a remote spot.

B. He was sent to the Columbia as a sign of recognition of his executive ability and initiative shown in the Northwest Company. This was the largest and most important of all the Company districts. He felt honored to accept this challenge.

III

A. Doctor John McLoughlin studied medicine in Scotland.

B. He studied medicine in Canada. (His brother, Dr. David, studied in both Canada and Scotland.)

IV

A. The Doctor's family accompanied him to the Columbia in 1824.

B. The family trailed the Chief Factor's party in a canoe caravan, but did *not* travel with him and his party.

C. The family came out in 1825, 1826, or 1827 when Dr. McLoughlin sent for them.

V

A. Mrs. McLoughlin was one-fourth Indian, being the daughter of a white man (Swiss Étienne Wadin) and his half-breed wife, Marie-Josèphe Déguire.

B. She was one-half Indian, the daughter of Wadin and a Cree Indian woman with whom he lived while in the Red River Country.

C. Her maiden name was Bruce, not Wadin; her father was Scottish, rather than Swiss.

Royal Family of the Columbia

VI

A. Mrs. McLoughlin had been a widow for several months following the murder of her husband on the *Tonquin* in 1811 before she and Dr. McLoughlin were married.

B. The McKay marriage was an informal union and Alexander McKay had abandoned her when he left for Astoria; Mrs. McKay and Dr. McLoughlin lived together for some time before the news of McKay's death came to them at Sault Ste. Marie. After the news reached them they contracted a marriage recognized as legal by the Hudson's Bay Company.

VII

A. John McLoughlin Jr. was brought into the Company by Governor George Simpson against his father's wishes.

B. Dr. McLoughlin brought his son into the Honourable Company even though he might be accused of nepotism.

VIII

A. Governor Simpson sent John to Stikine.

B. Chief Factor McLoughlin sent John to Stikine.

IX

A. Governor Simpson sent McLoughlin's son-in-law William Glen Rae to Yerba Buena.

B. McLoughlin sent Rae to Yerba Buena; again, nepotism?

X

A. Mrs. McLoughlin was relatively well educated; she had attended the Ursuline Convent in Québec where Marie-Louise McLoughlin had been a student, and, later, as sister St. Henry, a teacher and Mother Superior.

B. Since Mrs. McLoughlin was unable to sign her name (using an X when she signed a document), it is unlikely that she attended school in Québec.

XI

A. John Jr. died the night of April 19/20, 1842. (Letters of his father)
B. He died the night of April 20/21. (Letter of brother David)
C. He died the night of April 21/22. (Richard Montgomery)

XII

A. Dr. McLoughlin was involved in a liaison with "an Indian woman", resulting in an illegitimate son, Joseph.

B. Dr. McLoughlin was married to Joseph's mother according to fur company rules, just as he was later married to Margaret McKay.
There are numerous other points which could logically be discussed, but those cited above seem best to illustrate interpretive reading of *Royal Family of the Columbia*.

Interpretive reading of history is the intelligent sorting-out of various options presented by more than one historian, after which the reader has the privilege of making his own valid assumption or inference. The reading of history interpretively is infinitely more rewarding to the reader than is the arbitrary presentation of only one writer's viewpoint, which for diverse reasons of his own may be prejudiced, even bigoted. Interpretive reading is liberated reading.

Royal Family of the Columbia

FOREWORD

"THERE WAS A KING IN OREGON"[1]

King of Old Oregon, Emperor of the West, King of the Columbia, Great White Eagle, Savior of Oregon, Founder of Oregon City, Governor of the Pacific Slope, Patriarch of the Northwest, Benevolent Despot,—these are but a few of the honorary titles bestowed upon Dr. John McLoughlin, chief factor for the Columbia District of the Hudson's Bay Company from 1824 until 1845.

This twenty-one-year period has been labeled by some historians the "Age of McLoughlin",[2] for "almost every event and action in the whole territory was with reference to the Chief Factor and waited for final disposition on his decision."[3] The name of the Chief Factor became synonymous with the Hudson's Bay Company's westernmost outpost at Fort Vancouver.

To the reader of Pacific Northwest history the life of Dr. John McLoughlin is taken for granted. Every school child of Oregon and Washington knows of the White-Headed Eagle, the Father of Oregon, the kindly and hospitable doctor at Fort Vancouver who eased the path for hundreds of competitors and rivals—Americans— whether trappers, missionaries, or colonists. The school-age child may not understand the term "chief factor," but he has at least a partial knowledge of the character of the man who held that high position in the Hudson's Bay Company for more than twenty years.

The more mature reader is no doubt also aware of the paradox that the man personified: On the one hand, he as an official in the Honourable Company had the duty of discouraging Americans from settling in the Oregon Country; on the other, as a Christian he could not let those weary, bedraggled, often-destitute pioneers attempt a wilderness existence without adequate provision for food and shelter.

A telling of the legend of this man who himself became a legend is particularly timely for both child and adult alike in the 1970s, for 1975 was the year in which Vancouver, Washington, celebrated its sesquicentennial, and 1974 marked the sesquicentennial of Chief Factor McLoughlin's arrival in the Oregon Country, the year when he began both his reign and his rule over the Kingdom of the Columbia, a kingdom bounded only by the Rockies, the Pacific, Russian Alaska, and Mexico.

REFERENCES

1 Ben Hur Lampman, *Elks Magazine,* April 1925, pp. 36-37.
2 Horace S. Lyman, *History of Oregon,* II, p. 353.
3 *Ibid.,* p. 355.

London headquarters of the Hudson's Bay Company and the "Honourable Governor and Committee" at Number 3 Fenchurch Street, c. 1794.

Photo by Harrison Hornish

Royal Family of the Columbia

PART I

WHERE IT ALL BEGAN——THE KING'S ANCESTORS

17

Fort William c. 1812, the great entrepôt of the North West Company.

CHAPTER 1

THE FRASERS OF MOUNT MURRAY

Three mighty rivers crossed the lives of the Frasers and of the McLoughlins: The St. Lawrence was the core of the family domain. The Columbia and the Seine were tributary to the St. Lawrence, for on the banks of these rivers key members of this ruling family gained and lost power.[1] The "key members" can be identified as Dr. John McLoughlin, who ruled the district of the mighty Columbia; as his brother, Dr. David, who practiced medicine in Paris at the court of King Louis-Philippe, on the Seine; and last, but most certainly not least, as their older sister, Marie-Louise, later Sister St. Henry, who "ruled" on the St. Lawrence, where as teacher and Mother Superior she guided countless girls and young women, including numerous nieces and young cousins, branches of the Fraser clan, including several McLoughlins.[2]

Marie-Louise, or rather, Sister St. Henry, was the greatest of the three, for she "lost power" only on her death, July 3, 1846, whereas each of her brothers lost his prestige during his lifetime, John when he "quarreled himself" out of his position with the Hudson's Bay Company in 1845, and David when the February Revolution in 1848 brought the exile of Louis-Philippe and the advent of Louis-Napoléon.[3]

The Frasers, or ffrasers, were a proud, ancient clan of Scotland, extending back for several centuries. In the late seventeenth and early eighteenth centuries they had in the main been Jacobite partisans, fighting first for the "Old Pretender" and later for his son, the "Young Pretender," or "Bonnie Prince Charlie." An early Simon Fraser, a turncoat, from Stuart to Hanover, and back to Stuart, had during his Hanoverian period been recognized as the eleventh Lord Lovat by George II in 1730. However, again changing sides, he was arrested and sent to the block for treason by the same king after the battle of Culloden in 1746.[4] Wishing to die gracefully, the proud Lord of Lovat rehearsed the position he would need to assume at the block,[5] and when on the scaffold, efficiently inspected the axe's edge to be sure that it was sufficiently sharp.

Malcolm Fraser, born in 1733, the maternal grandfather of the three McLoughlin "rulers," was the son of Donald Fraser, who fought on the "other" (Hanoverian) side at the battle of Culloden and died there. He joined the Fraser Highlanders, a regiment of his distant cousin, Colonel Simon Fraser. son of the Simon who had lost his head on the block. With the Highlanders he fought in the French and Indian War (Seven Years' War), on the Plains of Abraham with the forces of General James Wolfe. In 1761 he settled on a Seigneury (seignory) near Québec at Malbaie, re-named Murray Bay in honor of his commander, General James Murray, who had been influential in securing the seigneury for him.[6]

Malcolm is said to have had earlier several Indian "wives," *i.e.,* woman by whom he had children, who took their mothers' names. Marrying a French-Canadian girl, Marie Allaire, he fathered four children; by another woman, Mary Dugros, who lived in his home for a period of years, he fathered four additional children. Mrs. Dugros was presumably his second wife, although his first wife was still living and there were no records either of divorce or of remarriage. Because of his military rank Colonel Malcolm Fraser's life on the seigneury was occasionally interrupted, as when he served in the English army in the American Revolutionary War, defending Québec against the forces of Benedict Arnold.[7]

Malcolm was an extremely well-organized and assiduous individual, keeping a detailed diary of General Wolfe's victories. Extracts of this valuable journal were published by literary and historical societies of Québec, attesting the probability that the Colonel possessed a certain degree to erudition and culture. Systematic and careful, he always made at least two copies of each document with which he was concerned so that he would have a copy for his file. At the age of seventy-nine, in 1812, he made four identical original copies of his fourteen-page will before leading a unit of militia to Québec to fight in the War of 1812.[8]

The story of the two who were to become the parents of the future chief factor and of his brother and his five sisters is one of those romances which ignore and defy class bias. Angélique, daughter of Malcolm Fraser, a seigneur of French and Scottish blood, took as her husband John McLoughlin, a mere cultivateur, or tiller of the soil, of Irish extraction. He was commonly believed to be her inferior intellectually as well as socially. The union, probably made in 1778, was considered a mésalliance, almost a Prince and Cinderella story in reverse. The little McLoughlin cottage at Rivière-du-Loup must have presented a sharp contrast to Mount Murray, Angélique McLoughlin's girlhood home, yet she is said to have adapted to her reduced life both gracefully and graciously.[9] Here their seven children were born. She is described as an excellent mother, keeping her children close to her spiritually, even though according to some writers the family was separated physically.[10]

Her father is presumed to have disinherited her both for marrying so far beneath her and for converting to Catholicism. To her staunch Scottish Protestant father the conversion was unforgivable. However, in 1786 he did give his daughter and son-in-law a farm at Rivière-du-Loup, fronting on the St. Lawrence River, when John, the third child, was sixteen months old.[11] While the gift of the farm was not mentioned in Malcolm's will as the reason for not leaving Angélique a legacy, it is assumed that that was probably the case. He did, however, bequeath small amounts to her children, giving 400 pounds sterling to be divided among her (five) "female children" and 200 pounds to each of her two sons, John and David. He understood the concept of bequeathing estates with remainders over and used it, as did his sons and grandsons later in their wills.[12]

Royal Family of the Columbia

The concept of the seigneur and his seigneury was that of French medieval feudalism. The seigneury of Mount Murray extended east from the Malbaie River along the St. Lawrence for eighteen miles to the River Noire (Black River) and was three leagues (nine miles) deep. No private owners had been dispossessed by the creation of this—and other—seigneuries. Originally the French government had retained the land from settlement for the refuge of fur-bearing animals. Tenant farmers on the seigneuries tilled the soil for the government with their few crude tools. It is interesting to note that the prestigious noble Frasers had no money. Their equipment for maintenance had to be bought by note.

In theory each seigneur declared homage to the governor, on his knees with head bared; he would also take an oath to serve the king. In reality the Crown required little of the seigneurs; if, in turn, the seigneurs required little of their tenants, they at least enjoyed the social distinction and prestige which accompanied the title. Feudal tradition, however, was observed in its minor aspects: On New Year's Day the tenants gathered at the manor house to pay their respects and to consume the Lord's whiskey and cakes. The seigneur was godfather to the firstborn of each tenant. By custom he enjoyed certain privileges, such as receiving Communion first, occupying a special pew, operating the only lumber and grist mills, the *corvée* (free labor of the tenants on roads of the seigneury), and possessing every eleventh fish caught in his streams. He could not dispossess the tenant from the land as long as the latter paid his nominal rent. He was regarded with great respect, even awe, as illustrated by a tenant's answer concerning the seigneur's status in earlier times, *"Monsieur, il était le roi, l'empereur, du village."* (Sir, he was the king, the emperor, of the village".)[13]

Because Malcolm willed Mount Murray to William, older son of his second marriage, he aided his eldest son, Alexander, in buying the seigneury of Rivière-du-Loup, on the south shore of the St. Lawrence, This gave him reason to visit frequently across the river; here he set up an ingenious system of signals from Kamouraska, straight across the river from Murray Bay, with friends in Malbaie. A long blaze meant good news; a half-smothered flame indicated illness; a large blaze referred to an adult, a small one to a child, while a suddenly extinguished flame meant death.[14]

It was often the character of the seigneur to act not only the role of the benefactor, but also of the tyrant. This latter part Malcolm played to the hilt with his family. In the presence of this headstrong figure his sons remained "mere shadows"[15] It was Alexander and Simon, born in 1761 and in 1769, respectively, who were effaced as long as their father lived. It was they who ceased all communication with each other in 1812. Dying in 1837 and in 1844, they had lived for twenty-five years at odds with each other, occasionally using as intermediary their niece, Sister St. Henry, or some other relative.[16]

One writer has drawn on his imagination and posed a hypothetical family reunion at Mount Murray. Here, in imagination, Malcolm sits at one end of a large semicircle, his grandson Dr. John at the other. Next to John is his favorite uncle,

Alberta Brooks Fogdall

Simon, while Simon's brother, Alexander, sits some distance away, for the two brothers are not speaking to each other. Between the brothers are Simon's only son, John; Cultivateur John McLoughlin, and his younger son, Dr. David; as well as Dr. John's children, John, Eliza, and David. Missing for some reason is Angélique. Missing also are Marie-Louise, who does not leave her convent, and Margaret McLoughlin, Dr. John's wife, who is quiet and reserved, and her stepson, Joseph, who is shy.

These individuals, the Frasers and McLoughlins of the hypothetical tableau, are the leading characters of this story.[17]

The "mere shadows" during Malcolm's lifetime emerged slowly after his death. Between the three sons and the daughter of Malcolm's first marriage and the two sons of his second was at least a generation's difference in age. Angélique, born in 1760, could actually have been the grandmother of her half brother John Malcolm, born in 1800. Gradually the four sons, Alexander, Simon, William, and John Malcolm, developed into separate entities and personalities once they were no longer overwhelmed by their father's presence.

The older sons, Alexander and Simon, especially, began to assume leadership in the extended family after Malcolm's death in 1815 at eighty-two. They were no longer young. Already fifty-four and forty-six, much of their lives was behind them. The younger sons, William and John Malcolm, emerged also, though less prominently than their half brothers.

Simon's personality emerged to the historian much more distinctly than that of Alexander and than those of his young half brothers. The fourth child and third son of his parents, he was probably educated first in or near Québec; later he studied subjects relevant to medicine at the University of Edinburgh for two years, but was not graduated. The years between 1789, when he left the University, and 1795, when he received a commission in the British army as a lieutenant in the Royal Highland Regiment, are not accounted for.[18] There is no record of his receiving a medical degree, although the prefix "Dr." ordinarily preceded his name. Was it simply typical of the times, when often a "doctor" had studied medical courses for a short time or had been apprenticed to a practicing physician for a long or even for a short period? It seems hardly likely, for Simon Fraser was greatly respected and his medical opinion highly regarded, particularly by his nephew John after he had received his own medical degree. Apparently he did not serve in the British army in a medical capacity.[19] In any case, he was wounded in Egypt in 1801, probably returning to Canada in 1802, for in 1803 he helped his nephew John, now a doctor, to secure an apprentice contract with the Northwest Fur Company as a physician.[20] He had probably married by this time (he was now thirty-four) and established a home at Terrebonne, near Montréal; it was under Simon's aegis and from Terrebonne that his nephew John's application for permission to practice medicine was dated April 1, 1803.[21]

Royal Family of the Columbia

Some historians record that Simon practiced medicine as an employee of the Northwest Company for a time; others made no mention of any connection with the fur trade. One, Richard Montgomery, mentioned that the favorite uncle of the White-Headed Eagle fought in Napoleonic wars from 1795 to 1803.[22] Montgomery also claimed this "fighting doctor" was both idolized and idealized by nephews John and David, was in fact "a veritable *beau idéal*" and that as children on frequent visits at Mount Murray, they had been taught the fundamentals of science and had been inspired to study medicine in emulation of their uncle, and to please both him and their Grandfather Fraser, who wanted the boys to go into a profession as "gentlemen" should do. One fur trader-adventurer in the family (Alexander) was enough! His grandsons must go into law or medicine. The story was told that for some time John was ambivalent concerning his future, but that David had made up his mind early to become a doctor.[23] Thus, Alexander's efforts—just how forceful they were is not known—to interest his nephews in fur trading came to nothing, in spite of the long walks together, the exciting adventure tales of the Northwest and Hudson's Bay fur companies, no doubt including that he had headed an expedition in 1802 sent by the "Marquis", Simon McTavish, of the Northwest Company to Hudson Bay to attempt to break the monopoly of the Hudson's Bay Company, the conflict between the two organizations.

No writer has ever suggested the possibility that Alexander's desire that the boys follow in his footsteps may have subconsciously lessened his interest in helping them (especially David) to finance their medical education. Simon, of course, was pleased. As it turned out John combined the desires of both uncles and grandfather by becoming both a fur trader and a doctor.[24]

Just what Alexander did for his own eleven children, four by his first wife, an "Indian Woman," Angélique Meadows, and seven by his second marriage to a French Canadian, Pauline Michaud, has not been documented, except that he lacked the money to educate his son and namesake and was forced to apprentice him as a clerk to the Northwest Company. In 1823 a letter from Dr. John to Dr. Fraser mentioned that young Alexander was paralyzed, and that he and his father were now reconciled.[25] (It would seem that Alexander had disagreements with several family members.)

The story of Simon's—and other Frasers'—financial involvement with McLoughlins comes more logically later as each individual most concerned is discussed. He played a significant part in their affairs for the rest of his life, unhappily for his health and for his peace of mind.

It was a source of unhappiness for many of the Fraser-McLoughlin clan that Alexander and Simon were at odds for a quarter of a century. Dr. John regretted the split, especially because his brother, David, was the unknowing cause. He tried to heal the breach between Alexander's and Simon's children; whether due to the Doctor's efforts or not, in 1842 Alexander's daughter (Betsy) married Simon's only son, John; the marriage took place five years after Alexander's death and two years before Simon's.[26] Presumably Simon did not object to the marriage, especially as Alexander was no longer living.

Simon died in 1844 and was much missed by Dr. John, with whom he had kept a regular correspondence. A portrait of him, hanging today in the old manor house of the Seigneury of Rivière-du-Loup,[27] shows him as a rather stocky individual, dignified, but with the suggestion of a twinkle in his eyes, as if he possessed a sense of humor in spite of his feuding brother and troublesome relatives. Today the manor house belongs to a granddaughter of Alexander, the daughter of his son William. The granddaughter, (Mrs.) Alice Fraser Prevost, found a packet of seventy-five or eighty letters in a drawer of a secretary in the manor house, evidently put there by her father, William. He had inherited the manor house (and the letters) when John, his cousin and brother-in law, died. It is these letters which have served as original source material for studying the inter-relationship of the Fraser-McLoughlin clan.[28]

It has been erroneously believed by many that the Fraser River, an important waterway of western Canada, was named in honor of the Simon Fraser of this story. However, the Simon Fraser so honored, the explorer, was a distant cousin who in 1808 explored the "Mighty river," previously named Tacoutche Tesse by famed explorer Alexander Mackenzie.[29] The Frasers were a prolific clan with a plethora of Simons, Malcoms, Donalds, Alexanders, Davids, and Williams. In the *Biographical Dictionary of Nor'westers*[30] are listed seven Frasers, four of them Simons; the fourth listed is the great explorer; none of them is the uncle of the McLoughlin "rulers."

REFERENCES

CHAPTER 1

THE FRASERS OF MOUNT MURRAY

1 Dr. Burt Brown Barker presented this thesis, almost a fantasy, in *The McLoughlin Empire and its rulers*, p. 22.
2 *Ibid.*
3 *Ibid.*
4 *Ibid.*
4 *Ibid.*
5 Reminiscent of Catherine Howard, Henry VIII's fifth queen, at her execution.
6 Barker, *op. cit.*, p. 57.
7 *Ibid.*, pp. 67—68.
8 *Ibid.*, p. 70.
10 *Ibid.*, pp. 11, 14.
11 *Ibid.*, p. 31, p. 31n.
12 *Ibid.*, pp. 290-291. "Remainder over" means making provision for the next estate, in case of the decease of the original legatee. Parts of the estate were to "remain over" for the next in line. Often the legatee was forbidden to sell.
13 *Ibid.*, pp. 57—59.
14 *Ibid.*, p. 67.
15 *Ibid.*, p. 72.
16 *Ibid.*, pp. 73-74, *passim*.
17 *Ibid.*, pp. 15-20.
18 *Ibid.*, p. 72.
19 *Ibid.* However, Richard G. Montgomery in *The White-Headed Eagle*, p. 4, stated that Simon Fraser served as a physician in the "Black Watch" regiment of the Royal Highlanders, in the British army. He also wrote that all of Malcolm's children were by his second wife. Since Dr. Barker published twenty-five years later (1959) than Montgomery (1934) and it is known that he had access to material not available earlier, it is logical to assume his is probably the correct version.
20 *Ibid.*, p. 73.
21 *Ibid.*
22 Montgomery, *op. cit.*, p. 4.
23 *Ibid.*, pp. 7, 13-15.
24 *Ibid.*, pp. 7-11.
25 Barker, *op. cit.*, pp. 162, 175.
26 *Ibid.*, pp. 73-74, 77-78.
27 *Ibid.*, p. 75.
28 Or at least as of 1958 it belonged to a descendant, (Mrs.) Alice Fraser Prevost. Now, 1970's, it has probably changed hands; hopefully, it remains in the Fraser family.
29 Dorothy Johansen, *Empire of the Columbia*, pp. 84-85.
30 In W.S. Wallace, *Documents Related to the Northwest Company*, pp. 443-446.

GENEALOGY

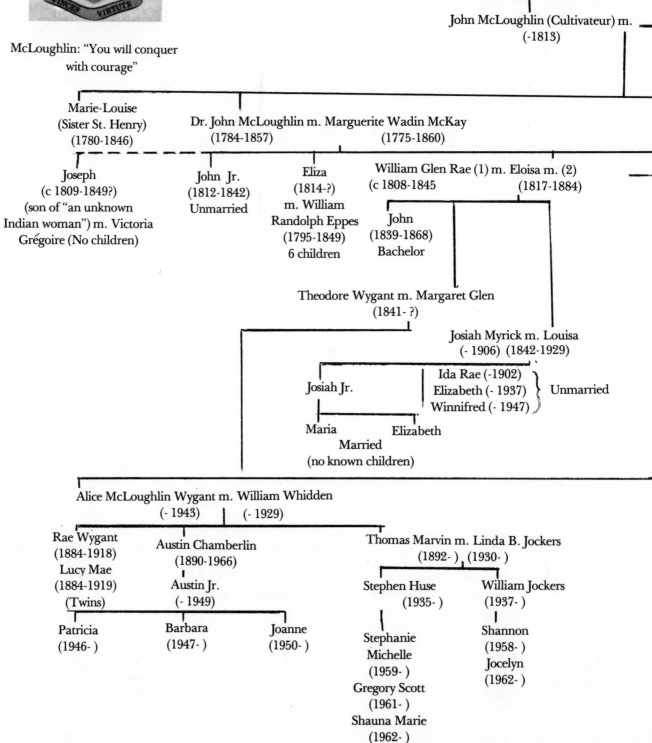

McLoughlin: "You will conquer
with courage"

John McLoughlin m. Mary Short

John McLoughlin (Cultivateur) m.
(-1813)

Marie-Louise
(Sister St. Henry)
(1780-1846)

Dr. John McLoughlin m. Marguerite Wadin McKay
(1784-1857)   (1775-1860)

Joseph
(c 1809-1849?)
(son of "an unknown
Indian woman") m. Victoria
Grégoire (No children)

John Jr.
(1812-1842)
Unmarried

Eliza
(1814-?)
m. William
Randolph Eppes
(1795-1849)
6 children

William Glen Rae (1) m. Eloisa m. (2)
(c 1808-1845   (1817-1884)

John
(1839-1868)
Bachelor

Theodore Wygant m. Margaret Glen
(1841- ?)

Josiah Myrick m. Louisa
(- 1906) (1842-1929)

Josiah Jr.

Ida Rae (-1902)
Elizabeth (- 1937)   } Unmarried
Winnifred (- 1947)

Maria   Elizabeth
Married
(no known children)

Alice McLoughlin Wygant m. William Whidden
(- 1943)   (- 1929)

Rae Wygant
(1884-1918)
Lucy Mae
(1884-1919)
(Twins)

Austin Chamberlin
(1890-1966)

Austin Jr.
(- 1949)

Thomas Marvin m. Linda B. Jockers
(1892-) (1930-)

Stephen Huse
(1935-)

William Jockers
(1937-)

Patricia
(1946-)

Barbara
(1947-)

Joanne
(1950-)

Stephanie
Michelle
(1959-)
Gregory Scott
(1961-)
Shauna Marie
(1962-)

Shannon
(1958-)
Jocelyn
(1962-)

Malcolm Fraser m. Marie Allaire
(1733-1815)

Angélique   Alexander   Simon
(1760-1842)   (1761-1837   (1769-1844

Elisabeth (Betsy) m. John (cousins)

Fraser: "I am prepared."

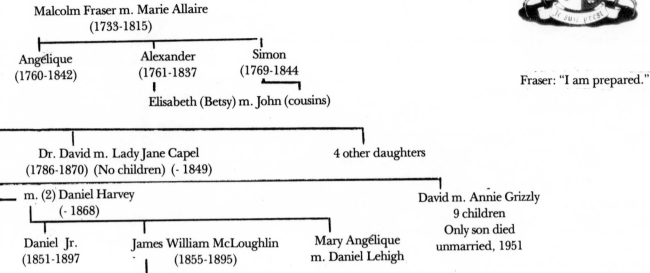

Dr. David m. Lady Jane Capel   4 other daughters
(1786-1870) (No children) (- 1849)

m. (2) Daniel Harvey   David m. Annie Grizzly
(- 1868)   9 children
                              Only son died
                         unmarried, 1951

Daniel Jr.   James William McLoughlin   Mary Angélique
(1851-1897   (1855-1895)   m. Daniel Lehigh

Matilda Eloisa
(1886-)
m. George Deering

Daniel Harvey   William Francis   James Vincent

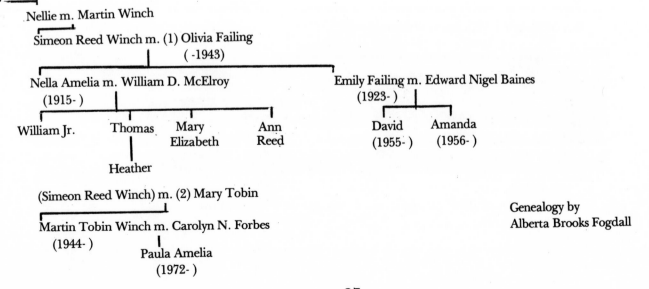

Nellie m. Martin Winch

Simeon Reed Winch m. (1) Olivia Failing
(-1943)

Nella Amelia m. William D. McElroy   Emily Failing m. Edward Nigel Baines
(1915-)   (1923-)

William Jr.   Thomas   Mary   Ann   David   Amanda
                   Elizabeth Reed   (1955-)   (1956-)

Heather

(Simeon Reed Winch) m. (2) Mary Tobin

Martin Tobin Winch m. Carolyn N. Forbes
(1944-)

Paula Amelia
(1972-)

Genealogy by
Alberta Brooks Fogdall

27

*Astoria, 1812,
with the American
flag flying.*

York Fort, on Hudson Bay, first Headquarters of Hudson's Bay Company

CHAPTER 2

THE McLOUGHLINS OF RIVIÈRE-DU-LOUP

The redundancy of such Christian names as John, David, Alexander, Simon, and Malcolm in the Fraser-McLoughlin saga makes clarification difficult. This is particularly true of the name John, which was popular with the McLoughlins, appearing a minimum of four times in four generations. With two Davids, and with a variety of Johns, John Malcolms, and Alexanders among the Frasers, a careful sorting-out and identification becomes essential.

Among the Johns the star of the story was the third in line of four John McLoughlins, representing four generations. The first was his grandfather, who was born in Ireland, married an Irish woman, Mary Short, and died in Rivière-du-Loup in 1812 at ninety-eight. Little is recorded of his life. They were the parents of four children, of whom the eldest was John. This John married Angélique Fraser, probably in 1778.[1] Of their seven children, it is the first, third and fourth—Marie-Louise, John, and David—who are the "rulers" and the subjects of this part of the story.

A common method of distinguishing the four Johns is from oldest to youngest: Grandfather John, Cultivateur John, John or Dr. John, and John Jr., the Doctor's son, born in 1812. The two Davids can be identified simply as Dr. David and David.

These three McLoughlin children have been labeled the "vindication" of Angélique's unequal marriage to Cultivateur John McLoughlin, who was so often described as a "simple soul" a "good" man, a "poor Irishman", definitely inferior to her in every way. He "meant well" but was unable to understand his brilliant children. They could have a spiritual and intellectual affinity only with their mother, who was so much her husband's superior. Both Barker and Montgomery have presented this view both directly and by implication.

Marie-Louise, the eldest, was said to be such a beautiful and fascinating child at the age of six that her grandfather Malcolm Fraser "was so charmed with her childish attractions that he declared she should not return with her parents... and almost by force retained her as his adopted child."[2]

Another writer, however, records that Marie-Louise was adopted (informally, at least) by a sister of her grandfather who had married a cousin, (another) William Fraser. These two were so completely captivated by the little girl that they "simply had to have" her. It was David and John who lived with the Malcolm Frasers a great deal of the time: "Angélique fell into the habit of leaving first John and later David with her parents for weeks at a time."[3] Another writer claims that the boys lived permanently at Mount Murray.[4]

In an attempt to analyze these paradoxical statements, one must consider two other contradictory claims: 1. That all Malcolm's children were by his second wife.[5] 2. That he was completely impartial, fathering four children by each wife.[6] If the latter is true, it is hardly credible that a stepgrandmother would be so attached to a child not related to her, during the very period 1791-1800, when she herself was giving birth to four children. All four of her children were younger than Marie-Louise, her stepgranddaughter.

If, on the other hand, the same wife was the mother of all eight children, she gave birth to them over a period of forty years, 1760-1800,[7] a phenomenon indeed! Even if she had produced the first child when she was twelve and the eighth at fifty-two, which is hardly likely, the reader's imagination is still stretched beyond the limitation of credibility.

Regardless of which set of Frasers she lived with, Marie-Louise's education seemed to be basically the same. Only the motivation was different: For a time she attended a Protestant school but changed to the Ursulines Convent, in Québec, because her guardians, the William Frasers, believed she would receive more "advantages" there. Or, if she was living with Grandfather Malcolm, she became interested in Catholicism and, wilfully, against his wishes, transferred to the Convent.[8]

As a student in a Catholic convent and with part of her family Catholic (her father, possibly mother, at least one grandmother, Marie Allaire) it was not too surprising that Marie-Louise decided to convert to Catholicism in spite of the Protestant upbringing received at the home of her guardian (whether grandfather or granduncle). Her parents willingly gave their permission, naturally, but her grandfather fought the conversion bitterly. Montgomery, who claims that she lived with the William Frasers, felt "the news was not slow in finding its way across to Mount Murray, and when the old seigneur, who *until then had taken scant interest* in his granddaughter (italics added), heard of her decision, his anger knew no bounds."[9] In 1798, at age eighteen, she decided to take the veil, still over Malcolm Fraser's violent protests, and two years later she pronounced her final vows.

Marie-Louise, later Sister St. Henry, taught French and geography and was one of the first teachers of English in the Convent. There was a great demand at this time for English teachers due to a large influx of English-speaking Catholics in Québec. Both her brothers, Drs. John and David, were interested both in her and in her work, providing her with such visual aids as globes and maps to facilitate her teaching. David sent the newest and latest equipment from Paris; the brothers jointly made it a project to collect unusual and intriguing games that only those with a knowledge of English could enjoy; this naturally increased the teacher's popularity. David also sent her plays from Paris for use in her French classes.[10]

Sister St. Henry exerted a great deal of influence on the lives of her pupils, for she was interested in helping them to become women who would lead worthwhile, useful lives. At one time as many as six nieces were among her students, three of whom themselves became nuns. She was described as having a cheerful disposition and happy nature, getting along well with her pupils.

Her work and life in a convent did not cause her to lose touch with her family, for her relatives' children, including John's daughters, Eliza and Eloisa, formed a link to the outside world. She kept in touch, too, with family members by almost constant letter writing. She was frequently consulted by her siblings and other relatives about family matters and seemed to have a talent for smoothing over difficulties. While she could not have her young male relatives as students, she was able to help them indirectly with advice given both in person and in letters. A case in point was that of Dr. John's son John Jr., who at one time was to be sent to Rivière-du-Loup, where her mother, Angélique, was still living. Her tender love and unusually strong filial feeling for her mother was always apparent, but it was especially so when in a letter of May 11, 1835, she begged her uncle Simon Fraser not to distress Angélique by sending young John to her mother, "who would die of sadness to see that child run wild in the country."[11]

She may have served as a substitute mother for Eliza, who was across the continent from her own mother. One of her strangest duties for her relatives was serving as intermediary in writing between her uncles Alexander and Simon, since they refused to communicate with each other.

The exact date is not recorded when Sister St. Henry became Mother Superior. In this capacity she had charge of the convent for a number of years before her death, described as the result of a "painful malady" July 3, 1846, aged sixty-six.

The Québec *Gazette* described her glowingly:

During the long period of forty-six years of religious profession, she filled at various times the office of Superior of the community, with rare talent, prudence and justice which merited for her the highest confidence and esteem. She will be long and deeply regretted, not only by the citizens of Québec, of every class and nationality, who have so often rendered homage to her virtues and fine qualities, but also by those strangers who have had occasion to visit that estimable institution, none of whom ever went away without expressing the highest admiration for the noble manners and the interesting conversation of this amiable lady.

Sister St. Henry's brother John had a portrait of her painted by artist and teacher of art F. G. Bowman, which today hangs in the convent. A description of the portrait mentioned her "eyes ever beaming with charity" and included the sentiment that "it was sufficient to have seen her once to remain impressed with the highest respect for her as a religious,[12] and at the same time attracted by the charm of her conversation, her presence, her manners, all denoting the accomplished lady whose mind was even superior to her exterior endowments."[13]

Second of the McLoughlins who "ruled" was John, the chief protagonist of this work. The first son after two daughters, he was no doubt "special" to both his parents. Probably Cultivateur John McLoughlin looked upon his first son as a pair of hands to help in the fields and as a successor who would one day take over the grueling work of a "cultivateur".

This boy was born October 19, 1784, in Rivière-du-Loup and baptized in Kamouraska, a nearby village to the south, on November 5 by a Catholic priest, Curé Trutault.[14] Given the names Jean-Baptiste, both French and Catholic, he was known in history only as John.[15]

John and Angélique were indebted to her father for the farm on which they lived and were always in very modest circumstances. In fact, the children spent almost as much time at their grandfather's home as they did at their own.[16] Malcolm Fraser was an Anglican, although as was the custom in Roman Catholic Québec, he was invariably referred to as a Protestant. He wanted his children brought up in his church and on July 27, 1796, wrote to his son-in-law:

> I feel it Rather hard that you should Compell a parent to bring his Children up in a Religion that he was not brought up himself & Consider that it is a weakness to Aquiese. However, If it is your Request I find myself Obliged to Agree With what you Request. Honored Sir I am your Dutifull Servant.[17]

John received a good grounding in Anglicanism, further advanced when he, his brother, David, and sister Mary Louise, went to stay with their maternal granduncle, Colonel William Fraser, also an Anglican. Here his Anglican background was strengthened. His sister, Mary Louise, who was adopted by the Frasers, became a Roman Catholic nun, Although this disturbed Grandfather Fraser, Colonel Fraser supported her. In modern-day context it is virtually impossible to understand the compliance of the children's parents in submitting to the edict of an interfering father, but in the context of 1796 and considering the awe of a simple farmer for his aristocratic father-in-law, it is perhaps less incomprehensible. Remembering too the gift of land from the Seigneur at Rivière-du-Loup ten years previously, it is almost understandable.

Royal Family of the Columbia

After his early education, whether it was in the village of Rivière-du-Loup, in Québec, at Mount Murray, or a combination of some or all of these, John, possibly influenced by his Uncle Simon and his Grandfather Fraser, decided to study medicine, as discussed earlier.

Burt Brown Barker disagreed with Richard Montgomery's thesis, expounded earlier, that John—and David—saw a great deal of their Uncles Simon and Alexander, for neither was at Mount Murray much during this period. Instead, Dr. Barker felt, John knew of their work and admired them from a distance. Alexander, especially, spent very little time at Mount Murry, for he had entered the fur trade as a clerk before 1789 and had become a wintering partner in the Northwest Company in 1799. His rotation vacation periods were few and would logically have come at the time of year when John was in school.[18]

However it came about, John began in 1798 to study medicine with Dr. Sir James Fisher of Québec, a prominent physician of excellent reputation. Because Dr. Fisher accepted a very limited number of students, his accepting John was a definite compliment to the fourteen-year-old boy. After spending four and one-half years with Dr. Fisher, John applied for his permission to practice medicine. This document, still extant, is irrefutable proof against the charge rather commonly made that John McLoughlin was not legally a doctor, having just picked up a smattering of medical knowledge here and there. It is possible that the origin of the charge is the fact that he obviously preferred other aspects of the fur trade to that of company "surgeon", and that his renown rests upon his humaneness and benevolence and upon his executive and administrative prowess, rather than upon his expertise as a physician, although his medical knowledge and capability were indispensable on many occasions throughout his life.

Evidence of John's being a lawful and qualified doctor of medicine assumed three forms: 1. His petition to practice medicine. 2. Supporting the petitioner. 3. The permit itself. Dr. Fisher in the affidavit April 30, 1803, certified that "John McLoughlin, a Canadian lived with me as an apprintice (*sic*) student in medicine, surgery, and pharmacy for four years and six months—during which time, he behaved honestly, he possesses talents, and I sincerely believe him a good subject of the British Government."[19] Another document strengthens the validity of his certification, that of two witnesses, whose signatures, unfortunately, are illegible, to his taking the examination, which, they said, he passed "creditably".[20] Additional proof is supplied by Maude E. Abbott in her *History of Medicine in the Province of Québec,* who states on Pages 256-257 that "Among the licentiates admitted by examination in 1803 was John McLoughlin of Terrebonne who had served his apprenticeship under Sir James Fisher."[21] She added that he was a Scotsman who was later a chief factor of the Hudson's Bay Company in Oregon while it was still British territory and that he "did noble pioneer work."

Strangely, Montgomery had no knowledge of the soon-to-be White-Headed Eagle's studying with Sir James Fisher; "where he went and exactly when, no one can say." He presented the "traditional" idea of John's going to the University of Edinburgh, basing the possiblity on F. V. Holman's *Dr. John McLoughlin,* but almost immediately dismissed the thought that "John, at only sixteen, could have journeyed so far from home to study medicine."[22]

Horace Lyman, among other reputable early historians, stated factually that John studied medicine in Paris.[23] This belief, stated at the turn of the century, has since been superseded. There was quite obviously no time in John's life, given the now-known facts, when he could have studied in Paris. It is probable that earlier historians confused John with his brother, David, who did study medicine in Europe and practiced in Paris.

Relevant to the controversy over whether John McLoughlin was "really" a doctor and, if so, where he studied, is a description of him, eulogistic in character, which appeared in an 1886 publication of *Oregon Pioneer Association Transactions:* "He had taken time to study medicine and was thorough in his knowledge of his science." The article added that he also had great general information and great knowledge of history; "hardly anyone could cope with him in this discipline."[24] To many Oregonians Dr. John McLoughlin was a hero, a paragon of all the virtues, and possessing absolutely no vices. They couldn't have "cared less" where the King of the Columbia received his medical training.

Leaving this second "ruler" of the McLoughlin family temporarily, in order to fit the third "ruler", Dr. David McLoughlin, into the picture, the narrative will return to him later, for this young medical student is, after all, the chief protagonist of the *Royal Family of the Columbia.*

The boy who was to grow up as a member of the "royal family" and to "reign", if not "rule", on the Seine as the personal physician to Louis-Philippe was born at Rivière-du-Loup in 1786, the fourth child and second son of Cultivateur John and Angélique Fraser McLoughlin.

Only two years in age separated David from his older brother, John. The two boys were described as "inseparable companions".[25] Whether they lived at Mount Murray permanently, spent most of the time there, or visited only occasionally, the two brothers were together a great deal, sharing many of the same interests. They were pictured tramping the fields together, riding, canoeing, perhaps occasionally accompanying their mother to visit their sister Marie-Louise in the convent at Québec, or going with their Grandfather Fraser to Montréal.

To the claim of some writers that Angélique and her children went frequently to Mount Murray to visit her father, Dr. Barker pointed out that though frequent visits would alleviate the monotony of farm life for Angélique, practical coinsiderations of distance alone would tend to invalidate this theory. Rivière-du-Loup is forty miles east of Malbaie and also on the opposite bank of the St. Lawrence. A modern steam ferry requires at least an hour to cross at Rivière-du-Loup; then it would have taken much longer. Roads were poor. The trips, if any, would have been mostly in winter, since members of the family were needed to do farm work in summer, and Canadian winters are cold.[26] In all likelihood the trips to Mount Murray were infrequent, but regardless of the frequency or infrequency of excursions, the two McLoughlin boys were usually together. As they grew older the affection between them deepened, John developing an almost paternal and protective attitude in spite of the slight age difference. In writing to David, John addressed him as "My dear David" and signed himself "Your affectionate Brother", unlike the customary stiff and formal opening and closure used frequently even in family letters. As a young man he accepted financial terms of the Northwest Company which were not favorable in his opinion only because he needed the money to help David with his medical education at the University of Edinburgh.[27] "There is one thing unmans my fortitude," he wrote to Simon July 13, 1808, "the fear that my brother David should not finish his education through want of means."[28]

Like his brother, David decided to study medicine; whether he was influenced by his grandfather and uncle, Malcolm and Simon Fraser, is a moot question. He could not know that he would be the unwitting cause of family quarrels: Frasers against Frasers and Frasers against McLoughlins, and, even more, a twenty-five-year silence between brothers.

Like John, David studied with Dr. Sir James Fisher, the result being that he was well prepared for advanced study at the University of Edinburgh. Their apprenticeships with Dr. Fisher overlapped one year, since David's extended from 1802 until 1807 and John's from 1798 to 1803.

In Edinburgh David was desperate for money. In fact, at one time he was very close to debtor's prison.[29] His Fraser relatives had been the first to suggest that he continue his medical study after completing his studies with Dr. Fisher; David had written his Uncle Alexander, while still in Québec, August 20, 1807, that his Uncle Simon had offered to pay one-third of David's educational expenses and that he would advance 100 pounds, and hinting that perhaps Alexander would do likewise. Alexander, offended, refused, no doubt pointing out that he had no money with which to help his nephew, and emphasizing that his own son Alexander had to serve as an apprentice clerk with the Northwest Company.

Malcolm, too, was in financial straits. In a letter to his son Simon of September 26, 1808, he lamented that it was impossible to help David "at this time" for many who were indebted to him had not paid him and he would have to sue. "...I tell you that I am obliged to keep out of sight for want of cash as I cannot at this time command ten dollars tho' there is more than 1000 due."[30]   Both Malcolm and Alexander asked Simon to send money to David, Malcolm guaranteeing reimbursement from them both.   He asked Simon to send David 50 pounds if possible, if not 30 pounds. Simon sent a draft for 100 pounds, which for some reason David did not receive.[31] John even asked for and received an advance for 100 pounds on his salary from the Company, which was sent to David. John had been reluctant to borrow, writing Simon August 11, 1808, "...nothing but my brother's situation could occasion my drawing money before it was due."[32]

David apparently took his studies at Edinburgh seriously, studying anatomy, surgery, chemistry, clinical surgery, the practice of medicine, dissection, botany, internal medicine, and related courses. In addition, he took two classes in midwifery. Most of the courses were of six months' duration and were taught by twelve different instructors.   In 1807-1808 he interned in the Edinburgh Hospital. On March 20, 1809, he received a diploma as surgeon from the College of Surgeons of Edinburgh and a degree in medicine from the University of Edinburgh, June 24, 1810.*

Dr. John revealed in letters of March 22, and of August 12, in 1812, to Simon that David was detained nearly eleven months due to the failure of his relatives to get money to him. At last, on May 9, 1811, he was permitted to take his examination before the Army Medical Board, receiving his commission as Hospital Mate Senior Service in the British army. On September 3, 1812, he was appointed Assistant Surgeon of the 61st Regiment on Foot.[33]

His regiment fought under the Duke of Wellington in six battles of the Napoleonic wars in a period of less than three years.[34] No doubt the experience in practicing medicine and surgery during this period was invaluable. It goes without saying that he probably received little experience in gynecology, obstetrics, or midwifery, those aspects of medicine which first gave him his "big chance" a few years later in France.

During this time no letters were received from David by his Canadian relatives—or at least there is today no record of such letters. His grandfather Malcolm Fraser (who died in 1815, leaving David 200 pounds sterling)[35] complained in a letter of November 10, 1812, that Alexander was the only one to receive a letter from David. This letter contained a payment on account to Alexander for money sent him. The reason money was sent to Alexander is unknown; there is no record that any other relatives were reimbursed.[36]

Only two months before, September 6, 1812, Alexander had written David a letter from Rivière-du-Loup. Apparently he felt extremely emotional as he wrote, a fact illustrated by his even-worse-than-usual punctuation and his incoherence—not to mention his grammar:

*See reference note 47 at the end of the chapter.

Having repeated wrote to you the judgment of your Silence bears a strong mark of ingratitude (to) your Poor Parents to whom you should have wrote. You most wrongfully impute your disappointment at Edinburgh to me mere Hasard brought me June last to the knowledge of a Bill you had drawn on your Uncle Simon in favour of a Mr. Ker of Edinburgh, which appeared Protested. it will I hope be paid...before you again Censur learn that Doctor Fraser had the transacting the remittance to you *with whom I hope I shall never again Correspond* (italics added)"—...You are too greedy a man to be told much about your family they are all well may a day come for you to enquire how they do.

I am most affectionately Your

The complimentary close seemed incongruous with the tenor of the letter's contents, and the fact that it was incomplete again indicates his disturbed emotions. His only address for David was "Medical Hosp. Portugal."[37] Apparently Alexander was the only relative who knew David's whereabouts.

This letter is the watershed in the relationship of Simon and Alexander, for they "never again Correspond(ed)." Whether David ever realized that the financing of his education was the principal cause of the brothers' feud is not known.

It is recorded that during the years 1812 and 1813 Dr. John, greatly disturbed concerning his brother's financial status, not knowing whether David had been able to complete his studies, or even where he was, had written at least one very sharp letter to Simon Fraser, implying blame that Simon had not succeeded in getting money to David; then in answer to a rather indignant letter from his uncle, he had written a letter of apology.[38]

David served in the British army until 1818, remaining on full pay until January 24, 1819, then on half pay until retirement from the service on January 24, 1824. He had been headquartered in France at the end of his service and he continued residing there. It is known that he was in Boulogne in 1820. Colin Robertson, a wintering partner first in the Northwest Company and later in the Hudson's Bay Company, dined with him and commented on the resemblance between the two brothers. There was a strong similarity, but David was much more "polished," Robertson felt. "What an astonishing difference a little intercourse with the world makes in the man's manners! Dr. McL. (David) is an elegant, gentlemanly young man, stands high at this place, and seems to be a great favorite with the good folks of Boulogne."[39]

Dr. John had visited his brother at the time of the London coalition meeting, 1820-1821, and received power-of-attorney rights to act for David concerning family property at Rivière-du-Loup.[40]

Alberta Brooks Fogdall

The event which resulted in a significant impetus to David's career was the impending birth of a child to a Mrs. Algernon Greville, daughter of Priscilla, Lady Lake, by her first marriage, to Sir Bellingham Graham. Her attending French physician had indicated that he could not save both mother and child. When Dr. David was consulted he said that he could deliver the infant with safety for both mother and child. "...Lady Lake (the mother of Mrs. Greville) was so pleased as well she might be that she fell on her knees at his feet—begging a Blessing of God on him this first brought him into notice in Boulogne and this family looked on David as one to whom they owed the Greatest obligations..."[41] Thus was Dr. David brought to the attention of the highest professional and social circles. At some time in the early 1820s, probably late in 1821, he established himself in Paris. In the year 1824 Louis XVIII was succeeded by his brother, Charles X; six years later there was a change of régime, one which was to have great influence in the life of Dr. David McLoughlin.

In 1830 the July Revolution resulted in the exile of the Bourbons to England and the accession to the throne of a distant cousin, the Duc d'Orléans, who became king as Louis-Philippe. Somehow, possibly through the influence of the Grevilles and their friends, David became one of the King's court physicians. His social position was attested by his nephew John Jr., then studying with David in Paris, in letters to his family in which John described a ball at the Tuileries to which Dr. David and he had been invited. David's home was on the rue de la Paix, a "good" address.

In November 1833 David, now forty-seven years old, married Lady Jane Capel, sister of the Earl of Essex. A few months later, for an unknown reason, John Jr. was suddenly sent home by his uncle in disgrace.

David and Lady Jane apparently continued to live happily in Paris; whether his marriage into an English noble family of ancient lineage was a love match or not, it no doubt enhanced his professional and social prestige.

Although the reign of the Citizen-King has been traditionally described as bourgeois and mediocre, it probably did not seem monotonous to David, for his royal duties in addition to his regular practice must have kept him busy. The life of the King, who was constantly exposed to assassination attempts, was a source of worry to the court physicians.

David may have been one of the seven attending physicians that hot July 12, 1842, who were bleeding with a blunt razor the King's heir, Robert, Duc d'Orléans, when he was fatally injured in a carriage accident.

Too, since obstetrics and midwifery appeared to be his forte, it is likely that he may have attended the King's daughter Marie-Christine, Princess of Württemberg, when she gave birth to an over-size infant in 1835.[42]

During his years in Paris David was awarded the Légion d'Honneur August 15, 1842. Tradition had had it that he received the honor much earlier, at the hands of

Napoléon. Later historians doubted it, for the time element was wrong. Possibly David had worked for a time in a French hospital as a prisoner; even if true, Napoléon was completely engrossed in preparations for his Russian campaign and the atmosphere was not conducive to the awarding of honors. The question was definitely settled when a researcher of the Honourable Company discovered in a copy of *Lancet,* a medical pamphlet of 1870, that 1842 was the date of the conferral.[43]

That David must have had a quite exclusive clientèle is attested by various Paris directories. For example, in 1848 the directory lists "MacLoughlin (David) Medical-legal consultations on some signs of true paralysis and on their relative value — Place Vendôme 22 — from 11 a.m. to noon." The Place Vendôme was then, as it is today, an exclusive and desirable address. That he was able to maintain an office there and keep even better than "banker's hours" undoubtedly proves the fact that he had "arrived" both professionally and financially. No doubt his position must have been considered an enviable one by many members of his profession.[44]

In addition to being "rich" he was an able writer on medical topics. In 1841 he published his first book in the field of his specialization, *Consultation médico-légale sur quelques signes de la Paralysie vraie et la valeur rélative.* In 1845 a second edition appeared. The *Catalogue de la Bibliothèque Nationale* lists other publications, *on the Premonitory Symptoms of Cholera* and *Result of an Inquiry into the Invariable Existence of Premonitory Diarrhea in Cholera, in a series of communications to the registrar-general.* The above were published in Paris (1841, 1845) and in London (1855, 1854).

The *Catalogue of the British Museum* included *Letter to His Grace the Duke of Somerset...relative to the question, Is there a Syphilitic Virus?* (London, 1864). There were many others, illustrating his interest in communicable diseases, particularly syphilis, and their prevention — especially in naval and military stations. Cholera, too, had particular interest for him as shown in his *Result of an Inquiry whether Cholera can be Conveyed by Human Intercourse, from an infected to a healthy locality; or from an infected to a healthy person.* (London, 1856)

No records are extant to show when David and Lady Jane left Paris and went to London. The 1848 directory is the last issue in which he is listed in Paris. It is logical to assume when the February Revolution of 1848 drove Louis-Philippe, Queen Marie-Amélie, and their family to exile in England and eventually brought in Louis-Napoléon and the Second Republic, that David found it advisable to follow his benefactor and patron to England. Too, his wife was English and he already had many English friends and acquaintances as well as relatives by marriage. Lady Jane died November 2, 1849, in England. There is no record of children.

In London several fashionable addresses were listed both for his residence and for his office: Brook Street, Chapel Place, Bruton Street W., and Cavendish Square.

In 1859 he was honored by election to the Royal College of Physicians. He died February 26, 1870, at the age of eighty-four; cause of death was listed as senile decay. Supposedly he never returned to his native Canada.

Before leaving David, the controversy regarding his dishonorable discharge from the British army should be mentioned. Again, there are no certain facts—only conjecture and assumption. The cause of a controversy between Dr. David and Sir James McGrigor, director general of the medical department of the British army, and David's superior, is still unknown. Possibly it was the fact that Sir James was chagrinned because David refused to return to his army duties as assistant staff surgeon to Sir James. The option was apparently his; he had served the time for which he had been commissioned. By 1826, the date when the dispute was at its height, he was settled in France, had a flourishing practice, and had no desire or reason to leave civilian life. Whether from McGrigor's vindictiveness or for some other reason, at the botton of David's "Return of Services" document is a statement that he was "gazetted to full pay 25th Jan., 1824, ordered to Chatham for duty—Refused to obey that order—Dismissed His Majesty's Service for a gross breach of discipline and disobedience of the order of His Royal Highness, The Commander in Chief dated 13, May 1824."[45]

The most unusal aspect of the controversy was perhaps the fact that David had somehow come to know the Commander-in-Chief, Prince Frederick, Duke of York, second son of King George III, well enough to ask him to arbitrate the dispute. This the Duke agreed, reluctantly, to do and came to a decision which vindicated David. One can imagine the disappointment and embarrassment of Sir James McGrigor, who was fifteen years older than David and the King's physician extraordinary, in addition to being medical director-general of the British army. David must have been pleased and relieved to have his record cleared.[46]

In looking back over David's life the reader must be impressed with his worldly success in Europe, especially when remembering that he was a foreigner of common birth (in spite of his Fraser ancestors), a mixture of Scottish, Irish and French-Canadian blood. His success would seem to refute emphatically the earlier fears of his relatives that he was not suited for medicine. He achieved success that his brother may have envied; he possessed social prestige in Paris and London that Dr. John sought—or so says Dr. Burt Brown Barker. Perhaps; but many, not only his admirers, but also those who attempt objectivity, would tend to feel that John McLoughlin was too "big" a man, inwardly as well as outwardly, for petty envy or jealousy; he achieved his own success and enjoyed his own prestige in a manner truly unique.

There are other McLoughlins, of course, whose stories are still to be told, but they are of the younger generation; unfortunately, a great "generation gap" existed

Royal Family of the Columbia

between them and the three McLoughlin "rulers" just described. Their stories follow. Because each family member is affected by many events involving other members, a certain amount of repetition results unavoidably. This reiteration will be kept at a minimum whenever consistent with presenting as nearly complete a story as possible of each individual.

Alberta Brooks Fogdall

REFERENCES
CHAPTER 2

THE McLOUGHLINS OF RIVIÈRE-DU-LOUP

1 Baker, *op. cit.*, pp. 23-25.
2 *Ibid.*, pp. 32, 95.
3 Montgomery, *op. cit.*, pp. 4, 5, 6.
4 Robert Johnson, *John McLoughlin; Patriarch of the Northwest*, p. 16.
5 Montgomery, *op, cit.*, p. 4.
6 Barker, *op. cit.*, p. 62.
7 *Ibid.*, pp. 61-62.
8 *Ibid.*, pp. 30-32; also, Montgomery, *op. cit.*, p. 12.
9 Montgomery, *op, cit.*, p. 12.
10 Barker, *op. cit.*, pp. 95-96.
11 *Ibid.*, pp. 97-98.
12 *Ibid.*, p. 105. Dr. Barker had interpolated "leader" at this point, which is unnecessary since the word "religious" is a noun as well as an adjective and is used in the Catholic Church to mean "member of a religious order."
13 *Ibid.*, pp. 99-100.
14 *Ibid.*, p. 23.
15 *Ibid.*, pp. 26-27.
16 Montgomery, *op. cit.*, p. 6.
17 Barker, *op. cit.*, pp. 26, 144.
18 *Ibid.*, p. 33.
19 *Ibid.*, pages unnumbered, between Appendices I and II, photostats, Plates 10, 11, 12.
20 Photostats (microfilm), Archives of Oregon Historical Society.
21 Published by McGill University Press.
22 Montgomery, *op. cit.*, p. 16.
23 Horace Lyman, *History of Oregon*, II, p. 359.
24 Oregon Pioneer Association *Transactions*, 1186, pp. 42, 56.
25 Montgomery, *op. cit.*, p. 13.
26 Barker, *op. cit.*, pp. 29-30.
27 *Ibid.*, p. 46.
28 *Ibid.*, p. 159.
29 *Ibid.*, p. 74.
30 *Ibid.*, p. 152; p. 162; p. 175.
31 *Ibid.*, p. 83.
32 *Ibid.*, p. 151.
33 *Ibid.*, pp. 84-85.
34 *Ibid.*, p. 83.
35 *Ibid.*, p. 291.
36 *Ibid.*, p. 86. Dr. Barker gave no documentation for these statements.
37 *Ibid.*, pp. 161-162.
38 *Ibid.*, Archives, Oregon Historical Society.
39 *Ibid.*, p. 83.
40 *Ibid.*
41 *Ibid.*, pp. 177-178. A letter from Dr. John McLoughlin to Dr. Simon Fraser, March 19, 1826.
42 *Ibid.*, p. 92.
43 Microfilm, Arhives, Oregon Historical Society; letters of Miss A. M. Johnson, Archivist of Hudson's Bay Company, London. (Correspondence to Burt Brown Baker, January—April, 1954).
44 A letter from John Fraser to his cousin Dr. John McLoughlin, April 20, 1834, microfilm, Oregon Historical Society archives.
45 The specific material re David is in Barker, *op. cit.*, pp. 88-94. French history—general knowledge.
46 Plate 17, document, pp. 275-276.
47 A copy (possibly the original) of David's dissertation in 1810 for partial fulfillment of his Doctor of Medicine degree is in the library of McLoughlin House. Hard-cover bound and written in Latin, it is dedicated to John, "brother and friend".

PART II

DOCTOR, FUR TRADER, KING OF THE COLUMBIA

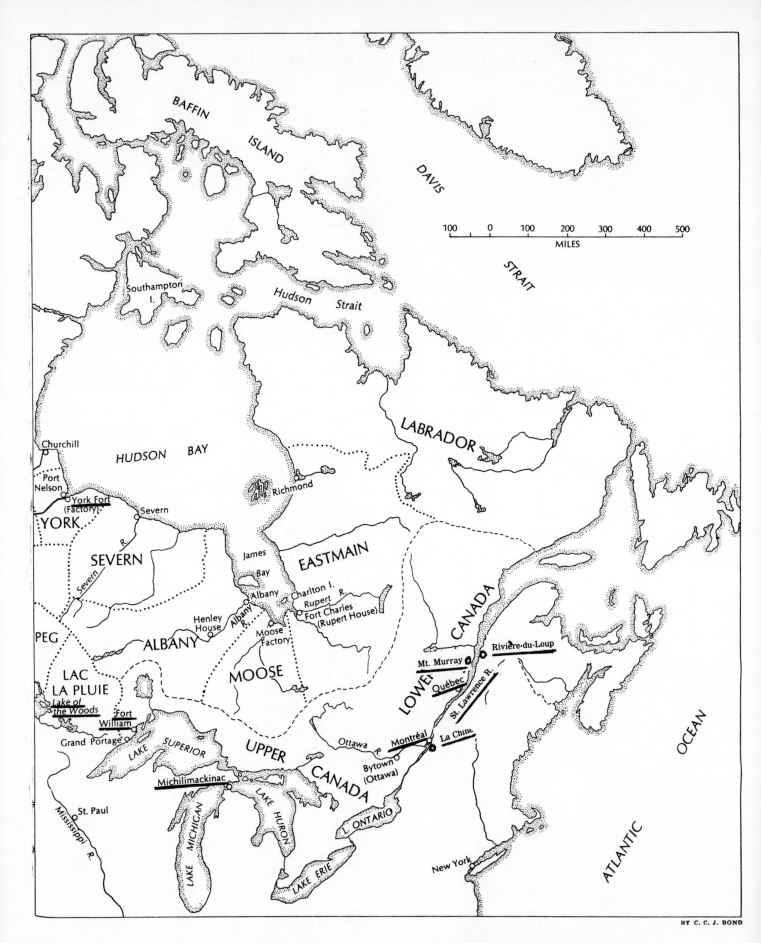

BAFFIN ISLAND

DAVIS STRAIT

100 0 100 200 300 400 500
MILES

Southampton I.

Hudson Strait

HUDSON BAY

Churchill

Port Nelson

York Fort (Factory)

Severn

YORK

SEVERN

Severn R.

LABRADOR

Richmond

James Bay

EASTMAIN

Albany

Charlton I.

Rupert R.

Fort Charles (Rupert House)

Henley House

Albany R.

Moose Factory

CANADA

Rivière-du-Loup

PEG

ALBANY

MOOSE

Mt. Murray

LOWER

Québec

St. Lawrence R.

LAC LA PLUIE

Lake of the Woods

Fort William

Grand Portage

LAKE SUPERIOR

UPPER

CANADA

Ottawa R.

Montréal

La Chine

Bytown (Ottawa)

Michilimackinac

St. Paul

Mississippi R.

LAKE MICHIGAN

LAKE HURON

L. ONTARIO

LAKE ERIE

New York

ATLANTIC OCEAN

ATLANTIC

BY C. C. J. BOND

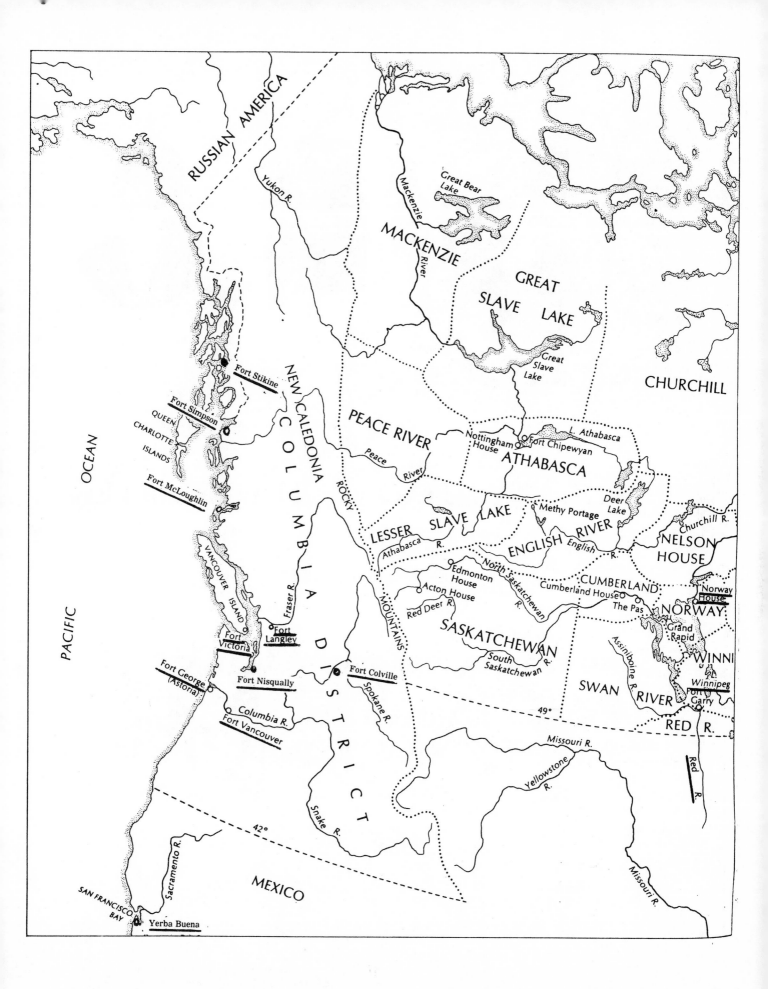

RUSSIAN AMERICA

Yukon R.

MACKENZIE

Mackenzie River

Great Bear Lake

GREAT

SLAVE LAKE

Great Slave Lake

CHURCHILL

Fort Stikine

NEW CALEDONIA

Fort Simpson

QUEEN CHARLOTTE ISLANDS

PEACE RIVER

Peace River

Nottingham House

Fort Chipewyan

L. Athabasca

ATHABASCA

Deer Lake

Fort McLoughlin

OCEAN

C O L U M B I A

ROCKY

LESSER SLAVE LAKE

Athabasca R.

Methy Portage

ENGLISH RIVER

English R.

Churchill R.

NELSON HOUSE

CUMBERLAND

Norway House

VANCOUVER ISLAND

Fraser R.

Edmonton House

Acton House

North Saskatchewan R.

Cumberland House

The Pas

NORWAY

PACIFIC

Fort Victoria

Fort Langley

Red Deer R.

Grand Rapid

WINNI

SASKATCHEWAN

D I S T R I C T

Fort George (Astoria)

Fort Nisqually

Fort Colville

Spokane R.

South Saskatchewan R.

SWAN RIVER

Assiniboine R.

Winnipeg L.

Fort Garry

Columbia R.

Fort Vancouver

MOUNTAINS

49°

RED R.

Missouri R.

Red R.

Yellowstone R.

Snake R.

42°

Missouri R.

Sacramento R.

MEXICO

SAN FRANCISCO BAY

Yerba Buena

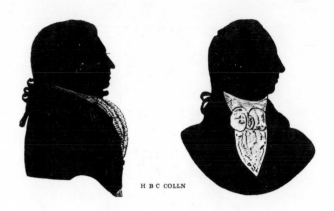

H B C Governors, remote in London

The Charter of 1670 begins with this initial surrounding the miniature of Charles II, by whom it was granted.

I   THE GRANTING OF THE CHARTER

CHAPTER 3

FROM STUDENT TO CHIEF FACTOR

In 1670, ten years after the restoration of the Stuarts to the English throne, Charles II, because he was influenced by those French promoter-explorers, Pierre Radisson and Médard Chouart, Sieur of Groseilliers, because he wished to repay his cousin Prince Rupert of the Rhine for services to the Royalist cause during the recent Civil War, and, because he was impecunious as always, "gave" Rupert and "seventeen other gentlemen" all the area drained by Hudson Bay, to be called Rupert's Land. To the organization called "The Governor and Company of Adventurers of England tradeing into Hudsons Baye," later simplified to the Hudson's Bay Company, the King granted more of North American than he or anyone else knew: "The whole trade of all those seas, streights, and bays, lakes, rivers, creeks, and sounds aforesaid...". This is the equivalent of most of modern Ontario and Québec, the whole of Manitoba, most of Saskatchewan, the southern half of Alberta, and most of the Northwest Territory—a total of 1,486,000 square miles.[2] The charter granted to this "Hudson's Bay Company" provided for the additional privileges of passing laws, sitting in judgment on civil and criminal cases in accordance with English law, using armed force when necessary, appointing officials, building forts, maintaining warships, and making war or peace on natives.[3] In return they had an obligation to look for a Northwest Passage and to pay each year to the King two elk and two beaver skins.[4]

For the first twelve years Prince Rupert was governor of the Honourable Company. Upon his death in 1682 the King's brother, James, Duke of York, replaced him, serving three years, until he succeeded to the throne in 1685. For the next seven years, until his imprisonment in the Tower, John Churchill, first Duke of Marlborough, was the Honourable Governor. Later the governance was vested in a board in London referred to as Honourable Governor and Committee as well as in a resident Governor and a council in North America.[5]

The Hudson's Bay Company was the oldest and the most prestigious of all the fur companies. Of all the English chartered companies only the Honourable Company is in existence today.[6] Hudson's Bay House at No. 3 Fenchurch Street housed the London headquarters, while York Factory (or "Ye House") on Hudson Bay was the original North American headquarters. Later a second headquarters was built at La Chine, near Montréal.

According to the original charter the company enjoyed a monopoly of the fur trade in the vaguely-defined Rupert's Land. Such a profitable monopoly could expect only to be challenged. In addition to expected resentment and contest from

Alberta Brooks Fogdall

France, which had most certainly established claim to some areas of North America, Canadian and other English companies, as well as private trappers, let it be known that any claim to monopoly was both invalid and unjust.

Most prominent of these aggressors was the Northwest Fur Company, a Canadian organization which by 1805 was already an amalgamation of several small Canadian companies which had been competing with one another. Promoted by Montréal merchant-capitalists, it was organized in 1784, reorganized in 1787 and again in 1804.[7]

Basically Scottish, it abounded with such names as MacTavish, McKay, MacKay, Mac (Mc) Kenzie, McDonald, McGillis, McDougal, McGillivray, and others, with variations. There were many Frasers too. Many of these Scotsmen were sons of the Highlanders who had fought under General James Wolfe in the French and Indian War, which in 1763 ended all French claims and challenges.

The Northwest Company, unlike the Hudson's Bay Company, which was a joint-stock company, began as a simple partnership and was interested in the area west of the Honourable Company's monopoly, the watershed of Hudson Bay.[8]

The younger company was daring and innovative, ambitious and energetic, vigorous and hardy, picturesque and lawless, far less conservative than its older competitor. Called contemptuously "Pedlars" by the Hudson's Bay men, the partners who controlled the company were experienced in the field, knowledgeable of the terrain, understanding of the life of the trapper, unlike the executives of the Hudson's Bay Company.[9]

Beginning in the area of the Red River (of the North), that is, in the Minnesota-Manitoba vicinity, the Northwest Company secured a foothold between 1807 and 1813 in the Northwest, filling a vacuum left by the Honourable Company, which in its turn challenged the "intrusion" by invading the Northwest Company's Athabasca precinct, north of Saskatchewan, building a colony at Red River on land "belonging" to Thomas Douglas, Lord Selkirk. A vast area of 116,000 square miles had become his property when he acquired control of the Honourable Company. It was the Company's purpose to build up a populous settlement in the valleys of the Red and Assiniboine Rivers. Obviously the Northwest Company contested the right of the HBC to the territory since (1) it cut across the main route of travel from the St. Lawrence to the Northwest, and (2) it contained one of the Northwest Company's main pemmican depots.[10]

Without going into tedious detail it is necessary to mention that the "Red River War" left devastation in its wake. Violence followed violence. Rival forts were built within sight of each other; traders broke each other's traplines; guerilla warfare followed, with kidnaping, thieving, and fighting at their worst. The Nor'westers took up arms; tensions were at the breaking point; both camps were in financial distress.[11]

48

Royal Family of the Columbia

Culmination of the mutual hostility was the Seven Oaks Massacre, near Winnipeg, June 19, 1816, at which the governor of the Red River Colony, Robert Semple, and twenty of his staff were killed.[12]

It was this massacre which served as catalyst to bring the British government, already disgusted with the cutthroat competition of its two subject companies, with the inefficiency, with the lack of profit, and with the waste of fur-bearing animals, ordered the two rival companies, British subjects all, to merge. Historian Frederick Merk described the depressing situation:

> Rupert's Land was strewn with the wreckage of battle. There was material wreckage in the form of exhaustion of fur preserves, the duplication of trading posts, and the multiplication of equipment and men. More difficult to cope with was the psychological wreckage, material bitterness and hate...and the propensity to waste and extravagance formed by the whole fur-trading communtiy.[13]

Caught as an innocent victim in the Seven Oaks-Red River Colony debacle was a thirty-two-old physician-fur trader of the Northwest Company, John McLoughlin. The massacre, perpetrated by half-breeds allied with the Nor'westers, was not even known to the future Chief Factor and his associates until several hours later. To save the Indians, who were innocent, from being blamed and punished, John McLoughlin and his superior, Kenneth McKenzie, gallantly offered themselves for bail to Selkirk as representatives of the Nor'westers. Selkirk refused bail, arresting both men and charging them with complicity in the murder of Governor Semple.[14]

While crossing Lake Superior to be tried, the canoe in which he was riding capsized and many of the men, including McKenzie, were drowned. Dr. McLoughlin was thought to be dead but was finally resuscitated with great difficulty. Legend has it that his already-graying hair turned white overnight as a result of the near-drowning. Fiction, no doubt, but the poor health suffered by the Doctor for the next few years he ascribed to this accident. Having no wish to avoid trial, the Nor'westers went voluntarily to York. McLoughlin's case was tried October 30, 1818, and after short deliberation the court completely exonerated him.[15]

To turn back a few years: After completing his medical education in 1803 John McLoughlin signed on as resident physician with the Northwest Company. From time to time he was depressed by and dissatisfied with his salary, wondering sporadically whether he should have gone to the West Indies at Simon Fraser's suggestion, or possibly to Detroit. He soon found that there was little variety in the diseases he treated, in the wounds of voyageurs he bandaged, and in the numerous half-breed infants he delivered; he came to feel that fur-trading itself would be more interesting and would present a greater challenge as his life work.[16] In a relatively short time, under the personal notice of William McGillivray, a partner of the Northwest Company, his duties combined those of physician and clerk, then gradually evolved into those of fur trader alone.[17]

In 1811 he had refused an offer to go to the Columbia perhaps because under the Northwest Company the Columbia District was a total loss, or perhaps because he had just assumed reponsibility for a wife and new family.[18] The next year he was a wintering partner, that is, a partner in the field. This was a position awarded to those traders who had served the company ably for some time. Romanticized by Washington Irving as "Lords of the lakes and forests," they spent the trapping seasons in the wilderness, usually at a post or a fort.[19]

The part played by John McLoughlin in the coalition of the Northwest Company and the Hudson's Bay Company has been variously interpreted, ranging from a highly significant role to one completely inconsequential.

In the fall of 1819 leaders of the Northwest Company gathered at Fort William, chief headquarters of the company and the station too of Chief Trader McLoughlin, to discuss the possibility and the pros and cons of a merger. While it was a stormy meeting with great diversity of opinion expressed, from it came a consensus that a coalition was the only alternative to chaos and annihilation. McLoughlin believed a union was feasible and insisted that terms must be fair to the wintering partners. Things drifted along until July 1820, when further plans were formulated at the annual meeting at Fort William.[20]

The rift between wintering partners on the one hand and the Montréal agents (or officers) of the Northwest Company on the other had widened to the point where each faction sent representatives to further its own interests in the coalition discussions in London. Dr. McLoughlin and Angus Bethune, Margaret's half nephew, carried eighteen powers of attorney for the wintering partners, while Edward Ellice and William McGillivray advocated terms which would benefit the company's agents. This tri-partite aspect complicated merger discussions which were already far from simple or easy to handle.[21]

According to one McLoughlin admirer, he "amazed the dignified directors of the Hudson's Bay Company by his forceful speeches and insistent demands. Who was this picturesque figure with white locks and flashing eyes, exhibiting a spirit born in the liberty of a new country! The young doctor stood out for better terms and his remarks made a profound impression upon the staid membership of the two companies."[22]

Burt Brown Barker wrote that McLoughlin and Bethune had no part in the merger, that the Hudson's Bay Company dealt directly with the Northwest Company agents, McTavish, McGillvrays, and Company.[23] Another historian believed that Dr.

McLoughlin was "elbowed to one side" in the settlement, that the eighteen powers of the attorney he carried were "not enough to win his case during the negotiations."[24]

At the meeting McLoughlin (among several others) was promoted to chief factor and assigned temporarily to the Lac la Pluie District.[25]

The claim was made that he was considered for governor but was passed over after consideration because he had been "too much" the Nor'wester and too concerned with the interests of the field employees. In addition, it was felt advisable to have an Englishman, rather than a Canadian, as governor.[26]

Briefly, what came out of the 1820-1821 meeting at No. 3 Fenchurch Street was a merger in which, according to some, the Northwest Company lost its identity with the retention of the name Hudson's Bay Company; much was said of a semantic difference between "merger" and "coalition."

However, the new Hudson's Bay Company, while not greatly different from the old, was not simply an enlarged version of it. The Northwest Company contributed a great deal to it both in method and personnel. The reorganization recognized and employed two distinct features of the younger company: (1) the formal financial partnership of the traders and (2) the regular participation of these partners in the management of the trade.[27] The Deed Poll of March 26, 1821, made a number of the wintering partners of the Northwest Company and a number of the field officers of the Hudson's Bay Company partners in the new company; they shared forty percent of the trade's profits, while sixty percent was shared by the proprietors.[28] Two ranks of officers were recognized: chief factors, of whom there were to be twenty-five, and chief traders, with a fixed number of twenty-eight. Of this total number of fifty-three officers or "commissioned gentlemen", thirty-two were from the Northwest Company. Regarding management in each of the two regional departments, the chief factors and chief traders were required to meet in council annually to determine police, promotions, methods, *etc.* This council was intended to support the resident governor (governor in the field).

The forty percent of the trade's profits belonging to the wintering partners was to be divided into eighty-five shares, seven shares to be retained by the company as a retiring fund, two to go to each chief factor annually, one to each chief trader.[29] The service "class" consisted of "servants" (voyageurs) and clerks, with various sub-divisions.[30] Each district had over it a chief factor and under him chief traders, chief clerks, first and second class clerks, apprentice-clerks, interpreters, voyageurs, and laborers.[31]

The Hudson's Bay Company was now augmented with more (often superfluous) posts and personnel of the former Northwest Company. (In most cases the posts were just that, not forts, for the Northwest Company posts as a rule had no military force at all, depending upon the good will of the natives.) The HBC territory was not limited to "Rupert's Land", but comprised in addition the entire Canadian West, including the "Oregon Country."[32]   This vast land mass was organized into four districts:

1.   Northern Department—Rupert's Land (plus New Caledonia until 1825).
2. Southern Department—the James Bay area and south to Upper and Lower Canada.
3. Montréal Department—Upper and Lower Canada (and later Labrador).
4. Columbia District—of special interest to this story, the entire Columbia River Valley (and after 1825, New Caledonia, which was roughly mainland British Columbia). At that time the Columbia District became the Columbia Department.[33]

William Williams was at first governor of the Southern and Montréal Departments; George Simpson governed the Northern Department and the Columbia District, with both field governors responsible to the Governor and Committee in London. In 1826 Williams was recalled and Simpson became Deputy Governor of Williams' territories and remained governor of his own departments, soon taking the title of acting governor-in-chief of the Honourable Company's North American lands.[34] In 1839 he received the full title.[35]

It is of interest to note that the newly-made chief factor was not so thoroughly absorbed in business while in London that he could not find time for pleasure. He crossed the Channel late in 1820 or early in 1821 to visit his brother, Dr. David, either in Boulogne or in Paris, probably the former.[36] According to Burt Brown Barker the Doctor returned to Canada, going back to France for the winter, but he presented no documentation for the claim.[37] Letters from Dr. McLoughlin to Dr. Fraser dated November 1821 (1820) and eighteen months later, May 1822, showed him in eastern Canada (St. Johns, Newfoundland, and Montréal) but do not contain information relevant to the above point.[38]

Not only did the Chief Factor enjoy France; he also shopped in London, for he loved fine clothes. Supposedly David had urged him to "play the game of dress and manners." The narrative continues that he outfitted himself with a new suit and hat in a fashionable haberdashery. He had brought with him a number of prime-quality beaver pelts carefully rolled inside a scarlet blanket; he insisted that the clothier make the new hat of his own pelts, not of skins of the Hudson's Bay Company, for he was still a loyal Nor'wester. The hat would thus be the silkiest fur hat in London! The tailor who made his suit was reportedly delighted with the great height, the wide shoulders, and the impressive barrel chest, all of which were so admirably suited for the extra-wide lapels newly in fashion.[39]

John McLoughlin, chief factor, had already proved himself a successful business man. It was also his happy destiny to become a family man. So far as is known he had not been involved romantically until about 1808 when he was twenty-three or twenty-four years old. As a result of either a liaison or of a "fur-trade marriage" a son was born in 1809, named Joseph, possibly for a maternal uncle of the Doctor. His mother, usually described only as "a Chippewa Indian of Red River descent," died at his birth.[40]

The question of Joseph's legitimacy is one that has interested historical writers. His younger half brother David, writing many years later (c. 1900), stated that his father had married for the first time in 1808.[41] One writer showed inconsistency when he referred to Joseph as John McLoughlin's "natural son" in the index and as "a son by his first wife" in the text.[42] Another, undecided as to Joseph's legitimacy, temporized by referring to the Doctor's "obscure affair" on page twenty-six, while on pages twenty-nine and thirty he speculated that a man with such a "lofty sense of moral values" as McLoughlin's (as well as with the pragmatic philosophy of protecting his future standing in the Honourable Company) would have contracted a marriage, fur-trade style, with the woman who was his first son's mother; consequently, in this way Joseph was legitimate in the same way as were his four younger half siblings.[43]

While at Fort William (Kaministikwia) romance of a permanent nature became part of the Doctor's busy life in the person of Margaret (or the French equivalent, Marguerite) Wadin McKay. She and her husband, well-known Alexander McKay, and their son and three daughters lived at Sault Ste. Marie, Ontario, connecting Lake Huron and Lake Superior, which was, like Fort William, within the area under the supervision of Chief Trader McLoughlin.

Controversy has existed as to whether Dr. John was attracted to Mrs. McKay before her husband's tragic death on the *Tonquin* in 1811, or whether their courtship began after a "respectable" interval following his death, with their marriage soon following. In any case, their first child, John Jr., was born August 18, 1812. One author discreetly postponed young John's birth until December 1812.[44]

It goes without saying that Herbert Beaver, discussed elsewhere, would present the most damaging interpretation, that John and Margaret were "married" before she learned of her husband's death.[45]

The new Mrs. McLoughlin was said to take Joseph as her own son, while her husband assumed the care of her three daughters. Tom, her only son, had gone with his father when the latter left to join the Astor expedition in 1810 and had remained in the Northwest.[46]

Three other children were born after John to the McLoughlins: Maria Elizabeth (called Eliza by her family), probably in 1814; Maria Eloisa in 1817, and David, named for his father's only brother, in 1821, while his father was attending the coalition conference in London.

Alberta Brooks Fogdall

Margaret McKay McLoughlin was nine years older than her new husband; at the time of their marriage they were twenty-seven and thirty-six. Born near Montréal, she was said by most historians to be a daughter of Étienne Wadin, a Swiss fur trader and merchant, who was born in Berne, and respected in both business and political circles, who came in Canada with the British army. However, she was not the daughter of his wife, Marie Josèphe Déguire, who "had some Indian blood" and apparently remained in eastern Canada, but of a "Chippewa or Cree Indian of the Red River Country,"[47] or possibly of a half-breed Chippewa, with whom Mr. Wadin lived[48] while in the fur country. Thus Margaret was either one-half or one-fourth Indian.

David McLoughlin, writing about 1900, however, gave his mother's maiden name as Margaret Bruce, daughter of a Scottish trader. Because his information concerning his family was so scanty, in fact almost nil (see Chapter 11), the first identification presented would appear to be more nearly valid.[49] One writer has based his description of Mrs. McLoughlin upon David's writing;[50] otherwise, the Wadin identification is favored by historians and by biographers of Dr. John McLoughlin.

According to legend Margaret was attractive, with light coppery skin, flashing black eyes, and long, lustrous, straight black hair which reached her waist. She was a happy person, with a calm, even disposition, the perfect foil, apparently, for her tempestuous, excitable husband. She was the only person, with the possible exception of James Douglas, who was able to calm him when his "Irish temper" caused him to lose control. She exerted a great deal of influence over him. Angered by a thoughtless or stupid action of an employee or of one of the natives, her attentive listening as she knitted, a word or two of quiet advice and a smile would quiet his storming up and down the room; he was disarmed, would laugh, kiss her quickly, and return to his work. For Margaret he would do almost anything.

She was a loving mother and an excellent housekeeper and manager. Most of all, she relieved her husband of all anxiety and worry concerning his home and family; he could be absent on his much too frequent expeditions knowing that all was well at home and was thus able to concentrate all his energies on his work.[51] They were an exceptionally well-suited couple, complementing each other in almost every respect.

Speculation as to Margaret's education consisted chiefly of the possibility that she had attended the Ursuline Convent in Québec, where Dr. John's sister Marie-Louise had been a pupil, then teacher, and, finally, Mother Superior. One writer even suggested romantically that she "may have learned something of her future husband long before she met him" from Marie-Louise.[52] This possibility has been contradicted by other historians, who pointed out that Margaret's father, her first husband, and her eldest daughter, Mary, were all Protestant, implying that Margaret was undoubtedly also Protestant, and therefore would not have attended a Catholic convent school. More significant, recorded documents have shown that she was unable even to write her name, using the simple X as her signature. This latter factor would seem to negate her having received a formal education.[53]

Her "Indian blood", whether fifty or twenty-five percent, prevented her from putting herself forward. Shy and retiring and perhaps suffering from a feeling of inferiority, she preferred to remain in the background, while her husband, and later the children, moved forward in the public eye. She was always there, in the background, quietly giving her husband the comfort and support he needed in his tense, energetic life. He was faithful to her all his life setting an example of marital fidelity for his employees, most of whom also had married Indian or half-Indian women.[54] He was even said to have treated her "like a princess." An unidentified missionary believed him to be as loyal as if (she were) a daughter of Victoria; his gallantry knew no bounds." A slight to Margaret was a slight to him. On one occasion, when the people of the Fort gave officers of the *Modeste* a picnic, the Doctor saw his wife walking alone carrying a basket; instantly, he ordered one of the men to go to her and he himself also went to her aid. Servants were under orders always to remove their hats in her presence.[55]

The new Chief Factor had been assigned at the London Conference to the Lac la Pluie (Rainy Lake) district; thus he continued to make Fort William his headquarters. However, he also served as a trouble shooter and ambassador-at-large, swinging around the circle of Rupert's Land, reconciling former not-too-happy Nor'westers to the new order of things. In short, he was, in effect, assistant to the new governor, George Simpson, as he persuaded his former co-workers that certain concessions to the Hudson's Bay Company had been necessary, even though it meant for the Northwest Company losing its name and separate identity.

This irksome, difficult task continued until 1822, when Mr. Simpson assigned him to Fort Frances, on the Lake of the Woods, a small fort about one hundred miles west of Fort William. Apparently the assignment to this seemingly unimportant fort was a stop-gap until a more appropriate and a more challenging opening was available. He was returned to Fort Frances following the 1823 council.[56] Finally, at the July 1824 council at York Factory—he was now almost forty—he felt that he surely would receive a major appointment at last. The Governor, on the morning of July 10, began the lengthy and rather tedious business meeting, leaving appointments of the officers to the last. Then, as the names and assignments were called off one by one, only one station and one name remained. Suddenly Dr. McLoughlin realized that Governor Simpson was announcing his appointment to the Columbia District. As the list was completed he realized too that Peter Skene Ogden was one of the three chief traders assigned to assist him on the Columbia.[57]

What was the reaction of Dr. John McLoughlin at York Factory to his long-awaited appointment? The traditional view has been that he was delighted; he was grateful for the honor, overjoyed at the challenge. Here was a whole new territory to be developed—and it was his responsibility.

> The Columbia's new chief sat transfixed. Had he heard aright? Was it actually he, John McLoughlin, who had been chosen to serve in the company's western empire?…At last the doctor was to have a post worthy of his competence…he rose to his majestic height, bowed his head, made the sign of the cross over his heart…gave thanks to Almighty God.[58]

Several other authors share a viewpoint polarized to the above: "Some of his associates thought he was exiled to the Columbia because of his partisanship."[59] That is, at the merger conference he had argued vehemently for better terms for the Northwest Company and for the wintering partners, as well as higher wages for the trappers and servants, who he felt had been grossly underpaid even though they risked their lives to secure the beaver skins. They were paid seventeen pounds a year and worked like beasts of burden.

A more extreme view was that the Company assignment was punitive, that John McLoughlin was being sent into exile to this remote, isolated section of the continent. Here he could be left in obscurity, forgotten; the Columbia was the "problem child" of the fur trade provinces. Here at so great a distance from London he could not "needle" the Honourable Governor and Committee about increasing the voyageurs' wages or improving their working conditions.[60]

"Dr. John McLoughlin, ex-Nor'wester, was banished to the Columbia because he dared contend for better terms for his company in the union of 1821…John McLoughlin had a much higher concept of duty (than had Simpson) to his fellow men…"[61]

Dr. McLoughlin's bitter enemy Herbert Beaver stated as his opinion that the Chief Factor was relegated to the hinterlands because of his unimportance. This viewpoint is perhaps the most uncomplimentary of all.[62]

Regardless of the reasons for his appointment to the Columbia, he began the long trek from York on July 27, just seventeen days after receiving the appointment. Deputy Governor Simpson was, as always, in a hurry and urged his employee to leave as soon as possible. He planned to overtake the Chief Factor after the arrival in York of a supply ship from England for which he felt he had to wait. When the ship still had not arrived by August 17, Mr. Simpson decided to wait no longer and set out; he hoped to break all existing speed records.[63]

Royal Family of the Columbia

It seems relevant to insert here another of the many controversies concerning the McLoughlins: Did the Chief Factor's family accompany him, or not? If not, how and when did they reach the Columbia?

Dr. Burt Brown Barker insisted that the two youngest McLoughlin children, Eloisa and David, and Mrs. McLoughlin accompanied the Doctor in 1824 to his new assignment; he gave no documentation.[64] Both Eloisa and David much later in their lives attested in separate accounts that they had made the trip west in 1824, but so much time had elapsed that their memories were not necessarily reliable.[65]

Richard Montgomery was equally insistent that the Chief Factor did *not* take any of his family with him in 1824:

....The start of his (McLoughlin's) long trek across America had been tinged with disappointment. Once he had become aware of the speed he would have to maintain to keep up the swift pace Governor Simpson was certain to set, he had reluctantly decided to leave his family behind. The probability is that he had not even been able to see them before his departure. What with extended conferences and elaborate preparations for the overland journey, he could scarcely have sandwiched a side trip to Fort Frances into the scant seventeen days at his disposal.[66]

In addition, there was no mention of the presence of a family either in the Doctor's meticulously kept records or in Governor Simpson's journal. The law of averages would assume a reference to a family in at least one of these records; the Governor, especially, would not have hesitated to express his disapproval of their presence.[67]

Montgomery admitted that he did not know how or when Mrs. McLoughlin and the children arrived. However, he described Dr. McLoughlin at the end of his first year on the Columbia (1825) as thinking often of his family back in Canada and knowing that he must have them join him as soon as possible. Strangely, though, they were there waiting on the boat landing at Fort Vancouver July 5, 1826, with their husband and father preparing to depart on a brigade, according to John Work (a clerk, later to be a chief factor) in his diary. They were sending John Jr. (according to Montgomery) with an express to be educated in the East. If the diary of John Work can be trusted, and there is probably no reason to doubt its authenticity and accuracy, the family *must* have arrived sometime between 1824 and 1826, possibly with an express returning from Canada.[68] But John Jr. was definitely *not* among the children on the boat landing that July 5. He had apparently not left eastern Canada, for as early as 1820 Dr. McLoughlin wrote of "my son" (being in Québec) and still in 1823 in letters from Dr. McLoughlin to his uncle Dr. Simon Fraser[69] he thanked Dr. Fraser for "the kind attention you have shown my little Boy," and letters of 1825[70] from the Doctor to his uncle mention John Jr. (and his sister Eliza) as continuing in schools in and near Québec, as do letters of 1826 from Governor Simpson at La Chine to Dr. Fraser at Terrebonne.[71]

Which children lived at Fort Vancouver? John Jr. did not; nor did Eliza; her father felt that she was too frail to make the long trip across the continent and to live in the rigorous frontier country. Letters prove that she remained in Canada to be educated at the Ursuline Convent in Québec; she married young and continued to live in Québec.[72] Of John and Margaret's four children, only Eloisa and David, seven to nine and three to five years of age, respectively (depending on which year they joined their father), lived at Fort Vancouver during the period 1824-1830.

John's eldest son, Joseph, received no education at all;[73] he was about fifteen when the move was made to Fort Vancouver, but he may or may not have moved there with his stepmother and small half sister and half brother. Of Margaret's children, Tom McKay was married and a father and already on the Pacific Coast when John McLoughlin was assigned to the Columbia. Tom's three younger sisters remained in Canada, all of them marrying early.[74]

In the perspective of more than 150 years it is no doubt immaterial, except as an exercise in historical interpretation, whether the family accompanied the Doctor in 1824, or whether they joined him in 1825 or in 1826 "when the Fort was ready."[75] Too, in the 1970s it may be irrelevant just how many and which ones of the family went to the Columbia and how many and which ones remained in the East. As Mr. Thomas Whidden, a great, great-grandson of Dr. John McLoughlin, wrote, "(I don't know) when Dr. John let his family join him at Fort Vancouver...(but) I'm sure that they all get along well in heaven, forgiving and peaceful with one another."[76] Perhaps that one sentence of his direct descendant can conclude discussion of this unsolved and probably unsolvable controversy.

Before discussing the "who" and "when", Chief Factor McLoughlin had been left as he was beginning the long journey to the Pacific Coast, with his superior, George Simpson, three weeks behind, but grimly determined to overtake him. In fact the Governor had patronizingly offered his subordinate a headstart, assuring him confidently that they would meet enroute, as of course they did.[77] Governor George Simpson was a man of his word.

At 7:00 o'clock, in the morning of September 27, the "Emperor" caught up with the "King" at Portage la Biche, near the Athabasca River, in the Rockies. Dr. McLoughlin was embarrassed to be caught still in camp. Maliciously the Governor pointed out with pride the speed with which he had traveled, almost implying that the Chief Factor was malingering.[78]

In his journal he expressed his disapproval, that passage which is quoted in every McLoughlin biography or textbook of Pacific Northwest history:

He was such a figure as I should not like to meet in a dark Night in one of the bye lanes in the neighbourhood of London, dressed in Clothes that had once been fashionable, but now covered with a thousand patches of different Colours...his hands evidently Showing that he had not lost much time at his Toilette, Loaded with Arms and his own herculean dimensions forming a tout ensemble that would convey a good idea of the highway men of former days.[79]

When the Governor and the Chief Factor arrived at Astoria (Fort George), near the mouth of the Columbia on the south bank, they realized that it was unsuitable as chief headquarters of the Columbia District. For one thing, it was badly run down. For another, a location was needed nearer to inland trade facilities, yet on the water. Also, there was insufficient space and the soil was not sufficiently fertile for the Company's agricultural plans.[80] Most important, however, was the strong possibility that when at long last the United States and Britain settled the boundary controversy all the area south of the Columbia would be American.[81]

At an earlier period Astoria had served its purpose for John Jacob Astor's fur company and for the Northwest Company in keeping the good will of the Chinooks, who had been the first tribe to sell pelts to the fur companies. Some of the natives felt very strongly about the loss they would suffer in losing the post. Now it would be difficult to prevent the "King George Men" from reaching and trading with the upper Columbia tribes. In revenge they pulled down the stockade and burned the fort in 1826 and 1827.[82]

Governor Simpson wanted the replacement for Fort George to be established at the mouth of the Fraser River, two or three degrees north of Astoria, where it would be more central to both the coast and the interior and could serve as a base for the China trade. Since he was the "boss", the Chief Factor knew he would have to yield in spite of his own eight years' seniority and his greater experience in the fields unless he could convince the Deputy Governor that Belle Vue Point, about ninety miles up the Columbia was more advantageous to the Honourable Company's interests.[83] The Deputy Governor "magnanimously" allowed Dr. McLoughlin to prove his choice superior by exploring as far as the foothills of the Cascades, while he himself would send an expedition up the Fraser. This "hair-raising" trip, made by a party of forty under the leadership of Chief Trader James McMillan and including Tom McKay, Mrs. McLoughlin's son, finally proved even to the opinionated Mr. Simpson that the Fraser was not easily navigable.[84]

In the meantime John McLoughlin explored to see whether ships could reach the confluence of the Columbia and Willamette. He sent swift canoes on the Columbia and made several trips north more than one hundred miles into the interior. He obtained all the information he felt necessary, found a practicable channel, and drew a map.[85] For pragmatic reasons the Governor yielded to his Chief Factor, agreeing that the new fort would be built at the site of the latter's choice, Belle Vue Point, so named in 1792 by Lieutenant William Broughton, a companion of George Vancouver, Mr. Simpson insisted, however, that the name be changed to Vancouver, patriotically preferring an English to a French name.[86]

The ultimate reason for building Fort Vancouver was one of political expediency for George Canning, British Foreign Secretary, had strongly intimated that Great Britain would attempt to retain the territory north of the Columbia, but felt it futile to continue to claim land south of the River. The Hudson's Bay Company, consequently, was instructed to "treat all people kindly" but to see that all white non-Britons remain south of the Columbia.[87]

The strategic site chosen was accessible to both the Columbia and the Willamette, with plenty of fertile soil for agriculture. It was the head of navigation, the convergence of three great fur trails: The Columbia from the east, the Willamette from the south, and the Cowlitz from the north, leading to Puget Sound and New Caledonia. It was near the scene of operations, yet accessible to the Pacific.[88]

The fort itself was originally built about one mile from the river; this distance was inconvenient, for it proved irksome to transport food and supplies from the distant boat landing. Water, too, was not easily accessible, having to be hauled too great a distance. Early in 1829 a new fort was built about one mile west on lower ground and closer to the river.[89] The first site is today occupied by the Washington State School for the Deaf.

During the period when Fort Vancouver was being built the Chief Factor did not waste time. While the work progressed he divided his time between Vancouver and Fort George. His frequent canoe trips on the Columbia transporting supplies and building materials resulted in his becoming friendly with the Indians along the route. He soon received the titles "White-Headed Eagle", due of course to his impressive mane of white hair, and "hyas tyee" (Great Chief).[90]

Dr. McLoughlin during the year 1824-1825 was "blessed" with the presence of his undefatigable superior. The Little Emperor had applied earlier to the Company London headquarters for a leave to return to England in order to marry; he had been refused and ordered to remain in North America until the Columbia District was well established.[91] By March 1825 the post was ready for occupancy, although far from completed.[92]

The Governor was delighted. With bark roofs in place to furnish shelter, and movable goods from Fort George ferried upstream "including 31 head of cattle and 17 hogs riding a specially constructed barge", Mr. Simpson was ready to christen the new post and be on his way east to Canada and ultimately to England.

Royal Family of the Columbia

At sunrise on March 19, 1825, the Governor "baptized (the post) by breaking a Bottle of Rum on the Flag Staff and repeating...in a loud voice: 'In behalf of the Hon'ble Hudson's Bay Co'y I hereby name this Establishment FORT VANCOUVER, God save King George the 4th!' With three cheers." Three rousing cheers went up from the assembled employees and Indians who then enjoyed "a couple of Drams" dispensed by the Governor. He had chosen the post's name as a pointed reminder to the United States that the first man to penetrate the Columbia this far had not been an American citizen, but a subject of Great Britian.[93]

He repeated emphatically to the Chief Factor instructions based on policies set up during the past year:

1. Stop all traffic in alcohol.
2. Develop the coastal trade so long neglected by the Northwest Company.
3. Open business with the Russians (*i. e.,* with the Russian Fur Company).
4. Finish building Fort Langley on the Fraser.
5. Sweep the country between the Columbia and United States territory clean of fur-bearing animals; that is, "trap it out."
6. Send brigades south to California.
7. Plant gardens.
8. Most of all, keep the expenses down![94]

Off the Governor went, leaving at 9:00 A.M. and heading east to the skirl of his ubiquitous bagpipes. He ran the legs off his subordinates in his characteristic headlong course back East. His group collapsed due to exhaustion on the central prairies, but he continued swiftly on to London. The Governor and Committee were much impressed with his whirlwind achievements and voted a 500 pound bonus to the Little Emperor.[95]

Meanwhile, back at the Fort, with his superior's repeated injunctions still ringing in his ears, Chief Factor John McLoughlin must have experienced a tremendous feeling of relief as the Governor sailed away, and accompanying his relief was the triumphant realization that he was now in fact, if not yet in name, the King of the Columbia.

REFERENCES

CHAPTER 3

FROM STUDENT TO CHIEF FACTOR

1 *The Beaver*, house organ of the Hudson's Bay Company, Tercentennial issue, Autumn 1970, p.6. These "seventeen other gentlemen included the Duke of Albemarle (the former Cromwellian General Monk), who was instrumental in Charles II's restoration to the throne; Anthony Ashley Cooper (Earl of Shaftesbury), and Sir Philip Carteret.

2 Douglas MacKay, *The Honourable Company*, p. 34.

3 Oscar O. Winther, *The Great Northwest*, p. 49.

4 Dorothy O. Johansen, *Empire of the Columbia*, p. 65.

5 MacKay, *op. cit.*, p. 46.

6 The form of the Hudson's Bay Company best known to the public today is probably its large department stores in Canada, located in Montreal, Winnipeg, Saskatoon, Calgary, Edmonton, Vancouver, and Victoria (MacKay, p. 311). HBC customers and the HBC itself refer to them familiarly as "The Bay."

7 Johansen, *op. cit.*, pp. 65-66.

8 *Ibid.*

9 MacKay, *op. cit.*, p. 106.

10 *Ibid.*, pp. 134-136, 138.

11 A.S. Marquis, *Dr. John McLoughlin*, p. 9.

12 Richard Montgomery, *The White-Headed Eagle*, p. 31.

13 *The Beaver*, p. 46 (from Merk).

14 Montgomery, *op. cit.*, pp. 31-32.

15 *Ibid.*, p. 33.

16 Burt Brown Barker, *The McLoughlin Empire*, p. 35.

17 Montgomery, *op. cit.*, p. 21.

18 Jane Tipton, *John McLoughlin, Chief Factor of the Hudson's Bay Company at Fort Vancouver*, p. 25.

19 MacKay, *op. cit.*, p. 107.

20 Montgomery, *op. cit.*, p. 39.

21 MacKay, *op. cit.*, p. 153.

22 Marquis, *op. cit.*, p. 10.

23 Barker, *op. cit.*, p. 43.

24 MacKay, *op. cit.*, pp. 152-153.

25 *The Beaver*, p. 50.

26 Montgomery, *op. cit.*, p. 47.

27 *The Beaver*, p. 46.

28 E. E. Rich, *The Hudson's Bay Company*, Vol. I, p. 406.

29 Montgomery, *op. cit.*, pp. 45-47.

30 Marquis, *op. cit.*, pp. 7-8.

31 Gordon Speck, *Northwest Explorations*, p. 365.

32 Horace S. Lyman, *History of Oregon*, Vol. II, p. 265.

33 Winther, *op. cit.*, p. 52.

34 *Ibid.*, pp. 53-54.

35 MacKay, *op. cit.*, p. 178.

36 Montgomery, *op. cit.*, p. 44.

37 Barker, *op. cit.*, p. 43.

38 *Ibid.*, pp. 171-173.

39 T. D. Allen, *Troubled Border*, pp. 22-24.

40 Barker, *op. cit.*, p. 16, is one example.

41 David McLoughlin, "Correspondence", Archives, Oregon Historical Society.

42 Robert Johnson, *John McLoughlin, Patriarch of the Northwest,* p. 120.

43 Montgomery, *op. cit.,* pp. 26, 29-30.

44 Allen, *op. cit.,* p. 40.

45 Herbert Beaver, *Reports and Letters,* p. 82.

46 Montgomery, *op. cit.,* p. 27.

47 Helen Krebs Smith, *With Her Own Wings,* p. 21.

48 Tipton, *op. cit.,* p. 40.

49 McLoughlin, *loc. cit.*

50 Johnson, *op. cit.,* pp. 27-28.

51 Montgomery, *op. cit.,* p. 181.

52 *Ibid.,* p. 26.

53 T. C. Elliott, "Margaret Wadin McKay McLoughlin", *Oregon Historical Quarterly,* Vol. 36 (December 1935), p. 342.

54 Smith, *op. cit.,* pp. 21-25.

55 Eva Emery, Dye, *McLoughlin and Old Oregon,* p. 331.

56 Montgomery, *op. cit.,* pp. 56-57.

57 Frederick Merk, *Fur Trade and Empire,* pp. 215-217.

58 Montgomery, *op cit.,* p. 58.

59 Johansen, *op. cit.,* pp. 127-128.

60 Allen, *op. cit.,* pp. 31-32.

61 Speck, *op. cit.,* p. 367.

62 Beaver, *op. cit.,* p. XII.

63 Montgomery, *op. cit.,* pp. 60-61.

64 Barker, *op. cit.,* p. 44.

65 Eloisa McLoughlin Harvey, "Recollections", Bancroft Collection Oregon Historical Society Archives.

66 Montgomery, *op. cit.,* p. 62.

67 *Ibid.,* p. 108. A compromise solution might be that the family trailed the Chief Factor in a canoe (or canoes). (Elliott, *op. cit.,* p. 346; Tipton, *op. cit.,* p. XIII.)

68 Montgomery, *op. cit.,* pp. 96-97.

69 Barker, *op. cit.,* pp. 171-172; 173-174.

70 *Ibid.,* pp. 174-175.

71 *Ibid.,* pp. 181-182.

72 *Ibid.,* pp. 171-172.

73 H. H. Bancroft, *History of Oregon,* Vol. I, p. 37.

74 Montgomery, *op. cit.,* p. 326.

75 Smith, *op. cit.,* p. 24.

76 Letter from Thomas Marvin Whidden to the author, dated October 17, 1972.

77 Montgomery, *op. cit.,* p. 62.

78 *Ibid.,* p. 63.

79 For example, MacKay, p. 187; Montgomery, p. 63; Johansen, 128; Winther, p. 57, *et al.*

80 Stewart Holbrook, *The Columbia,* p. 62.

81 Horace S. Lyman, *History of Oregon,* Vol. II, p. 362.

82 Johansen, *op. cit.,* p. 126.

83 Montgomery, *op. cit.,* p. 71.

84 *Ibid.,* pp. 72-73.

85 Lyman, *op. cit.,* p. 367.

86 Montgomery, *op. cit.,* p. 74.

87 Arthur L. Throckmorton, *The Oregon Boundary Question,* p. 24.

88 S. A. Clarke, *Pioneer Days of Oregon,* Vol. I, p. 180.

89 John B. Horner, *Days and Deeds in the Oregon Country,* p. 89.

90 Montgomery, *op. cit.,* p. 76.

91 David Lavender, *Land of Giants,* p. 118.

92 Montgomery, *op. cit.,* p. 81.

93 Lavender, *op. cit.,* p.122 (quoted from the Simpson Journal).

94 *Ibid.,* p.123.

95 *Ibid.*

Fort Vancouver, Columbia River, an unsigned, undated watercolour that, judging from the buildings, might date from the early 1850s. The view faces stores and shop buildings at west of enclosure; at right, with cannon in front, is the Chief Factor's house.

S.S. Beaver Model

64

CHAPTER 4

LIFE AT THE PALACE

THE KING'S DOMESTIC POLICY

In the sense that "a man's home is his castle" Fort Vancouver was John McLoughlin's palace. He planned it. He built it. He and his beloved wife lived there for approximately twenty years. It was home for some of his children and for several months of three of his grandchildren.

In a wider sense it was a palace also for members of the Chief Factor's staff and for the visitors who came there through the years, whether traders, missionaries, or pioneers. The McLoughlin residence was truly palatial with its baronial dining hall, the huge mahogany dining table, the damask napery, the flat silver, the Spode china, the Waterford glassware, all of which were the setting of the multi-course gourmet dinners served there. More than a palace, it was also a refuge, on oasis in a desert of loneliness, discouragement, and fatigue, "a sanctuary of civilization in the heart of the savage western country."[1] Its description as the New York of the Pacific was not inappropriate. Its commercial importance as the convergence of three principal fur trails was not overstated.[2]

What was the external appearance of this great Fort Vancouver? Not all historians agree on its dimensions, but in general it has been described as a parallelogram 750 feet by 450 feet and enclosed by a stockade twenty feet high. There was a bastion in the northwest corner mounting two twelve pounders, while in the center against the front wall were several eighteen pounders. These cannon were chiefly for appearance and seldom, if ever, put to use.

Enclosed in a quadrangle were the homes of the married officers, the Chief Factor's residence dominating the others. Of French-Canadian style, the white one-story house, built about eight feet above the ground for storage space, contained ten rooms. A flight of stairs led up from each of a veranda into a central hallway. In front of the Chief Factor's home were flowers in abundance, while trellises were covered romantically and practically with grape vines.[3] Behind the residence were a kitchen, a wash house, and several other outbuildings, as shown in a model at the Fort Vancouver Visitors Center. Over the compound flew a Union Jack.

The interiors of the unpretentious small houses were of rough, unpainted lumber. The partitions were of planed boards, while the floor boards were unplaned except in the McLoughlin home and in the main office. In general the houses consisted of only two rooms, one used as kitchen and dining room, the other as sitting and sleeping room. Although scantily furnished, with chair, table, and bench, they were warm and relatively comfortable.

A short distance outside the stockade a village of more than sixty houses, built in rows so as to form streets where children could play, for mechanics, laborers, and voyageurs, stood on the bank of the Columbia. Two or three families with their Indian slaves lived in one house.

Approximately forty other buildings lay within the stockade, including a pharmacy, a stone power house, a chapel used both for religious services and as a school, offices, warehouses for furs, English goods, and other commodities, workshops for mechanics, carpenters, blacksmiths, coopers, wheelwrights, tanners, and others. This was no place for idlers. The Chief Factor had no use for a lazy or an idle man. If at the moment there was nothing for a voyageur to do, he was sent to work in the gardens, the orchards, or, later, the mills. The work day began early, and ended at six o'clock five days a week and at five o'clock on Saturdays, when the workers received their rations.[4] Sunday was, of course, a day of rest and of attending religious services in the chapel.

The smiths had the never-ending task of keeping the tools and machinery in order, each day making fifty axes and hatchets for the Indians and for traders. The three bakers were under constant pressure to provide bread for all the land workers and sea biscuits for the crews of the Columbia Department's coasting vessels. Clerks worked from morning to midnight on the annual accounts, checking and re-checking figures to show that the Department was doing well.[5]

Entrance and exit to the Fort for wagons and carts were by two wide double gates which were locked and guarded by two tall sentries in kilts. Back of the Fort, still within the enclosure, were fields of grain, a large vegetable garden, and fruit orchards.[6] Also belonging to the Fort, but outside the stockade, were several large farms planted with wheat, peas, and potatoes, as well as pasturage for sheep, horses, and cattle. Agricultural yields in 1832 were described as "1800 bushels of wheat; 1200 bushels barley; 60 bushels peas; 400 bushels Indian corn, and 6000 bushels potatoes."[7] Agriculture and grazing were but two facets of the Simpson-McLoughlin policy of making each post self-sustaining; Fort Vancouver, especially, as the great entrepot of the Columbia Department must sustain not only itself, but also furnish subsidiary posts with needed foodstuffs and supplies. However, all industries, whether farming, lumbering grazing, raising cattle, or dairying, were merely ancillary to fur trading, having perhaps a relationship parallel to that of the spokes of a wheel to its hub. Later, when the fur industry declined and finally became extinct, these secondary industries assumed primary importance.

While the officers of the Fort as a rule dined fashionably with the Chief Factor, the voyageurs and laborers were given rations, which lacked in quantity, quality, and variety. Described by one writer, they consisted of eight pounds of salted salmon and eight quarters of potatoes per person per month, as well as undetermined amounts of peas and tallow per week. Understandably, the men found it essential to draw on their meager annual wage of seventeen pounds out of which they had to buy clothing and incidentals to supplement their food rations.[8] Typical of this historical period, class prejudice was all-pervasive.

One humble but necessary task was the weekly beating of the furs; this chore was often assigned to the half-grown children of the Fort. The Doctor's eldest child, Joseph, all too frequently, he felt, performed this chore, though reluctantly. Whenever possible he inveigled his half sister Eloisa and little Billy McKay, Tom's son, into helping him at this boring, dusty job.[9]

Everyone at the Fort was expected work hard—most of all, the Chief Factor himself. He was under constant pressure, some of it imposed by George Simpson, but a great deal of it self-imposed.

He was described by an unknown writer in an *Oregonian* of April 12, 1888, as a "rustler" (hustler?) whose work went on "regular as clock work." The elderly Scottish gardener, Robert Bruce, rang a huge bell, suspended on three poles, the size of that of a village church, each morning, at four o'clock in the summer and at eight in the winter. Clerks worked diligently, taking few liberties indeed with the Chief Factor. He spoke; they listened. His letters revealed the tremendous amount of detail he had to supervise. He made decisions on policy (within the principles laid down by his superiors), gave detailed orders as to location and shifting of men, horses, trappers, coastal steamers (later), boatmen; he had also to plan for and build additional forts, sawmills and gristmills and to supervise the manufacture and sale of the mills' products. He indicated to what use the soil should be put, which products each post was to produce, and the constant exchange of goods among the posts in his domain so that each fort in the Department was sufficiently supplied with men, food, horses, trapping materials, and goods to use in exchange with natives and others. It was he who must determine the rate of exchange of goods for pelts. It was for a while necessary to set the exchange to meet competition of the Rocky Mountain Fur Company and other American traders.[10] According to a television series, "America," the English at one time paid Indians one dollar a pelt and sold it for ten dollars. American fur traders paid the natives three or four dollars per pelt, forcing the British to increase their payments accordingly in order to meet American competition.[11]

The Chief Factor was forced against his better judgment to allow certain practices which he disliked, for obvious reasons, such as selling guns to the Indians. However, when an American company sold guns to the natives, Dr. McLoughlin felt forced to do so, even though it violated his principles. Similarly, the Americans sold second-hand clothes to the Indians, who loved to "dress up" in them. McLoughlin, in response, ordered new clothes for his men and sold their worn clothing to the natives. It was necessary for the Company to maintain Indian allegiance and friendship.[12]

Alberta Brooks Fogdall

After Fort Vancouver was completed and in operation the Chief Factor built several other posts in quick succession. The purposes of this multiplicity of forts or posts were to contain supplies, to produce food so that each area could be as self-contained as possible in order to eliminate the expense of importing goods from England, and to serve as bases for shipping furs and pelts to England via the Pacific rather than overland to the American east coast and across the Atlantic. This last factor was McLoughlin's own innovative policy. An additional function of posts was, in effect, to serve as a claim to the disputed territory, a claim not merely for the Honourable Company, but for Great Britain, when the boundary should at last be settled.

All the forts built by Chief Factor McLoughlin in the Columbia Department were important, but Fort Vancouver was the headquarters and nerve center of the Company's business. Runners were dispatched with news and orders to various outlying posts: fifty horses were needed to outfit a brigade up the Snake; a warning was sent that an American trader had slipped up the river to The Dalles; a chief trader at a post was to reduce Company prices temporarily; instructions to another chief trader, who was leading a trapping party to northern California that he was to meet Michel La Framboise, one of the Company's most intrepid voyegeurs, and his men at the Umpqua; to a chief trader at a New Caledonia (British Columbia) post that leather was needed at Fort Colville—and so on. Dr. McLoughlin had the posts so organized that all had a year's supply of essentials in reserve, in case of emergency. The brigades and the overland expresses, the mail and supply ships from London—all arrived and departed. Visitors were greeted, entertained, and sent on their way. Fort Vancouver was a metropolis; other forts were its satellites.[13]

As part of his policy of recouping losses of the Columbia Department suffered under the Northwest Company, Chief Factor McLoughlin greatly extended the old Northwest trade by sending large trapping parties out under Tom McKay, François Ermatinger, Michel La Framboise, Chief Traders Peter Skene Ogden and John Work, and others. Voyegeurs were also sent below the Columbia, east to Montana, southeast into present Wyoming, Colorado, Nevada, and Utah, and south into the northern half of California.

After New Caledonia was added to the Columbia District, forming the new Columbia Department, in 1825, John McLoughlin's kingdom was a domain synonymous with the watershed of the mighty Columbia. Trapping done in this northern area had to be handled differently because the northern Indians were treacherous. In the North the Company used vessels, which plied back and forth along the coast, stopping at the larger villages, permitting only a few natives at a time aboard ship.[14] Memory of the tragedy on the *Tonquin* in 1811, a massacre in which Mrs. McLoughlin's first husband was killed, was still fresh in many memories.

Royal Family of the Columbia

The relationship of Hudson's Bay Company men with the natives was many-faceted and complex. One of John McLoughlin's greatest talents was his knack for handling the Indians, combining firmness and kindness. Early in his career he had forbidden the selling of liquor to natives, knowing that they simply could not function after imbibing "firewater". Earlier it had been customary to give, sell, or exchange liquor in dealing with the Indians to make them more tractable, but experience had proven that more trouble than good resulted from the practice. The ruling against the sale of liquor was difficult to enforce. On two separate occasions the Chief Factor simply bought the entire liquor cargo from the ships' captains to avoid the natives' exposure to it. In addition he found employment for some of the crew members who wished to remain for a time, and who, the Doctor knew, must not be idle.[15]

Because he felt certain of his ability to keep the river Indians friendly, there were for a time no blockhouses at the Fort; only a few guns, intended for appearance, were mounted. Yet he was a realist. Occasionally his handling of the natives required more than his customary kindness and justice. Showmanship was called for and the Doctor made strategic use of it.

He had begun to hear disquieting rumors of frequent Indian councils in the thick woods across the Columbia. His "spies" reported that new, strange faces were beginning to appear among the old, familiar ones. It was feared that a number of them might storm the Fort's stores which were heavily stocked with new goods. According to Indian logic it was much simpler to storm the gates and forcibly take the goods than to go through the tedious process of trapping beaver and exchanging pelts for the articles they wanted. Dr. McLoughlin accepted the challenge and sent out native runners with orders to call a council meeting at the Fort of all tribes with whom he usually dealt.

The curious natives flocked by scores to the grounds outside the stockade, squatted on their heels, and waited. The showman-host kept his guests waiting for a full hour until they began to feel uneasy. During the hour interval a Scottish trader, at the Doctor's orders, marched slowly back and forth in front of the gates playing mournful tunes on his bagpipes. Bagpipes were wholly new phenomena to the Indians; they came to believe the bare-kneed musician could produce "bad medicine" which could harm them. The strategy was effective. When the Chief Factor finally appeared, his piercing eyes, his long snow-white hair, his magnificent frame of six feet, four inches, his barrel chest, his dignified mien and authoritative manner awed them. He was plainly capable of friendship, but equally capable of destruction—depending on their behaviour. They were convinced of their need for his friendhsip; they were won over and glad to promise peace and friendship, as well as furs, to the Factor-Doctor. This was but one of several times that the Hudson's Bay man was forced to take a strict upper hand with the natives.[16]

Alberta Brooks Fogdall

Le Bon Docteur ("The Good Doctor") was indefatigable in caring for the Indians when ill. For eight years there was no other doctor at Fort Vancouver and the Chief Factor was often worked to the point of exhaustion caring for his employees and the natives. The Indian was more than usually susceptible to the white man's diseases for he had developed no immunity. Referred to as the "cold sick" and as the plague, it was potent in the years 1829-1832. The origin of the mysterious disease was not known for certain. Among its symptoms were chills, fever, and the ague, which indicate a degree of similarity to those of twentieth-century influenza, or "flu". Frequently the sick were sent to the sweathouse for treatment.[17] Some survived. Many died. Peter Skene Ogden, doughty Company chief trader, served the Indians by himself, lighting their funeral pyres in order that the flames could purify and devour the diseased bodies.[18] The Doctor, too, was ill during an epidemic but sent a clerk with quinine to help the ill.

One possible source of the diseases which appeared endemic to the lower Columbia Indians was their encouragement of prostitution among their girls and young women, whom the braves often took shipside, first exacting payment, then leaving the females on board overnight or for several days. Often infected with venereal disease, the women and girls passed the disease on to the Indian males. Germs and infection were also spread by old castoff garments that sailors gave to the natives. The next generation could be affected and weakened—and, so, the endless cycle.[19]

In 1833, in answer to a request of the Chief Factor, the London Committee sent two young Scottish doctors, Merideth Gairdner and William Frazer Tolmie, to serve as post physicians at Fort Vancouver. They were, as could be expected, welcomed cordially by the Chief Factor and immediately found a great deal to do, as there were many ill Indians and trappers. Too, whenever medicine did not consume all their time they were expected to take on clerical duties.[20] Dr. Tolmie was much impressed with the equipment Dr. McLoughlin had collected for his infirmary. In his journal he listed surgical instruments for amputations, two midwifery forceps, catheters, eye instruments, bandages, and other quality equipment.[21] He was assigned to Fort Nisqually as a chief trader, and was afterward at Victoria.[22]

In 1840 Dr. Forbes Barclay arrived to replace Dr. Tolmie when the latter went to Fort Nisqually. Dr. Barclay, a graduate of the Royal College of Surgery of London, would later serve as councilman and as mayor of Oregon City and a superintendent of the Oregon City public school.[23]

The most significant Caucasian-Indian relationship was understandably that of marriage. It was taken for granted that the French Canadian voyageurs, as well as the English and the Scots, would take Indian wives, for there were no white women available. Furthermore, no white woman would be able to stand the exhausting, rigorous journey across the continent or the crude, hard pioneer life if she did survive the long trip — or so the white man felt. Thus, Indian wives were the result of the process of elimination.

More than this negative advantage, however, there were significant positive advantages:

1. While social life was peculiar due to the absence of white women, it would have been virtually non-existent without Indian wives.

2. Indian wives brought protection to their husbands, since Indian women were less vulnerable to attack from their own race than white women would be.

3. Marriage connections brought business to the white trappers, guaranteeing them a food supply as they traveled.

4. Indian wives helped their husbands to learn and understand the language and customs of various tribes, promoting friendship and good will.

5. Indian women were hardier than their Caucasian counterparts, better able to bear children and to take care of households in frontier country.[24]

In general, the Indian and half-Indian girls made good wives and housekeepers, adjusting relatively fast to the white man's life-style. Mrs. McLoughlin interested herself in training some of these girls in the household arts, helping them to make the important transition in their lives more easily.[25]

These unions were held as binding even if later the Company employee returned to "civilization" and reared a new, white family. Frequently the courts upheld the first (Indian) alliance and supported the claims of the children of the first marriage to an estate.[26]

The marriage of John and Margaret McLoughlin was one of this type. A company marriage, even though blessed by neither church nor state, was binding and legal. In a sense the Honourable Company *was* both church and state, providing both legal and moral restrictions for many years.

The marriage form was referred to as "consent of marriage". It was included with other documents and records which were sent to London each year as part of the official report. A typical document follows:

In presence of the undersigned witnesses I Archibald McKinlay a clerk in the service of the Honbl Hudson's Bay Company late of Scotland and now residing at Fort Vancouver Columbia River do voluntarily and of my own free will and accord take Sarah Julia Ogden daughter of Peter Skene Ogden to be my lawful wife and the said Sarah Julia Ogden also voluntarily and of her own accord take the said Archibald McKinlay to be my (her?) lawful husband.

Witnesses

Arch'd McDonald
Alex C. Anderson
Ft. Vancouver
June 1840

Archibald McKinlay
Sarah Julia Ogden
John McLoughlin
C. F. HB co. [27]

Relevant to the "consent of marriage" probably signed in 1811 is the renewal form signed thirty-one years later, November 19, 1842.

'...John McLoughlin...of one part and Dame Marguerite Wadin, his legitimate spouse, of the other part' wished to renew consent of marriage'...said spouses have declared for their legitimate children the late John McLoughlin, in life, doctor, Miss Eliza McLoughlin, Miss Eloisa McLoughlin, and Mr. David McLoughlin, the wife not being able to sign, the husband has signed for her. Witnesses were James Douglas, Forbes Barclay, and D. McTavish. [28]

It is of interest here to cast ahead about seventeen and one-half years to the death of Margaret McLoughlin, March 2, 1860. It was of so little importance that in the (Salem) *Oregon Statesman* of that date only one and one-half lines of microscopic print at the bottom of the seventh column of the second page recorded the fact that Margaret McLoughlin had died that day. Even more ironic, the *Pacific Christian Advocate* of March 3 devoted one and one-third lines at the bottom of the second column of page three as it announced the death of Margaret *McPherson*. [29]

However, in spite of being almost totally ignored in death, the widow of the "Father of Oregon" was allowed by "civic permission" to be buried beside her husband in the gardens adjacent to the Catholic Church "within the limits of Oregon City," just as three years earlier Dr. McLoughlin had been buried with "civic recognition" in the church yard. Both special documents were signed by Amory Holbrook, Mayor of Oregon City. [30]

Royal Family of the Columbia

On June 24, 1842, Father Blanchet had performed a marriage ceremony for a former Company servant and his Indian mate, formalizing their fur-company marriage. Present as witnesses were their "now legitimate" children:

Julie, 23; Antoine, 19 on November next; Sophie, 16; David, 13; Félix, 12; Étienne, 8. Nous avons donné la benédiction nuptiale en présence du Gouverneur McLoughlin et de Mr. Peter Skene Ogden.[31]

Because the HBC charter required it and because Dr. McLoughlin believed in the value of education for both the children of Fort families and for native children of the area who were interested in learning from the white man's books, he opened the first school west of the Rockies at the Fort in the autumn of 1832, with John Ball, a Dartmouth graduate and New England teacher and lawyer, who had come with Nathaniel Wyeth's expedition, as teacher. He and the Chief Factor seemed to be kindred spirits, both enjoying the intellectual discussions of the Bachelor's Hall.[32]

Mr. Ball had immediately been put at ease and made to feel at home at the Fort by the hospitable Doctor when he first arrived. However, because his New England conscience would not permit him to stay for several months without giving some service in return he offered to teach the children of the Fort. After at first refusing hospitably, Dr. McLoughlin at last agreed. In his autobiography Mr. Ball described the boys as "all half-breed since there are no white women." He described Mrs. McLoughlin as "a Chippewa woman of Lake Superior" and Amelia Douglas as "the lightest woman, a half-breed woman from Hudson Bay."

In regard to his pupils, he found the boys "docile and attentive and making good progress, for they are precocious..."[33]

Among his students were David McLoughlin, eleven, the Doctor's youngest child; and Billy McKay, a grandson of Mrs. McLoughlin. There were about twenty-four students (probably all boys) ages six to eleven, representing several languages, or at least several dialects, or patois, including Cree, Klickitat, Nez Percé, Chinook, a French and Indian mixture, and others. English and French were taught and the boys were required to stay and work after school if they were guilty of using any language during the day other than French or English.[34]

Mr. Ball found the "gentlemen of the Fort...pleasant and intelligent, a circle of a dozen or more usually at (the) well provided table, where there was much formality..." According to the teacher "the old doctor" visited the school occasionally and seemed "much pleased and well satisfied."[35]

Mr. Ball left Vancouver March 1, 1833, going to the Willamette Valley to try farming. He was succeeded by Solomon H. Smith, another New Englander who had come to the Northwest in the Wyeth expedition.[36] Mr. Smith, who had had some training in medicine and some business experience, taught for two years, married

Celiast, daughter of a Clatsop chief, and joined the French Canadian settlement at French Prairie, where he taught for a time.[37] Today the graves of Solomon and Celiast Smith and of their son Silas and of his wife may be seen in the Pioneer Cemetery at Clatsop Plains behind the Pioneer Presbyterian Church, which was founded in 1846.[38]

Religion played a significant role at the Fort both for the Company and for the natives. John McLoughlin, born of a Catholic father and of a Protestant mother who had converted to Catholicism at her marriage, had been christened by a Catholic priest. A few years later his maternal grandfather, Malcolm Fraser, insisted that John and his siblings be reared as Protestants. He apparently remained a Protestant throughout his young and middle adult life.[39] It is known that he read the Anglican service on Sundays and feast days at the Fort as was required by Company policy. The Factor's bilingual ability was advantageous in religious as well as secular matters. When in September 1836 the Rev. Herbert Beaver arrived to be the resident company chaplain, McLoughlin turned the services over to him.

Beaver demanded the right to teach the catechism of the Church of England in the school McLoughlin had established and the two of them quarreled over this. McLoughlin further irritated Beaver by holding catechism classes for the children of the French-Canadian employees of the company, in the afternoon after Beaver's services.

Influenced by his sister, the Roman Catholic nun, McLoughlin appealed to the Company for Roman Catholic priests, using Governor Simpson as a "intermediatory."[40] Motives other than religious existed, for the Company realized that religion exerted a moral and a restraining force on the natives. Other things being equal, a religious Indian would be better behaved and more easily handled than a non-religious Indian. In addition, Catholic, as contrasted with Protestant, missionaries were far less likely to encourage the coming and the settlement of "meddlesome Yankees." Another advantage from the Company viewpoint of Catholic, as opposed to Protestant, missionaries was shown later in the fact that they took little or no interest in local politics, and did not "meddle," which most emphatically could not be said of the Protestants.[41]

Catholic priests, however, did not arrive until November 24, 1838, while Dr. McLoughlin was on furlough. Father François Blanchet and Father Modeste Demers had come overland with the Company annual express and soon set up temporary missions at Fort Vancouver and at Cowlitz, as well as in the Willamette Valley. By January 6, 1839, they were sufficiently established that Father Blanchet conducted the first Roman Catholic service in the present state of Oregon.[42]

Royal Family of the Columbia

The Chief Factor was determined to bring religion to the natives, to teach them Christian principles. He was able to accomplish his goal even before the missionaries arrived "through the rare combination of force, benevolence, and lofty example."[43]

Among the first of the "Christian principles" which Dr. McLoughlin hoped to inculcate in the natives was the cruelty and indignity of slavery. Enslavement of Indians by fellow Indians was not at all unusual, even as relatively late as 1839. Every spring the Klamaths came to Champoeg with prisoners to sell. A girl could be purchased for fifteen blankets, a boy for only five.[44] (This seems contrary to the traditional concept of the relative value of male and female; is it that a female, already subservient to the male, possessed both innate and acquired slave characteristics?)

The Chief Factor in his report to the Honourable Governor and Committee in 1837, answering the charges of American emissary William Slacum, wrote,

> It is incorrect that we encourage slavery, and on the reverse we avail ourselves of every opportunity to discourage it. Though we cannot prevent Indians having slaves, we tell the masters it is very improper to keep their fellow beings in slavery. Moreover we have redeemed several and sent them back to their own country this very season. Some Indians of this vicinity had captured two families in the Willamette. By our influence they were liberated.

Some HBC servants (employees) had slaves. McLoughlin could not force his subordinates to give them up, but he strongly encouraged them to pay the Indians for their work. In some cases in which Company employees freed their slaves and sent them back to their own tribes, they were treated much worse there and wanted to return to the Fort.[45]

Underlying, rather than tangential to, any relationship with the Indian natives, whether marriage, education, religion, or slavery, was, and is, racial prejudice. John McLoughlin, a paternalist at heart, had "a just appreciation of the Indian character. In his eyes a savage was never a monster, but a man, the offspring of our common mother nature...Being...their superior McLoughlin conducted himself as such..."[46] The Chief Factor treated them as a kindly father treated his children, using punishment and reward when appropriate. The Indians admired him and accepted his words as truth because he always kept his promises. Because of his stern yet kindly Indian policy, which had drastically ameliorated conditions, even small parties were able to travel safely in the middle and late 1830s. HBC insignia were even borrowed by travelers as protection. The Honourable Company did not anger the natives because they did not want to settle, as did the American immigrants.[47]

Alberta Brooks Fogdall

The epitome of racial bigotry was expressed by the renowned historian H. H. Bancroft, writing in the 1880s:

It has always seemed to me that the heaviest penalty the servants of the Hudson's Bay Company were obliged to pay for the wealth and authority advancement gave them was the wives they were expected to marry and the progeny they should rear. What greater happiness to the father, what greater benefit to mankind than noble children! I never could understand how such men as John McLoughlin, James Douglas...could endure the thought of having their name and honors descend to a degenerate posterity.

He continued in the same vein, indicating the vast chasm between the white and red races:

Surely they were possessed of sufficient intelligence to know that by giving their children Indian or half-breed mothers, their own Scotch, Irish, or English blood would then be greatly debased...they were doing all concerned a great wrong. Perish all the Hudson's Bay Company thrice over, I would say, sooner than bring upon my offspring such foul corruption, sooner than bring into being offspring of such a curse.

He then placed "John McLoughlin father beside John McLoughlin son," and added, "...tell me what there is in all the wide universe that would pay this strong, high-souled gentleman for having taken so vile a copy of himself..." He felt that the "superior intellectuality of the father developed in the son superior brutality."[48] Much more of the same trend followed. Mr. Bancroft was no doubt simply expressing the late nineteenth-century viewpoint of a majority of the Caucasian division of humanity which saw itself not as merely *different* from other groups, but as *superior*.

Later, after the arrival of the Roman Catholic priests, a chapel was built. Here the catechism was taught on week days and prayers said on Sundays. The Doctor was said to have been an interesting sight on Sundays as he strode from his home to the chapel, his wife and two or three children with him, the wind blowing his long white hair, a dramatic blue cape flowing from his shoulders, a gold-headed cane in his hand. One writer commented unkindly but perhaps truthfully on the strange contrast Margaret made with her husband: Nine years his senior, as she aged, the "Indian characteristics" were emphasized. Her short, stout figure and her plain clothes were "lacking in womanly grace" and all the more unattractive next to his "straight-as-an-arrow, well-dressed," tall, erect figure. Nevertheless, he loved her devotedly and treated her chivalrously. She was interested whole-heartedly in her husband's benevolences, always seeking out sick immigrants to help; often she sent clothing and food because "It is a duty put upon us by our Heavenly Father."[49]

On June 24, 1842, Father Blanchet baptized John and Margaret McLoughlin:

Le vingt-quatre juin, dix-huit cents quarante-deux, nous avons baptisé Jean-Baptiste McLoughlin et son épouse, Marguerite McLoughlin, née entre les sauvages infidèles de la Calédonie...[50]

It is not difficult to imagine that Dr. McLoughlin felt as if he were "going home"—back to the religion of his father and of his paternal ancestors, the religion in which he had been baptized as an infant. The Reverend A. Hillabrand, a Catholic priest, clung to the interesting theory that Dr. McLoughlin was always basically Catholic. T. C. Elliott, however, stated that not until Christmas morning, 1842, did he (Dr. McLoughlin) partake of holy communion and enter (the) membership of the Catholic Church and that up until 1839 or 1840 he had been affiliated with the Church of England.[51]

Another source stated that the Doctor made his "abjuration and profession of Faith" to Father François Blanchet November 18, 1842, that he made his confession and had his marriage blessed by the Church and prepared for his first communion by fasting during the four weeks of advent.[52]

T. C. Elliot suggested that the Doctor's return to Catholicism may have been partly due to the fact that those who were attempting to rob him of his Oregon City land were Protestant (chiefly Methodist).[53]

In spite of his closeness to the Chief Factor, James Douglas remained Protestant, as did Dr. Tolmie, Mr. Ogden, and most of the Doctor's close associates. However, John McLoughlin was credited with effecting some conversions, an outstanding example being that of Peter Burnett, first American governor of California, who was said to have discussed Catholic doctrine with Dr. John and to have borrowed books on the subject from him, particularly Milner's *The End of Religious Controversy*. After "impartial and calm investigation" Mr. Burnett was convinced that Catholicism was the only true faith.[54] He joined the Catholic fold in 1846. Mrs. Burnett soon followed; they later were married (again) in the Catholic Church.[55]

Yet despite his devotion and his fidelity to his religion, Dr. McLoughlin seemed to be completely devoid of bigotry and religious prejudice. At Fort Vancouver he made it possible for the French Canadians and the natives to follow their own religious preference, in this case Catholicism, while he also held a Protestant service.

In a later chapter his ecumenical spirit is illustrated in his land donations to both Catholic and Protestant churches. Apparently he possessed a broad concept of religion, feeling that the spirit of worship was more important than its outward form. His lack of bigotry and his tolerance were shown by the scrupulousness with which he cared for an orphan daughter of a Company employee, meticulously placing her in a Protestant school because her father had been a Protestant.[56]

That John McLoughlin was successful in his capacity as superintendent of the vast activities of the Columbia Department was confirmed by his superior, Governor George Simpson, who in 1828—1829 made his first visit to Fort Vancouver since its completion in 1825; he was greatly pleased with the progress made there by the Chief Factor and wrote to the London Committee:

> Never did such a change of system, and a change of management, produce such obvious advantages in any part of the Indian country, as those which the present state of this Establishment in particular, and of the Columbia Department as a whole, at this moment exhibits.[57]

This is perhaps the most complimentary remark ever made by the Governor concerning his often-dissenting subordinate; it was during a later period, after 1840, that irremediable differences arose and exacerbated.

The Chief Factor's personal financial status improved early in his Fort Vancouver years. The Company had begun to advance him money January 1, 1822; on June 1, 1828, financial reports showed that he owed more than 484 pounds, while one year later, for the first time he was out of debt, the accounts revealing a credit of a little more than seventy-eight pounds.[58]

The Hudson's Bay Company in 1830 represented a culmination of many years' efforts to organize the Columbia country. It was an economic system measured by profits and losses; it was also a strategic system of forts and garrisons and unstable frontiers to be controlled. It was a way of life; its daily, weekly, and yearly routines had to be adapted to the circumstances of each locality.

Competition with American merchants was a serious, but not an insurmountable problem during the early period of the McLoughlin rule. The Chief Factor found the Columbia Department involved in a two-front commercial war with Americans: 1. Encroachments of trapping parties beyond the Rockies into the Snake and Flathead regions, and 2. American ships cruising the waterways and the coast of the Pacific. This second front was the more disturbing of the two to the Company and to the Chief Factor, for the waterway intrusion extended from the lower Columbia to the limits of navigation at the Cascades.

Royal Family of the Columbia

One continuing irritant of American aggressiveness was the persistent undercutting of the HBC, one example being the practice of giving the natives one blanket for each beaver pelt, as compared with the Honourable Company's paying one blanket for five pelts. The Chief Factor was able to hold to the original terms in the interior but was often forced to meet the Americans' exchange rate along the coast and on the lower Columbia.[59]

The first serious threat from the Americans came in 1829 when Boston brigs *Owyhee* and *Convoy* entered the Columbia to trade. The loss of the Company ship *William and Anne* with its cargo of trade items further handicapped Dr. McLoughlin's ability to compete with the American traders. As a result the two Boston brigs carried away 2900 beaver and otter skins when they returned east in July 1830.[60]

The second American menace was Nathaniel Wyeth, Boston trader in fur at Fort Hall and in Salmon at Wapato (Sauvie Island).

The company employed several methods of combatting their American rivals. One effective means was strategically located forts such as Nisqually (1834) at the head of Puget Sound; Langley (1827) at the head of Fraser; Simpson (1831, 1834) and McLoughlin (1834), both on the coast, north of Vancouver Island and near the Alaskan border. Fort Colville (Colvile), named for Arthur Wedderburn, Lord Colville, then the London governor of the Company, was also of great importance.

Fort McLoughlin and Simpson, along with later additions Stikine and Taku, were intended to combat American coastal trade. Colville, in the interior, facilitated shipments and reduced the costs which Simpson had considered outrageous at Spokane House, which Fort Colville replaced. In addition, the neighboring Blackfeet Indians were expected to serve as a buffer against American traders.

The year 1834 marked the tenth anniversary of John McLoughlin's appointment to the Columbia. To honor the occasion and the Chief Factor, Governor Simpson piloted through the Council of the Northern Department a resolution voting the Doctor a gratuity of 500 pounds and an additional allowance of 150 pounds per annum for the years 1830, 1831, 1832, and 1833 for his professional services as post physician during the plague epidemics.[61]

Although for reasons to be discussed later, Chief Factor McLoughlin was opposed to the use of Company trading vessels as substitutes for posts, the London authorities organized a marine department, headed by Captain Aemilius Simpson, cousin of the resident Governor.[62] (Captain Simpson was also given credit for bringng from England a packet of apple seeds which were planted at the Fort and carefully nurtured; the resulting tree still exists today, the first of an orchard at the Fort. At the Fort's Visitors Center it is a favorite subject of souvenir postcards.)

Alberta Brooks Fogdall

In 1827 came the *Cadboro*, in 1828, the *Vancouver* and the *Broughton*; the *Néreide,* which McLoughlin rejected and sent back to London, appeared in 1834 and returned in 1836 bringing the Beavers. The famous *Beaver,* first steamer in Pacific waters, came in 1836.[63] All these plowed waters superintended by John McLoughlin. Thus, much to his displeasure, he was saddled with seven vessels for coastal trade and for trips with cargo to China or to England.

In 1832 he had brought up a plan "for the rearing of Cattle on a large scale" by Company servants under his supervision. The plan was rejected at that time, but in 1838 was introduced by the Honourable Committee to McLoughlin in London as the Puget's Sound Agricultural Company, to be operated under the Commmittee's auspices. Dr. McLoughlin, although by this time reluctant to undertake the new venture, added it to his other duties.[64]

There were several purposes for the creation of the PSAC. Most important, it was to fulfill the contract which the Company had with the Russian American Fur Company to sell it agricultural products at stipulated prices.[65] Also, the PSAC was a means of laying the Company's—and Great Britain's—claims to the disputed area north of the Columbia.[66]

The new company was to be established at Nisqually and at Cowlitz, in modern southwest Washington. It was legally independent, although the Chief Factor managed its affairs and HBC stockholders owned it exclusively. Unfortunately, it was not a complete long-range financial success, due partly to the poor soil at Nisqually and also to uncertainty over the boundary settlement.[67]

In 1836 the Chief Factor had been ordered to take a furlough, to go to London for a meeting with the London Governor and Committee at which Governor Simpson would also be present. He did not go, for he had not been well and he felt that there was too much to be done and that there were too many problems for him to be absent:[68] 1. While the great influx of American colonists did not come until the 1840s, even in 1836 the Fort was inundated with missionaries and with American "pests" and competitors such as Ewing Young, Hall J. Kelley, and Nathaniel Wyeth. 2. The unpopular and troublesome Beavers were present. 3. The Russians were showing opposition to his program of expansion.[69]

The year 1837 saw the arrival in the Willamette Valley of California cattle and also of numerous American females, the latter in the second group of Methodist missionaries. The same year the Columbia Department sent a bumper crop of pelts, worth 26,735 pounds, to the Company's London salesrooms. Again in 1838 there was a huge crop, so that stockholders in the Company received twenty-five percent dividends. These, however, were the last big crops of furs, for there was a change of emphasis. As a result of diversification, other crops replaced beaver pelts.[70]

Finally, on March 22, 1838, leaving his assistant and protégé, James Douglas, in charge, Dr. McLoughlin left for London—his first and only furlough in all his years

Royal Family of the Columbia

of service with the Honourable Company.[71] He disregarded the Governor's orders to proceed to London via Cape Horn, claiming that his health would not permit the long sea trip. It is also possible that he chose to travel overland in order to visit his seventy-nine year-old mother at Rivière-du-Loup and his sister Marie-Louise (Sister St. Henry) and his daughter Eliza Eppes, both in Québec.[72]

In London he did his best to dispel the Committee's notion that a beaver-filled wilderness still reached unbroken from the Rockies to the Pacific. Fort Vancouver, rather than being the center of the fur trade, was now a major distributing point. Furs from all over poured into it—from Russian Alaska, Northern California, Montana, old Fort Hall, and many other points. In return Vancouver sent back English cloth and hardware, boatloads of flour, dried peas and potatoes, smoked meat, dried salmon, fruit and other products raised on the ever-growing farms outside the stockade.[73]

Also in London, in spite of the added responsibility of the PSAC, arrangements were made at the Chief Factor's instigation to lease the strip of Russian territory containing two posts, Stikine on the river of that name and Taku to the north, located between Sitka and the Taku River. (Plans were made also for the organizing of the Puget's Sound Agricultural Company.)[74] By May 1839, after a visit with his brother, Dr. David, in Europe, Dr. McLoughlin was back in Montréal with his son David, who had accompanied him from England. He came back triumphantly, ready to resume his duties, with a sizeable increase in salary due to the growing importance of the Columbia Department and to his added responsibilites of the PSAC and the two new Russian posts.[75] He already had well-organized plans for developing the Agricultural Company and had sent instructions to Vancouver for Dr. Tolmie, who would go to Fort Nisqually the next year as chief trader, and to others working on the projects at Cowlitz and Nisqually.[76]

Taking a brief respite from the pressure of work at the Fort, it seems that a glimpse into the lives of a few of those who were affected by and had a part in determining and carrying out the Chief Factor's domestic policies might add to the reader's understanding. The most important of the Doctor's staff was James Douglas, who would one day succeed John McLoughlin and eventually even Governor George Simpson. Far more than an employee, he was more like a son or younger brother to the King of the Columbia. His wife, Amelia, half-breed daughter of Chief Trader William Connolly, Douglas' superior at Lake Stuart, in New Caledonia, was a great favorite at the Fort and much loved by Mrs. McLoughlin; the two women were most companionable. The fact that Amelia understood and could speak some English while Margaret could not was a "plus-value."[77]

Alberta Brooks Fogdall

Born either in Scotland or Jamaica of a "well-born" Scotsman and a Creole mother, James was said to be a direct descendant of Scottish nobility, even of royalty, for one of his ancestors was that Douglas who was Earl of Angus, called Black Douglas or Black Angus because of his swarthy coloring.[78]

As a result of the Northwest and of the Hudson's Bay Companies' policy of infusing new blood into the trade, chiefly from Scotland and the Orkney Islands, "the finest lads came from the isles and glens." Among these was James Douglas, who arrived in 1819 at the age of sixteen.[79]

On hand to greet him upon his arrival at the Northwest Company depot, Fort William, on August 6 was Chief Trader John McLoughlin, future King of the Columbia. No doubt remembering the friendliness and kindness shown him by Company partners Simon and William McGillivray when he had entered the Company, he, in effect, reciprocated by making young Douglas his protegé. Nineteen years older than the newcomer, the Doctor apparently took a paternal interest in the young Scotsman, later training him as his assistant, and eventually as his successor. For thirty years or more their names were closely linked, as indeed they have remained to the present.[80]

There was slight physical resemblance between the experienced McLoughlin and the man to whom he taught the fur trade. Both were tall, but there the resemblance ended. In contrast to the older man's blue eyes, the long hair prematurely turning white, and the fair complexion, the Scot was, like his royal ancestor, extremely dark—skin, eyes, and hair—and like the same ancestor, nicknamed "Black Douglas." While Dr. McLoughlin had a barrel chest and was of substantial build, James Douglas was described as "slim and regally erect." Both men loved fine clothes and were elegant in their dress when the occasion demanded.

The two men shared, of course, many attributes, notably those of clear thinking, of business acumen, of organizational ability, and, most of all, of honesty and integrity. They differed basically in temperament, however, the Chief Factor being emotional and sentimental and motivated often by personal factors. He was impulsive, quick-tempered, often irascible, behaving occasionally in such a fashion as to regret his impetuosity later. An outstanding illustration was his caning of Chaplain Herbert Beaver early in 1838. James Douglas, on the other hand, was cool and calculated, seldom if ever acting rashly, was much less ruled by his emotions and by personal factors than was his friend and superior.[81]

James Douglas had been an apprenticed clerk with the Northwest Company for a year at the time of its coalition with the more prestigious Hudson's Bay Company. At this time he became a clerk second class. During the next ten years he served as clerk at posts at McLeod Lake and at Stuart Lake (Fort St. James) before going to Fort Vancouver as Chief Factor McLoughlin's assistant and accountant. That Governor George Simpson was aware of Douglas' promising qualities was shown when he noted in his *Character Book* of 1832 that the young Scotsman was a likely candidate for rapid advancement. By 1835 he was a chief trader, and by 1840 a chief factor in the Columbia Department.[82]

As with so many "facts" in history, there is a lack of consensus as to when James Douglas joined Dr. McLoughlin at Fort Vancouver. Lyman (page 360) quoted the Chief Factor as saying, in 1823, "Come with me, lad, you shall be like a son to me." With which he whisked the "lad" off to Fort George with him in 1824. Montgomery, however, claimed that Douglas visited the Columbia for the first time in 1826 (page 153). Both Montgomery and E. E. Rich, editor of *McLoughlin's Letters* (page 312), stated that Douglas was appointed by the Council of the Northern Department in June 1829. While the three viewpoints are not necessarily mutually exclusive, there is undoubtedly a conflict of interpretations. James Douglas came to the Columbia Department, probably at the suggestion of his father-in-law and at the request of Dr. McLoughlin. He arrived at his new assignment early in the spring of 1830.

James and Amelia Douglas became the parents of thirteen children, of whom one son and five daughters survived childhood. Their marriage on April 17, 1828, was "according to the custom of the country," a fur-trade marriage. On February 28, 1837, they were married according to the rites of the Church of England by the Reverend Herbert Beaver, chaplain at Fort Vancouver.[83] Dr. McLoughlin, who felt pressure to remarry Margaret, refused to have a ceremony at which Beaver officiated—for obvious reasons. However, he and Margaret were remarried with James officiating at a civil ceremony in his capacity as justice of the peace. Dr. McLoughlin, foreseeing that there could be trouble with increased American immigration, in 1835 had managed to secure through an act of Parliament the right to appoint justices of the peace at various posts in the District.[84]

No doubt a high point in James Douglas' life was his serving as acting chief factor of the Columbia Department for more than a year, 1838-1839, during Dr. McLoughlin's absence. This added responsibility was an undoubted challenge as for this extended period of time Mr. Douglas transacted the Company's business in the Columbia Department in an efficient and competent manner, in emulation of his mentor and superior. Among the vast bulk of business which he supervised was the sad service he performed in sending a Company messenger to overtake the Reverend Jason Lee, enroute to Washington, D.C., in western Missouri with the news of the tragic deaths of Mrs. Lee in childbirth and of their newborn son.

A happier duty was his reception of Catholic missionaries Fathers François Blanchet and Modeste Demers, long desired by French Canadian settlers, and arranged for, after several earlier and unsuccessful requests, by Chief Factor McLoughlin while in London.[85]

Alberta Brooks Fogdall

In 1840 Douglas headed the party which escorted William Glen Rae, John McLoughlin Jr., and Mrs. Rae (Eloisa McLoughlin) to Fort Stikine on the Alaskan coast; after opening the post (or, rather, re-opening it following transfer from the Russian Fur Company) he continued north to Fort Taku, where he superintended building operations.[86]

From 1839 through 1841 James Douglas shared Dr. McLoughlin's enthusiasm for extending the fur trade to California. This extension materialized in the establishment of the Company post at Yerba Buena (San Francisco), discussed elsewhere.[87]

Douglas accompanied Governor Simpson in 1841 to Sitka.* In a letter of Mr. Simpson to London Governor Andrew (Lord) Colville on November 15, he wrote, "Douglas...has long been under the Doctor and has acquired much of his mode of management, with perhaps a little more system; and being less over bearing in his disposition, will I think be very fit for the charge of this Depot (Fort Vancouver) whenever the Doctor may withdraw...".[88] It was evident that Governor Simpson much preferred James Douglas to John McLoughlin as a colleague and subordinate.

Because of the great influx of Americans settling along the Columbia, Company officials feared that Fort Vancouver would be in American territory following the long-deferred boundary settlement; they searched for some time for a more advantageous site. The southern end of Vancouver Island pleased both Simpson and Douglas as they rounded it on their way to Sitka. Soon Sir George (he had been knighted recently by Queen Victoria) ordered Chief Factor McLoughlin to have a fort built on the Island and to see that all Company property was transferred from Fort Vancouver to the new location as speedily as possible.[89]

The next year Dr. McLoughlin sent Douglas and six others to Fort Nisqually where they boarded the Company schooner *Cadboro* and continued to study the southern Vancouver Island area. Douglas chose the exact site and a year later with fifteen men took the Company *Beaver,* the first steamship on the North Pacific, back to the Island where he superintended the construction of the new fort.[90]

Finished in 1843, the fort had at first been named Fort Adelaide, honoring the consort of William IV, Queen Victoria's uncle and predecessor. Later it was renamed Victoria for the twenty-four year-old queen.[91] From this Hudson's Bay post grew the present city of Victoria.

In 1842-43 James Douglas served his long-time friend by wringing confessions from Urbain Héroux and Pierre Kanaquassé of their guilt in the murder of John McLoughlin Jr.

Douglas, a Chief Factor since 1840, remained at Fort Victoria as its first officer, cooperating with Dr. McLoughlin during the transitional period of moving

*An original diary of James Douglas (read August 27, 1974) is in the Provincial Archives, Victoria, British Columbia. Of special interest is "Continuation of the Voyage to Sitka (1841-1843)."

personnel, supplies, documents—and memories too—from Vancouver to Victoria. After the White-Headed Eagle's resignation in June 1845 James Douglas succeeded him, his succession being the culmination of Dr. McLoughlin's long-range plan for his protégé.[92]

In 1845 Sir George Simpson was vehemently ordering Dr. McLoughlin to complete the transfer from Vancouver to Victoria. McLoughlin moved slowly; each move toward the abandonment of the Fort was a reluctant one.[93]

For reasons explained later the Governor and Committee in London acting jointly with Governor Simpson and the Council of the Northern Department ordered the aging Eagle (almost sixty-one) to share the control of the Columbia Department with Chief Factors Douglas and Ogden. This meant that the 1845-46 Outfit (year's business) was to be supervised by this triumvirate. The White-Headed eagle was hurt by the decision but yielded gracefully. In any case, he was accustomed to working with James Douglas; Ogden interfered very little in administration of the Outfit, preferring active work in the field.[94]

James Douglas' career "might have been designed for history textbooks and empire-building oratory. There can be few parallels to this story of virtue triumphant and industry rewarded." So said Douglas MacKay, late editor of *The Beaver,* house organ of the Hudson's Bay Company, in his *The Honourable Company* (page 233).

Even after the boundary was settled the British government feared a rush of American settlers to Vancouver Island and dreaded the formation of another provisional government "to embarrass both British and United States Governments." To prevent this possibility Her Majesty's Government in 1849 assigned to the HBC the responsibility for founding a colony on Vancouver Island. The Company was made trustee of the natural resources and was to promote the colony, hoping that it would appeal to Englishmen, rather than to Americans. Because the trip around Cape Horn from England was long and unpleasant the colony did not prosper. The California gold rush of 1849 further hindered interest in the colony; later, however, the gold rush in the Fraser River Valley after 1858 brought a new interest and gold seekers to British Columbia.

The fact that Douglas played the dual role of Company agent and Chief Factor, and (soon) also had the additional office of governor of Vancouver Island, and that the governing council was composed almost entirely of Company officials resulted in an unrepresentative government and in a glaring conflict of interests. In 1859 Douglas resigned from the Company, serving only as (the first) Governor of the Crown Colony of British Columbia, following the union of Vancouver Island with (mainland) British Columbia and before British Columbia became part of the Dominion of Canada in 1871.

In 1863 James Douglas, the swarthy Scotsman, was honored with a knighthood by his Queen. Sir James resigned in 1864, enjoying thirteen years of "patriarchal retirement" before his death in 1877.

"On the narrow stage of frontier colonial statesmanship he rose far above the minor scuffle of pioneer politics. His devotion to order and his respect for the conventions of office, even the flavor of autocracy which he brought to his administration of public affairs, were in the Simpson-McLoughlin tradition of the old Company."[95]

A charming couple arrived to live at the Fort on September 6, 1836. Not "visitors," because they were British subjects, they were to be part of the palace staff. They were literally the answer to the Chief Factor's prayers, or so he thought. Herbert and Jane Beaver had been seven months on their way from England.[96]

It had taken the Company's London officials and Governor George Simpson six years to fulfill their promise to send a chaplain-missionary to Fort Vancouver, even though the license of 1821 required the Company to provide moral instruction for the natives.[97] The Doctor had been most impressed that the Methodist missionaries were teaching the Indians not only religion, but also how to till the soil. Although he preferred a Roman Catholic priest as chaplain, he considered a Church of England clergyman acceptable; perhaps he would be practical like the Methodists.

The Beavers had not been expected until later, and by an overland express; instead, they had come on the Company's barque *Néreide*. The Company officials in London had made preparations, sending, the previous May on the annual supply ship *Columbia,* Bibles, registers, a surplice, an altar cloth, a silver communion service (marked with the Company coat of arms), and miscellaneous other appropriate articles.[98]

Witty Peter Skene Ogden made a play on words, using the chaplain's rather unusual name, that "amongst the many good things their honors from Fenchurch street sent us... was a clergyman and with him his wife, the Reverend Mr. Beaver, a very appropriate name for the fur trade." The chaplain was described as having a highly pitched voice, a poor delivery, "an unbounded capacity for lazy living—a most unprepossessing individual." He would have been called "cocky" if he had lived a century later. He had had experience as a British army chaplain which had far from broadened his bigoted outlook. On the contrary, "by comparison the uncompromising Methodist missionaries were freethinkers."[99]

The arrival itself was hardly propitious. They bore an "air of martyred condescension." They were fulfilling their "pious duty." Moreover, here they were: "English, clean, and neat." It looked as if they had stepped into the midst of "barbarians, savages, and squalor. Douglas disliked them on sight." If Douglas disliked them, one can be sure that the "head man", with his quick temper, his strong emotions, his violent likes and dislikes, found the Beavers thoroughly distasteful.

Superciliously they looked about them. They commented on the Indian village in the distance, referring to the small houses as pigsties. Pointing to two women a few feet away, Mr. Beaver asked that the "two gaudy creatures" be "let out" before he and Mrs. Beaver approached. Since the "gaudy creatures" were Mrs. McLoughlin and Mrs. Douglas, Dr. McLoughlin was, according to his nature, "close to apoplexy."

The Beavers were horrified at the Indians they had been hired to teach and refused to go near them until they "cleaned up."[100]

Basically there seemed to be three causes of the great gulf between McLoughlin and Beaver: 1. Personality or attitude, 2. Control of the school at the Fort, and 3. Condition (or lack of condition) of matrimony at the Fort.[101]

To elaborate on the above: The personality clash was probably due to the chaplain's constant air of condescension, superiority, and fault-finding. His insulting and contemptuous attitude to all and about everything at the Fort made him—and his wife—decidedly unpopular. Opposed to his bigotry and other personality defects was the Chief Factor with his decided views and strong, explosive nature. He had wanted a Roman Catholic priest. Did he purposely not make lavish, or even adequate, preparations for the new additions to his official family? The Beavers believed so and complained constantly of conditions: the noisy persons next door; they were entitled to a separate house. There were no servants—Mrs. Beaver was required to perform "menial tasks." They were served baked fish when they wanted boiled fish, and so it went.[102]

On the second point, control of the school, the Beavers did not want to associate with the Indians or their children at all, but at length reluctantly did so. Mr. Beaver insisted on attempting to convert the Roman Catholic children, giving them the Book of Common Prayer and teaching them the Church of England catechism. In disgust, McLoughlin, though not himself Catholic at this time, taught the Catholic children in his home at night. Of course Beaver disliked and resented the Doctor's "high-handed interference."[103]

The third point of disagreement was the most potent of all—matrimony was practiced, or not practiced, at the Fort. Beaver believed, and did not hesitate to proclaim his belief freely and loudly, that the men, including the officers, even Douglas and the Chief Factor, were "living in sin." As a self-appointed judge he stepped far beyond his boundary of his responsibility, referring frequently to Mrs. McLoughlin as a "kept mistress", or as the "Chief Factor's woman." He and Jane felt that it was "presumptuous for those living in a 'state of concubinage' to inhabit the same house as the 'married chaplain'."

His frequent letters and reports back to England frequently slandered Mrs. McLoughlin. One paragraph mentioned her as "the kept mistress of the highest personage in your service at this station put forward to associate with, and entertain, respectable married and unmarried females from the United States of America."[104]

The Beaver bigotry was incredible. One example was his refusal to read a religious burial service for a sixteen-year-old half-breed girl who had died unbaptised.

Dr. McLoughlin, in sympathy, read a Church of England service; again, Beaver was furious at the Doctor's "interference."

This clash of personality, purpose, and religion had to erupt eventually. The depth and extent of the reciprocal antipathy prevented either from even attempting to understand the other. Beaver was a product of the nineteenth-century English aristocratic tradition that the squire and parson ruled the social order, which included directing the education of the children. He felt himself "subject to no man, sometimes forgetting that he was subject to God." In his formative years the issue of Roman Catholic emancipation in England and Ireland had reached its crisis, which possibly explained Herbert Beaver's attitude toward Catholicism at the Fort.[105]

Rather difficult to reconcile with a staid Church of England clergyman and his wife was the statement that Beaver shocked many by his "explosions of profanity," and his frequent hunting with his dogs. Mrs. Beaver, surprisingly, or not, was described as "rather fierce" and was "masculine to the extent of actually wearing breeches."[106]

The rule at the Fort was that all mail going out from residents was to be left unsealed so that the Chief Factor or someone delegated to do so could check the contents. Herbert Beaver resisted this rule, claiming that he was not a subordinate of the Chief Factor, but responsible directly to London. Dr. McLoughlin became quite deaf to Beaver's rantings and ravings and scathing criticisms—the food, the living accommodations, the Indian "slaves," morals, *etc.*, perhaps following a "I'll just consider the source" philosophy.

The mutual antagonism reached a climax early in 1838. James Douglas had allowed Mr. Beaver to marry him and Amelia the previous year, but the Chief Factor had refused categorically to allow him to marry Margaret and himself.[107] One day, McLoughlin, incensed by a report Mr. Beaver had written to London in which he referred to Mrs. McLoughlin as "the kept mistress of the highest paid personage in this establishment", demanded from Beaver an explanation. Beaver refused, and McLoughlin in a rage seized the clergyman's walking stick and beat him about the shoulders with it. Such an action was a serious offense in England.[108] The next day at an auction the repentant White-Headed Eagle apologized publicly to Beaver, who stiffly and indignantly rejected his apology.

The Chief Factor departed on furlough a few days later, leaving, happily, no doubt, to James Douglas the joy of the mighty Beavers' company and the responsibility of dealing with their idiosyncracies and ever-increasing unpleasantness. Douglas, while he had no liking for the chaplain and his wife, did not find them as intensely repugnant as did Dr. McLoughlin. He tried conscientiously at least to "get along" with the annoying couple, to keep them at a distance when possible, but when not possible to be coolly courteous, and to keep the relationship as free from friction as his considerable tact and diplomacy allowed.

Royal Family of the Columbia

Even with the hated McLoughlin out of the way, Beaver's complaints continued: Douglas, Dr. Tolmie, William Glen Rae, Joseph McLoughlin, and others absented themselves from his church services; there were "indecent interruptions" to his worship service; "a large Bell, distant twenty-five yards from my quarters, is rung for the reading of Roman Catholic prayers by Chief Factor McLoughlin, who... with the most glaring inconsistency, is a constant attendant on the Protestant form of worship."[109] One wonders whether Chief Trader Douglas rang the "Catholic bell" in his superior's absence.

Mr. Douglas, writing as acting-Chief Factor in Dr. McLoughlin's absence, felt it wise to write in his report to his London superiors denials of many of Beaver's allegations. Included among these he stated, "The intrusion of Dr. McLoughlin's private affairs into a public report is decidedly in bad taste, and I deeply regret that Mr. Beaver sullied these pages with unhandsome reflections upon Mrs. McLoughlin, who is deservedly respected for her numerous charities, and many excellent qualities of heart."

Mr. Douglas continued in his report, denying another accusation of the chaplain that he had worked and was working "hard and diligently" (without commensurate pay). Mr. Douglas found this completely untrue, feeling that Mr. Beaver did not perform even the minimum duties expected of him.[110]

The Beavers must have realized long before they had spent two years at the Fort that they were ill-suited to frontier life. They departed late in 1838, arriving in London in May 1839. The clergyman had planned to prefer charges against John McLoughlin upon reaching London, but the Chief Factor had already left England to return to his duties on the Columbia.

July 31, 1839, Mr. Beaver wrote to the (Anglican) Bishop of Montréal, protesting his treatment at Fort Vancouver, saying, "We had made up our minds to dwell among *red* savages, but not among *white* ones...." He wrote to the London Company officials that he hoped "for that person's sake" that a successor would not be sent. The Company reportedly paid the chaplain 110 pounds as full settlement of any claims he might have against the Hudson's Bay Company.

Apparently it was ten years before a successor was sent, this time to Fort Victoria. After his experience with the Beavers, John McLoughlin stated that he wanted no more Anglican chaplains sent by the Company. Soon he had the welcome presence of Catholic priests.

It is only just to attempt to understand the viewpoint of Herbert and "Haughty Jane" Beaver. He did, after all, come from England with the parochial concept of responsibility and authority. To him Fort Vancouver was his parish and he as clergyman had the last word. Dr. McLoughlin was *not* his superior and therefore could not give him orders. Such was his belief and he acted upon it.

Worthy of consideration too was his efficiency in maintaining parochial registers. So well done were they that his records of baptisms, marriages, and burials were used until the turn of the century.[111]

On balance one must admit his possession of a few redeeming qualities. Perhaps dealing with a man of such strong character as Dr. McLoughlin was in itself an insurmountable handicap for the English couple. Quite probably, also, the narrow life which they had led left them with a complete lack of preparedness for the abrasiveness of frontier living.

In explaining the "Beaver Affair" to Governor Simpson and the London officials, James Douglas, acting in Dr. McLoughlin's absence, summarized the qualifications of a clergyman for a frontier community as heterogeneous as the Honourable Company's Columbia Department:

> A Clergyman in this Country must quit the closet and live a life of beneficent activity, devoted to the support of principles, rather than of forms; he must shun discord, avoid uncharitable feelings, temper zeal with discretion, illustrate precept by example, and the obdurate rock upon which we have been so long hammering in vain will soon be broken into fragments.[112]

It goes without saying that the Reverend Mr. Beaver did not possess these requisite qualities.

Since considerable space was devoted to Sir James Douglas and to the Reverend Herbert Beaver it seems only fair to mention a few other individuals who shared the life of the royal family, both business and personal.

François (Francis or Frank) Ermatinger and his brother Edward were sons of Lawrence Edward Ermatinger and grandsons of Lawrence Ermatinger, who died in 1789 (birth date not given). A Swiss merchant, Lawrence Ermatinger had made his way from London to Montréal in the late 1750s or early 1760s and achieved some success in the fur trade.

From this respected family came Edward and Frank, born, respectively, in 1797 on the island of Elba (Napoléon's first place of exile) and in 1798 in Lisbon.[113] The two brothers were educated in England and in 1818 were apprenticed to the Hudson's Bay Company. Edward retired from the fur trade in 1830. His son, Judge C. O. Ermatinger, writer and editor, wrote "A Tragedy on the Stikeen in '42," concerning the murder of John McLoughlin Jr.[114]

Frank, unlike his brother, spent nearly forty years in the service of the Honourable Company, first as a clerk and, later, chief trader. Governor George Simpson in 1830 described him as a "bustling, active, boisterous fellow." He was tremendously active in Company expeditions, going to California in 1841, and on various trips into the Snake, on one accompanying Tom McKay and Nathaniel Wyeth to the latter's new Fort Hall, an important way station for American immigrants. Tom and Frank then superintended the building of Fort Boise to serve as competition to Fort Hall.[115] After the HBC bought Fort Hall from Wyeth, Frank served as factor there for a time and was said to have made it a miniature Fort Vancouver.[116]

It was Frank whom Eloisa labeled "the finest gentleman at the Fort;" it was he who said that he would wait for her to grow up and marry her. Since Eloisa's father definitely rejected his suit, Frank married Catherine Sinclair, a daughter of Eloisa's half sister Mary McKay and Chief Trader (later Factor) James Sinclair not long after Eloisa's marriage to William Glen Rae.[117] Frank was about forty-one at the time of Eloisa's marriage, consequently old enough to be her father. There was of course an even greater age difference between him and his eighteen-year-old bride, Kate.

Frank retired from the Company in 1853 and died in 1868 in Canada.[118]

Michel La Framboise ("raspberry" in French) would be termed a "character" today. He had the reputation of having "a girl at every post", or should it be "a girl at every portage"? As mentioned elsewhere he was a "tease" and loved to joke with "the Princess", Eloisa. Complimented by the Chief Factor as the "safest boatman on the river" and by historian David Lavender as "one of the West's unsung giants," he, too, had been aboard the *Tonquin,* but unlike Alexander McKay had been fortunate enough to escape.[119] Like his Chief he was a master at controlling the natives because of his unerring use of the rifle and a "wife" in nearly every coastal tribe who tended to smooth out the relationship of her "husband" with her own particular tribe.

He was considered an outstanding brigade leader of "proven ability." He and Chief Trader John McLeod together established a trading post on the Umpqua River, in southern Oregon, the only HBC post in the Oregon Country south of the Columbia. Dr. McLoughlin's purpose was to subdue the Indians of that vicinity and also to divert the supply of furs of that area into Company channels.[120]

Michel La Framboise and other voyageurs presented a picturesque appearance in their soft buckskin trousers, tanned and fashioned by Indian squaws. They wore their long black hair loose and cut shoulder length, undoubtedly with the same knife that carved their meat at dinner, skinned pelts, or carved a toy for an Indian child.[121] Whether in a canoe or a bateau (a large boat which could transport heavy freight) these voyageurs and boatmen made a valuable though generally unacknowledged contribution to the success of the fur industry as well as the color and glamor surrounding the beginnings of Pacific Northwest history.

It is highly possible that Peter Skene Ogden should not be equated with a mere voyageur; perhaps this snobbery is justified, for Mr. Ogden was of a "highly respected" family, his father being Chief Justice Isaac Ogden of the province of Québec. Justice Ogden, an American tory, had once lived in Newark, New Jersey, but after spending some time in England and marrying a loyalist, Sarah Hanson, he had changed his residence to Canada.[122]

Peter Skene Ogden, born in 1774, entered the service of the Northwest Company in 1811, being transferred to its Columbia Department in 1818. In 1820 he was made a wintering partner.[123] In 1823, now an employee of the reorganized Hudson's Bay Company, he was promoted to the rank of chief trader and in 1824 assigned to Spokane House, working under Chief Factor McLoughlin in charge of the Snake Country trade.[124] In 1835 he achieved the rank of chief factor and continued to work under John McLoughlin; the two men enjoyed an unusually close working and personal relationship.[125]

Ogden has been described as below average height, stocky in build, with a dark complexion and an odd, highly pitched voice; he was a wit and loved to play practical jokes. Picturesque and resourceful, he was extremely popular with the voyageurs, who call him "M'sieu Pete."[126]

At some point in his life he was "educated in the law," following up to a point his father's profession.[127] Just how much practical value his legal studies had for him in the fur trade is questionable. As a matter of fact, he revealed his reckless nature in his belief that necessity knew no law and that the *lēx nõn scrĩpta* was the only guide a fur trader needed.[128]

Described as "a strong-armed, vigorous trader of the old school" he headed the Snake River trapping expeditions composed of motley groups of frontiersmen of approximately one hundred who hunted on a free-lance basis and sold their furs to the Company.[129] He considered the day that brought American fur traders, and especially his American counterpart, Jedediah Smith, into the Snake Valley "that damned all cursed day."[130]

When news of the Whitman massacre was brought to Fort Vancouver on December 6, 1847, Ogden could have simply done nothing: After all, Oregon was now an American Territory—and he was not involved. However, he left the next morning and on December 19 at Walla Walla summoned the Cayuse chiefs to a meeting.[131] He met with them in a council and demanded the return of the hostages, American women and children; otherwise, he told them, there would be a retaliatory war which would result in their extermination.[132] Because of the influence Ogden had always had over the Indians and their respect for him, and because they were afraid not to obey him they turned the white families, forty-seven persons, over to him five days later. Ogden bought their freedom by paying the Indians $500 worth of guns, blankets, shirts, and trinkets.[133] Ogden had nothing to do with the punishment of the perpetrators of the massacre, an indication that the HBC recognized the

Royal Family of the Columbia

validity of the Provisional Government. It was months later before the confessed murderers were brought to Oregon City for trial and were hanged in 1850.[134]

It was said the Mr. Ogden liked and admired Narcissa Whitman, but that he disliked "missionarying." As for his private life, he was twice married, first to a Cree Indian, later to a Spokane, who lived with him seven years at Fort Vancouver. After the McLoughlins were married by a priest in 1842 the Doctor tried to persuade Mr. Ogden to have a legal, preferably a religious, ceremony for his wife and himself. Ogden bluntly refused, feeling that his open support of and his companionship with his wife and the care of their children counted more than any words a clergyman would say over them.[135] Unfortunately, his refusal deprived his family of its legal right to Ogden's estate.

His second wife was "Princess Julia", daughter of a Flathead chief. For her Ogden paid fifty ponies. She was a very unusual woman and most helpful to her husband in his relationships and business dealings with the Indians. She was the heroine of many daring adventures, such as rescuing her infant daughter, Sarah Julia, from a party of hostile American trappers; saving a valuable raftful of fur pelts by towing them across the rampaging Snake when no horse would cross it; and swimming the Snake in March to get a goose for her sick child, to name only a few courageous acts of derring-do.[136]

Unlike John McLoughlin, Peter Skene Ogden did not become an American citizen, but in his will spoke of himself as "of Montréal, Canada." He died September 17, 1854, "leaving many descendants and an estate of fifty thousand dollars." He is buried in Mountain View Cemetery in Oregon City. His monument was erected twenty years after his death by the Oregon Historical Society and the Oregon Pioneer Association.

"He did not found colonies; he explored no new empire; he received no titles." He was a loyal officer of the Company and was "a great-hearted gentleman whose name will live in the story of the Northwest." Ogden, Utah, is named in his honor, as is also Peter Skene Ogden State Park in Central Oregon.[137]

These are but a few of the many members of John McLoughlin's official family, those who were part of the life of the King's palace—Fort Vancouver.

Discussion of John McLoughlin's work as head of the Columbia Department after 1840 comprises another chapter. But life at the Fort was not all grim work and worry. Far from it. There was time for leisure, time to be spent in pleasure, and what better pleasure was there than eating delicious food?

There were approximately twenty domestic servants at the Fort, all of them men, many working as house servants in the Chief Factor's residence, in the kitchens, the laundry, and the dining room.

Alberta Brooks Fogdall

In the immense dining room men in formal attire dined at the long table graced with fine china, glass, and silver (after 1839 engraved with the monogram "J. Mc." silver which he had purchased in Edinburgh while on his furlough in 1838—1839), two silver candelabra twenty-four inches high, and large china and silver serving dishes.[138]

Always served in courses, a sample menu consisted of a hearty meat, rice and vegetable soup, fowl, a variety of meats, perhaps lamb, tripe, or pork; fish, either salmon or sturgeon, swimming in rich butter and cream sauces. Desserts often included rice pudding, apple pie, melons, grapes, and cheese; always there were fresh bread and hot biscuits. Wine was served as an accompaniment to a fine dinner. The host was most temperate, drinking no alcoholic beverages whatsoever, except an occasional small glass of wine as a toast to a special guest. He occasionally used snuff, but did not smoke. Regularly a Scottish bagpiper was stationed behind the Doctor's chair, at his beck and call for special music, indicating the Chief Factor's Scottish Fraser ancestry.[139]

A typical group of diners, seated in strict precedence, might include James Douglas at the host's right, Peter Skene Ogden, the captain of a supply vessel from London, David Douglas, famous botanist; a captain of a trading vessel berthed in the river, Jedediah Smith, Rocky Mountain Fur Company man with an adventure to relate; John Ball, the first teacher in the Oregon Country; Bostonian Nathaniel Wyeth, who hoped to compete with the Honourable Company; Tom McKay, and visiting chief factors and chief traders.[140] Only ranking officers were privileged to dine regularly with Dr. McLoughlin, for life at the Fort was governed by the etiquette and precision of a military fort.

After dinner there were fellowship and stimulating conversation in the smoking room, called the Bachelors' Hall. The Chief Factor could speak knowledgeably and at length on a diversity of fields other than fur trading. Talk was of world affairs, of art, science, philosophy, religion, and politics. Peter Skene Ogden and Tom McKay, among others, could always be counted on to have rousing tales of daring adventures with which to regale their listeners.[141]

Nor was culture lacking; in fact, this last outpost of civilization was a cultural oasis in a savage wilderness. Dr. McLoughlin had a fine collection of books called the Columbia Library, undoubtedly the finest—perhaps the only one—west of the Rockies. Dr. William Frazer Tolmie, after his arrival in 1833, arranged and circulated the books for officers and guests. Visitors were amazed to find on the shelves the works of Sir Walter Scott, Cervantes, and Shakespeare, as well as of a variety of historians (for history was the Chief Factor's favorite reading), medical texts, and a five-volume set of the *History of Scotland*. Cosmopolitan newspapers, including the London *Times* and the Edinburgh *Journal,* were also available.[142] Also in the Bachelors' Hall were a museum and an armory which displayed weapons and curiosities of "both savage and civilized life."[143]

Dress was a significant factor in the social life of the "royal court." The King of the Columbia, with his six-foot, four-inch figure and tremendous chest, was the ideal model for the attire he adopted. His favorite daytime costume was usually a black broadcloth suit with wide satin lapels, often topped by a dark blue overcoat with brass buttons. On Sunday the coat might be replaced by a navy blue cloak draped dramatically about his "patriarchal shoulders." With his majestic figure and long, flowing white mane he was the personification of regal dignity. Loving fine dress, in the evening for formal occasions he achieved additional elegance in black velvet knee breeches with gold or silver buckles. He loved dancing and delighted in wearing a narrow, long-tailed coat, a satin vest with ruffles, white kid gloves, and dancing pumps.[144]

Officers of the Company at times enjoyed emulating their superior in sartorial matters, but they also liked to wear semi-Indian attire, one might even say an early-day "mod" costume, made by their wives, of tanned deerskin trimmed with beads and fringe. Some of the wives had been educated in Canada and had a natural aptitude for the traders' life, accompanying their husbands on their journeys, usually in bright, gaudy, beaded attire. Occasionally they would wear English dress, but with moccasins.[145]

Princess Eloisa, the King's younger daughter, loved beautiful clothes, and possessed a most fashionable wardrobe. A "Noah's Ark", a massive cedar chest bound with zinc-lined copper, kept in a large closet, was packed with carefully folded and perfumed dresses of silk made by London dressmakers, silk hose, hand-made lingerie, Indian shawls, Chinese crepes, brocades, French embroidery, and Parisian bonnets. The gowns were fashioned with voluminous skirts containing ten to twelve dress widths, with fitted bodices pointed in front, and with bell sleeves. Eloisa's doting father was proud of his beautiful daughter and had the means with which to gratify her wishes.[146]

By contrast there was the pathetic ingenuity which the Company servants had to use in order to prolong the life of their scanty supply of clothing. For them, existing on a meager wage, it was a necessity to save every pence possible. An example was their stockings which, new in October, reached in the calf; in January they came an inch or two above the ankle, and by April barely reached the ankle. Measures responsible for this anomaly involved cutting off part of the foot as holes developed progressively in the toe, and sewing it across. By April all of the foot of the sock was gone and what had once been the leg of the sock was now covering the voyageur's foot. This was genuine economy.[147]

Alberta Brooks Fogdall

The elegance of the Company's resident Governor was outstanding. George Simpson was the prototype of *haute couture,* its high priest *par excellence.* Arriving at the head of the annual HBC express from Canada, he traveled in great splendor and high style to impress the natives. As soon as his scouts sighted the Fort a guide unfurled the Union Jack. Next a lively march was struck by buglers and bagpipers, who always accompanied the Little Emperor. One of the bagpipers, apparently his favorite, Colin Fraser, had difficulty becoming accustomed to the rapid travel and in the first years with Mr. Simpson was so exhausted he had no wind to pipe with. He piped in canoes and bateaux on both lakes and rivers; he played a leading part in the ceremonial approaches to the various posts. Upon landing, Colin, in full Highland costume, marched between the Governor and the guide who was carrying the Company flag. His Highland marches stirred the Scots at the posts and impressed the natives with the solemnity of the occasion and the importance of Governor Simpson.[148]

The doughty little Governor always rode in the lead canoe wearing his attention-getting scarlet-lined velvet cape, his ruffled choker, and, of course, a high beaver hat. Everyone, from the humblest laborer to the Chief Factor, attired in his finest, stood at the boat landing to pay homage to the Great Man. With the bagpipers marching and playing he walked about, shaking hands condescendingly with the men present.

An alternate costume for the Governor was a suit of dark blue or black, a white shirt, the collar of which was a high as his ears, a frock coat, velvet stock, straps on the bottom of his trouser legs, and the ubiquitous beaver hat "worth 40 shillings." Over the black frock coat he often wore a long coat of Royal Stuart tartan lined with scarlet.[149]

There were numerous red-letter days to provide variety and a change of pace from hard, steady work: holidays, parties, weddings, potlatches, brigades in which familes might also participate, arrival of the express, and the coming of mail and supply boats from England.

Holidays at the palace were bright and gay; Christmas was a particularly gala occasion. On holidays the employees' rations were doubled; work was kept at a minimum. There was unceasing merriment from Christmas Day until New Year's Day.

The celebration in 1839 was especially festive. The Chief Factor had returned from his year's furlough in Europe and eastern Canada; Eloisa had been married to William Glen Rae, a clerk at the Fort, early in 1838 before her father left in March and was now the mother of a son, John, a few months old. She and her mother stood at tables piled high with gifts and graciously dispensed English candies, cakes, and coffee. The Great White Eagle greeted each guest personally.

Royal Family of the Columbia

Attractive young people moving among the guests included the Doctor's son-in-law, Mrs. McLouglin's granddaughter Catherine Sinclair Ermatinger,[150] James and Amelia Douglas, and Maria, half-breed daughter of Chief Factor Pierre Pambrun of Fort Walla Walla, later to be married to Dr. Forbes Barclay and to live next door to the McLoughlins in Oregon City. Good cheer abounded. Five hundred guests dined at long tables in the immense dining hall. Greens and holly-leaved Oregon grape were everywhere, adding to the beauty of the huge room. Great logs blazed in the enormous fireplace.[151]

In spite of the fact that Governor Simpson made known his disapproval of the let-down of work and waste of time and money and did not hesitate to express his displeasure, the Chief Factor continued his practice of celebrating the Christmas holidays generously and lavishly. The Christmas feasts consisting of joints of beef, cheeses, salmon, sturgeon, not to mention trout, and wild game such as goose, crane, plover, swan, duck, blue-ruffled grouse, quail, deer, and elk, were unbelievably exotic and would have done justice to a banquet of Henry VIII or even of Lucullus. Wines, ales, and ciders were also available for temperate enjoyment.[152]

Following this gourmet repast there was dancing; the exercise must have been both welcome and essential after the consumption of such vast quantities of food. The Doctor loved to dance. As he led the dancing with Margaret he looked a fashion plate in flowing peruke and flowered waistcoat.[153] Strangely, Margaret's attire was not described. Perhaps she wore a bouffant gown of Christmas red brocade.

Brigades were a diversion as well as an all-important part of the business of fur trading, a red-letter-day activity. By tradition on these special occasions those departing took a glass of wine to wish each other well. As a rule wives of the officers of the Fort accompanied their husbands on this combined business and pleasure journey. The Indian and half-breed women rode astride, in contrast to white women, who rode "lady-like", side saddle. Mrs. McLoughlin had a special saddle, built high both in the front and in the back. Amelia Douglas, wife of James Douglas, was often in attendance on the Queen of the Columbia, who rode with her husband at the head of the long procession. Always she wore a colorful costume, perhaps a crimson shawl and a fine blue broadcloth petticoat of European origin, with heavily beaded leggings and moccasins. The horse brigades were gay, with the bright dress of the trappers and the habits of their Indian wives, tiny bells tinkling at their saddle skirts.[154]

After Eloisa, the only McLoughlin daughter at the royal residence, reached her 'teens she also participated in the brigades, sometimes riding with her father, while her mother, in her quiet, retiring manner, gladly rode behind, yielding to her daughter the status of First Lady of the Fort.

Eloisa possessed the finest horse on the Columbia, a blond Cayuse, with pinkish eyes and blond mane and tail, given to her father by the chief of the Walla Wallas. On special occasions, such as a brigade, the horse was decorated with waving plumes. The tall blonde girl on the blond horse, with the tall, stately King of the Columbia, his long white hair and dark cloak streaming from his shoulders, composed an impressive picture for the natives who watched the regal cavalcade pass. The pomp and circumstance was not incidental, but was carefully planned; the Chief Factor, with his flair for the dramatic, realized the importance of impressing upon the Indian mind the tremendous force and power of the great Hudson's Bay Company. He was both literally and figuratively the monarch of all he surveyed—and of much more.[155]

Often the destination of those accompanying the brigade was the lush green Willamette Valley and beyond. Ever since 1832, when the Chief Factor had visited the Valley for the first time he returned each October with the brigade. With Margaret and Eloisa in bright colors at his side he rode in the lead canoe. After crossing the Columbia, at the landing they mounted horses sent from Tom McKay's farm and rode to Champoeg, in the Willamette Valley. This annual event of seeing the voyageurs off on another season of fur hunting and trapping, of enjoying horse and canoe travel in the mild October climate, and of sharing in the action and color of the excursion was eagerly anticipated each year.[156]

Fort Vancouver has been compared by the historian H. H. Bancroft with a feudal castle. In his metaphor this feudal life in the wilderness contained an "Arcadian simplicity" in the early years. The subordinate posts in the Columbia Department were dependent baronies, while the leaders of trapping parties were "chiefs who sally forth to do battle for their lords." Every summer the huge fortress gates opened to receive "not armored knights but brigades of successful trappers returning with the year's fur harvest."[157]

Each spring as the ice began to break up around the inland trading posts the wintering partners loaded their season's take. At the northernmost post the trappers would leave their winter quarters carrying their furs on horseback to the next station on the long line of march. At each station more men joined the cavalcade, which continued to grow in numbers until a vast quantity of furs from the Inland Empire had been collected.

When they reached the banks of the upper Columbia, the voyageurs left their horses and loaded their valuable pelts on canoes to begin the long journey to the lower Columbia and to Fort Vancouver. More men and more furs were added at each successive fort. At last they reached Fort Walla Walla, the last station before the Vancouver headquarters. To these fur trappers Vancouver was the center of the universe and was truly deserving of its nickname, "New York of the Pacific."[158]

A brigade coming to and going from Fort Vancouver was a small army with experienced leaders, usually consisting of from fifteen to twenty-five white men and fifty or more half-breeds, French Canadians, Hawaiians, and Indians, many of them from the more distant tribes. Of the local Indians only a few Walla Wallas, Cayuse or Flatheads occasionally joined for the adventure. Clerks often went along to study the business as preparation for promotion.[159]

By the time the brigade neared Fort Vancouver the canoes and the bateaux were twenty-five across led by a single bateau of Company officers in charge of the Union Jack, which floated proudly from the masthead. (Possibly the British flag had the large letters HBC in the lower right corner as does the one on display currently in the Fort Vancouver Visitors Center.)

Just before reaching the final bend before the Fort the voyageurs stopped, drew up at a bank, donned their best clothes of bright colors, gay ribbons and beads, and carefully combed their hair, tying it with ribbons. Again taking to their canoes, they formed perfect straight lines across the current. Singing the familiar, wild songs of the oar, their paddles flashed rhythmically in the sun, as Mt. Hood loomed white and proud in the distance.[160]

> Dans mon chemin je rencontre
> Deux cavaliers, très bien montés,
> L'on ton larridon danae,
> L'on ton larridon dai;
> Deux cavaliers, très bien montés,
> L'un cheval, l'autre à pied.

Here the boatman is citing the superiority of his mode of travel over those of the two knights whom he met on his way, one on horseback, the other on foot.

This return of the *coureurs de bois* (hunters) took place each year on the June flood; experienced people at the Fort knew when to expect them. Ordinarily an employee would be stationed at the landing to watch for their arrival.

Soon the cry "Brigade!" would go up and everyone including the Chief Factor would assemble to greet the returning traders. Reunions were exciting and joyous, with delectable food and perhaps a little wine for such a special occasion. There were always "tall tales" to tell.

Now the voyageurs could enjoy a respite. They could relax a little during the summer; others could now take the responsibility for the pelts, for cleaning, sorting, and shipping them, along with other goods, and laying in other supplies and guns in preparation for the next brigade, which would depart in the fall.

By 1839 fur brigades were a thing of the past. The fur country had been trapped out, by the HBC and by American, Pacific and Rocky Mountain Fur Companies. Men no longer cared to wear beaver hats, which were now replaced by silk. Ingeniously McLoughlin established a supply business, sending Tom McKay and Frank Ermatinger to American fur traders' rendezvous to sell or exchange goods. This was, incidentally, against Company rules, to allow, even to encourage, free-lance trading, but the practice continued for some time. Diversification, started immediately after the completion for Fort Vancouver, was flourishing. At Willamette Falls, a rapidly growing settlement, Dr. McLoughlin had opened a branch store for the Company.[161]

Another red-letter day came in the late summer, when the homeship with letters and newspapers arrived from England for the "exiles" at the Fort. A gala event always, the Chief Factor would give a festive banquet in the large dining room, to be followed by genial conversation in the Bachelors' Hall.

The Company ship, after weary months at sea, coming from London around the Horn to the Columbia would come to the Columbia bar. Once over the bar, it anchored at Baker's Bay, near present Astoria. A longboat was lowered, one of the officers would hurry to old Fort George, now reduced to a mere lookout station. Indian paddlers took the officer with his packets to Fort Vancouver; the HBC ship continued to lie in the bay waiting for a favorable wind to bring its cargo of supplies on to the Fort, where a watchman was on the alert. Soon Dr. McLoughlin was on the dock welcoming the officers, taking them to his own residence for relaxation and refreshment.[162]

Also in summer there was the annual trip to Champoeg to visit the mission. The Chief Factor always took Mrs. McLoughlin and, frequently, other family members. The trip was broken by making a portage at Willamette Falls, where by 1839 Dr. McLoughlin had two houses which he had built to substantiate his land claims. His fleet of canoes was filled with beds, bedding, tea, coffee, sugar, bread, cake, wines, and a number of servants, including a cook.

Traders set up long tables on which delicious edibles were set out. The French Canadians were very proud of their Indian wives' cooking, especially of their bread. Fruits, vegetables, venison hams, and gingerbread were just a few of the delectable items on the groaning tables.

Dr. McLoughlin was held in great respect, even reverence, by the Canadians, since he was also Canadian and spoke their provincial French. He was the center of attention in any gathering. In his element, standing in his dark blue cloth coat with its double rows of silver buttons, he shook hands heartily with the fathers and sons and kissed affectionately the cheeks of mothers and daughters.[163]

Life for the King of the Columbia was to be lived to the fullest, whether he was working with the utmost efficiency or enjoying at leisure the company of his family, of his friends, or of his fellow workers.

Royal Family of the Columbia

REFERENCES

CHAPTER 4

LIFE AT THE PALACE

THE KING'S DOMESTIC POLICY

1 Richard Montgomery, *The White-Headed Eagle*, p. 160.

2 Dorothy O. Johansen, *Empire of the Columbia*, p. 127. Also numerous other sources.

3 Oscar O. Winther, *The Great Northwest*, pp. 59-61, and A. S. Marquis, *Dr. John McLoughlin, The Great White Eagle*, pp. 13-14.

4 Winther, *op. cit.*, p. 59; Marquis, *op. cit.*, p. 14; Robert Johnson, *Dr. John McLoughlin*, pp. 58-59.

5 Cecil P. Dryden, *Give All to Oregon*, pp. 36-37; Johansen, *op. cit.*, pp. 128-135; Montgomery, *op. cit.*, p. 161.

6 Johnson, *op. cit.*, pp. 58-59.

7 Letter of McLoughlin to John Work from Fort Vancouver, March 1, 1832, in the *Oregon Historical Quarterly*, Vol.XV, pp.206-207

8 Johnson, *op. cit.*, pp. 60-61.

9 Eloisa McLoughlin Harvey, "Recollections-Dr. John McLoughlin," Ms., Bancroft Library; transcript, Oregon Historical Society Archives.

10 *Scrap Book*, Vol. 38, p. 76; article from *Oregonian*, April 12, 1888.

11 Television series "America" with Alistair Cooke, January 9, 1973.

12 Helen Bowers, "Trade and Administrative Policies and Practices of John McLoughlin,"p.7.

13 Johansen, *op. cit.*, pp. 129-131.

14 Robert E. Pinkerton, *The Hudson's Bay Company*, p. 304.

15 Jane Tipton, *John McLoughlin, Chief Factor of Hudson's Bay Company at Fort Vancouver*, p. 41.

16 Richard Montgomery, *Young Northwest*, pp. 118-120.

17 *White-Headed Eagle, op. cit.*, pp. 139-142.

18 Gordon Speck, *Northwest Explorations*, p. 369.

19 Horace S. Lyman, *History of Oregon*, p. 390.

20 W.H.E., *op. cit.*, pp. 183-184

21 *Ibid.*, p. 185.

22 Microfilm, Oregon Historical Society, October 16, 1972.

23 Historical marker at Barclay House, Oregon City.

24 Tipton, *op. cit.*, p. 39.

25 Tipton, *op. cit.*, p. 41.

26 Burt Brown Barker, *The McLoughlin Empire and its Rulers*, p. 61. The first (Indian) family of Alexander Fraser, an uncle of Dr. McLoughlin, won its claim to the father's estate against the second (Caucasian) family in a court of law.

27 T. C. Elliott, A Hudson's Bay Company Marriage Certificate," *Oregon Historical Society Quarterly*, Vol. X, pp. 325-328.

28 *Ibid.*, p. 329.

29 Microfilm, Oregon Historical Society, October 16, 1972.

30 Elliott. "Margaret Wadin McKay McLoughlin", *Oregon Historical Quarterly*, Vol. 36 (December 1935), p. 329.

31 *Catholic Church Records of the Pacific Northwest Coast*, Volume II, *Vancouver*, p. 96, from pp. 5-6 of original records.

32 *W.-H. E. op. cit.*, p. 176

33 John Ball, *Autobiography*, pp. 92-93.

34 Johnson, *op. cit.*, pp. 118-119.

35 Ball, *loc. cit.*

36 *W.-H. E.*, *op. cit.*, p. 178.

37 Johansen, *op. cit.*, p. 146.

38 Visited by author July 31, 1973.

39 Harvey, *loc. cit.*

40 Jessett, Herbert Beaver, Letters and Reports, pp. xix-xx.

41 Johansen, *op. cit.*, pp. 173-174.

42 *W.-H. E. op. cit.*, pp. 252-253.

43 *Ibid.*, p. 76.

44 Eva Emery Dye, *McLoughlin and Old Oregon*, p. 117.

45 Frederick Merk, *Fur Trade and Empire*, pp. 354-355.

46 Hubert H. Bancroft, *History of the Northwest Coast*, Vol. II, pp. 434-435.

47 George W. Fuller, *A History of the Pacific Northwest*, pp. 209-210.

48 Bancroft, *op. cit.*, pp. 650-653.

49 (Mrs.) Eliza Wilson, Oregon Sketches", p. 20, quoted by Theressa Gay in *Life and Letters of Mrs. Jason Lee*, p. 155.

50 *Catholic Church Records, op. cit.*, p. 97, from p. 7 or original record.

51 Edwin V. O'Hara, *Catholic History of Oregon*, p. 35.

52 *Catholic Church Records, op. cit.*, p. 93.

53 *Washington Historical Quarterly*, Vol. 3, part 1, October 1908, p. 72.

54 Nard Jones, *Marcus Whitman: The Great Command*, p. 272.

55 *Quarterly of the California Historical Society*, Vol. 45, pp. 125-126.

56 Johnson, *op. cit.*, p. 115.

57 *The Beaver*, house organ of the Hudson's Bay Company, fall 1970, tercentennial issue, p. 51.

58 Burt Brown Barker, ed., *McLoughlin's Financial Papers*.

59 D.W. Meinig, *The Great Columbia Plain: A Historical Geography 1804-1910*, pp. 89-91.

60 William Rea Sampson, *John McLoughlin's Business Correspondence 1847-1848*, p. XXI.

61 Meinig, *loc, cit*.

62 *The Beaver, op cit.*, pp. 52-53.

63 *W-H. E., op. cit.*, pp. 52-53.

64 *The Beaver, op cit.*, pp. 52-53.

65 Tipton, *op. cit.*, pp. 86-87.

66 Johansen, *op. cit.*, p. 134.

67 *W.-H. E., op. cit.*, p. 259.

68 Katharine B. Judson, *Early Days in Old Oregon*, p. 67.

69 *W.-H. E., op cit.*, p. 213.

70 David Lavender, *Land of Giants*, p. 189.

71 Sampson, *op. cit.*, p. XXIV.

72 *W.-H. E., op. cit.*, p. 242.

73 Lavender, *loc, cit*.

74 W.-H.E., *op. cit.*, pp. 246-250.

75 E. E. Rich, *The Hudson's Bay Company* 1670-1870, Vol. II, p. 689.

76 Judson, *op. cit.*, p. 68.

77 *W.-H. E., op. cit.*, p. 155.

78 Lyman, *op. cit.*, p. 360.

79 Douglas MacKay, *The Honourable Company*, p. 231.

80 *W.-H. E., op. cit.*, pp. 38, 39, 49.

81. Lavender, *op. cit.*, p. 82.

82 MacKay, *op. cit.*, p. 233.

83 Rich, *op. cit.*, p. 314.

84 Bancroft, *op. cit.*, Vol. I, p. 48.

85 *W.-H. E., op. cit.*, p. 241, pp. 247-248.

86 Rich, *op. cit.*, p. 312.

87 *California Historical Society Quarterly*, Vol. 28 (1949), p. 255.

88 Merk, *op. cit.*, pp. 246-247.

89 *W.-H. E., op. cit.*, p. 277.

90 MacKay, *op. cit.*, p. 233.

91 Marquis, *op. cit.*, p. 21; Lavender, *op. cit.*, 213.

92 George Woodcock, "Far Western Outposts: Vancouver Island and British Columbia," *History Today*, September 1971, p. 661.

93 Merk, *op. cit.*, p. 247.

94 Rich, *op. cit.*, p. 313.

95 MacKay, *op cit.*, pp. 233-235.

96 *W.-H. E.*, *op. cit.*, p. 217.

97 Johansen, *op. cit.*, p. 159.

98 G. Hollis Slater, "New Light on Herbert Beaver," *British Columbia Historical Quarterly*, Vol. VI, January 1942, p. 19.

99 *W.-H. E.*, *op. cit.*, p. 217.

100 Robert Ormond Case, *Empire Builders*, pp. 63-67.

101 Herbert Beaver, *Reports and Letters of Herbert Beaver 1836-1838*, introduction, pp. XVI-XX.

102 James Douglas Reports on the Beaver Affair," *Oregon Historical Quarterly*, Vol. 47, March 1946, p. 18.

103 Beaver, *loc. cit.*

104 *Ibid.*, p. 84.

105 *Ibid.*, p. XVI.

106 *Scrap Book, loc. cit.*

107 *W.-H. E.*, p. 239.

108 Bancroft, *op. cit.*, pp. 50-53.

109 Beaver, *op. cit.*, p. 4.

110 *Ibid.*, p. 141.

111 Slater, *op. cit.*, pp. 21-22.

112 James Douglas Reports..." *loc. cit.*

113 W. Stewart Wallace, *Documents Relating to the Northwest Company.* pp. 438-439.

114 *Oregon Historical Quarterly*, Volume 26 (1914), p. 15.

115 Wallace, *op. cit.*, p. 439; Frank C. Robertson, *Fort Hall: Gateway to the Oregon Country*, pp. 166-167.

116 Robertson, *op. cit.*, p. 95.

117 Elliott, *op. cit.*, p. 338. See reference note 152.

118 Wallace, *loc. cit.*

119 Robertson, *op. cit.*, p. 146, 120. *W.H.E. op. cit.*, pp. 185-186.

120 *W.-H. E.*, *op. cit.*, pp. 185-186.

121 Evelyn Sibley Lampman, *Princess of Fort Vancouver*, pp. 10, 11.

122 Lyman, *op. cit.*, Vol. II, p. 334.

123 Wallace, *op. cit.*, p. 489.

124 Winther, *op. cit.*, p. 69.

125 *W.-H. E.*, *op. cit.*, p. 91.

126 Johnson, *op. cit.*, p. 52.

127 Johansen, *op. cit.*, p. 130.

128 Johnson, *loc. cit.*

129 MacKay, *op. cit.*, p. 253.

130 Johansen, *op. cit.*, pp. 138.

131 MacKay, *op. cit.*, pp. 253-254.

132 Johansen, *op. cit.*, p. 222.

133 Jalmar Johnson, *Builders of the Northwest*, p. 47.

134 Bancroft, *op. cit.*, *History of Oregon*, Vol. II, p. 97.

135 *City of Portland*, Vol. I, p. 72.

136 Dye, *op. cit.*, pp. 137-140.

137 MacKay, *op. cit.*, p. 254.

138 Barker, *The McLoughlin Empire*, p. 321.

139 Helen Krebs Smith, *With Her Own Wings*, p. 36.

140 Philip H. Parrish, *Historic Oregon*, p. 254.

141 Judson, *op. cit.*, pp. 104-106.

142 John Walton Caughey, *History of the Pacific Coast*, p. 214.

143 Robert Johnson, *op. cit.*, p. 63.

144 Dye, *op. cit.*, p. 331.

145 George W. Fuller, *History of the Pacific Northwest*, p. 119.

146 Dye, *op. cit.*, pp. 110-111.

147 T. D. Allen, *Troubled Border*, pp. 172-173.

148 Rich, *op. cit.*, p. 361.

149 Lavender, *op. cit.*, p. 118.

150 See Elliot, *op. cit.*, p. 337.   Some mystery enveloped the Sinclair-Ermatinger wedding, which took place August 10, 1841, according to Elliott, rather than 1838 or 1839, as a few others stated.   A Methodist missionary, Joseph Frost, was called to Fort George, where James Birnie of the HBC was in charge, to marry Catherine Sinclair and Frank Ermatinger, who had come nearly 100 miles from Fort Vancouver.   Elliott raised the question of an elopement, feeling since Dr. McLoughlin had been opposed to Ermatinger's marrying his daughter Eloisa, that he was also opposed to his marrying his stepgranddaughter Catherine.(See Note 119.)   If the (Frank's) marriage took place in 1841, as Elliott believed, obviously Catherine (if she was present in 1838) was still Catherine Sinclair.

151 Marquis, *op. cit.*, pp. 25-57.

152 Ben Hur Lampman, *Elks Magazine*, April 1925, p. 37.

153 Dye, *op. cit.*, p. 22.

154 Quotation from Narcissa Whitman's "Journal", in *Oregon Pioneer Association Transactions*, Vol. for 1877-1883, p. 68.

155 Dye, *op. cit.*, pp. 61-62.

156 *W.-H. E.*, *op. cit.*, p. 194.

157 Bancroft, *History of Oregon*, *op. cit.*, Vol. I, pp. 45-46.

158 Montgomery, *Young Northwest*, *op. cit.*, pp. 121-122.

159 Robert Johnson, *op. cit.*, pp. 48-49.

160 Parrish, *op. cit.*, pp. 86-87.

161 *Ibid.*, p. 88; Johnson, *op. cit;* p. 66.

162 *Young Northwest*, *op. cit.*, pp. 122-126.

163 Dye, *op. cit.*, pp. 114, 116, 118.

Royal Family of the Columbia

CHAPTER 5

VISITORS AT THE PALACE

THE KING'S FOREIGN POLICY

Visitors at the Fort were a source either of great pleasure or of intense annoyance, depending upon the viewpoint. To some of the staff they were a nuisance, consuming valuable time which should have been devoted to business. Remarks of Chief Trader Peter Skene Ogden, frequently called upon to serve as guide for numerous visiting celebrities, were typically derogatory: "...five...Gent. as follows 2 in quest of Flowers 2 killing Birds in the Columbia and 1 in quest of rocks and stones." Since many of these men came armed "with letters from the President of the U. States" Ogden reasoned that "it would not be good policy not to treat them politely," but in his opinion they were "a perfect nuisance."[1]

Dr. McLoughlin, however, took a more hospitable attitude toward the Fort's guests, assisting those who needed help in any way possible. A typical example of his Good Samaritan character was his assistance to and hospitality toward Jedediah Smith, discussed in another chapter. His extended concern and sincere friendship for the Whitmans, the Spaldings, and the Lees, as well as for hundreds of others, were an innate part of his make-up, the outward expression of his generosity and magnanimity.

Missionaries, fur traders, scientists: A representative of the third group was David Douglas, a famous botanist. Indubitably he was Ogden's target when he protested the presence of "Gents...in quest of Flowers." Sent by the Horticultural Society of London, he was Fort Vancouver's first guest, arriving even before the first fort was completed. Nevertheless, he was received hospitably. He had passage on the Company ship *William and Anne,* arriving at the mouth of the Columbia February 12, 1825, but it was nearly two months later, April 7, before the ship could enter the river at Astoria (Fort George) and could continue to Fort Vancouver.[2]

The young Scotch scientist became very popular with many of the Fort's officers, because of his friendliness. In turn he admired Dr. McLoughlin for his integrity and kindness. When the roof of the hut to which Mr. Douglas was assigned at Fort Vancouver began to leak, the Chief Factor invited him to his own home[3]

Dr. McLoughlin's sense of humor in regard to the visiting botanist was revealed by an ingenious device when both men happened to be at Fort Colville in 1826. The visitor had the habit of wandering at random as he collected specimens. The Chief Factor, to protect the younger man, informed the Indians that Douglas was the "grass man", possessing "great powers over flowers and shrubs". This caused the young

Scotsman for whom the Douglas fir is named to seem so awesome to the natives that he was able to travel freely without fear of molestation.[4]

While still at Fort Colville, Mr. Douglas went out on one of his collecting expeditions. After walking twenty miles or so, he sat down to rest, falling asleep in the warm 86° temperature. When he awoke it was very late; he would have preferred to remain there and to continue his hunt the next day, but feeling that Dr. McLoughlin would be uneasy if he did not return, he trudged back in the dark over mountainous terrain, reaching the post about midnight. He found the Chief Factor anxious about his safety and on the point of sending two Indians after him. The Doctor laughed heartily when he heard the scientist's story.[5] A strong fellowship had grown between the two men. It was part of the McLoughlin policy to show the natives that all white men, whether King George men or Boston men, were under his protection and that of the Honourable Company and that he, John McLoughlin, working under the aegis of the Company would see to it that any natives who molested white men would be punished. His protective treatment of David Douglas was only one exemplary action of the policy.[6]

Another illustrative recipient of the McLoughlin hospitality and bounty was the Reverend Samuel Parker. Sent to Oregon by the American Board of Commissioners for Foreign Missions (representing Presbyterian, Congregational, and Dutch Reformed denominations), he spent several months, from the fall of 1834 to April 1835, as a guest of Chief Factor McLoughlin at Fort Vancouver.[7] His treatment there in view of his later conduct was much better than he deserved.

A graduate of Williams College in 1806, and later a pastor of Presbyterian and Congregational churches in New York state, and a teacher at Ithaca Academy, he became restless at age fifty-four, and no longer "encumbered" with a wife, he applied for an appointment to Oregon. His principal assignment was to look over the Oregon Country, give advice as to a propitious site for a mission, meet the Whitman-Spalding party and guide them further west.[8] The Whitmans and the Spaldings crossed the Continental Divide on Independence Day (1836), expecting to be met soon at a fur traders' rendezvous on the Green River by a party headed by Parker. Instead they were surprised by a party of Nez Percés and Flatheads with two Company men and two chiefs, "Lawyer" and "Rottenbelly", bearing a message from Parker blithely informing them that he had decided to investigate the northeast branch of the Columbia. He gave them none of the advance information which was his obligation and his assignment to do. Eventually, he simply sailed back to New York, leaving the four younger missionaries to shift for themselves.[9]

Both Dr. Whitman and Mr. Spalding were justifiably disappointed and irritated at Mr. Parker's callous selfishness and irresponsibility; Mr. Spalding because he was worried about Eliza's frail health, the Whitmans because they in a sense considered themselves protégés of the older man, who was in part responsible for their marriage.[10]

Royal Family of the Columbia

However, when previously a guest at Fort Vancouver, these deplorable character traits of Mr. Parker's had not yet been revealed. He had stopped at Fort Vancouver expecting a complete lack of comfort in this wilderness post and was thoroughly amazed to be lodged in "well-furnished, quarters"; he wrote that he had "access to as many volumes of books as I have time to read; and opportunity to ride out for exercise and to see the adjoining country (and to enjoy) the society of gentlemen, enlightened, polished and sociable."[11]

When he left the Fort he was given clothing, goods, and provisions to "pay my Indians...my guides and interpreters." Upon asking for his bill the chief clerk replied that there was no bill but "(he) felt pleasure in gratuitously conferring all they had done for the benefit of the object in which I was engaged."[12]

Mr. Parker, who was sometimes called the "plug hat missionary" because of his immaculate appearance, was among the passengers on the maiden voyage of the first steamboat on the Columbia. In 1836 when the HBC steamer *Beaver* sailed down the Willamette to Tom McKay's farm in the Valley all the Company dignitaries within calling distance accompanied Fort Vancouver's chief factor on the history-making, gala excursion, including James Douglas, Peter Skene Ogden, Archibald McKinlay, John Work, and Pierre Pambrun, among others. Perhaps the White-Headed Eagle had in mind that the missionary would carry back to the United States a story of the progress being made by the Company in the Pacific Northwest.[13]

It should be noted that the Chief Factor's charitable benevolence to American visitors was not always viewed favorably by Company officials in London. Doctor McLoughlin was informed that they wished the "rites of Hospitality" to be shown "at our Establishment to Strangers when properly introduced...(but) we are averse to keeping open house for the Entertainment and accommodations of people who have no claim upon us..."[14] (Not too unreasonable, really.) As quoted elsewhere, whenever the Chief Factor was impugned with extravagance or even with disloyalty to the company in befriending Americans, his answer invariably was to the effect that as a Christian and as an humanitarian his conscience demanded that he assist a needy fellow man. He would sometimes, as well, offer the additional and more pragmatic defense that it was to the Honourable Company's advantage to keep the friendship of the ever-increasing numbers of Americans who crossed the continent (particularly after 1840, for the Company might soon be at the Americans' mercy), at least until the so-called "joint occupation" agreement finally expired and the boundary west of the Rockies was legally settled by international diplomacy.

Other missionaries, too, visited Fort Vancouver, that opulent Palace on the Columbia, and were received with the same kindness and cordiality as were the Reverend Mr. Parker and hundreds of other guests, both lay and clergy. In 1834 the Reverend Jason Lee and his nephew the Reverend Daniel Lee led west a party of

Methodist mssionaries and lay workers. They had come with Nathaniel Wyeth, who had made his first trip to the Oregon Country in 1832 and had been welcomed then, as now, by the Chief Factor.[15] Tom McKay, Mrs. McLoughlin's son, had conducted the Lee party part of the way from Fort Hall, which had been built by Wyeth.[16]

The story goes that in 1831 four Nez Percés and Flatheads had made the rough overland trip to St. Louis asking for "Black Robes" and the "whiteman's Book of Heaven". Protestant missionary societies, ever eager to steal a march on the Black Robes, answered the dramatic petition, among them the Missionary Society of the Methodist Episcopal Church. One of the first to respond to the Missionary Society's call for volunteers was Jason Lee, who was formally dedicated to the mission's task;[17] Daniel Lee, also an ordained minister, was appointed his uncle's colleague.[18]

Jason Lee had been recommended by a former teacher, Dr. Wilbur Fisk, "the most powerful Methodist leader in America," and at that time president of Wesleyan University, Middletown, Connecticut.[19] Born in 1803 in Stanstead, Lower Canada, of New England parents, Mr. Lee was large and strong, a man of great endurance. He was devout, practical, friendly, but lacked the firmness needed in his responsible position.[20]

Dr. McLoughlin, hospitable as ever, invited the Lees to hold services at the Fort. En route Jason had conducted a service of public worship in a grove near Fort Hall at the request of Tom McKay. His sermons at Fort Vancouver were to a congregation of international character: English, French, Scottish, Scotch-Irish, American, Indian, Hawaiian, half-breed Indian, and even Japanese, for there were three survivors of a wrecked junk found in 1833.[21]

With motives probably more pragmatic than romantic, the Oregon Missions Board had decided that Anna Maria Pittman, eldest of George Washington and Mary Spies Pittman's thirteen children, of New York, would be a worthy mate for the Reverend Mr. Lee. Born in 1803, the same year as her future husband, she had helped her mother rear one child after another. Like Narcissa Whitman, she was an "old maid" before she married. She had her heart set on serving in the mission field and, like Narcissa, while awaiting the opportunity, became a teacher. On January 6, 1836, she was chosen a "Teacher for the Oregon Mission." It may have been at this time that it was suggested to her that she had been selected as a wife for the Reverend Mr. Lee.[22] Apparently even at age thirty-two she was not so eager to "catch a husband" that she was pleased. On the contrary, the opposite seemed to be true.

She was to be given a salary of $300 a year and was to have $100 for an "outfit". All her traveling expenses to Oregon would be paid by the Board.[23]

Passage was arranged for the Oregon party on the *Hamilton,* which was to sail from Boston to the Sandwich Islands (Hawaii).

Since the married condition was almost obligatory for male missionaries, and inferring that the Mission Board was *ipso facto* categorically opposed to its missionaries marrying Indian or half-breed women, it was a policy to send (white) women of marriageable age as teachers. Some of the women were already fiancées of members of the mission, whom they may or may not even have met. The presence of these young white Christian women was felt to have a beneficial influence on the native women of the mission area.[24]

It is interesting to note as further confirmation of Miss Pittman's lack of desire to marry, her refusal to let the Reverend Rufus Spaulding, in charge of buying supplies for the missionaries, buy her a double mattress. This additional implication that she was committed to Jason Lee incensed her. As a possible early-day "libber" she insisted on a single mattress on principle. In a letter to her parents written from Boston on July 17, 1836, she wrote, "I would not have it and made him get me a single one. They seem determined to have me doubled, I will take care of number one and that is enough."[25]

All had to be on board by 8:00 A.M., July 28, but the boat did not put to sea until the next day.[26] Anna Maria found many things to keep her busy on shipboard. She wrote letters, read books, and studied her French books in order to be able to converse more easily with the French settlers she expected to meet. In addition she made four dresses and a patchwork spread and knit two pairs of stockings. For exercise she jumped rope and walked the deck whenever the weather was suitable.[27]

Her birthday (the thirty-third) was September 24; she wrote a diary-type letter to her parents in which her religious fervor shines through: "33 years of my life forever gone, and alas how little of that time has been spent doing good. Oh if my life is spared another year I trust I shall be enabled to do something for God, who has done so much for me..."[28] The boat docked December 24 and Christmas was spent in Honolulu, an extremely strange Christmas to New Yorkers, with open windows and lush green growth instead of chilling blasts and glittering white snow.[29]

The traveling missionaries were guests of resident missionaries of Oahu. The winter was spent in Honolulu; perhaps the climax of the stay was attending the wedding, with all its colorful ceremonies, of King Kamehameha III to his favorite, Kalama. One of the unmarried girls, fellow-missionary Susan Downing, a friend of Anna Maria's, had the honor of making the wedding cake. His Majesty had heard of the American custom and wished to add a new feature to the Hawaiian marriage feast.[30]

On April 8, 1837, the party left on the *Diana.* There were severe gales, high seas, loud winds. The travelers caught sight of Oregon exactly a month after setting sail, but the *Diana* did not dare go close, for it could not cross the sandbar at the mouth of the Columbia, which could be crossed only at high tide. Finally, on May 12, with everything lashed tight against the breakers, the ship crossed the bar and dropped anchor at Baker's Bay, near Fort George. Anna Maria described the locale: "scenery is good the birds are singing, the hills are covered with spruce pine and hemlock trees..."

Everyone went ashore the next day, glad to be on land. They were surprised and happy, perhaps slightly apprehensive, to see an Indian advancing toward them followed by several squaws.[31]

On May 13 they weighed anchor and proceeded up the Columbia. There were difficulties navigating the channel and the brig ran aground on May 15; however, on May 17 the *Diana* reached Fort Vancouver.[32] In a letter to her brothers and sisters Miss Pittman wrote on May 18:

> Yesterday we arrived at Fort Vancouver about 3 o'clock P.M. Dr. McLaughlin (sic) came on board and heartily received us. They was (sic) expecting us; the next morning we were landed, and conducted to the Dr's dwelling, a very handsome one story house, with a piazza clear across, with a winding stair on each side...the house stands high from the ground...we was introduced to Mrs. McLaughlin she is half white, their daughter Maria (Eloisa) 21 years of age is as white as I am, a lovely girl. she speaks french and english; they are very clever.[33]

The newly-arrived missionary also described her first dinner at Fort Vancouver in the same letter:

> We were all seated around a long table 18 of us, the table set with blue. Our first course was Soup, the next boiled salmon, then roasted ducks, then such a roast turkey as I never saw or eat it was a monster, it was like cutting of slices of pork, then wheat pan cakes, after that bread and butter and cheese all of their own make, and excellent too...traveling and high living agree with me. I have gained 11 pounds of flesh since I left home——This is a delightful coutnry I am much pleased with it.[34]

"Everyone" was now awaiting Jason Lee's arrival. No doubt Anna Marie was included in that indefinite pronoun, although she would not have wanted to admit it.[35] He too had been notified at some time that Miss Pittman was being sent out with the possibility of becoming his wife. When Dr. McLoughlin announced that Mr. Lee would soon arrive at his (McLoughlin's) request to meet and conduct his party to the mission in the Willamette Valley, about sixty miles south of the Fort, members of the group began to cast sly and mischievous glances toward Anna Maria. She was embarrassed by their teasing remarks.[36]

The Reverend Mr. Lee had been introduced to Anna Maria in New York City. Neither had seemed favorably impressed with the other at that time. She tried hard to maintain her composure as the young minister approached. Dr. McLoughlin introduced Mr. Lee to the party, leaving Anna Maria to the last. She is supposed to have blushed, which "added to the charm of her manner" and Mr. Lee seemed "pleased."[37]

After spending a most pleasant week at the Fort, the Methodist missionaries left on May 25 for the last stage of their 22,000-mile journey.[38] It was probably arranged in advance that Anna Maria would ride in Mr. Lee's canoe. In any case, she stated in a letter, "I went with Mr. J. L. in his canoe." It took the party three days to reach the mission site, sailing past Portland, and spending the second night at Willamette Falls, where they were met by an HBC employee (perhaps Tom McKay) with horses on which they completed the journey.[39]

Upon arriving at the Mission everyone immediately became busy. Thirty Indian children under the care of the Mission, seven of whom were ill, some seriously, lived in the rough log house. Consisting of two rooms, a kitchen and a schoolroom, the shelter was devoid of most of the usual comforts; the children had only mats and blankets on the floor to serve as beds.[40]

Everyone had his or her assigned tasks. Even some of the men had certain domestic duties. Adjusting quickly to the new mode of living, the women soon created a pleasant homelike atmosphere in the former bachelor quarters. Apparently Jason Lee approved of the change, for Anna Maria, in the same letter of June 5 to her parents, wrote "...Mr. Lee he says he feels now as if he was home with so many females around him, the men seem much pleased..." She also described caring for an Indian who had been shot, with a part of his jaw and throat torn away, a chest wound, and fragmented bone in one arm. It speaks well for her courage and consecration, for she seemed to take matter of factly an experience which might have been traumatic, or at least terrifying, to a young woman so protectively reared and sheltered as Anna Maria.[41]

Of especial interest to her parents must have been the following information, which she earnestly asked that they keep confidential:

> ...you will be anxious to know if there is any prospect of my having a Protector, let me tell you there is. Mr. J. Lee has broached the subject, it remains for me to say wither (sic) I shall be his helpmate...I look unto the Lord...it is an importation (important) station to fill..
>
> ....
>
> ...I expect to give my heart and hand to J. Lee. When this union will take place I am not prepared to say, but probably soon.[42]

She wrote that she would not have written them the news just yet, but that she "thought proper to relieve your minds, that you may not think I am alone." and that she had an opportunity to send the letter "by way of California" and did not know when there would be a later opportunity for her to get a letter through to the east coast. She asked them not to forget her, and to write; there was a strong implication that she did not expect to see them again. She asked them to "pray for your unworthy daughter." She was happy and if she could be "useful here among these wretched race of Adams sons and daughters here I will toil here I will live and die and be buried."[43]

It is of interest to note that in answer to the question of Mr. Lee's curious colleagues as to whether he would or would not marry Anna Maria, he had a stock answer:

> Though a lady should travel the world over in order to become my wife, yet
> I would never consent to marry her, unless upon *acquaintance* I should become
> satisfied, that that step would be conducive to our mutual happiness and
> the Glory of God.[44]

Jason Lee had a "Noble view of marriage." He would when he married make his wife "comfortable and happy," never giving her any reason to regret that she had become his wife. He was both "practical and sensible" and felt it wise for economic reasons to postpone marrying. After his conversion and his engaging to go as a missionary to the Oregon Country he felt it unfair to be married until he had started his work in this dangerous and uncivilized territory.

In his diary he confessed that at Fort Vancouver he still felt the prejudice against Anna Maria that he had felt a year or more earlier when they had met in New York City, and that though he considered her to possess "good piety and deep sense" he could not "fancy her as a wife." However, he would postpone a decision until they had become acquainted.[45]

Perhaps it was on their canoe trip from Fort Vancouver to the mission that his attitude toward her had begun to change. It was only two weeks later that he asked her to marry him.

The wedding was to take place Sunday, July 16 (1837) and on the week before, Anna Maria gave Jason Lee her written answer to his proposal in a poem, based upon Ruth I: 16, 17, the devotion of Ruth to Naomi. The first stanza follows:

> Yes, where thou goest I will go,
> With thine my earthly lot be cast;
> In pain or pleasure, joy or woe,
> Will I attend thee to the last.[46]

July 16 had previously been chosen as the date of the first public communion service in Oregon. Susan Downing (who had baked the royal wedding cake in Honolulu) and another missionary, Cyrus Shepherd, were also to be married. This triply impressive Sabbath Day was to have, they hoped, a beneficial influence on white men who were living with Indian or half-breed women without benefit of clergy. In a short talk Jason Lee mentioned that he had talked to them before of the importance of marriage and of its being blessed in church, and now he was about to practice what he preached.

As he finished speaking he stepped down from his improvised pulpit and led Anna Maria to the altar; Daniel Lee performed the marriage service according to the Methodist Episcopal discipline. The new bridegroom then married Cyrus and Susan. A third ceremony was then performed for Charles Roe, an American settler, and a Callopooya Indian called Miss Nancy.[47]

One author describes the wedding ceremonies as being performed in the firs near the mission house, while natives and voyageurs watched interestedly.[48]

The singing of hymns, offering of prayers, and a sermon by the minister-bridegroom followed; he then read and explained the creed of the Methodist Episcopal Society, baptized Charles Roe and received him into the church. (Nothing was said about baptizing the new Mrs. Roe.)

At this point Daniel Lee presided at the Communion of the Lord's Supper. Many were said to be extremely moved by the lengthy service.[49] There followed a conversion (from the Quaker faith) and a "feast of love" in which each member of the congregation "brought in testimony for the Lord, and bore witness to the truth excelency (sic) and importance of the religion of Jesus Christ." Even some Roman Catholic neighbors described the wicked lives they had led and expressed a desire to live better to save their souls. A hymn and a prayer concluded the service.[50] For Anna Maria, with her deep religious conviction, it was probably a perfect wedding day, as well as a most unusual one.

There was no honeymoon or wedding trip immediately following the ceremony, for there was too much work to be done. A few weeks later, however, in order to combat the fever and ague which apparently afflicted the mission each year, the Lees and the Shepherds took a delayed wedding pack trip to the coast, which required four days each way. Apparently they were in the Tillamook area, for mention was made that they attempted to preach to the "Killemook" Indians, an earlier version of "Tillamook." Here they enjoyed clam and fish bakes. "Frequent dips into the surf" were said to "invigorate their ague-racked bodies" and improved their health "materially".[51]

Apparently the Lees' marriage was a happy one, for in a letter to her mother dated March 25, 1838, Mrs. Lee mentioned how painful the imminent separation from her husband would be and referred to Jason as her "dearest half."[52]

In 1835 Mr. Lee, after one year in Oregon, had sent such a glowing report of his first year's work to the Mission board that the next year it sent men and women to help him. This was, of course, the group in which Anna Maria had come in 1837.

He—and the others—worked hard. On Sundays he preached to the French Canadians. On weekdays he and his helpers built a mission house and planted crops. Fifty-two Indian children came for instruction. Because the group of 1836-1837 made it possible to expand the operation he established a station at the Dalles where the Indians had permanent villages.[53]

At the end of three years (1837) Mr. Lee felt greatly frustrated, for he felt that he was spending the greater part of his time providing for the natives' physical and secular needs, when he yearned to care for their spiritual needs. Still, he felt he must have more missions among the Indians and also felt a call to "redeem" the Catholics.

For this reason, in the spring of 1838, he went back East to urge the recruitment of "respectable, Protestant, American" settlers. He was so successful in arousing enthusiasm that $100,000 was subscribed to send back the "Great Reinforcement" of fifty persons, of whom eighteen were children. These additional workers and colonizers returned with Jason Lee on the *Lausanne,* making the journey around Cape Horn, arriving in Oregon in the spring of 1840; some of the families were sent to the Clatsops (later to Clatsop Plains); others went to Nisqually and to the Falls of the Willamette. There were now five Methodist missions, including the original settlement.[54]

It was this trip which caused the separation to which Anna Maria had alluded in the March 25, 1838, letter to her mother. Jason had not wanted to leave his bride of eight months, especially at this time, for she was expecting a child in June. She, however, insisted that he should go—it was his duty; it was the will of God; she would be fine. She worried about the effect of a rigorous trip on his health, for he had not been feeling well for some time.

Before he left, on March 26, she gave him a seven-stanza poem of farewell, beginning

> Must my dear Companion leave me,
> Sad and lonely here to dwell?
> It 'tis duty thus that calls thee,
> Shall I keep thee? No, farewell;
> Though my heart aches
> While I bid thee thus farewell.[55]

The couple communicated as best they could, knowing that they would be separated for at least eighteen months. Each took advantage of the service of any messenger who might be going in the appropriate direction.

Anna Maria did not feel at all well, but she continued to work at the numerous tasks about her home and her seemingly endless work with the natives. Finally June came and on the evening of the twenty-third, after a long painful labor and the use of forceps, she gave birth to a boy. The infant lived for only about thirty-six hours, dying Monday, June 25. At about six o'clock the next morning Anna Maria also died. No reason was given for the death of either mother or child. It seems logical to infer that the long period of hard work, causing chronic exhaustion, plus the hardships all pioneers, especially women, were necessarily forced to undergo, and the grief and worry brought about by the painful separation from her husband were all contributory to her death and, indirectly, to the child's, even if there were not specific medical or obstetrical problems as additional factors.

This was the first death among the mission workers. In fact, Anna Maria had the honor of representing several historical "firsts"; the first white woman to see Willamette Falls, the first white bride, the first white woman to bear a child in the Oregon Country, and the first white woman to die there.[56]

She was buried the next day with her baby in her arms. Much later, her remains were moved, with those of her child, along with the original tombstone, to the Lee Mission Cemetery at Salem. The stone, a white marble slab, was purchased by Jason while still in the East and brought back by him in 1840 on the *Lausanne*. Today, it is understandably time-and weather-worn, but still legible. Surprisingly, since it was presumably Jason who composed the epitaph, an error was made in the date of her arrival in the Oregon Country, that she "landed in Oregon June 1837," whereas she had "crossed the bar" of the Columbia on May 11 of that year.[57]

Arrangements were made to notify Mr. Lee of the tragedy through the HBC at Fort Vancouver. James Douglas, in charge there during Dr. McLoughlin's furlough, sent an express to reach the missionary, picking up several letters of sympathy along the way. Many individuals took part in the relay, including several Indians. Stops were made at several HBC posts, including Fort Hall. One problem was finding runners who were willing to make the life-risking trip from Fort Hall. No one wanted to undertake the journey for less than five dollars a day, but finally a young man was engaged to take the packet of letters of Mr. Lee and was given a draft for two hundred fifty dollars as payment. Finally, on September 8 (1838) Mr. Lee was overtaken at the Shawnee Mission near Westport, on the Missouri River (today a part of Kansas City).[58]

To say that he was grief-stricken is unnecessary. His letter expressed, in the flowery, embellished style of the day, his sorrow, and his belief that his wife and his son were in heaven; he mentioned the interesting statistic, historically speaking, that her grave was "beneath the first sod that was ever broken in Oregon for the reception of a Missionary of the Cross, of a *white* female, or a *white* child."[59]

Anna Maria's parents did not know of their daughter's death until a letter came from the Missionary Society some time in October. Jason Lee was to give them more detailed information later.[60]

Mr. Lee, to honor his deceased wife, followed a custom of the time, that of giving the name of a prominent person in the Methodist Church to an Indian child of the Mission.   While in Marlborough, New York, he received thirty dollars from collections and subscriptions to educate an Indian girl at the Lee mission.   This girl was re-named Anna Maria Pittman in honor of the Methodist leader's missionary-wife.   Anna Maria Lee was further honored by namesakes in other families, in particular by Cyrus and Susan Downing Shepherd's new daughter, born in the autumn of 1838, who was given the name Anna Maria Lee.[61]

On July 26, 1839, while still in the East, Jason Lee married for the second time. His bride was Miss Lucy Thompson (or Thomson) of Barre, Vermont, who had recently given a valedictory address on missions and missionaries as she was graduated by Newbury Seminary.[62]

It was apparent from a letter written by Mr. Lee on November 27-28 to Mrs. Pittman from the *Lausanne,* while on the return trip to Oregon, that the latter had been deeply hurt by her son-in-law's remarriage.   Actually, it had been thirteen months since Anna Maria's death, a long interval between marriages in that day.

Mrs. Pittman apparently felt that he should not have taken another wife until he had at least seen her daughter's grave.   Jason riposted, while he could understand the "feelings of a fond mother," that she was the only person who felt that he should not have married at that time; indeed, he said, "more than a score...of my most judicious and inteligent (*sic*) friends...not only *advised*; but *urged* the measure; and begged of me, not to return to Oregon alone, but to choose a suitable companion to accompany me."   Among those urging his remarriage were a bishop, ministers, and other missionaries, whose judgment he felt to be more valid and objective than that of his former mother-in-law.

Perhaps the new Mrs. Lee had accompanied her husband when he called on Mrs. Pittman, which may or may not have been unwise and tactless.   Possibly Mrs. Pittman had been discourteous or cold to her daughter's successor, for Jason wrote that Mrs. Lee (Lucy) was not to blame (for his remarriage).   He implied that Anna Maria would have herself wanted him to remarry, for to "promote my comfort, was the grand object, to which your Maria and my Maria had devoted herself..."

Too, Jason objected to Mrs. Pittman's discussing "our family matters," with one of his friends, an action which he felt to be embarrassing and demeaning.

Mrs. Pittman had asked him to send Anna Maria's possessions to her.   He replied that he would send her clothes and anything else desired, if Mrs. Pittman would send him a list, except Anna Maria's watch, which he wanted as a souvenir of her, and spoons which Anna Maria had bought in the Sandwich Islands (and which Mrs. Pittman had specifically asked for).   These he and Anna Maria had used together and he wished to keep them.

Royal Family of the Columbia

The letter contained an addendum dated December 11 (1839) from Rio de Janeiro, in which he described their voyage around the Horn as very rough; he added that "Mrs. Lee was...prostrated for several weeks."

The whole tone of his letter, while direct, even blunt, was respectful and affectionate. He hoped Mrs. Pittman would continue to consider him her son; he considered her his "Dear Mother" and hoped that she would reconcile herself "to the course I have pursued." He would always be interested in her welfare and he hoped she would correspond with him. Again he showed his wish to keep their affairs private:

> As the above is upon a subject which concerns nobody but ourselves, I must utterly refuse my consent, to your showing it to anyone, except Father Pittman, and when you have both read it, let it be committed to the flames. This is the first letter I have attempted to write since we embarked.
>
> Ever yours,
> Jason Lee[63]

Mrs. Pittman's reaction to his letter is not known. A second letter was written by Jason to Mr. and Mrs. Pittman September 23, 1841, from Fort Vancouver. He apologized for being so slow in sending their daughter's things, but cited that he had been extremely busy. He felt "most of Maria's Dresses, &c. (were) not...worth sending." He sent some shells she had "brought from the S. I. (Sandwich Islands), "a lock of her hair, a gold locket with locks of hair of her friends a "Waiter" (probably a tray) which she had brought from the Islands and had been heard to say she would like to send to her mother, and the "Beaver and Otter which were put in to fill up the Box." Separately he wrote that "the little Clothes in the Box were suppose to be those worn by your little grand Son, during his short sojourn on earth; and the patch work we presume his Mother intended for a covering for her Son." He mentioned that he had never heard from any of Anna Maria's family, which was very disappointing to him. Asking his former parents-in-law to let him know if they ever needed any help from him, he closed by saying that he hoped still to have the privilege of signing himself "Yours (*sic*) Dutiful Son *Jason Lee*."[64]

In a letter from "Walamette" August 2, 1842, Mr. Lee explained that the box he had packed had not been accepted for shipment for lack of space; he had tried again to ship it, but it was not accepted; it was now at Fort George and would be sent soon.

The news which Jason sent was that his second wife, Lucy, had also died.

> I can now look upon two graves, and reflect, that I have lived in perfect peace and harmony with the inmates of both, and that I am now standing *alone,* having no one to share my sorrows or participate in my griefs, Be it so. Heaven is just, and I bow with submission. Never was man blessed with two better wives....

117

He added that Lucy had left him with an infant daughter, Lucyanna Maria, named for both of her father's wives. Again he called the Pittmans his "Dear Parents" and signed himself their "Dutiful Son".[65]

Little Lucyanna had been born February 26, 1842. Her mother died a little more than three weeks later, on March 20; the immediate cause of her death was given as pleurisy. Only three years later Jason died in eastern Canada; Lucyanna was reared by the Reverend and Mrs. Gustavus Hines, who had cared for her since her mother's death.

Jason Lee's daughter was graduated from Willamette University in 1863. For a time she was an instructor there, later marrying Professor Francis H. Grubbs of Willamette; she died in 1881. Their only child was a daughter, Ethel, who in 1936 was living in Portland, the only descendant of Jason Lee.[66]

Today in Salem a small fenced-in section of the Lee Mission Cemetery contains the graves and markers of (right to left) Anna Maria Lee, Lucy Thompson Lee, Lucy Lee Grubbs, and Francis Grubbs. The stone of Anna Maria is more than one hundred years old; the other three match each other and are quite modern in design.[67] There is no grave or marker for Ethel, yet if she were still living she would probably be one hundred or more years old. The central figure of this family, Jason Lee, is not there; he was buried in eastern Canada.*

For the purpose of this work the Lee story is ended. What was the effect, if any, of the Lee missions on the Honourable Company's Fort Vancouver, upon its chief factor, John McLoughlin, and, indirectly, upon his family?

Back in 1834, on his first trip to the Oregon Country, Jason, then a guest at the royal palace of Vancouver, had been advised by the King of the Columbia not to locate his mission among Flatheads, north of the Columbia, even though it was some of their tribe, or a related tribe, the Nez Percés, who had asked for missionaries. The Chief Factor explained that because the Flatheads were almost continuously at war with the Blackfeet, their territory was dangerous even for traders, and much more so for missionaries and settlers. Also, the nomadic life-style of the Flatheads made it difficult for missionaries to support themselves in such isolated country. No doubt Dr. McLoughlin also had in mind the Company policy of discouraging Americans from settling north of the Coluumbia, hoping of course that the boundary would be settled at the Columbia, particularly if not too many Americans had settled to the north. Mr. Lee did not decide impulsively on the Willamette site. He wished to know the "identicle (*sic*) place that the Lord designs." A disadvantage was that influenza epidemics of 1829-1832 had practically wiped out the Indian population there. Outweighing this negative factor, to Jason and Daniel Lee, was the favorable location of the southern part of the Willamette Valley, "so situated as to form a central position from which missionary labors may be extended in every direction among the

*See footnote 137 on p. 132.

natives and those immigrants who may thereafter settle in that vast and fertile valley." He decided on a site about ten miles north of present-day Salem.[68]

As always John McLoughlin was kind and willing to go out of his way to be helpful. He was interested in the success of the missions; he believed in converting the natives. However, he knew the true situation with the Methodist Mission: conversions had been few; both natives and Americans had been ill; some had died; some had become discouraged. Why had Mr. Lee gone east in 1838?[69]

In May 1840 a lone canoe arrived at the Fort; Jason Lee had arrived to visit the Great White Eagle. When the Chief Factor learned that fifty more Americans were soon arriving on the *Lausanne* he began to feel—perhaps suspect—that the nature of the Willamette missions was changing gradually from a society to save Indian souls to an organization to build American colonization.[70]

Nevertheless, with his usual thoughtfulness and cordiality, Dr. McLoughlin sent a pilot boat to assist the missionary ship *Lausanne* and guide it in the Columbia to the boat landing. In addition, he sent milk, vegetables, "a bag of fresh bread and a large tub of fresh butter."[71] The boat docked about 6:00 o'clock in the evening. The Chief Factor was waiting at the landing to receive them and invited the ship's company—fifty-four—to take tea at his home. They were provided with "comfortable quarters and abundant table" at the Fort. Furthermore they were Dr. McLoughlin's guests for several weeks. He invited the visiting ministers to preach at the Fort's Sunday services and insisted that Daniel Lee and his fiancée, Miss Maria Ware, be married at his residence with Jason Lee performing the ceremony.[72]

The Methodist missions lasted only a few more years. In addition to the problem of natives uninterested in religion, there were too many missionaries for the number of natives left to be taught and there was intra-mission conflict over spiritual and secular needs and over some of Lee's methods.[73] One of his strong beliefs was the value of manual training for the young natives, that this secular training was a force in saving their souls. Out of this educational beginning eventually grew Willamette University, a Methodist college at Salem, chartered in 1853.[74]

In 1843 the Society suspended Mr. Lee. Ill and exhausted as he was, early in 1844 he went to Honolulu, then sailed to Mexico, went overland in a Mexican stagecoach, caught a Gulf mail packet to New Orleans, and sailed up the Mississippi in a steamboat. He was in New York City, Washington, D.C., then back in New York pleading his case in the debilitating heat for two weeks, often to vindictive questioners. At last he was publicly vindicated and allowed to keep his title "Missionary to Oregon." He tried to preach a few times, but the old fire was gone. His clothes hung on his gaunt frame. The pain in his lungs and intestines was intense. He died at forty-one, March 14, 1845, in his birthplace, Stanstead, Lower Canada.[75]

Further ramifications of the Methodist missions as they affected John McLoughlin and the Company will be discussed in a later chapter in another context.

Certainly the Chief Factor perceived that the far-reaching purpose and result of the missions was colonization, for to the missionaries Christianizing must be accompanied by civilizing; civilizing was followed by colonization and settlement.[76]

The Society Board rule was to pay return transportation to the mission workers only after ten years of field service. After ten years of arduous labor cultivating the land, raising herds of cattle, building grist and saw mills, and the multitudinous other tasks under primitive conditions, many workers preferred to remain in the Oregon Country rather than to lose the benefits of ten years' labor. That fact, plus the emphasis of the Board on the recruitment of married couples and of marriageable female teachers and on bringing "the right kind of people" to Oregon[77] revealed an ulterior motivation for all to see. Only a moron would have lacked the insight to make a valid inference, and Chief Factor John McLoughlin was most emphatically not a moron.

It is not difficult to perceive why Dr. McLoughlin, even disregarding his own innate Catholic leanings, would prefer the presence of Catholic, to Protestant, missionaries, since the former of course had no families, and thus had less interest in colonization than had the Protestants[78] Nor did Catholic priests, as a rule, involve themselves in politics, whereas the Protestant (and American) missionary-settlers brought their politics with them and adapted them to the pioneer environment.

Among the most interesting visitors to the Palace on the Columbia were the Whitmans, Dr. Marcus and the former Narcissa Prentiss of Plattsburg and Angelica, New York. With them were the Reverend Henry Harmon and Eliza Hart Spalding and five others, including two Nez Percé boys.

For the Whitmans the transcontinental journey was also a wedding trip; they had been married (she in a "practical" black dress) seven months before the party's arrival on September 12, 1836. Narcissa had been a teacher but had always yearned to go to the mission field; she was an "old maid" of twenty-eight when she entered into a marriage which was at first a pragmatic "arrangement" made in order to effect the missionary goals of both Marcus and Narcissa. Marcus was no impetuous youth, but a man of thirty-two.[79]

The marriage had been suggested by the Reverend Samuel Parker; the two met and became engaged in one week,[80] although it was understood that the wedding could not take place for at least a year, for Marcus and Mr. Parker were first to make a preliminary exploratory trip, which they accomplished in 1835.[81]

The first white women to cross the continent, Narcissa and Eliza had marveled at the beauty of much of the country, especially Narcissa, whose health was excellent in spite of her pregnancy, and whose nature was exuberant. Eliza, whose natural fragility had been heightened by the stillbirth of a daughter several months previously, was much quieter, and more retiring than her ebullient sister missionary.[82]

Royal Family of the Columbia

The party had enjoyed the unusual experience of being met at the fur trappers' rendezvous at Green River, just west of the Continental Divide, by Joe Meek; at twenty-six, he was already beginning to be "a legend in his own time." Six or seven other "cleaned-up" trappers accompanied him. They had even shaved, some for the first time in months. They wore "decent" buckskin breeches.[83] Many of the mountain men hadn't seen a white woman for years; most of the Indians in the welcoming party had never seen one. They were captivated by Narcissa and Eliza, the white men perhaps more so by the blond, buxom Narcissa; the Indians, however, seemed more attracted to Eliza, dark and thin, sensing that Eliza had a more sincere interest in them than had the other woman.[84]

While at the rendezvous the Whitmans and the Spaldings received the letter (previously mentioned) of the Parker defection, delivered to them by two HBC men, Tom McKay and John McLeod, who had escorted Nathaniel Wyeth from Fort Hall, which he had just sold to the Honourable Company. The missionary party took advantage of Mr. Wyeth's return to Boston, sending mail with him to their families and to the Board.[85]

The party proceeded westward with escorts McKay and McLeod, arriving at Fort Hall on August 3. The fort was a "sprawling horror" of logs and adobe with no windows; it had none of the opulence the party had been told Fort Vancouver contained and was thus a disappointment. It was not as comfortable even as Fort Laramie, but they were thankful at least to be within walls.[86]

And so it was on to Tom McKay's Fort Boise (Fort Snake), across the swift, deep Snake River, then on to Fort Walla Walla (Fort Nez Percé), and at long last to the New York of the Pacific. Here they were welcomed at the boat landing with Old World courtesy by the Chief Factor and by his second-in-command, Chief Trader James Douglas. The ladies were escorted almost at once to the McLoughlin residence and soon the party was enjoying a substantial midday meal.[87] The food served at the Fort was ambrosia,[88] its variety heavenly, especially so after two months on a steady diet of dried buffalo meat of which Narcissa had written, "...I can scarcely eat it, it appears so filthy."[89] An ordinary breakfast might consist of salmon, roast duck, potatoes, bread and butter, coffee or cocoa. For dinner the missionaries always had a delicious soup, which might be followed by venison, pork, fresh salmon or sturgeon, a variety of vegetables, luscious fruits and melons, rice pudding, apple pie, and cheese. Narcissa was much impressed when each course was served on a clean plate. Some visitors found it courtly, if incongruous, occasionally to see roast grizzly bear served in proper sequence on fine china.[90] The battered camp dishes were forgotten in the presence of late Spode china and the Waterford glass. Woman-like, she no doubt worried that she might gain too much weight.

One bit of Palace fare which Narcissa was unable to eat was "black pudding". Made "of blood and the fat of hogs, well spiced and filled into a gut," it was completely distasteful to her and to the other Americans.[91]

121

The Indian natives about the Fort, mostly Chinooks, were interested in the visitors' customs. Standing about, watching their arrival, they noted men helping women out of the boat. And the women didn't even carry the baggage! The interest was mutual. Many of the children were completely naked, the visitors noticed. Their flattened heads made them objects of pity to the missionaries. Their presence, the Union Jack flying in front of the King's palace, the British men-of-war *Columbia* and *Néreide* lying at the wharf, the singing of the voyageurs—all served to remind the Americans that they were indeed in a foreign country.[92]

In line with the Hudson's Bay Company's policy of encouraging Americans to settle south of the Columbia, and also because of his sincere interest in their welfare, Dr. McLoughlin had urged the Whitmans not to settle among the Cayuse, who were known to be treacherous and sly. Dr. Whitman, however, had an almost fanatical belief that he and his work were desperately needed by the Cayuse tribe. He had long ago decided to establish a mission among them at Waiilatpu ("Rye Grass Meadow"),[93] twenty-five miles east of Fort Walla Walla. The Spaldings planned to work among the Nez Percés (Pierced Noses) one hundred and twenty-five miles northeast of the Whitmans, at Lapwai, near present-day Lewiston, Idaho. Here the natives were teachable. They wanted their children to be educated; often the adults learned from their children. Both stations were established in what today is called the Inland Empire.

After a few days' rest Dr. Whitman and Mr. Spalding left the Fort for their respective destinations, leaving their wives at the Fort, where they would be safe and comfortable for a few weeks until shelters were built at the mission sites. Dr. McLoughlin was insistent that Narcissa, especially, should remain; since she was pregnant the Doctor felt she should not be exposed to the hardships and dangers of the isolation of the North. Here at Vancouver she would be safe and well cared for.[94] In a letter to her mother Narcissa wrote "No person could have received a more hearty welcome or be treated with greater kindness than we have been since our arrival."[95]

Narcissa did not pamper herself or waste time, however, while a guest at the Fort. Efficiently she set about teaching literature and music to nineteen-year-old Eloisa, whom she described as "an interesting young lady."[96] Narcissa, whom Mrs. McLoughlin considered "One of the kindest women in the world," had a fine voice and enjoyed teaching singing to Eloisa and teaching new tunes to some of the Indian children at the Fort.[97] Eloisa in turn taught Narcissa and Eliza something of fur trading, the lore of the sea otter, the bear, the fox, and the beaver. Of interest was the story that Eloisa, with all the opportunity to do so, did not herself wear furs; she knew too well how the pelts were obtained, what a laborious and dangerous task it was for the trapper. The Company's motto *Pro pelle cutem*[98] was, unfortunately, both realistic and relevant.

Royal Family of the Columbia

Mrs. McLoughlin was a gracious hostess to the two missionary-wives; their friendliness and utter lack of condescension toward her contrasted sharply with the racial bigotry and the supercilious attitude toward their half-breed hostess of Jane Beaver and her husband, who had arrived at the Fort six days before the missionary party.[99] Narcissa rode frequently in the afternoon with Mrs. McLoughlin. She added to the Fort's supply of garden seeds from seeds which had been given to her in Cincinnati. Mrs. McLoughlin in turn gave Narcissa sprouts which she could plant in her mission garden.[100]

Both Margaret and Eloisa, as well as Amelia Douglas, watched with interest as Eliza Spalding spun, wove, painted, knitted, and crocheted; apparently she was as versatile in the domestic arts as Narcissa was talented in music.[101] Eliza, while less physically attractive than Narcissa, was better educated, of a calmer temperament than the intensely emotional Narcissa, and perhaps surer of her religious convictions. There was sometimes an element of disharmony between the two, although it was more evident when their husbands were present. In fact, the two men had several times shown their antagonism on the journey, causing embarrassment and a feeling of unease among other members of the party. The origin of the antipathy was in Spalding's proposal of marriage to Narcissa and her rejection several years before. Mr. Spalding, incredibly sensitive due to his illegitimate birth, felt that Narcissa had considered herself superior to him. He more than once questioned her fitness to serve as a missionary.[102]

An interesting aspect of the extended visit at the Fort of the missionaries' wives, especially of Narcissa, was the attempt to "liberate" the woman of the Fort, that is, the half-breed wives of the officers, particularly of course, Mrs. McLoughlin and Mrs. Douglas. Custom and the Chief Factor's own orders did not allow Indian or half-breed wives to dine with the men of the Fort. They were said to lead such isolated lives as to approach the life-style of an Oriental harem.[103] "Gentlemen who came to the Fort never saw the family. We never saw anybody." So wrote Eloisa many years later as a woman of sixty-one.

As a matter of course Eloisa and her mother had taken their American guests to the women's mess room, while their husbands ate in the huge dining hall with the Fort's officers. Soon, however, due no doubt to the persuasiveness of their wives, Dr. Whitman and Mr. Spalding began coming for the midday meal to the women's dining room. They preferred the more leisurely dining pace there to the rushed eating of the men, who felt forced to eat quickly in order to return to their work. This was the first time that the McLoughlin women and Mrs. Douglas had ever eaten in mixed company. Mrs. McLoughlin, due to her race and her shy, reserved nature, was at first so ill at ease and embarrassed that she could not eat. Gradually she became less shy, but she was never completely at ease in the men's presence. Eloisa, by contrast, thoroughly enjoyed masculine company and is said to have vowed that when she married there would be no separation of the sexes at her table.[105] The two white women might possibly be considered early-day advocates of women's rights. Narcissa wrote in her journal, "Mrs. McLoughlin wishes to go and live with me her Daughter and Mrs. Douglas also. The Lord reward them for their love and kindness to us."[106]

On November 3, about two months after their husbands had left to establish missions, Narcissa and Eliza rejoined them, going by bateau on an eighteen-day trip up the Columbia. Marcus took Narcissa to a lean-to he had completed. The Spaldings, less fortunate, had a tent of animal skins. Before Christmas both couples were settled at their missions, eager to get the "main Presbyterian show" started on its work of training the natives in agricultural methods, as well as teaching them to read, and converting them by explaining the Bible.[107] The two missionaries had nearly exhausted their supplies by this time and were greatly relieved when the Chief Factor, with his usual generosity, agreed to replenish their goods at a nominal sum; every summer the brigades went north with goods for the interior. He asked the two Americans only that the missions not employ men at wages higher than the Company's usual rates. Since the Presbyterians' funds were at low ebb, the request was hardly necessary.[108]

When answering Company complaints Dr. McLoughlin justified his generosity in assisting the Americans with the pragmatic rationalization that if he refused help they would import supplies from the Sandwich Islands, which would attract Adventurers...to open shop in opposition to us."[109] In addition, the Doctor's innate sympathy and beneficence could not allow suffering.

Much of the remainder of the Whitman and Spalding stories is well known to readers of Pacific Northwest history. Both missions in the Inland Empire had initial success. The Spaldings were among friendly Nez Percés who showed some adaptability to Christian discipline and developed, even though reluctantly, interest in agriculture. In contrast, the Cayuse, at Waiilatpu, although speaking the Nez Percé dialect, and related to them, were untrustworthy, arrogant, and troublesome. Mr. Spalding emphasized strongly the secular aspects. He and Marcus Whitman had a number of disagreements, perhaps exacerbated by their old differences, the former wanting more stress on changing the Indians' secular lives, the latter wanting to encourage white settlement, feeling that the natives would learn from the whites. Mr. Spalding wanted to change the Indians' life-style first, postponing white settlement until the Indians were ready for it. Their differences reached a climax in 1840. As a result of complaints received, the Board dismissed Spalding and ordered the mission closed. Before the orders were received in the fall of 1842 the two men had reconciled and Dr. Whitman left on the long journey to persuade the Board to rescind its orders, and to discuss future policy.[110]

Royal Family of the Columbia

While her husband was gone Narcissa was not safe alone with three adopted half-breed children, one of them Joe Meek's daughter Helen Mar. On at least one occasion a native made an abortive attempt on their lives; Archibald McKinlay, Chief Trader at Fort Walla Walla, took Narcissa and the children to Walla Walla, keeping them until Methodist missionaries at The Dalles invited the refugees to stay with them. There were occasions too when Narcissa took refuge from danger with the kindly McLoughlins at Fort Vancouver.[111]

In 1843 the "Great Migration", en route to the Willamette Valley, stopped at Waiilatpu. It was but one of countless groups, large and small, which used the Whitman mission as a refuge and a way station. With this in mind the Board rescinded the closure order and Marcus upon his return turned Waiilatpu into a provision center, rest station and hospital for immigrants of the next three years. The last pioneer wagons had barely left the mission in 1847 when the Cayuse on November 29 put an end to the courageous work of the mission,[112] bearing out the repeated warnings Dr. McLoughlin had given the Whitmans. Fourteen persons were slaughtered, the Whitmans and twelve others of the mission household. About fifty-three women and children were abused and held captive until ransomed by the Hudson's Bay Company's Peter Skene Ogden. It was two and one-half years before the guilty were caught; they were tried and hanged in Oregon City on May 21, 1850. Dr. John McLoughlin was among those who testified under subpoena for the defense. He was asked merely to corroborate that he had repeatedly warned the missionaries against the Cayuse.[113]

There was, of course, a complexity of factors behind the massacre. The deep-rooted cause was probably the character of the Cayuse themselves and the fact that the Whitmans did not really understand these people they wanted so much and tried so desperately to help. They were harsh with the natives when they broke the white man's moral code or ignored rights of privacy and possession, concepts which they didn't comprehend. Yet the Whitmans were meek when mistreated by the Cayuse; if struck by an Indian, Marcus turned the other cheek, figuratively at least. On the other hand, if a native stole from his garden he was whipped as punishment. Even though Dr. Whitman knew of the tribal custom of putting to death a medicine man whose patients died, he risked his life repeatedly by attempting to cure their illnesses.[114]

In addition, immigrants who stopped at Waiilatpu in 1845 and 1847 brought with them diseases not serious to Caucasians but which killed the Indians, who had no immunity, in epidemic numbers. In addition, the ever-increasing number of white settlers foretold only one thing to the Indians—white civilization, which meant the end of their civilization, the disappearance of their land.

An immediate result of the tragedy was the beginning of the Cayuse War, first of a series of Indian wars which continued for thirty years. A far-reaching result was the expediting of legislative action by Congress, caused by public indignation, to make Oregon a territory, a goal which had been sought for several years by impatient American pioneers.[115]

What contribution did the Whitman-Spalding missions make to the development of the Northwest? Just as in the case of their sister (Methodist) missions in the Willamette Valley and elsewhere, conversions seemed, with some exceptions, to be of only temporary value. As already indicated, their civilizing, i. e., colonizing, had positive and permanent results. Definite educational contributions were made at both Inland Empire missions. The Spaldings made progress in educating the Nez Percés. It was Henry Spalding who introduced that symbol of culture, the printing press, into the Pacific Northwest. Sent from Boston to Honolulu, thence to Fort Vancouver in 1839, it was delivered by a Company brigade to Lapwai. Using a practical alphabet devised by scholar and linguist Asa Bowen Smith, Mr. Spalding printed a Nez Percé text of the Book of Matthew. He also adapted the popular "Catholic ladder" for Protestant use in educating and converting the Nez Percés.[116]

At Waiilatpu, too, education was of primary importance as a means of conversion. The Whitmans undertook the teaching of white children, as well as Indian. Countless orphans whose parents had died en route to Oregon were given a home and an education by Marcus and Narcissa. In recognition of this emphasis on education, Whitman College at Walla Walla, Washington, was named in his honor.[117]

Toward the end of their lives the health of both Marcus and Narcissa was at the breaking point. Ten years at Waiilatpu had thoroughly exhausted the once vivacious Narcissa: the burden of running a large household, caring for sick and hungry Indians and immigrants, teaching numerous children, above all the constant harassment by the natives—these had, not surprisingly, caused her health to deteriorate. Most of all, the drowning of their only child, two-year-old Alica Clarissa, in 1839, was a blow from which they never completely recovered.[118]

During Marcus' long absence Narcissa had gone to Fort Vancouver to be treated by Dr. Forbes Barclay, who had succeeded Dr. Tolmie. Dr. Barclay diagnosed her illness as enlargement of the right ovary and prescribed iodine and at least a month's rest at the Fort.[119]

Narcissa had arrived at the Palace on the Columbia Sunday, June 4, 1843, feeling strangely antagonistic toward the Chief Factor: first, because the HBC brigade which she accompanied had traveled on the Sabbath, a fact of which she disapproved and, equally, a situation which she was powerless to change; second, Dr. McLoughlin, she knew, had re-entered the Roman Catholic Church the previous year.[120] (To the Protestant missionaries, whether Methodist or Presbyterian, Catholicism was as reprehensible as heathenism. The competition for the privilege of saving the heathens' souls was strong. Moreover, the Indians found the Catholic religion easier to understand; there were no divisive sects and creeds to confuse them. The Catholic priests taught the natives only as much as they were capable of understanding. Both Catholics and Protestants frightened their potential converts by telling them of the damnation awaiting them if they accepted the faith of the other.[121])

The McLoughlins welcomed Narcissa as warmly as ever, but she did not reciprocate for the reasons indicated and also because there were interesting political developments taking place in Champoeg, in the Willamette Valley, and she felt left out, being "innured" at the Fort. The middle of July she and Helen Mar Meek, who had stayed with Narcissa as she had moved from fort to fort, left in a Company bateau, sailing down the Columbia to the mouth of the Willamette and on to the Valley. She accompanied a *bon voyage* party to Fort George, still an HBC post, to say farewell to the Reverend Daniel Lee and Mrs. Lee, who were returning to the States. In the Tualatin Plains Joe Meek was delighted to see his daughter and was amazed at her growth. In October Jason Lee escorted Narcissa and Helen Mar back to The Dalles, as "Husband" (as Narcissa called Marcus) would be returning from Boston and was to meet her there. Jason was eager to talk with his Presbyterian friend to learn news from the East and to know how Marcus had fared with the Mission Board. At the Cascades portage, about forty miles below The Dalles, Narcissa contracted a heavy cold and felt ill all the way to The Dalles.[122]

The homecoming would not be a pleasant one. All was confusion. The mission was no longer a mission but a "chaotic inn for emigrants." The vanguard of the emigrant train had broken into the house for supplies and had left it open to thieving Cayuse, who had also burned the gristmill. Marcus, distraught and pulled in a hundred directions, had stayed at Waiilatpu long enough to make some repairs and lay in more supplies; he had returned from the East by way of Lapwai because he had heard that the Spaldings were ill of scarlet fever.[123] He found them recovering and the Spalding children well. Henry Spalding told Marcus that the fever had at last burned out all his feelings of enmity and jealousy. Marcus continued on to The Dalles to meet Narcissa, bone-weary from his six-thousand mile trip; he was limping. Jason Lee was there and had to hear the bad news from Marcus that the Methodist Board planned to recall him. Narcissa's appearance no doubt shocked her husband, who as a doctor must have realized the seriousness of her condition. He disagreed with Dr. Barclay's diagnosis and felt that she suffered from "aneurism of the main aorta below the heart."[124]

The family had been enlarged by Marcus' nephew Perrin Whitman. Three needy families were to be cared for also, invited missionary-style by Marcus to stay with them. Narcissa's health continued to deteriorate, hastened by the scanty fare available. She knew she had to steel herself each fall against another emigrant train. In 1844 the seven Sager children, ranging from five months to fourteen years, whose mother had died on the Oregon Trail, were left for Narcissa to care for.

The Cayuse were becoming even more restless. Even some of the Nez Percés at Lapwai were being disaffected by Tom Hill, an educated Delaware Indian who had married a Nez Percé. Fluent in both English and Nez Perce, he repeatedly related how eastern tribes had lost their lands after being infiltrated by missions. After the missions came the settlers—the point of the tale was plain to all. A commanding individual, he could summon a thousand followers, including several chiefs; by contrast, Spalding was fortunate to have two hundred in his congregation. The Nez Percés began to loom as threatening to the Spaldings as were the Cayuse to the Whitmans.[125]

In a sense the news of the massacre, while shocking, was not totally unexpected at Lapwai. The Spaldings, more fortunate than their friends, were helped by friendly Nez Percés to escape to the Willamette Valley.[126]

Late in February 1848 a group of volunteers under Colonel Cornelius Gilliam, wanting to avenge the Whitmans, visited the shambles of Waiilatpu. The bodies of the dead had been disinterred by coyotes and half devoured by animals. Perrin Whitman helped to identify his uncle and aunt. Some of the more sentimental cut locks of Narcissa's hair to keep, made a deep grave for all and piled stones high on the mound.[127] Joe Meek was evidently in the group, a short time before he left for Washington, D.C.; he found little Helen Mar's body dug up by wolves and lovingly and sadly re-buried it. He helped to bury Narcissa's remains after cutting off a number of locks of her blonde hair for her friends.[128]

Soon after the massacre all missions, both Catholic and Protestant, were ordered closed and armed escorts conducted some of the mission families out of the interior to safety.[129]

Gentle, frail Eliza Spalding died in January 1851 and Henry remarried two years later. As a substitute for preaching, his favorite pastime, he wrote "lectures" for the Walla Walla *Statesman,* the *State's Rights Democrat* of Albany, and eastern religious periodicals.[130]

With the discovery of gold in 1859 the interior was reopened. When his daughter Eliza's husband staked a claim, he accompanied his son-in-law, farmed for a while, then received a teaching position in an Indian school established by the government in Lapwai. Later he also preached there. He was delighted when many of the Nez Percés remembered him.[131]

He died August 3, 1874, at Lapwai among the Nez Percés. A missionary working among the tribe asked him on his deathbed, "Do you feel that Jesus is with you?"

He replied, "Jesus only. Oh, how I love Him!"[132]

Today sculptures of John McLoughlin, Marcus Whitman, and Jason Lee stand in Statuary Hall of the nation's Capitol attesting that they, along with others who preceded and followed, whether missionaries, mountain men, or settlers, did their part, not just in "saving Oregon for the United States," but in the making of a nation.[133]

Not all visitors at the King's palace were as welcome or as hospitably received as the missionaries discussed or as many other secular visitors, such as Nathaniel Wyeth, to whom Dr. McLoughlin was a genuine friend and host, even though he had to fight the American and break him in business. There were some, on the contrary, who were highly unwelcome, for justifiable reason, or at least the Chief Factor felt that he had valid reason for being, if not inhospitable, at least cool and distant. The reference is of course to Hall Jackson Kelley and Ewing Young, who bitterly hated the Chief Factor. Suffice it to say, Dr. McLoughlin still sheltered Mr. Kelley, fed him, gave him medical aid, and paid for his passage to the Sandwich Islands:[134] All this, in spite of the fact that Kelley in his capacity as the "Prophet of Oregon" formed the Society for Encouraging the Settlement of the Oregon Territory, claiming that the Northwest was legitimate American territory, and inveighing bitterly against the Hudson's Bay Company and its personified symbol, Chief Factor John McLoughlin.[135] It seems that another of Mr. Kelley's grievances against Dr. McLoughlin, petty as it was, was that he was not invited to Bachelors' Hall at the Fort, as was Nathaniel Wyeth.[136]

The visitors here discussed represent only a minute sampling of the humanity who poured into the disputed territory of the Pacific Northwest, most of them "enemy" Americans, who, almost as a matter of course stopped at Fort Vancouver, expecting kindness, hospitality and assistance of countless kinds. In almost all cases they received the welcome and the aid they so desperately needed, for the King of the Columbia was not one who could turn the destitute and the needy away from the palace gates.

CHAPTER 5

VISITORS AT THE PALACE
THE KING'S FOREIGN POLICY

1 Jane Tipton, *John McLoughlin, Chief Factor of the Hudson's Bay Company at Fort Vancouver*, pp. 82-83.

2 T. C. Elliott, "John McLoughlin and his Guests," *Washington Historical Society Quarterly*, Vol. 3, No. 1, October 1908, p. 64.

3 *Ibid.*

4 Elliott, *op. cit.*, pp. 65-66.

5 *Ibid.*

6 Tipton, *loc. cit.*

7 Elliott, *op. cit.*, p. 67.

8 Nard Jones, *The Great Command*, p. 43.

9 *Ibid.*, pp. 106-107.

10 *Ibid.*, pp. 142-143.

11 Tipton, *op. cit.*, p. 84.

12 *Ibid.*

13 Richard Montgomery, *The White-Headed Eagle*, p. 216.

14 Tipton, *loc. cit.*

15 Dorothy O. Johansen, *Empire of the Columbia*, pp. 148-149.

16 Theressa Gay, *Life and Letters of Mrs. Jason Lee*, p. 12.

17 Johansen, *op. cit.*, p. 161.

18 *Ibid.*

19 Jones, *op. cit.*, p. 37.

20 Johansen, *loc. cit.*

21 *Ibid.*

22 Gay, *op. cit.*, p. 28.

23 *Ibid.*, p. 29.

24 *Ibid.*, p. 26.

25 *Ibid.*, p. 121.

26 *Ibid.*, p. 35.

27 *Ibid.*, p. 38.

28 *Ibid.*, p. 129.

29 *Ibid.*, pp. 44-45.

30 *Ibid.*, p. 46.

31 *Ibid.*, p. 151.

32 *Ibid.*, pp. 152-153.

33 *Ibid.*

34 *Ibid.*, p. 153.

35 Jones, *op. cit.*, pp. 51-52.

36 *Ibid.*, p. 58.

37 *Ibid.*, p. 53.

38 Cecil P. Dryden, *Give All to Oregon*, pp. 57-58.

39 Gay. *op. cit.*, p. 156; a letter from Anna Maria Pittman to her parents, June 5, 1837.

40 *Ibid.*, p. 55.

41 *Ibid.*, p. 157.

42 *Ibid.*, p. 158.

43 *Ibid.*, pp. 158-159.

44 *Ibid.*, p. 59.

45 *Ibid.*, pp. 58-59.

46 *Ibid.*, pp. 60-61.

47 *Ibid.*, pp. 62, 64-65. But Charles H. Carey, *A General History of Oregon*, I, p. 292, says that "Miss Nancy" was a (half-breed) daughter of Tom McKay.

48 Dryden, *loc. cit.*

49 Gay, *op. cit.*, pp. 66-67.

50 Diary of the Reverend Jason Lee, *Quarterly of the Oregon Historical Society*, Vol. 17, pp. 410-412.

51 Gay, *op. cit.*, pp. 68-70.

52 *Ibid.*, p. 166.

53 Johansen, *op. cit.*, p. 162.

54 *Ibid.*, p. 162-3.

55 Gay, *op. cit.*, pp. 76-77.

56 *Ibid.*, pp. 84-86.

57 *Ibid.*, pp. 91-92.

58 *Ibid.*, pp. 86-90.

59 *Ibid.*, p. 90.

60 *Ibid.*, p. 91.

61 *Ibid.*

62 Jones, *op. cit.*, pp. 169-170.

63 Gay, *op. cit.*, pp. 187-193. Letters from Jason Lee to Mrs. Pittman.

64 *Ibid.*, pp. 194-196. Letter from Jason Lee to Mr. and Mrs. Pittman.

65 *Ibid.*, pp. 197-198. Letter from Jason Lee to Mr. and Mrs. Pittman.

66 *Ibid.*, p. 199, n. 2, n. 3.

67 Visit of author, August 9, 1973.

68 Johansen, *op. cit.*, pp. 161-162.

69 Montgomery, *op. cit.*, p. 262.

70 *Ibid.*, p. 261.

71 *Ibid.*, pp. 261-262.

72 *Ibid.*, pp. 263-264.

73 Johansen, *op. cit.*, p. 164.

74 Oscar O. Winther, *The Great Northwest*, p. 208.

75 Jones, *op. cit.*, pp. 282-283.

76 Johansen, *op. cit.*, pp. 164-165.

77 *Ibid.*

78 Montgomery, *op. cit.*, pp. 269, 295-296.

79 Jalmar Johnson, *Builders of the Northwest*, p. 31.

80 *Ibid.*, p. 30.

81 Jones, *op. cit.*, p. 48.

82 *Ibid.*, pp. 67-68.

83 J. Johnson, *op. cit.*, pp. 34-35. This account of the meeting at Green River differs from that of Nard Jones (see reference note 9), although they are not mutually exclusive.

84 Jones, *op. cit.*, p. 113.

85 *Ibid.*, pp. 117-118.

86 *Ibid.*, p. 122.

87 *Ibid.*, pp. 143-144.

88 J. Johnson, *op. cit.*, p. 36.

89 Jones, *op. cit.*, p. 147.

90 Earl Pomeroy, *The Pacific Slope, A History*, p. 18.

91 Eva Emery Dye, *McLoughlin and Old Oregon*, p. 25.

92 Montgomery, *op. cit.*, p. 222.

93 Dye, *op. cit.*, p. 29.

94 Montgomery, *loc. cit.*

95 Elliott, *op. cit.*, Vol. 3, No. 1, October 1908, p. 71.

96 George W. Fuller, *History of the Pacific Northwest*, p. 119.

97 Tipton, *op. cit.*, p. 46.

98 Fuller, *op, cit.*, p. 26.

99 Montgomery, *op. cit.*, p. 221.

100 Jones, *op. cit.*, p. 148.

101 Fuller, *op. cit.*, p. 27.

102 Johansen, *op. cit.*, p. 171.

103 Dye, *op. cit.*, pp. 25-26.

104 Eloisa McLoughlin Harvey, "Recollections—Life of Dr. John McLoughlin," Manuscript, Bancroft Collection; typescript in Oregon Historical Society Archives.

105 Montgomery, *loc. cit.*

106 Tipton, *op. cit.*, p. 45.

107 J. Johnson, *op. cit.*, pp. 39-40.

108 Montgomery, *op. cit.*, pp. 222-223.

109 David Lavender, *Land of Giants*, pp. 78-79.

110 Johansen, *op. cit.*, pp. 170, 171-172.

111 Jones, *op. cit.*, pp. 266-267.

112 Johansen, *op. cit.*, pp. 172-173.

113 Montgomery, *op. cit.*, pp. 315-316. However, Nard Jones in *Great Command*, p. 366, wrote that the trial began May 22 and the criminals were executed June 3.

114 Johansen, *op. cit.*, p. 222.

115 *Ibid.*

116 Winther, *loc. cit.*

117 *Ibid.*

118 Johansen, *op. cit.*, pp. 171-172.

119 Jones, *op. cit.*, p. 274.

120 *Ibid.*, pp. 274, 272.

121 Johansen, *op. cit.*, p. 175.

122 Jones, *op. cit.*, pp. 275, 277-279.

123 *Ibid.*, pp. 279-280.

124 *Ibid.*, p. 284.

125 *Ibid.*, pp. 292-293.

126 Johansen, *op. cit.*, p. 222.

127 Jones, *op. cit.*, p. 363.

128 Stanley Vestal, *Joe Meek; The Merry Mountain Man*, p. 286.

129 Jones, *op. cit.*, p. 364.

130 *Ibid.*, pp. 366, 370.

131 *Ibid.*, pp. 368-369.

132 *Ibid.*, p. 371.

133 *Ibid.*, p. 372.

134 Montgomery, *op. cit.*, pp. 204, 205-206.

135 Johansen, *op. cit.*, pp. 141, 144.

136 Frank C. Robertson, *Fort Hall: Gateway to the Oregon Country*, p. 172.

137 According to Catherine Zorn of Salem, Oregon, president of the Marion County Historical Society, in a letter of March 28, 1974, and Norman Winslow, attorney, also a member of the Society, the body of Jason Lee was moved to Salem soon after 1900 and was interred inside the enclosure of the Lee Mission Cemetery.

PART III

THE KING'S FAMILY
PRINCES AND PRINCESSES OF THE COLUMBIA

The text on the plaque reads:

OWYHEE CHURCH

THE BUILDING WHICH STOOD ON THIS SITE HAD MANY USES. IN 1832 JOHN BALL, FIRST SCHOOL TEACHER IN OREGON COUNTRY, OPENED A SCHOOL FOR THE FORT'S CHILDREN.

WITH THE ARRIVAL OF FATHERS DEMERS AND BLANCHET, THE FIRST ROMAN CATHOLIC MASS WAS CELEBRATED IN THIS BUILDING.

THE BUILDING WAS NAMED OWYHEE CHURCH IN HONOR OF THE HAWAIIAN EMPLOYEES WHO USED IT AS A CHURCH FROM 1844 TO 1848. DR. McLOUGHLIN EMPLOYED A CHRISTIAN NATIVE FROM HAWAII TO MINISTER TO THEM. HIS NAME WAS "KANAKA WILLIAM."

Courtesy Harrison Hornish

Royal Family of the Columbia
CHAPTER 6

JOSEPH——THE KING'S ELDEST, MYSTERIOUS SON

"Man of mystery" might well describe the Doctor's first-born child, Joseph. Little has been written concerning this son, and even that small amount of information has been revealed by relatively recent research.

The identity of his mother remains shrouded in obscurity. Known only as "a Red River Indian woman," she died at Joseph's birth.[1] Questions have arisen as to whether Dr. McLoughlin and Joseph's mother were married, or whether the boy's birth resulted from a liaison. McLoughlin's detractors, of whom Herbert Beaver, discussed elsewhere, was the prototype, preferred to believe the latter possibility. Other authors, far more numerous, believed the former to be the truth. Montgomery, known for his admiration for McLoughlin, seemed ambivalent in his opinion. Referring to the Doctor's and the Indian woman's relationship as "an obscure affair" on page twenty-six of *The White-Headed Eagle,* on page twenty-nine he stated, "Whether or not the child was illegitimate is a moot question and one which most writers on the early West have...evaded." Later he added, "Surely the doctor's character, as revealed by his own high sense of morality, would suggest a...marriage." Robert Johnson in *John McLoughlin* also showed ambivalence when he referred to Joseph as "a son by his first wife" on page 120, yet in the index, page 301, described Joseph as a "natural" son. A third, Burt Brown Barker, in *The McLoughlin Empire,* apparently believed that Dr. McLoughlin was married to Joseph's mother, for he implied a marriage when he referred to Margaret McKay McLoughlin as the Doctor's *second* wife (page 362).

Dr. McLoughlin, being unable to care for an infant, left the child with friends, Angus Bethune, also of the Northwest Company, and his wife, at St. Mary's. Joseph came to the Oregon Country in 1825.[2]

If he came to Oregon in 1825, it must have been with Mrs. McLoughlin and the other children, for after Margaret McKay was married to Dr. McLoughlin she was said to have "accepted the lad as her own," much to the gratification of her husband. When Chief Trader McLoughlin returned to Fort William in 1818 from York Factory and from other travels connected with his position he was happy to be with his integrated family.[3]

Joseph was said to admire his stepbrother, Tom McKay, about twelve years his senior, almost to the point of idolatry. An expert rider, Joseph often accompanied Tom, an expert with the rifle, on many "hair-raising" expeditions into the wilderness, in the 1840s, accompanying him to the Sacramento Valley. His Indian blood was held against him, whether with realism or bigotry. According to his father he was "too much the Indian" and hampered by his lack of education. The Doctor felt that Joseph was suited only for farming and hoped that he would settle down in the Willamette Valley.[4]

A writer of historical fiction concurred somewhat in an evaluation of Joseph. In *Tall Brigade* Hermia Fraser portrayed Joseph as slow and rather dull, with little or no education. He yearned to become a chief trader but his father discouraged him, insisting that he should become a farmer. Tom McKay, when he first became acquainted with Joseph, was not favorably impressed, considering his stepbrother rude, impatient, and quick-tempered. Tom also found him to be sullen and easily disgruntled and frequently complaining that it was difficult to get ahead in a fur company because hard work and ability mattered little, since "fools" were often chosen for the best positions and that to get ahead one must have influential friends.[5]

Even though with the help of writers of historical fiction Joseph's personality and character do not emerge with clarity; there are a few incidents in his life, possibly apocryphal, which have been recorded by an "old timer". One was reported in the form of a riddle: Question: "Where did Jumpoff Joe Creek in Josephine County get its name?" Answer: "From Joseph McLoughlin, who on one of his many expeditions fell over the edge of a bluff as he was returning in the darkness to his camp. He was seriously injured but recovered slowly, always retaining some reminders of the accident."[6]

In another work of historical fiction Joseph was said to have for one of his tasks at Fort Vancouver the beating of the furs, a job which he thoroughly detested. This work had to be done weekly in order to keep dust and moths from the furs. In order to get the unpleasant task done more quickly, he tried regularly to inveigle his younger half sister into helping him. She is supposed to have complied, although reluctantly. Expert horseman that he was, he reciprocated by teaching her to ride.[7]

Apparently the beating of furs was sufficiently important that Dr. McLoughlin as ruler of the Columbia District instructed the chief traders and chief factors working under him to beat them regularly: "The Snake Beaver was full of sand and evidently they had not been beaten since Freemen gave them in; this ought not to be in a country like this we ought to be very particular and beat our furs from time to time...". He wished that the furs of the Pacific could be as clean as those "on the other side of the Mountain."[8]

The story is told that Joseph and Eloisa more than once had to cooperate in helping John Jr. to bed when he returned intoxicated from a "night on the village."[9] No doubt the story is aprocyphal, for during the time this could logically have taken place John was not at the Fort, as explained in another chapter.

Joseph apparently bore out his father's belief that he had a propensity for farming, for it is recorded that as a farmer in the Valley he served on a committee to draft a code of laws for the Provisional Government and moved its adoption at a meeting July 5, 1843.[10]

The Reverend Herbert Beaver, as noted elsewhere, denigrated Joseph, verbally chastising him severely for absenting himself "in a very marked manner" from the Reverend Mr. Beaver's Anglican church service and for "at a time of public worship holding a conventicle in the office..."[11]

Royal Family of the Columbia

An example of inadequate early research on the subject of Joseph McLoughlin is found in a history by Horace Lyman, published in 1903. In a brief biographical account of Dr. McLoughlin, the author stated that one surviving child, Joseph, lived in Spokane, Washington.[12] It is obvious that he confused the Doctor's eldest son with his youngest. It was David who lived in Porthill Idaho, near Spokane, dying at eighty-two in 1903. There was confusion as to the date of Joseph's death, it being given variously as 1846, 1848, and 1849. T. C. Elliott, a prolific historical writer of the 1930s, wrote on page 342 that Joseph died December 14, 1848, at "about 38," yet on page 388 gave Joseph's life span as 1808-1846.[13] Most historians, it seems, agree on 1809 and 1848 (or 1849) as his birth and death dates. Regardless of the exact date of his death his grave cannot be found in the Catholic Cemetery in St. Paul, Oregon, today. He was buried in the original St. Paul's Cemetery which was closed about 1875 when a new road was built through it, resulting in the disappearance of the sites of the graves of Joseph McLoughlin, Louis Labonte, Étienne Lucier, and other early French Canadian settlers.[14]

Joseph was married, though the date is not recorded. His wife has been identified as Victoria, the daughter of "a Mr. McMillan," probably James McMillan, the redoubtable chief trader and later chief factor of the Hudson's Bay Company, whom Dr. McLoughlin in 1827 sent to build a fort on the Fraser River—Fort Langley, which commanded both the lands and the waters of the fur-bearing north. Joseph's wife was the widow of Étienne Grégoire (also called Grigman) before her marriage to Joseph.[15]

Another proof of his married state is found in a letter of 1850 ordering "Victoria McLoughlin" to appear "instanter" at the county probate court, "then and there to accept or renounce your right as executrix of the estate of your late husband's...Given under my hand with my private seal (there being no official seal yet provided) at office July 2, 1840," and in another legal document in which Joseph revoked all previous wills and testaments and dictated a new will leaving everything to his "wife and executrix, Victoria" and directs "a (funeral) ceremony with all Catholic rites and interment in Cemetry (*sic*) of the Catholic Church situated in County of Champoeg, Oregon Territory according to the rites and Ceremony of the Catholic religion and with that solemnity which my means admit of." Another document assigned the well-known Judge Matthew P. Deady to administer the estate.[16]

The assumption is that since his wife was sole heir, there were no children. Since, as far as is known, John Jr. had no children, and since David had only one son, who died a bachelor, Dr. John McLoughlin had no grandchildren bearing his name. The McLoughlin name died with David's son in 1951. There are no descendants of Dr. McLoughlin named McLoughlin, although there must be one hundred or more descended from his daughters and from David's daughter's living today. Because of the family name being different, it is more difficult to trace today's "McLoughlins," but an effort will be made later to do so.

Alberta Brooks Fogdall

REFERENCES

CHAPTER 6

JOSEPH——THE KING'S ELDEST, MYSTERIOUS SON

1 Dr. Burt Brown Barker, *The McLoughlin Empire and its Rulers,* index, p. 362.

2 David McLoughlin, "Correspondence," Archives, Oregon Historical Society. Angus Bethune (often spelled Bathein) was the son of Mrs. McLoughlin's half sister, Veronica Wadin.

3 Richard G. Montgomery, *The White-Headed Eagle,* p. 35.

4 S. A. Clarke, *Pioneer Days of Oregon History,* I, p. 87.

5 Hermia Fraser, *Tall Brigade,* pp. 48-49.

6 News clipping, probably from the *Oregon Journal,* n. d., Archives, Oregon Historical Society.

7 Evelyn Sibley Lampman, *Princess of Fort Vancouver,* pp. 34-37.

8 Frederick Merk, *Fur Trade and Empire,* p. 252.

9 Lampman, *op. cit.,* pp. 262-263.

10 Montgomery, *op. cit.,* p. 299; Barker, *op. cit.,* p. 329n.

11 Herbert Beaver, *Reports and Letters,* p. 4.

12 Horace S. Lyman, *History of Oregon,* III, p. 253.

13 T. C. Elliott, *Oregon Historical Quarterly,* Vol. 36. (1935), pp. 342, 388.

14 Although the McLoughlin grave and others in the original cemetery were leveled by the highway, a short distance away (in St. Paul) a large cross, a boulder, and a bronze plaque mark the putative site of Joseph's grave, as well as of those of Labonte, Lucier, and nine other French Canadian early Oregonians. This monument and the "new" St. Paul Catholic Cemetery were visited by the author May 13, 1973.

15 Fred Lockley, *Columbia River Valley,* in an interview (1928 or 1929) with Louisa Rae Myrick, daughter of Joseph's half sister Eloisa.

16 Letter with heading "Territory of Oregon, County of Yam Hill," *"Scrap Book,"* Archives, Oregon Historical Society.

CHAPTER 7

JOHN JR. ——— THE CROWN PRINCE

The story of the short life—and the death—of John and Margaret McLoughlin's eldest son is even more nearly incredible than those of other members of the McLoughlin family, strange as they also are shown to be.

Called most appropriately *enfant terrible*, he became the burden of both the McLoughlin and Fraser families, particularly of Dr. Simon Fraser, that generous uncle of Dr. John who assumed the responsibility of supervising the education and finances of two generations of McLoughlins—his nephews John and David and of John's children, particularly of John Jr. and of Eliza. In addition, he oversaw to some extent the lives of other nieces, nephews, grandnieces and grandnephews, all related to Dr. John.

Born August 18, 1812, John's birth date has been used by historians to reckon the approximate date of his parents' marriage, or "consent of marriage" as "sometime in 1811," whether before or after she learned of the murder on the *Tonquin* of her first husband, is not known.

While some historians arbitrarily assign "either Lac la Pluie or Fort William" as his birthplace, Dr. Burt Brown Barker felt that it could have been Lac la Pluie or Vermillion Lake or Fort William, as there are records showing correspondence dated 1812 and supplies received the same year at all three posts.[1]

In 1821 as Dr. McLoughlin went to London for the merger, he left John, aged nine, at school in Montréal, asking his uncle Simon Fraser to "look after John" from his home in nearby Terrebonne.[2] John did not do well in school, and as his father returned east in 1822 he looked for another school in Montréal but was unsuccessful in finding one which he felt was better. He was not feeling at all well and in his letter of May 15, 1822, told of writing his will, making Dr. Fraser executor of his estate. John Malcolm Fraser, his half uncle, sixteen years younger than he, was his financial agent at Montréal. He made at this time provision for his mother, for other relatives, and especially for the education of his children.[3]

During this period Dr. Fraser expressed his belief that John Jr. was too slow in his studies, that he could not, the Doctor felt, succeed as a physician, that "boys of mixed blood lacked steadiness and the application necessary to pursue the long course of the study of medicine...."[4]

In a letter of September 14, 1823, the Chief Factor wrote his uncle from Lac la Pluie that he (Simon) was to feel free and "perfectly at liberty to adopt the plan you chuse...for my Son's Education." He expressed the deep obligation he felt to his uncle for the trouble he was taking. He regretted that Dr. Fraser was suing his brother Alexander for money owed him. Knowing that the original disagreement between his uncles was caused by worries over financing education for members of the McLoughlin family, Dr. John no doubt felt responsible. He requested in a postscript that his uncle send him "smallpox vaccine for the natives of this quarter."[5]

John's behavior, never commendable, deteriorated under restraint. He caused trouble repeatedly, leaving school without permission, even mercilessly beating a younger boy. The schoolmaster asked Governor Simpson, whose La Chine headquarters were only nine miles from Montréal and who had visited the school before, to meet with him. At the meeting John became abusive, threatening to attack the teacher, Mr. Jones. The latter asked Mr. Simpson to take John out of the school, for he would not keep him "even one week longer, not even if I were paid 500 pounds for it."

Governor Simpson had had a rather favorable impression of John before the incident at school and had felt that he might take him into the Honourable Company. Now he felt quite differently. Writing from LaChine on March 14, 1828, he described the incident and added, "I had a very high opinion of this young man...but I have never been so grossly deceived in a Young Man, and regret it exceedingly on account of his father for whom I have a very high regard."[6]

A letter from John in Montréal asking Dr. Fraser to send his summer clothes also carried the news that he was "learning Book Keeping and the French grammar (and)—begun the Arithmetic from barter till as far as the end of cube root..."[7] He had been given a chance after all by the Governor and was working in the Hudson's Bay Company counting-house (probably part time) at La Chine.

Dr. Simon answered the boy's request by sending the clothes, scolding him for being so careless in leaving them and, in a rather "washing-my-hands-of-you" manner, giving him much advice as to his future conduct: "...apply to your studies with the greatest possible assiduity this besides the strictest propriety of behavior on all occasions...is the only means you have to advance your future welfare."[8]

A letter from Dr. John's sister, Sister St. Henry, to Dr. Fraser, dated February 29 (?), 1829, expressed her delight in seeing her nephew the day before and showed that she was favorably impressed. (It is easy to imagine that John was on his best behavior when he visited the Sister at the Ursuline Convent, in Québec.) She noticed with satisfaction

> that my nephew is imbued with the paternal care which he had received
> from you, he loves to say, My dear uncle, has always treated me as his son,
> and I myself love him as my father, I hope that he will not forget your
> lessons and that he will make proof of his gratitude. By his behavior, the
> simple and innocent manners of that child please me very much.[9]

Royal Family of the Columbia

John became very restless during this period and wrote twice, the last time April 27, 1829, to his father for permission to go to Fort Vancouver. Dr. McLoughlin refused permission February 1, 1830, scolding him for asking a second time to go to the Columbia. Beginning "My Dear Boy," he continued

> you ought to know that if I conceived it to your advantage I would have acced'd to your wish and I have written to my friends to consider what Business you are qualifi'd for and to place you accordingly...you are not yet sufficiently advanced in your education—and if they leave you at school I desire you will particularly apply yourself to study the English and French Grammar so as to be able to write in both languages correctly.

He praised the boy for improving his writing, but tempered his approval by adding that it was not as good as his sister's (Eliza's).

> (this) shews you did not apply as much as you ought....you are now a Man...and if you feel that pride and ambition to Rise in the world, you must see that the only way you can succeed is by Applying yourself Most diligently to your Education. You must employ every Moment that you have to spare from your meals and sleep to improve yourself and take pains to do *with all care imaginable as well as you possible can.*

He urged his son to exert himself and admonished him that he must have his own "Real Anxious Desire to Learn". He must also be particularly careful to do everything Dr. Fraser "Desires" and "also your schoolmaster as a complaint from them would Expose you to my Displeasure."[10]

This letter was written more than three months after John had left Canada for Europe. October 25, 1829, he had written from Québec to Dr. Fraser that he would leave "the 26th of this month...I have not went down to Rivier du Loup."[11] From Paris nearly two years later he again wrote his granduncle announcing that he was preparing for an examination to be taken in three months. In a postscript he wrote that he had received a letter from his father who said that he had not known that John was in France until Governor Simpson told him.[12]

The question arises as to how John got to France. Since he was just past seventeen and one-half it is not likely that he planned, executed and financed the trip. His father did not know he had gone to France. However, an examination of the Chief Factor's account with the Company at LaChine revealed that his funds had been charged 32-2-0 pounds for "Cash paid passage of his Son from Québec to London"; then, "Cash paid passage of his Son from London to Paris, 17-5-6 pounds."[13] This would indicate that the Doctor had, as he said he would do February 1, 1830, "written to my friends to consider what Business you are qualified for and to place you accordingly". The "friends"[14] had decided to send John to his uncle, Dr. David McLoughlin, to study medicine with him. They had authority to use money from Dr. McLoughlin's account for the purpose of his son's education.

From Paris John wrote to John Fraser, Simon's son. As is true of many McLoughlin letters, both father and son, they are very difficult to read: little or no punctuation, frequent misspelling, no or little paragraphing, general illegibility resulting in necessary interpolations and bracketed guesses. However, in this particular letter the reader learned that John was very happy in Paris: "I spent the winter very gay. I have been to balls even (where) the Royal family was and also I had a moment's conversation with the Prince (King Louis-Philippe)."[15] He would frequently write a few snatches of French in his letters, unfortunately as ungrammatical as his English.

Over a year later, June 26, 1832, he wrote to Dr. Fraser of disturbances in Paris. Two years after Louis-Philippe began his reign a republican insurrection took place. John and a cousin, David Michaud, watched the street fighting and saw men killed, a new experience for both of them.

John's remarks concerning republicans and Carlists, i. e., putting them in the same category, showed a lack of historical knowledge and political insight. Perhaps his views relected those of his Uncle David [16] who would no doubt tend to be ultra-conservative and consequently lack understanding of other than the conservative-bourgeois viewpoint.

In February 1833 John wrote two letters,[17] the first, to John Fraser ambiguously dated "24 Feb. 18, 1833,"—the other, to Simon Fraser, dated, in the complimentary close, "24 Feb. 1833". His address was 8, rue de la Paix, his uncle's home, a most desirable address. In the first he again mentioned the gay life he was living, "having been to the Kings Bals" and of having been presented to the King. In the second he begged Dr. Fraser to write to him, told his granduncle how hard he was studying, having "passed the examination of Bachelier-en lettres...a credit." In fact, he was the one who "had passed the best of the whole," for he had "answered to every question put to me by the 'examinators.' " In addition, he was then "preparing two more examinations for the month of July." He hoped to "enter one of the hospitals in summer. I study from ten in the morning till three and then rest till six and from then I study for three hours more during that time I study chemistry anatomy Physiology Physics; but I devote more of my time to anatomy for the study of it pleases me more than the rest." Sensing that he might not be believed, he asked Dr. Fraser to ask his Uncle David how he was doing "...for you might think that I am not telling the truth or I am praising myself to much so I advice you to write to him...."

Royal Family of the Columbia

John wrote in the second letter that he had received a letter from his "dear sister" (Eliza) who announced her marriage to William Randolph Eppes. He also expressed much concern because he had written to "Papa" twice a year for three years "and sometimes more, and still not one of them (letters) has reached him...I hope by this time that he have received one he is very uneasy, in every one he has written he complains that I am forgetting him. He may be sure that I never (torn) I am writing to him at this moment."

One interesting feature of John's letters is that he often asked whether Miss "So and So" was married, or "Remember me to Marguerite—if she is not married". He seemed to have many feminine friends, relatives, and acquaintances.

In a letter of August 8, 1833, he described the third anniversary of the July Revolution, the event marking the change from the régime of Charles X to that of the Citizen-King, Louis-Philippe. Included in the festivities were the playing of bands, the reviewing of troops, and the displays of fireworks, which he witnessed in the "company of some ladies".[18] This letter he has whimsically signed "John *Mac*Loughlin."

Not conducive to subduing the extravagance of which John was no doubt justifiably accused was a letter to him from John Fraser, dated August 1833, which related the story of a "Voyageur who came down in his canoe tells me he served three years under your father at Columbia where he says he was then acting as Governor, as Mr. Simpson seldom goes as far as that; and his property there is very considerable, he is *very, very rich*..." John Fraser also mentioned that his father (Dr. Simon) had aged ten years since the death of John Fraser's younger sister, Mary, and "fears he will be carried away by that sickness ('the Cholera of this Country')."[19]

A letter of April 20, 1834, from John Fraser to Dr. McLoughlin answering the Doctor's letter of March 1, 1833, in which he remarked on the speed with which the letter arrived (thirteen months), mentioned several letters from John Jr. in Paris telling that he was applying himself well and pleasing his Uncle David. Neither of the correspondents could have known that a few months before, Dr. David McLoughlin had become so displeased with John that he had put him out of his home and sent him back to Canada. In fact, the Doctor, even in a letter of February 1, 1835, still believed his son to be in Paris: "I had a long letter from John he says he is Studying and on his own account I hope he is. I suppose by this time he has taken his Degrees. Whether he will settle in France or come back to Canada I cannot say."[20]

Just thirteen days later, John, writing from Montréal, was asking again for money—for four or five pounds—of John Fraser. Then enclosed was a note asking for ten pounds and, after that request, "do not disappoint me, if you cannot send all send at least half of it."[21]

The rejection of John by Dr. David seemed to come suddenly; the reason has never been revealed. It is possible that when Dr. John visited his brother in Paris in

1838, bringing young David back with him, that the two Drs. McLoughlin had at least one heart-to-heart talk, in which John's uncle told his father the cause of the drastic action.[22] If so, Dr. McLoughlin never revealed it. Several times, it seems, John had brought his uncle's disapproval on himself. Dr. David had written complaints of John's conduct in a letter to his brother. Before sending the letter he had shown it to John. Instead of its causing John to discontinue his objectionable behavior, it had the opposite effect, and within the next four days he committed such an atrocious act that his uncle refused to keep him any longer.[23] John was about twenty-one and one-half at this time, certainly no longer a child.

In the same letter (February 14, 1836) Dr. McLoughlin had the opinion that extravagance was probably the cause of John's dismissal: "…Which obliged my Brother to send him away and as he is spending more Money than is necessary and Neglecting his Studies It is Evident that what has Occurred to him has not affected him as it ought…."[24]

Yet Dr. McLoughlin's account in London showed that only 700 pounds was spent in four years for John's education in Paris. Of this, 100 pounds was probably spent for the passage home. This leaves an average of 150 pounds a year, which could hardly be considered extravagant in view of the high social circles—even royal—in which Dr. David McLoughlin—and to a certain extent, John—moved. Furthermore, since Dr. David was said to have an income of at least 10,000 pounds yearly, the charge of extravagance seems hardly valid.[25]

It seems that John had received an allowance of twenty-five pounds per year of his father's money, allotted by his Uncle David. This was for "Clothing and Pocket Money." Since his lodging, food, and payment for his teachers were all taken care of, his father felt this amount was ample; however, he had told the "boy" that "if he Exerted himself at His Studies and that his Uncle was pleased with his conduct and it was Necessary, My Brother would Increase his Allowance…."[26]

In a letter of the same date as quoted above (February 14, 1836), but to John, not Simon, Fraser, Dr. John showed his concern and embarrassment at his heir's behavior: "As you may suppose I was much affected on Learning that John had so misconducted himself that my Brother had been obliged to send him Back to your father who certainly at that time of his life ought not to be harrassed (sic) with the care of other peoples Children, and what makes it Worse John is no longer a Child and his Errors are the less pardonable…"

He added that he had sent John to France to "Learn how to Earn his livelihood in a Respectable manner and giving him Money to spend in Disipation would not only have been Wrong, but would have Destroyed the very Object for which he was sent he writes me an Apology for his Misconduct but he does not write me what it was he did which obliged his uncle to send him away…. There never was so far as I know a

Young (Man) from this Country who had so fine a Prospect to begin life with and how he has thrown it away."

That Dr. John McLoughlin was heartsick and disappointed because of John's conduct is easy to understand. It was only one of so many heartaches in store for him, both within and outside his family.

As he thought almost continuously concerning John Jr. he tended to rationalize the cause of John's latest disgrace; in a letter a year later, February 4, 1837, to Dr. Simon he indicated that he saw a connection between his brother David's marriage (November 1833) and John's dismissal a short time later, early in 1834; Dr. David had praised John's seriousness in his studies in a letter to the Chief Factor shortly before his marriage, but had sent him away shortly afterward.[27] Perhaps this was specious reasoning on the part of John's father; perhaps it was wishful thinking.

Because of the snail's-pace communication of the period, a little backing-up is in order at this point. For many years Simon Fraser had yearned to be relieved of the responsibility of educating and financing McLoughins, especially of wayward, troublesome John Jr. As early as 1827, when he was fifty-eight years old, he was worn out, physically and emotionally. He was completely disenchanted with John and with having to cope with him and his escapades and misdemeanors. He had wanted then to send John to Québec under the care of his (Simon's) half brother, John Malcolm Fraser, then only twenty-seven and better able to come to grips with "Problem John," Simon felt. The plan did not materialize, however.[28]

In 1835 Dr. Fraser was still saddled with John and his problems, even more than before, for John had moved into the Fraser home at Terrebonne as he returned from France. He decided to send John to his brother Alexander (with whom he had not communicated for twenty-three years) at Rivière-du-Loup and to his sister Angélique (Dr. John's mother).[29] Since both Alexander and Angélique were older than Simon, it is difficult to follow his rationale, but perhaps he simply felt it was someone else's "turn" to shoulder the burden.

Reference was made to Simon's hoped-for plan in Sister St. Henry's reply to his letter May 11, 1835. "I am extremely sorry for the trouble and sadness which my nephew gives you, but for heaven's sake, do not send him to Rivière-du-Loup. My uncle Alexander is too infirm to take care of the conduct of the young man. My Mother can barely see to distinguish objects, she is unable to walk alone, besides her sensitiveness increases with the years, she would die of sadness, to see that child run wild in the country, for charity's sake, My dear Uncle, place this child at some estate of your vicinity, do not abandon him, I beg of you, he would fall from excesses to excesses...."[30]

So John remained on in Terrebonne with Simon Fraser for the time being. Soon, however, Dr. Simon persuaded John's sister Eliza and her husband, William

Randolph Eppes, to care for John, and on June 17, 1835, Sister St. Henry reported in a letter to her uncle that "He (John) is staying with his sister M. Eppes (Eliza), and seems to be fond of her."[31] Dr. Fraser must have heaved a huge sigh of relief.

Even in his sister's home John had to buy clothes. The begging letters continued. Dunning letters were written to Dr. Simon from several of John's creditors, a confectioner, a student with whom John had boarded and not paid, and Mr. Neysmith (a merchant), to name a few.[32] Thoroughly disgruntled at the whole situation, Dr. Fraser answered one such letter curtly and to the point: "Dear Sir In reply to yours of the first, I am in no way obliged to pay the debt in question I have the honor to be *etc., etc.*"[33]

In a letter to John Fraser, June 23, 1835, John repeated a request for some clothing, asking John to remind his father, for "...he seems not to have payed any attention to it." He needed boots, for "Mine are full of holes and worn out....Who is to pay for washing-woman bill....I have let you know the articles I want—a *hat,*—a *blue surtout*—a pair of Boots, a dozen of socks and a couple of Pair of *drawers* and cash to pay for my passage to Rivière-du-Loup...." A postscript adds "....if you could see me....My coat is torn and I have not a single farthing to pay to get it mended and I have to pay for my washing and I have nothing to do it with."[34] Poor John! Nearly twenty-three years old and as dependent as a child!

Because communication between Canada and Fort Vancouver was so slow—it took two years to receive a reply to a letter—it was Dr. David McLoughlin, in Paris, who was consulted about "What to do with John," rather than John's father. For example, Simon, in a letter to his niece Sister St. Henry, suggested "...you as well as Mr. and Mrs. Eppes should write to receive counsel from David. Mr. Eppes could send John to Montréal to finish his studies there or in the United States."[35] There had been considerable discussion as to the advisability of John's continuing his medical studies at McGill University, in Montréal.

There were several difficulties in the way, however; John needed a diploma, or a certificate, or some sort of credentials from Paris showing the extent of his study there in order to matriculate at another school. He repeatedly requested his Uncle David to send him something official, but for some reason received neither credentials nor even a reply to his letters. From Montréal, March 14, 1835, he wrote to Dr. Simon, "I am sorry to say that I have not as yet received any letters from Paris if no letter comes in the course of this month I will not be admitted to pass this session I shall be forced to wait till next year. I have written to him (Dr. David) several letters and I do not know what hinders him...."[36]

Now, having been at his sister's home for about a month, he seemed to fit well into her household, so far as is known. On July 7, Dr. Fraser wrote to his niece Sister St. Henry, hoping that her nephew John would appreciate the kindness Mr. and Mrs.

Eppes showed him, "...he has talents instead of being a despicable being by his extravagance and his laziness; he could if he wanted to become useful instead of making his family blush, he could do them honor....I repeat again that I would be greatly obliged to Mr. Eppes if he would take care of his brother-in-law. He is much better fitted for that job than I, he is young, I am too old and I am prejudiced against John."[37]

From Rivière-du-Loup, August 28, 1835, John made a different type of request of John Fraser; this time he asked for dental instruments: "Will you be so kind as to purchase for me a Davier et un déschaupain (Déchaussoir) in fact a complete set of Instruments for extracting teeth...I can make a little money with my profession so as to enable me to continue my classes."[38]

January 6, 1836, he was back in Québec, presumably at Eliza's, writing to John Fraser for "a couple of vials of vegetable Pulmonary Balsam, as soon as you can....I have not been any better since I wrote you last...If I was not unwell I should not be so troublesome—suffering under such a disease I cannot do otherwise."[39] Reverting to type, he asked John to ask his father, Dr. Simon, to send him "some money to get little articles that I want."[40]

John Fraser showed his father this last begging note, and as a result came a letter aptly described as a "classic in vilification".[41] All the anger, frustration, disgust, and worry which had been building up for thirty or more years of financing, supervising, and fretting about two generations of McLoughlins (and also of Frasers), particularly of John McLoughlin Jr., were present in Simon's letter to his wretched grandnephew. It follows in part:

> From your remaining in Québec I am convinced that you are depraved beyond any hope of reform...the sooner and farther you go the better. I do not know any business you have in Québec. I suppose you have imposed on your uncle Lt. C. Alexr. Fraser by some plausible story and obtained money from him you have perhaps obtained it from your now old grand Mother deprived of what she cannot spare or you live on the credulity of some unfortunate tavern keeper that would be swindling (swindled?) I have had so bad an opinion of you that I think you equal to any species of meanness You perhaps live on Mr Eppes who if he is not a very saint...and fond of his wife beyond what husbands commonly are must curse the hour he became the husband of the sister of such a wretch as you are you appear to me to be born to disgrace every being who has the misfortune to be connected with you. If you have any the least affection for your father mother brothers you well retire to some distant far country that you may never more be heard of.

Alberta Brooks Fogdall

Dr. Fraser continued that he would ask chief Factor Keith to give John passage to the Columbia; if Mr. Keith should refuse John could as a last resort "go up as a common Voyageur this in my opinion is the only means left to save you from destruction your sister and her children from the disgrace you will finally bring on all those who have the misfortune to be related to you."

Dr. Fraser then related an incident from the past when John at eight had "the habit...of soiling your breeches and remaining in that condition for days...I blamed your mother for this filthy habit I am convinced I was wrong the blame lay solely on your innate perversity in school at Terrebonne."

He added that he had been urged at that time by two teachers to remove John from the school as he "corrupted the morals of the other boys...that you would eventually corrupt and destroy my son... you went on from bad to worse....Young as you were when you went to France your reputation was such that I could find no situation for you in Canada....your reputation always prevented every application." He continued, piling charge upon charge:

> You know better than I do what character you brought from France you have been kept at school for a number of years in fact till and after you were 21 years of age you must know that you are illiterate to that degree that if by any favor you should pass an examination for a Physician you would infallibly disgrace the Profession You really possess considerable good qualities your invincible indolence and perverse disposition have marred your good qualities I write these lines more in sorrow than in anger....you are incorrigible.

Simon again advised John to write to his Uncle David for advice "to decide what is to be done with you." Also, he might "apply to Lt. C. Alexr. Fraser (the brother with whom he had not communicated since 1812) to take on him the superintendency of your affairs for my part I will not be accessory to your father's money being spent in a manner worse than useless." He signed himself "your unfortunate uncle."[42]

From Fort Vancouver, in a letter dated February 16, 1836, and enclosed in a letter of February 14 to John Fraser, Dr. John wrote to Dr. Fraser of John Jr.'s "Very contrite letter" and in a postscript regretted that "you sent John to my poor Mother, He may give her trouble."[43]

When Simon Fraser told young John to "go to a far distant country" he probably had Spain in mind, for he knew Dr. David McLoughlin was trying to get a commission in the Spanish army for John, as well as for another nephew, David Michaud.[44] Whether John knew of it or not, he had something else in mind. Feeling cut adrift from all family, and completely at loose ends, he committed yet another foolish act when he joined in July 1836 the harebrained filibustering expedition of self-styled "General" James Dickson (or Dixon). Calling himself "liberator of the Indian Nations" Dickson planned to cross the Great Lakes, liberate the Indians of the Red River colony, which was under the control of the Hudson's Bay Company, put together an army of half-breed Indians, go on to Santa Fé. From there the Army would go west, set up an Indian kingdom in California of which Dickson would be the monarch; John McKenzie, half-breed son of Chief Factor Alexander McKenzie of the Athabasca district was to serve as Secretary of State and Brigadier General. Half-breed sons of two other chief factors and one chief trader were to be officers in the liberating "army."[45] (John was, of course, only one-fourth Indian, since his father was Caucasian and his mother one-half white.)

September 1, 1836, John wrote from Sault Ste. Marie, describing the vicissitudes of the expedition, especially the narrow escape from drowning when crossing Lake Erie. Because of his part in getting some of the boats safely across the Lake, because of "the devotion which I have shown, the commander has given...the commission of major in the cavalry." He signed the letter "John McLoughlin-Major."[46]

His next letter to John Fraser, which he said might be his last, again described his hardships:

In a common bateau with 20 men coasting a lake of 500 miles long living on corn and pork....exposed to cold....I anticipate more yet which will be worst (sic) these men that I had was the worst of all those living under the face of Heaven I could not get them to work without hard treatment I assure you that before I get to red river I shall break some of their bones and I will do it with the greatest pleasure for they deserve it, they give me more trouble than they are worth. The weather is very severe....We have had some snow about two inches....[47]

In this same letter John made a rather unusual request of his cousin: to order for him a cavalry uniform, the coat of which must be "red worked with silver lace on the chest and collar with large silver epaulettes and two pairs of pantaloons one black and the same as he (the tailor) already made for me with gold lace on the sides. In fact just an English Life guard dress do not be afraid of the Expense. I shall pay it."[48]

To make the proverbial long story short, the expedition failed as it was bound to do from its very nature, but also because of Governor Simpson's well-executed defense of the Red River Country.[49]

The governor, most astutely, "set them at variance with each other" and broke up the party of leaders of the second echelon, *i.e.,* John and the other young men, half-breed sons of partners in the Honourable Company. He offered them positions at scattered posts as he felt that "by detaching them you will have less difficulty in managing the others."

Governor Simpson authorized taking John into the Company as surgeon at 100 pounds a year. He asked John and the others to meet with him at La Chine April 25, 1837. Simpson's offer was accepted.

The Council of the Northern Department assigned John to Fort McLoughlin in June (1837), but Dr. McLoughlin ordered him to Fort Vancouver, feeling more comfortable—understandably—to have John under his supervision.[50]

The Doctor's letter of February 4, 1837, revealed that he knew nothing of the foolhardy adventure in which his son was then engaged, for he referred to Simon's statement in an April 1836 letter that he did not know how John had supported himself "last winter" (1835-1836); Dr. McLoughlin stated that John had been paid more than 84 pounds from his Company account. The Chief Factor mentioned that Governor Simpson had refused John passage on a Company express to Vancouver; neither would he allow John's even entering "the Service as a Common Voyageur," which Dr. Fraser had desperately suggested as an almost-last resort in his "Classic in vilification" letter of January 12, 1836.[51] Dr. McLoughlin did not blame Mr. Simpson for his refusal, for he considered it John's fault. "Is he such a fool as to suppose that people will Engage a person in this Service who has shown so Untractable a Desposition as to Disagree with his Relations and Guardians When people Engage others they only Engage those who are anxious to do their Duty...."[52]

John Fraser's April 16, 1837, letter to John acknowledged the receipt of five letters written from July 20 to October 11 in 1836; as John requested, John Fraser passed on messages to their common relatives, to all except Eliza, "seeing the feeble state of health she was in at the time, which might have occasioned the most fatal consequences...." He also urged his reprobate cousin to "join your Honorable Father who waits anxiously for his lost son...he will receive you with his arms open, he will soothe the pain and suffering you are feeling, he will restore you to yourself and make a new man of you."

John Fraser also reprimanded John for being so easily taken in by "your Dixon" (Dickson): "...is it honorable for you or anyone to follow a degraded vagabond one whom the world abhors and despises....?"[53]

This letter, written just nine days before John met Governor Simpson at La Chine and accepted employment, could not have been received yet by John, and hence could not have affected his decision to "go straight," but the Frasers, both Dr. Simon and John, must have been highly delighted, nevertheless.

At long last the Doctor and his prodigal son were reunited. John had written to John Fraser en route to Vancouver, August 8, 1837. He wrote from Norway House, on Lake Winnipeg, an important communication and distributing center both between Montréal and the West and between York Factory, on Hudson Bay, and western posts and forts. The letter comprised mostly his experiences on the filibustering expedition, but at least it indicated his eventual arrival at his destination on the Columbia.[54] As on some other occasions he capriciously spelled his name "Maclaughlin"; apparently he enjoyed variety.

Eleven months later (July 29, 1838), John wrote again from Norway House to John Fraser, indicating that he had been at Fort Vancovuer, that he had, in fact, spent the previous winter there "and came out this spring with my Father. (Dr. McLoughlin at that time was on furlough and en route to London and Paris.) It is no joke to cross the Mountains in the Spring Snow eleven (feet) deep."[55]

During the Chief Factor's absence in Europe, 1838-1839, John worked under James Douglas, then a chief trader, "second man" at the Fort. Mr. Douglas must have been satisfied, even pleased, with John's work, for he sent him across the mountains with both the 1838 and 1839 expresses.[56]

One year later another letter was written from Norway House, this time from David McLoughlin, who wrote to Dr. Fraser, July 11, 1839. He was en route from Europe to Fort Vancouver, having returned with his father. He had arrived just in time to say good-bye to John and his father as they left by canoe for York Factory; "therefore I am unable to tell you how My Brother is getting on."[57]

John Jr. himself wrote to John Fraser March 15, 1840, apparently contented with his life, and happy and excited about a new adventure to take place the next month when he was "ordered to go off in a few days to the coast to establish a new post."[58]

By October 24, 1840 (1839?) things seemed to be going very well, as both David and John were working for the Honourable Company with their father at Fort Vancouver. Dr. McLoughlin in a letter to his cousin John Fraser described his sons "as attentive and smart at their work as most young men…young men ought to be Kept Employed As certainly most Young Men are ruined by not being Kept Busy as Idleness is the Root of all evils…."[59]

The date October 24, 1840, must be an error; it should probably be October 24, 1839, for it is accepted by historians that John left for Fort Stikine April 22 and arrived June 1, 1840. In any case, he had worked for a time as a clerk at Fort Vancouver, supposedly in the stores, presumably working with accounts, and as far as is known, very satisfactorily. Whether he actually did work as a surgeon is not known. It is certain that he did not complete his medical studies, but he may have had as much training as many other practicing "doctors" of the nineteenth century.

It is of interest here to note that John's employment by the Hudson's Bay Company was entirely the responsibility of Governor Simpson. Not only did the Chief Factor have nothing to do with bringing John into the Company, but he was definitely opposed to it. Governor Simpson had brought John into the Honourable Company against his Chief Factor's wishes and even without consulting him. Dr. McLoughlin was not hesitant to point this out to his superior a few years later.

However, since Mr. Simpson had brought John Jr. into the Company, as previously mentioned, the "boy's" (twenty-five years old in 1837) father wanted his son with him, for obvious reasons. Because John did do well at Fort Vancouver, the events which ensued seemed logical.

It would be ideal if the curtain could be rung down at this point in the drama of the life of John McLoughlin Jr. Unfortunately, the drama had not yet reached the dénouement; in fact it had not even arrived at the climax. The story must be continued.

One of the posts which had come into the possession of the Hudson's Bay Company along with the strip of land leased from Russia was Fort Stikine (Stikeen). Since this came under Dr. McLoughlin's supervision he sent John to serve as assistant to his son-in-law William Glen Rae, who was in charge; his daughter Eloisa McLoughlin Rae also accompanied her husband to his new post. The party consisted of about "twenty labouring servants" and also Chief Trader James Douglas, McLoughlin's protégé, assistant, and soon-to-be successor. The trip took approximately five weeks, April 22-June 1.[60]

The next year (1841) Governor Simpson sent William Glen Rae to California to establish a new post at Yerba Buena (San Francisco), leaving John in charge as chief clerk with an able assistant, Roderick Finlayson. When Simpson visited Fort Stikine in October 1841 he seemed quite satisfied with John's management, sufficiently satisfied that he took Finlayson from Stikine to fill in at Fort Simpson.[61]

At the time that the Company took possession of Stikine the Russians expressed amazement as they relinquished control that such a small force was to be in charge, especially considering the isolation of the fort and the rough character of the natives of the area.[62]

Mr. Simpson, or rather Sir George Simpson, for he had been knighted in 1841, had left a man named McPherson with John as a replacement for Finlayson. According to John he "had no education at all" and was utterly worthless as an assistant.[63]

Thus John McLoughlin, inexperienced and with both a temper and a temperament unsuited to be left in unsupported command of twenty-two ill-disciplined Iroquois and French Canadian half-breeds, was left surrounded by unruly, unfriendly natives.

Eloisa, who had gone to Stikine with her husband and John in 1840 and had left it—most gladly—in 1841, described the Fort as "a miserable place."[64] No doubt she wondered at the wisdom of leaving her explosive twenty-nine-year-old brother in charge of such a dangerous, isolated post.

Royal Family of the Columbia

There were only flat rocks and no trees around close....The Indians were very troublesome. We never opened the gate to receive more than one Indian at a time to trade...We had a trough made with two boards for half a mile to bring in water....the Indians got drunk and would destroy the trough so that we could not get water....They were buying liquor and fighting all the time among themselves outside the Fort....Of liquor a big hogshead four feet high was emptied in one day. It was on the occasion of a feast.[65]

Several days of wild carousing on the part of the turbulent native staff preceded April 20, 1842.[66] The entire staff had drunk too much; hot-headed John had had trouble with some of the French Canadians and Kanaka (Hawaiian) employees, who decided to kill him.[67]

John was sensitive to the ominous atmosphere and is said to have written in a letter to his father that he knew the men would kill him that night, but that he would die bravely, "like a man." In an entry of his journal he wrote gloomily, "I am still amongst the living of this troublesome post—though report says that I am going to be dispatched to the Sandy Hills."[68]

According to depositions taken later by Sir George Simpson from four men at the post, John's behavior had been reprehensible on the day of the murder; he had been drunk by midday and had continued drinking rum steadily until 1:00 A.M. when he went to quell a disturbance in a cabin of one of the men. Failing to find the man he sought, he returned, got a rifle (was to intoxicated to load it), and searched the bastions and balcony. When he went into the courtyard four shots rang out and John fell dead.[69]

There were other descriptions. One, stated succinctly "...the violent death of a young trader at Fort Taku (sic) on the coast of Alaska, in the territory leased from the Russians by the Hudson's Bay Company....was the result of a drunken dispute among the Indians in which, accidentally, young McLoughlin has been shot."[70]

Jim Stuart of the staff of the Portland *Oregonian* felt that "Murder was not an attractive word in 1842 when *bon vivant extraordinaire,* son of revered John McLoughlin, was murdered at Fort Stikine, B.C." Citing "many contradictions in the character and personality" of John Jr. who emerged as "something of a rounder not averse to an occasional snifter and a well-turned ankle," Mr. Stuart mentioned that John's one-fourth Indian blood "lowered his social status" in spite of the advantages of being Dr. McLoughlin's son.[71]

Sir George Simpson maintained that young John was drunk and licentious, had engaged in brawls, had lived with native women, had neglected his work, and had not kept up his accounts.[72] His allegations were no doubt colored by the very unfavorable impressions that John had made on him during his school days in Canada, his disgrace in Paris, the Dickson débâcle, and all his other escapades and foolishness. It was understandably difficult, if not impossible, for Sir George to believe that John might have changed, that perhaps at long last he had grown up.

Letters written later by John's brother David and by his father told a different story. In essence the letters agreed, the main point of difference being the date of the murder, David choosing April 20/21, the Doctor, 19/20. Three letters were written to John Fraser which are still extant—David's on March 19, 1843, his father's on April 12, 1843, and February 17, 1844. David wrote

> It is with the greatest pain that I am under the necessity to relate the circumstance which led to the dreadful calamity which has befallen us by the murder of My Brother John he was shot down on the night of the 20/21 April in his own Fort & by his own men. John was in Charge of a Post on the Coast within the Russian Territories consisting of 22 men Sir G Simpson on passing there last fall took his assistant from him....I am bewildered how this affair will be brought to a proper conclusion as Sir G Simpson is such a dunce as to have formed his opinion on the reports of the Murderers who were pleading to alleviation than truth yet there it is on the words of these Villians he published his reports without consideration without a doubt these wretches have told him the truth and poor John was shot as a means of self preservation....

> Poor John he had a great deal of trouble the short time he was in this world, & if he remained in Canada this would never have happened He is (?) such a determined man and I am partly convinced it has been the means of his untimely end. Our people here are such beasts they take every advantage of insulting their Masters especially when there is a favorable opportunity.

David stressed the fact that John could not have been drunk as charged, that "The Wine which was sent to him, allowance for the year was found almost complete...." He also refuted the charge that John had been remiss in his bookkeeping. On the contrary, "his accounts (were) well kept up and his journal brought up to the day he was Murdered...."[73]

Dr. McLoughlin (in his letter of February 17, 1844), after congratulating John (Fraser) on his marriage to his cousin Elizabeth Fraser, daughter of Alexander, discussed his son's murder; much of what he wrote repeated the information of his letter of April 12, 1843. He explained that John's assistant stole a large quantity of "Liquor which they gave to the men which made them Drunk, particularly the Steward who being noisy the deceased ordered to be tied, in doing which the deceased assisted but this making the fellow abusive The man who shot the Deceased made a remark which irritated the Deceased he struck him when the fellow ran away calling aux armes aux armes."

The Chief Factor continued his description, telling that John had gone to get his "riffle" and was shot "from behind a corner." To murder, the killer added insult and injury, rushing "from his lurking place and put his foot on his (John's) throat while he was writhing in the agony of Death and finished him by beating in his head with his riffle." The Doctor added that the "Murderer is sent to Sitka to be tried by the Russians as the Deceased was murdered on Russian Territory. I have not yet heard the result." Like David, Dr. John reiterated emphatically that John was not a drunkard, that the fort was in excellent order, and that the account books were kept up-to-date.[74]

Dr. McLoughlin maintained that John had not been drunk or licentious, that in spite of his orders forbidding the men to bring in native prostitutes, they had defied him, bringing the women to the barracks at night and had stolen merchandise from the stores to pay them. When John threatened to expose them, the crew managed to get him drunk and provoked a brawl as a cover for murder.[75]

The Chief Factor felt that it was absurd to believe in the depositions taken by Sir George, for the men who made the depositions were utterly untrustworthy and of dubious character. Dr. McLoughlin was acquainted with some of John's staff, knowing them far better than a remote superior could possibly have known them.[76]

John's father was careful also to point out that while working both at Fort Vancouver and at Fort Stikine, John had acquired the reputation of being a good disciplinarian.[77] Dr. McLoughlin also emphasized the fact that since Sir George had not hesitated to transfer Finlayson to Fort Simpson, he must have been satisfied with John's management; in fact, he had expressed his pleasure at John's work. Too, Sir George had been sufficiently impressed with the dangers from unruly and bloodthirsty Indians surrounding the Fort that he encouraged fifteen men to take Indian wives.[78]

Back at Fort Stikine wild confusion followed the murder. If Sir George had not stopped there April 25 on his return from Sitka and the Sandwich Islands it is likely that quarrelsome natives would have completely sacked the Fort. He was surprised as he arrived to see the flag at half-staff. Since three (or four, or five, depending on the actual date of the murder) days had elapsed it was very difficult to sift the facts. More than that, four shots had been fired simultaneously;[79] was there one killer, or were there four?

Time was pressing. Simpson took the depositions hurriedly and, probably, superficially. With the natural prejudice he had against John, and remembering his instability and his escapades, he no doubt felt it was unnecessary to make a thorough investigation.[80] The truth was evident, he felt. Too, as usual, he was in a hurry.

Sir George decided that Urbain Héroux, a French Canadian, was the one who had fired the final shot. Finally, Héroux confessed; Sir George took him to Sitka and released him the next day. After all, both the murdered man and the murderer—or murderers—were drunk. Was John worth all this fuss and time-consumption? Previously, Simpson had dismissed an Iroquois, Pierre Kanaquassé, of the charge that he had made an earlier attempt on John's life. Dr. McLoughlin was furious at Simpson's handling of John's murder as trivial and inconsequential.[81]

Legal complications and red tape added to the already-confused situation. The strip of land on which Fort Stikine was located was legally a "sort-of" No-Man's land; since neither Canada nor Russia had a court of criminal jurisdiction, there was nothing that could be done,[82] or so said Sir George Simpson.

Not so—Dr. McLoughlin. It was not until June that he learned of his son's death in a letter from Governor Simpson. In addition to all the charges the Governor made, he added that "any Tribunal by which the case could be tried would find a verdict of 'Justifiable Homicide'."[83] Even if all the facts Sir George cited were true, which they probably were not, there was no excuse for the brutality of his tone.

Not only was the Doctor grief-stricken at the death of his son; he was also hurt and indignant at the Governor's injustice and hard indifference. He felt "let down" as a father and also as an officer of the Company. He felt in the latter capacity that the affair must be examined carefully so that justice would be done; that an example should be set so that the men would see that they could not murder officers with impunity—that John's murder would be followed by others unless justice was done.[84]

In his role as a father, he wanted his son vindicated of the charges Simpson had made. In a letter to the Honourable Governor and the Honourable Committee in London, the Doctor wrote on April 28, 1884, "Sir George Simpson mistakes me It is not Revenge I seek But the vindication of the character and conduct of a son who was murdered because he followed his Instructions and Did his Duty who instead of being done Justice to as was his Due, had his character and conduct unjustly aspersed by the improper manner in which Sir George Simpson took the Depositions."[85]

The true story will probably never be known, for Sir George Simpson had a great deal of influence; neither he nor the London rulers of the Honourable Company wanted unfavorable publicity. They were averse to having the Company's "dirty linen" washed in public and they asked Dr. McLoughlin to say as little as possible. This, quite naturally, made the Doctor furious.

His conscience, his sense of justice, and his love for his son would not let him give up. He made every effort to bring the murderers to justice, a very elusive justice. Chief Factor James Douglas and Chief Trader Donald Munson were sent by McLoughlin on errands and private investigations, wasting countless Company hours. After the Russians refused jurisdiction McLoughlin, rather than let the murderers go free, transported at his own expense two suspects and eleven witnesses across the Rockies to Lower Canada, paying for their food, travel and jail expenses. There too the courts refused jurisdiction, saying that a trial, if any, could take place only in England. Finally McLoughlin, his finances strained, gave up.[86]

He wrote series after series of vituperative letters; over and over he repeated his bitter charges against Simpson. Letters which were supposed to deal with business matters were filled instead with the same subject: Sir George Simpson's handling—or mishandling—of the murder case of John McLoughlin Jr. By his redundant accusations and his rehashing of details, he foolishly played completely into Sir George's hands.[87] The Governor continued to hold his attitude of tolerant rectitude, maintaining that McLoughlin's feelings were running away with him and that he was neglecting his work.[88]

A biased statement, slanted in favor of the Honourable Company, appears in a book of that title written by Douglas MacKay, long-time employee of the HBC: "Sir George's unwillingness to engage in wholesale reprisals against the natives, which Dr. John McLoughlin demanded, completed the bitterness between him and his Chief Factor in Oregon. Sir George knew, as all the fur trade knew, that the son was erratic, that his Indian blood did not equip him to deal as a trader with the natives where rum was involved."[89]

Both men, now mutually antipathetic, continued writing to the Governor and the Committee in London. McLoughlin bombarded them with letters of invective against Simpson. Finally, the Company became tired of the matter. It began to criticise McLoughlin for some of his policies, policies to which Sir George had long been opposed. McLoughlin's only recourse, he felt, was resignation.[90]

One beneficial result came of the whole tragedy—the decision to eliminate the selling of liquor to the natives. The elimination of liquor had been Dr. McLoughlin's practice for some time. Now at last it became official and agreement was made with the Russians that they too would cease selling "spirits" to the Indians of the Russian-American border area.[91]

Before leaving the subject of young John, the mischievous-child-who-never-grew-up, the *enfant terrible* who made two related families—and even Sir George Simpson—most unhappy at times, it is interesting, almost amusing, to read a "far-out" interpretation of the life and death of this strange young man.

Given the classification of historical fiction is a story by T. D. Allen[92] which makes Governor Simpson the "compleat" villain in a strange tale of intrigue and conspiracy which ended in murder.

In his story Allen portrays Simpson as totally evil, all vice, no virtue, completely without any redeeming qualities whatsoever. From the outset the author shows Simpson as jealous and resentful of McLoughlin—the small man's envy of the tall man's height. He consequently plotted for years against the Chief Factor. First, in 1824, when Dr. McLoughlin, his wife, and two of their children, John and Eloisa, came to the Columbia from Canada, the Simpson party met the McLoughlin family at Portage la Biche, much to Simpson's malicious glee and to the Doctor's discomfiture, for the latter had had a head start of three weeks over Simpson, who had had to wait at York until a Company ship with instructions came in. Simpson sent McLoughlin on an errand which would keep him absent for several hours and attempted to seduce Mrs. McLoughlin (whom Simpson considered the Doctor's "kept woman," rather than his wife), who at that period of her life was said to be very beautiful. She repulsed the Governor so definitely and so contemptuously, even slapping his face, that he vowed to avenge himself upon this lowly half-breed and her towering husband.

Seeing young John at sixteen in school in Lower Canada and understanding the boy's character and personality, Simpson realized that John was a perfect tool for his long-range plan. Following the Dickson misadventure he brought John into the Hudson's Bay Company, later sent him to Stikine, took Rae away, sending him to California, and later took Finlayson also, leaving a "worthless" substitute. Stikine, with its macabre setting, the rum-soaked natives and unruly staff, was the perfect locale for the culmination of his plot, the death of John, which would result in great grief for John's father, as well as disgrace which would bring about the Doctor's severance from the Company.

To embellish a fanciful tale even further, a few years previously in Montréal, John had fallen in love with "Susette," a girl of Swiss, French and Cree extraction. They became engaged and were to marry following John's return from Paris. In the meantime, with John out of the way, Simpson seduced Susette, disgracing and "ruining" her. Feeling that she could now not marry John, she committed suicide, telling John the pitiful story in a "suicide note". She asked John to be sure to make public what Simpson had done—to her and to other girls—so that he should not receive the knighthood[93] he was ambitiously angling for, for he was not worthy of the honor.

Simpson found out, or suspected, that Susette had written a letter to John in which she "told all" and which might foil him in his ambitions, both social and professional. Realizing the combustive nature of the occupants of the post at Stikine, he felt he would not have to wait long for the explosion. (Perhaps he even bribed one or more of the half-breed staff to stir up trouble, or even to do the actual shooting—?)

The day on which the murder took place John once more read Susette's tragic letter, and sensing the murderous atmosphere, decided to enclose it in a letter which he had just written to his father. The Chief Factor, John felt, could deal effectively with the wily Simpson.

Dr. John McLoughlin, "King of the Columbia," with his famous gold-headed cane. This portrait by Louise Lolli Wilson is displayed prominently near the entrance of the Fort Vancouver Visitors Information Center.

Photo by Harrison Hornish, Lake Oswego, Oregon

Once believed to be John McLoughlin made while he visited in Paris, current historians believe it to be of John's brother, Dr. David, who lived in Paris for some years while court physician to Louis-Philippe.
Photo from Oregon Historical Society Archives, Portland.

Angélique Harvey, Eloisa's only daughter by her second marriage.
Photo by Harrison Hornish, courtesy of Wayne Randolph, curator, McLoughlin House, Oregon City.

The reconstructed Chief Factor's residence, July 1976.
Photo by Leonard Bacon, Portland, 1976

All photos from Oregon Historical Society archives

The dining-room has the magnificent mahogany table and many of the twenty-four chairs used at the Fort.

The parlor contains the original Cogswell portrait, an exquisite lacquered Chinese cabinet of Mrs. McLoughlin, and a grand piano shipped from Boston around Cape Horn in 1851.

Photo from Oregon Historical Society Archives, Portland.

163

The bookcase contains several valuable books, nucleus of the "Columbia Library" arranged by Dr. William Frazer Tolmie at Fort Vancouver about 1833. The mortar and pestle are said to be from the apothecary shop at the Fort. Note the copy of the Cogswell portrait of McLoughlin.

Photo from Oregon Historical Society Archives, Portland.

The four upstairs bedrooms are furnished authentically for the mid-nineteenth-century period. One of the beds is believed by some to have belonged to the McLoughlins. Note the foot warmer, the cradle, and the quilted bedspread on the spool bed. Another room contains a trundle bed, which fits under an ornate hand-carved four-poster bed.

Partially restored Fort: stockade, 1966; bastion, 1973-1974; bakery, 1975. Taken from the top of the Interstate bridge with telephoto lens in 1975. Arrow marks the site of the first fort (now site of Washington State School for the Deaf), built in 1824-1825 and rebuilt at present Fort Site in 1829-1830. Note the seeming anachronism of a plane, probably from nearby Pearson Airfield

Photo by Steve Small for the Vancouver *The Columbian*, 1975

Little-known copy of a daguerrotype; the date is not certain, but it would have to be after 1839, when the daguerrotype process was developed. Note the severe facial expression and the "stock" (extremely high collar).

Photo from Oregon Historical Society Archives, Portland.

Margaret Wadin McKay (Mrs. John) McLoughlin.
Photo by Harrison Hornish, courtesy of Wayne Randolph, curator, McLoughlin House, Oregon City.

David, youngest child of the McLoughlins, at approximately eighty years of age
Photo from Oregon Historical Society Archives, Portland.

Cabin built by David for his Indian wife and nine children at Porthill, Idaho, near the Canadian border

Photo from Oregon Historical Society Archives, Portland.

The McLoughlins' home, minus its roof, was moved up steep Singer Hill to Oregon City Heights in 1909.

Photo from Oregon Historical Society Archives, Portland.

McLoughlin House today in McLoughlin Park on Center Street, on land given by McLoughlin to Oregon City. It is a National Historic Site and popular tourist attraction.
Photo from Oregon Historical Society Archives, Portland.

The statue of Dr. John McLouglin in the Statuary Hall of Fame of the Capitol in Washington, D.C., honors him as one of the two official representatives of the State of Oregon. (The Reverend Jason Lee is the other.)

The house at Willamette Falls, where it was built in 1845-1846

Photo from Oregon Historical Society Archives, Portland.

York Fort, on Hudson Bay, first Headquarters of Hudsons Bay Company

Christening of the first Fort Vancouver by George Simpson, March 19, 1825, a diorama formerly in the Fort Vancouver Visitors Center Museum. This scene was re-enacted March 19, 1975, as part of the Sesquicentenial observance.

Drawing of Fort Vancouver in 1853 by Gustavus Sohon. Original is in the United States War Department archives, Washington, D.C.

"Palace of the Columbia" c. 1860 in badly run-down condition. Members of the McLoughlin family were its first occupants.
Archives of Fort Vancouver Historical Society in Clark County Historical Museum, Vancouver, Washington

From a recent (1976) painting of Fort Vancouver c. 1845 by Richard Schlect for the National Park Service, Harper's Ferry, West Virginia. On display in the Fort Vancouver Visitors Center. Fort Vancouver was the administrative headquarters for the vast Columbia Department, directing the activities of numerous posts, forts, and ocean vessels.

Photo by Harrison Hornish, courtesy National Park Service, Fort Vancouver Visitors Center

All Roads Led to Fort Vancouver
Center of Commerce and Culture . . .

Royal Family of the Columbia

Simpson arrived at the Fort almost immediately after the murder and helped in supervising the preparation of the body for burial. He saw the letter and suggested that it be buried with John "in a pocket over his heart." The suggestion coming from Sir George Simpson was tantamount to a command; needless to say, it was followed.

When John's father arrived later it was too late for him to learn of the letter and note. The whole tragedy was irreversible.

Thus ends a fanciful and, so far as is known, an imaginary version of the death of John McLoughlin Jr., one that was engineered by a spiteful, vengeful, and powerful official as a means of vengeance against a subordinate. It is, of course, possible, but surely not probable. And yet it is no more a fantasy than many events known actually to have occurred.

The year 1842, the year of the death of John and Margaret McLoughlin's eldest son, was doubtless the year which marked the beginning of the McLoughlin family's grief. Dr. John's mother, Angélique Fraser McLoughlin, died three months later; in 1844 his benefactor and favorite uncle, Dr. Simon Fraser, died; his son-in-law William Glen Rae committed suicide under mysterious and suspicious circumstances in June 1845; July 1846 saw the death of his favorite sister, Marie-Louise; the revolution of 1848 drove his brother, Dr. David, from his position at the French Court; the next year David's wife, Lady Jane Capel, died; the Doctor's son, Joseph, and Margaret's son, Tom McKay, both died (probably) in 1849; finally, their only remaining son, David, also in 1849, resigned from the Hudson's Bay Company, left Oregon City and began the life of a wanderer, eventually "going native".[94]

It is interesting to speculate on the guilt in John's death. Was it his "Indian blood"? Historians and other writers of an earlier era, less liberal, less liberated, bigoted, and racist, often felt that non-Caucasian blood doomed its "victim" from the start. A less-than-first-class status was inevitable.

Was it William Glen Rae? Apparently he was a "nice" man; he meant well, but he was weak. He required detailed instruction and constant supervision to give him security in his work. He was not the ideal person to train another weak young man, particularly one as hot headed and erratic as John. Who sent Rae to Yerba Buena anyway? Some say McLoughlin; some say Simpson. Since Simpson was opposed to the Yerba Buena post from the start, it seems likely that McLoughlin sent his son-in-law to California; the transfer was doubtless considered a promotion. It was probably a matter of poor judgment. John Jr.'s father should have realized it was unwise to leave his son at Stikine; and yet, he had done very well at Vancouver—perhaps the Chief Factor felt that his twenty-nine-year-old son was at last ready for responsibility.

Was it Simpson? After all, he hired John to work for the Company against the father's wishes. Did he, rather than the Chief Factor, send John to Stikine? Some historians say so. It was certainly he who removed reliable Roderick Finlayson. The

179

murder would proably not have occurred if Finlayson had remained. Certainly, Dr. McLoughlin felt that this was true, as shown in his letters in which he repeatedly attributed guilt to Simpson for having arbitrarily and unnecessarily transferred the capable assistant.

The question of the identity of one guilty person will probably never be settled. There are too many factors, both personal and impersonal, involved, and too much of the human element, incomprehensible and unpredictable.

Young John McLoughlin was buried in the Fort Vancouver cemetery, outside the stockade and very near the then-location of St. James Catholic Church. His mortal remains were to occupy at least three sites, appropriate indeed for this youth who had been so restless in life.

His remains, and those of two others, were moved in the 1850s to make room for the Army Post road, and again in the late 1960s when Highway I-5 was built, by-passing Vancouver as it goes from Portland to Seattle. St. James Church, too, was moved to its present-day location in downtown Vancouver. The exact location of John's grave is not certain today, but it is probably among several rows of graves whose crosses are marked "Unknown" in the military cemetary adjoining St. James Cemetery, near Barnes Veterans' Hospital in the Fort Vancouver section of the city of Vancouver.[95]

Casting ahead approximately one hundred years, a bronze marker was unveiled at the site mentioned (now covered by Highway I-5) on June 12, 1938, by the Oregon Society of the Daughters of 1812. The marker honored Pierre Pambrun, a chief trader of the Hudson's Bay Company who died in 1841, William Kitson, a British soldier of the War of 1812, and Dr. John McLoughlin Jr.[96]

Dr. John and Margaret McLoughlin would have appreciated this attention to their wayward prodigal son. Perhaps there is an element of retribution in the honor, too, for after all, young John did reform for a period of his life, after his return to Fort Vancouver.

Most of all, John himself would have smiled at that prefix "Dr.," knowing that he never did finish his medical studies. Now, instead of the prefix as a mark of distinction between father and son, the title belongs to him too—for all time.

1 Burt Brown Barker, ed., *Financial Papers of Dr. John McLoughlin*, p. 43.

2 Barker, *The McLoughlin Empire and its Rulers,* Letter from Dr. McLoughlin to Dr. Simon Fraser, pp. 171-172. The letter was dated "Novr. 1821," but changed by the editor to 1820.

3 *Ibid.*, pp. 107-108.

4 *Ibid.*, p. 109.

5 *Ibid.*, pp. 174-175.

6 *Ibid.*, p. 109. Also, letter, pp. 186-187.

7 *Ibid.*, p. 187, letter July 2, 1828.

8 *Ibid.*, p. 188, letter dated only July 1828.

9 *Ibid.*, pp. 188-189.

10 *Ibid.*, pp. 190-191.

11 *Ibid.*, p. 189.

12 *Ibid.*, pp. 191-192.

13 *Ibid.*, p. 111.

14 *Ibid.*, pp. 111-112. The "friends" were Simon Fraser, Governor Simpson, and his brother-in-law Chief Factor James Keith (at La Chine).

15 *Ibid.*, pp. 192-193. Letter May 18, 1832.

16 *Ibid.*, pp. 194-195.

17 *Ibid.*, pp. 196-198.

18 *Ibid.*, pp. 199-200.

19 Archives, Oregon Historical Society.

20 Barker, *op. cit.*, pp. 203-204.

21 *Ibid.*, p. 205.

22 (Same as number 23.)

23 *Ibid.*, pp. 222-224. Dr. John McLoughlin stated these factors in a letter to Dr. Simon Fraser, February 14, 1836. He still did not know the cause of John's dismissal. He stated in this letter "...my Brother does not write what it is and he ought to have done so." This letter, written more than two years after John was sent home, points up the utter slowness of communication more than one hundred years ago.

24 *Ibid.*

25 Archives, Oregon Historical Society.

26 Barker, *op. cit.*, pp. 220-222.

27 *Ibid.*, pp. 232-235.

28 *Ibid.*, pp. 184-185. Letter to Governor George Simpson, October 16 1827.

29 *Ibid.*, p. 117, p. 117n.

30 *Ibid.*, p. 210.

31 Archives, Oregon Historical Society.

32 Barker, *op. cit.*, pp. 211-212, p. 207, p. 215.

33 *Ibid.*, p. 216.

34 Archives (microfilm), Oregon Historical Society.

35 Barker, *op. cit.*, pp. 215-216. Letter, July 7, 1835.

36 *Ibid.*, pp. 204-205.

37 Archives (microfilm), Oregon Historical Society.

38 *Ibid.*

39 *Ibid.*

40 *Ibid.*, Also, Barker, *op. cit.*, p. 218.

41 Feature Article in Portland *Oregonian*, November 12, 1950.

42 Archives (microfilm), Oregon Historical Society. Also, Barker, *op. cit.*, pp. 218-220.

43 Archives (microfilm), Oregon Historical Society. Also, Barker, *op. cit.*, p. 224.

44 Barker, *op. cit.*, p. 119.

45 *Ibid.*, pp. 119-120; pp. 235-238.

46 *Ibid.*, pp. 228-229.

47 *Ibid.*, pp. 230-231.

48 *Ibid.*

49 *Ibid.*, p. 121.

50 *Ibid.*, pp. 121-122.

51 *Ibid.*, pp. 232-235.

52 *Ibid.*

53 *Ibid.*, pp. 238-239.

54 *Ibid.*, pp. 239-241.

55 *Ibid.*, pp. 241-242.

56 *Ibid.*, p. 122.

57 *Ibid.*, p. 243.

58 *Ibid.*

59 *Ibid.*, p. 246.

60 Richard G. Montgomery, *The White-Headed Eagle*, p. 260.

61 Barker, *op. cit.*, p. 123.

62 Agnes C. Laut, *Conquest of the Great Northwest*, p. 338.

63 E. E. Rich, ed., *McLoughlin's Fort Vancouver Letters*, Second Series, 1839-1844, p. xxx (intro.).

64 David Lavender, *Land of Giants*, p. 213.

65 Eloisa McLoughlin Harvey, *Life of Dr. John McLoughlin*, Ms., Bancroft Library. Copy in archives of Oregon Historical Society.

66 There is disagreement as to the exact date of the murder. Most historians use April 20/21, including Burt Brown Barker (p. 123); Montgomery [*W.-H.E.*] says 21/22 (p. 286); David McLoughlin and his father, writing to John Fraser March 19 and April 12, respectively, both in 1843 do not agree, David citing 20/21 and Dr. McLoughlin 19/20. Thus any of the three dates seems possible.

67 Charles Ermatinger, "Tragedy on the Stikine," *Oregon Historical Quarterly*, XV, pp. 126-132.

68 Lavender, *loc. cit.*

69 E. E. Rich, *The Hudson's Bay Company*, II, pp. 713-714.

70 George Bryce, *The Remarkable History of the Hudson's Bay Company*, 22, p. 406.

71 The Portland *Oregonian*, December 17, 1950.

72 Rich, ed., *McLoughlin's Fort Vancouver Letters*, Third Series, 1844-1846, pp. 11-12.

73 Barker, *op. cit.*, pp. 247-249.

74 *Ibid.*, p. 251.

75 Lavender, pp. 213-215.

76 *McLoughlin's Fort Vancouver Letters*, *op. cit.*, Second Series, p. xxxii.

77 *Ibid.*, p. xxx.

78 Rich, *The Hudson's Bay Company*, *op. cit.*, pp. 712-713.

79 Montgomery, *op. cit.*, p. 286.

80 *McLoughlin's Fort Vancouver Letters*, *op. cit.*, p. xxxi.

81 Rich, *The Hudson's Bay Company*, *op. cit.*, pp. 714-715.

82 *McLoughlin's Fort Vancouver Letters*, *op. cit.*, p. xxxii.

83 *Ibid.*, p. 344.

84 Robert C. Johnson, *John McLoughlin: Patriarch of the Northwest*, pp. 247-248.

85 *McLoughlin's Fort Vancouver Letters,* Second Series, *op. cit.,* pp. 11-12.

86 Lavender, *op. cit.,* p. 214.

87 *Ibid.,* p. 215.

88 Rich, *The Hudson's Bay Company, loc. cit.*

89 Douglas MacKay, *The Honourable Company,* p. 215.

90 Lavender, *op. cit.,* p. 215.

91 Helen Tipton, *John McLoughlin, Chief Factor of the Hudson's Bay Company at Vancouver,* Ms., p. 11.

92 T. D. Allen, *Troubled Border,* pp. 227-230.

93 Governor George Simpson had already been knighted by Queen Victoria in January 1841. MacKay, *op. cit.,* p. 213. (Montgomery says 1839 [pp. 273-274]).

94 Barker, *op. cit.,* pp. 49-50.

95 Information given in an interview with Mr. Robert Clark, historian at Fort Vancouver, National Park Service, Department of the Interior.

96 *The Oregon Historical Quarterly,* 39 (1938), p. 327.

Courtesy, Harrison Hornish—model of the Chief Factor's House in Museum at Fort Vancouver Visitor Center.

Royal Family of the Columbia
CHAPTER 8

ELIZA, THE KING'S ABSENT DAUGHTER

Maria Elisabeth, the older of the McLoughlins' two daughters, might be considered even more of a mystery than her half brother Joseph. Affectionately called Eliza by her family, she remained in eastern Canada for her education and, later, her marriage when her family went to the Pacific Coast.[1]

Unlike Dr. Burt Brown Barker, who believed that it was Eloisa who "is seen only vaguely," then relegated her to eighteen lines,[2] spending nearly four pages discussing Eliza, this writer found Eloisa appearing as a distinct personality, mainly, no doubt, because she lived in the Pacific Northwest with her family, except for the few years which she spent at school in Québec, and also because a number of her descendants in the fourth, fifth and sixth generations have been relatively easy to trace, many of whom live on the west coast, and with whom it has been possible to become acquainted, to converse, to correspond, and to become familiar with family legends passed down from generation to generation.

By contrast, so far as is known, Eliza was never at any time in the Oregon Country; the names of her children are known, but further than that there is only obscurity. While there must be many of her descendants living today their names and whereabouts are unknown. In addition, while there are transcripts of interviews with both Eloisa and one of her daughters extant and available for study today, there is nothing extant of Eliza's; none of her letters has come to light.

Maria Elisabeth McLoughlin, first daughter and second child of Dr. John and Margaret McLoughlin, was born either at Lac la Pluie or Fort William in 1814, which was also the year her father was made a wintering partner in the Northwest Company and assigned as chief trader to be in charge at Lac la Pluie.[3]

She was not mentioned in letters back to the Frasers and other family members in Canada until 1825, probably because her parents' marriage was a "fur company marriage," and while legal and binding to the couple themselves, it was not the formal religious marriage ceremony of eastern Canada, so that the Doctor was probably hesitant to mention his marital status to his relatives. In a letter of March 15, 1825, Dr. McLoughlin in a letter to Dr. Simon Fraser mentioned "my daughter she is I presume with my sister" though not by name. Another letter of the same date, also to Dr. Fraser, spoke of financial arrangements for "the Education and support of my two children (John and Eliza, presumably)."[4]

In a letter of March 19, 1826, to Dr. Fraser he mentions leaving "My Daughter at the Nunnery (Ursulines Convent) till I go down."[5] From Terrebonne, April 20, 1827, Dr. Fraser wrote this to his nephew,

Alberta Brooks Fogdall

I wrote last Spring to your sister (Sister St. Henry) and sent her 25 pounds which I thought sufficient to defray the expense of your daughter at the Nunnery for a Year, but your sister really astonished me by sending me an account of 80 pounds for a year. I wrote her that I thought it highly exorbitant, I have since referred her to Mr. Simpson, and refused to sanction the system she follows....[6]

The outcome of the disagreement concerning tuition charges has not been recorded. Presumably, Governor Simpson paid them from Dr. McLoughlin's account.

Governor Simpson had written from La Chine (new Hudson's Bay Company headquarters near Montréal) to Dr. Simon the previous November (1826) that he had called on "my Friend Dr. McLoughlin's...sister and Daughter while at Québec and was happy to find that the Young Lady had made great progress in the different branches of education to which her attention has been directed; she is extremely fortunate in having been placed under the care and protection of a lady so well qualified to store and improve her young mind..."[7]

The Governor was correct. Eliza was indeed fortunate to be with her aunt, Sister St. Henry. Since she could not receive an adequate education and at the same time be with her family on the Columbia, it was a perfect "second-best" for the lonely girl that she could be at the Ursulines Convent with her warm, gentle and affectionate aunt as a teacher and also have her as a mother-substitute. It must have been no small comfort to her parents to know that their daughter, although the distance of a continent away from them, was being loved and cared for.

In a letter from Sister St. Henry to her Uncle Simon, May 18, 1826, she mentioned that "the little girl" worried her father, that her teacher found her advanced—also that Eliza "expects to write her brother (John), she often speaks...of the kindnesses of her Uncle (Simon)...."

The Doctor's sister reported in the same letter that Eliza's father wanted her to "apply herself to Music." Sister St. Henry said that she had often told "the little one that her music will be of some value to her as for a life of work, she is not strong."[8]

Nearly everyone seemed concerned about Eliza's frailty and delicacy. Her father had felt that she was not strong enough to make the trip across the country and that her health would not stand up in the rigorous Oregon wilderness. It is possible that the reason her father wanted her to study music was that he felt she would be subjected to less pressure than if she studied heavier courses. Today's "Libbers" would most certainly have taken umbrage at the good Doctor's instructions for his daughter's education in a letter to Dr. Fraser in 1825 from Fort George (Astoria): "I will be obliged to you to use your will and pleasure...as to my daughter...my object is not to give her a splendid Education but a good one—at least a good Education for a Girl."[9]

Royal Family of the Columbia

The reader can no doubt infer even through the run-on sentences and unconventional capitalization that Dr. McLoughlin, although he loved his daughter, most certainly felt that the mind of a female was undeniably inferior to that of a male.

In 1829 Eliza's health had not noticeably improved apparently, for her aunt wrote to Dr. Fraser "The health of his (her brother John's) daughter is delicate this obliges me to allow her to take walks it seems that her health gains by it as well as her manners, everything in her is noble and agreeable."[10]

Eliza was married at eighteen, some time in 1832. Strangely, her Fraser relatives learned of her wedding in Québec from her brother John Jr., writing to them from Paris, February 24, 1833: "I received a letter from my dear sister in which she announces me her marriage with Mr. Epps (Eppes). I hope she will be very happy with him...it seems that the gentleman is very respected in Québec by all his friends."[11]

Eliza's bridegroom was William Randolph Eppes. Born in 1795 (thus almost twenty years Eliza's senior), he led the usual peripatetic life of the British army officer. He joined the Army in 1811, became a Deputy Assistant in 1821, Assistant Commissary General in 1827; during this time he served in Portugal, on Malta, in the West Indies, on the Gold Coast, in Canada, and in Newfoundland. He was probably stationed in Canada 1829-1837. Mr. and Mrs. Eppes took her brother, John Jr., to live with them after his return from Paris and before the Dickson episode. They were apparently kind to him and he was as happy there as it was possible for him to be.[12]

Six children, five daughters and one son, were born to the Eppeses between 1835 and 1849, the youngest daughter born after her father's death.[13] One cannot help wondering how giving birth to six children affected Eliza's frail and delicate health.

Eliza received financial help from her father both before and after she became a widow. Amounts varying from 50 pounds to 400 pounds were paid to her in 1841, 1843, 1852, and each year until 1857, when Dr. McLoughlin died. Reason for the nine-year gap is not known. In addition, as a widow she received a pension of 70 pounds a year paid at Québec and 16 pounds for each child.[14]

Looking backward about thirty-five years—in the three-year period 1812-1815, Dr. John lost his father, Cultivateur McLoughlin; his paternal grandfather, John McLoughlin; and his maternal grandfather, Colonel Malcolm Fraser. This meant that within a short period there were three estates to be settled, with all the attendant intricacies and complications. These events would be irrelevant to the story of Eliza except that Dr. John inherited considerable land and money and, perhaps feeling sentimental and nostalgic for his former home, and also wishing to make a profitable investment, he bought three farms in Rivière-du-Loup, probably when he visited there in 1817 and 1818. The farms, totaling 676 acres, were later supervised by the Doctor's half uncle, John Malcolm Fraser.

In 1855 or 1856 Eliza wrote her father that John Malcolm no longer wished to superintend the three farms and that they were deteriorating for lack of care. Dr. McLoughlin wrote to John Malcolm, asking him to sell the farms, but did not include power of attorney. Later he sent power of attorney but received no acknowledgment. Tiring of the delay and the waiting, he sent Eliza power of attorney in a letter of July 23, 1856. However, a postscript asked Eliza not to sell the farms if John Malcolm was willing to do so. He also sent a second power of attorney to the latter. Eliza ignored his directions and sold the farms over Fraser's protests. Dr. McLoughlin then sent money to Fraser, asking him to redeem the farms, returning the purchase price to the buyer. Dr. McLoughlin's death, September 3, 1857, left the affair unsettled. The ending was clouded with loans, debts, and partial payments. The solution has never been recorded.[15] Possibly Eliza kept the money, for there is no mention in the inventory of the estate of the farms or of proceeds of their sale in the Chief Factor's meticulously kept accounts. He gave Eliza in his will a life estate in the farms with a remainder over to her children. Just how all of this worked out for Eliza and for the purchaser of the farms is still another of the several mysteries of the McLoughlin saga.

Royal Family of the Columbia

REFERENCES

CHAPTER 8

ELIZA, THE KING'S ABSENT DAUGHTER

1 David McLoughlin, "Correspondence," Archives, Oregon Historical Society.

2 Burt Brown Barker, *The McLoughlin Empire and Its Rulers,* p. 127.

3 W. Stewart Wallace, *Documents Relating to the Northwest Company,* p. 288.

4 Barker, *op. cit.,* pp. 175-177.

5 *Ibid.,* pp. 177-179.

6 *Ibid.,* pp. 182-184.

7 *Ibid.,* pp. 181-182.

8 *Ibid.,* pp. 179-180.

9 *Ibid.,* pp. 175-176. The letter was written March 15, 1825.

10 *Ibid.,* pp. 188-189. The letter was dated February 29, 1829, which was an error, since 1829 was not a "leap" year.

11 *Ibid.,* pp. 196-197. It seems likely that William Randolph Eppes was connected with the Eppes and the Randolph families with which Thomas Jefferson was related, but research did not result in documentation of the possibility.

12 *Ibid.,* p. 213. The letter was from Sister St. Henry to Dr. Simon Fraser, June 17, 1835.

13 *Ibid.,* p. 129.

14 *Ibid.*

15 *Ibid.,* pp. 129-131; 311, 312 and 313.

Bastion of reconstructed Fort Vancouver built in 1974.

Royal Family of the Columbia
CHAPTER 9

ELOISA, THE KING'S FAVORITE CHILD——HER FAMILY AND HER DESCENDANTS

Compared with the life of Eliza, that of the McLoughlins' third child, Maria Eloisa, or simply Eloisa, was an open book. Commonly considered her father's favorite, she has also been the favorite of writers of historical fiction.[1]

Eloisa was born at Fort William, on Lake Superior, in 1817* and may have come with her father and mother to Fort Vancouver in 1824.[2] It is also possible that she came with her mother and her younger brother, David, a year or two later.[3]

Like her older brother and sister, John and Eliza, she received the greater part of her education in Canada, though exactly which years she spent there have not been specified. Both the girls were placed by their father under the care of his sister Marie Louise at the Ursuline Convent in Québec as boarding students.[4] Eliza had remained in Québec, never traveling to the Columbia. Eloisa returned to Québec from the Northwest sometime before 1833, for Dr. McLoughlin in a letter to his cousin John Fraser reminded him, "...when you go to Québec I hope you will go to see my sister and my Daughter Eloisa."[5] (However, she herself in her "Recollections" did not mention attending school in Québec.) This letter was written March 1, 1833, just five days after a letter from John McLoughlin Jr. to John Fraser in which he mentioned the marriage of Eliza, which had taken place the previous year.[6] Thus the education of the two sisters at the convent may have overlapped for only a short time, due partly to the three years' difference in their ages.

Much of the information concerning Eloisa comes from original source material, some of it her own recollections, given in 1878 when she was sixty-one years old.[7]

Another original source of information on Eloisa is a series of interviews of one of her daughters, Maria Louisa Rae (Mrs. Josiah Myrick). These interviews were conducted by Fred Lockley in 1929 for his column in the *Oregon Journal*.[8] At this time Mrs. Myrick was eighty-seven, a fact which should be taken into consideration in evaluating the validity of her recollections. She can probably be forgiven for referring to her great-granduncle Simon Fraser as Samuel, for saying that her father, William Glen Rae, died in 1844, rather than in 1845, and that it was (Dr.) John and (Dr.) David, rather than their sister Marie-Louise, who were brought up by their Fraser grandparents; however, the last-mentioned statement is controversial; perhaps she was not mistaken.

*Her tombstone in Lone Fir Cemetery, in Portland, gives her birth date as February 3, 1818.

As for Eloisa herself, in the interview taken by Amos Bowman for the Bancroft Library she stated that she and her younger brother, David, accompanied their parents to the Columbia in 1824.[9]

It is possible, although she may have "remembered" from hearsay, rather than from actual fact. Many reasons, noted elsewhere, have been cited against the probability of the Chief Factor's family accompanying him to the Columbia in 1824.

The favorite of her father, whom she was said to resemble, her fair skin and blonde hair contrasted strongly with the copper-tinted skin and black hair of her part-Indian mother and of her darker-complexioned siblings. At fourteen she was taller than her mother, already showing herself to be the feminine version of her six-foot-four father. Whether she was blue-eyed like her father, as some writers have indicated, or brown-eyed, is uncertain, and probably not exactly crucial at this point. According to Eva Emery Dye, early writer of Oregon history, she had "creamy-tinted skin" and "satiny hair" (color not stated), "her mother's dark eyes," but "the form and features of her father;" she was "fair, imperious, and commanding." At twenty-one she was tall, graceful, a star in a land of dusky women. She "queened it" over the Columbia.[10]

It is interesting to note that at sixty-one she was described by her interviewer, Amos Bowman, as "tall, with white hair, dark eyes, strong frame, good features, and a slight French accent."

As she grew up at Fort Vancouver, excluding the period when she was in Québec, she was popular with the Company clerks and voyageurs. Called "Princess" by some of the men, she enjoyed their deferential teasing. Michel La Framboise, whom Dr. McLoughlin called "the safest boatman on the River", especially, enjoyed teasing her when she was a child, laughing with her, telling her that he was waiting for her to grow up so that he could marry her.[11] It was, of course, only banter, since a French Canadian voyageur would certainly not marry the King's daughter. Class consciousness and the caste system were an aspect of life taken for granted on the frontier. An illustration of what is today called "racism" was Eloisa's being forbidden to play with any child who did not have at least one fully-white parent.[12]

François Ermatinger, a clerk in the Company store, was another of her favorites. Always courteous, he talked with her as if she were grown up. She considered him "the finest gentleman at the Fort."[13]

As Eloisa reached her teens she became aware of, and greatly disliked, her mother's retiring nature and humility; as she became a "young lady" she almost unconsciously assumed the role of "Lady of the Pacific Coast," a status her mother gladly waived.[14] Perhaps she was an early-day "Libber" who saw no reason for women to take for granted their inferiority and subservience to men.

Eloisa looked forward to breaks in the Fort routine, such as brigade arrivals and departures, the coming of various ships, especially of the Company mail ship; and canoe and bateau excursions on the Willamette and the Columbia. Most of all she loved the trips to the numerous weddings and potlatches given by Indian chiefs for their "princess" daughters. The singing of the gay "songs of the paddle" by the boatmen, gay in striped cotton shirts and wide red belts from which hung tobacco pouches and razor-sharp hunting knives, enhanced the gala atmosphere and the fun-making.

Usually the entire family of the Fort and most of the staff attended, for it was wise and politic that the Chief Factor for business reasons maintain friendly relations with nearby native tribes. Many of the weddings were those of Company "gentlemen," *i.e.,* clerks and chief traders, to half-Indian girls, many of whom were offspring of chief traders and their Indian wives; other marriages were between "gentlemen" and full Indian "princessess," that is, daughters of important Indian chiefs. Here the caste system reared its ugly head, for mere "servants" of the Honourable Company (laborers, voyageurs) tended to marry Indian girls of less importance—girls whose fathers were not chiefs.[15]

One royal, or at least semi-royal, wedding attended by the official family of the Fort and many of its personnel was that of one of the seemingly-inexhaustible supply of daughters of Comcomly, one-eyed chief of the Chinooks. One daughter, "Timmee," had already been given in marriage to Tom McKay, the Chief Factor's stepson. Another, the "Princess of Wales," had a daughter called the "Filly" whom she was determined that either Governor George Simpson or Dr. McLoughlin should marry as a "second wife."[16] Still another daughter had been wed to Chief Casseno of the Multnomahs, and yet another to Duncan McDougal, a former Astor partner.

The daughter who was the bride on this particular red-letter day was Koale-yoa, whose husband-to-be was Chief Trader Archibald McDonald, from Fort Langley, one of the posts under the McLoughlin command.

As the bateaux and canoes of the cavalcade of Fort Vancouver wedding guests sailed gaily along to the splash of the paddles and the songs of the boatmen Eloisa's mother reminded her not to show surprise at the "beauty" of the bride, for the Chinooks practiced head-flattening. It was difficult for inexperienced Caucasians to become accustomed to this practice, although Eloisa had seen the wife of her half brother Tom McKay (sister of today's bride) several times. Potlatches were well worth attending, for various chiefs vied with each other in giving presents, for he who made the largest number of valuable gifts achieved the highest status. Chief Comcomly's potlatches, always lavish, were eagerly anticipated.

As the bateaux arrived at the landing of the Chinook village opposite Fort George (Astoria), Mrs. McLoughlin, the children, and all others waited respectfully in the boats, for only the Chief Factor and the prospective husband were allowed to walk down the aisle formed by two lines of Comcomly's slaves standing motionless as statues. This exclusive path was thick and solid with rich beaver and otter skins. As Chief Factor McLoughlin and Chief Trader McDonald walked impressively up the aisle they were met by Chief Comcomly, who with royal dignity escorted the bride, placing her hand in that of her bridegroom.

Members of the Chief's family were appropriately and royally attired for these festive occasions. Comcomly habitually wore a cocked hat which had been given to him by the British commander of the *Raccoon*. His torso was covered by a laced coat, also from the Royal Navy, while he carried an old sword for further effect. If son-in-law Casseno was present, he was no doubt attired in the scarlet coat of a British soldier and wearing on his head a battered silk hat trimmed with eagle feathers.

The "Princess of Wales," short and stout, often wore a sort of kilt or short petticoat of woodrat skins, with a bib of the same pelts, a blue shawl given her by Mrs. McLoughlin, and a red kerchief on her head.

The "Filly's" favorite covering—or uncovering—consisted of red and blue tattoos artistically arranged to form the Honourable Company's seal, a rampant elk on each breast; in the middle, a shield with four beavers, topped by an alert fox, while underneath, on her abdomen was loyally displayed the Company's motto "Pro pelle cutem" (a skin for a skin). Somehow room was also found to display effectively and patriotically the Union Jack.

Comcomly's policy was one of friendliness toward both the "King George Men" and the "Boston Men". In return, the British and the Americans desired to be on good terms with the Chinooks, both for trade advantages and in the interst of peace in the Valley.[17]

Nearly every morning from the first bright day in May until the Oregon Country rains of October, Mrs. McLoughlin and Eloisa sat on the full length veranda. The older woman was never idle. Always there was a needle and thread in her busy hands; she embroidered numerous caps, scarves, smoking-bags and other articles. She was meticulous in her handicraft, doing fine, soft, even work. By contrast, Eloisa, unlike her patient mother, always seemed to tangle the skeins. Impatient with herself, she was also impatient with her mother's patience. How could her mother bear to do needlework so patiently? It was so monotonous! Her quiet, unassuming mother, understanding her rebellious daughter, would often say sympathetically, "You are like your father, child, not patient like me."[18]

Early in the spring of 1838, when Eloisa was twenty-one, she was married to William Glen Rae, a tall, handsome young Scotsman. Born sometime between 1805 and 1810 in the Orkney Islands, he had served the Hudson's Bay Company at various posts, coming to the Columbia Department's principal headquarters in 1837 as chief clerk.[19]

In spite of the disagreements between Dr. McLoughlin and Mr. Beaver, Marie Eloisa McLoughlin and chief trader William Glen Rae were married by the chaplain early in 1838. Mrs. Beaver designed and supervised the making of the white dresses worn by the flower girls and the bridesmaids, no doubt to impress upon the inhabitants her idea of "civilized" ways. It was a gala occasion in the life of the fort. Undoubtedly the service was held in the mess-room, as were all the church services during Beaver's time.

Although historians have emphasized the conflict between McLoughlin and Beaver, the fact that the chaplain baptised 124 persons during his two year stay indicates that he must have been found acceptable by a large number of those living at the fort. Very few of the inhabitants were Church of England, yet they brought their children and came themselves to have him perform this sacrament.

Beaver was designated by the Company as "missionary to the Indians", but he did little in this capacity. He and Mrs. Beaver did adopt a little Indian girl, but she died while in their care. They were genuinely upset and wanted to send to England for a tombstone.[20]

Some time previous to her marriage François Ermatinger, by then a chief trader, had asked Eloisa's father for her hand. Dr. McLoughlin had made it very clear that marriage between Frank and Eloisa was out of the question. Obviously he did not consider Frank, as did Eloisa, "the finest gentleman at the fort." There may have been several reasons why Dr. McLoughlin did not wish his daughter to marry Frank; no doubt one reason was that he felt that Ermatinger, now forty, was too old for Eloisa. Apparently Frank recovered from his disappointment, for in August 1841 he married Mrs. McLoughlin's granddaughter Catherine Sinclair, whose father was a Hudson's Bay Company chief trader, later, factor.[21]

After his marriage to Eloisa, William Glen Rae was promoted to chief trader and in 1840 was sent to establish a new post at Fort Stikine which the Company had received (as noted elsewhere), in an agreement with the Russian Fur Company. With him went Eloisa and as Rae's assistant her brother John Jr., whose story has already been told.

In 1841 when her husband was sent to open and organize the first (and last) Company post in California, he preceded Eloisa, who planned to join him when he was established. She sailed down the coast in the controversial little steamer *Beaver*, and on it, March 21, 1841, gave birth to her second child, a daughter named for both the baby's father and her grandmother, Margaret Glen. Eloisa's first child, John, had been born in 1839, while they were still living at Fort Vancouver.

Eloisa and her new baby stopped at Nisqually where she stayed for three days with Mrs. John Work, wife of the factor there, one of the most reliable and capable of the Company officers. After partially regaining her strength, Eloisa went on to Fort Vancouver, carrying her baby on horseback as far as Cowlitz landing, then going by boat to her parents' home at the Fort. Where her little son, John, was during this time has not been clarified. Here she stayed until her husband sent for her to join him at

Yerba Buena, on San Francisco Bay. She, the baby, presumably little John, Dr. McLoughlin, and Governor Simpson made the trip together, as the two Company officers wished to inspect the new post.[22]

The next year, at Yerba Buena, a third child, Maria Louisa, was born to the Raes, and in 1845 a second son, Willie, or Billie, was born just a few days before his father's death. This child lived only a very short time and was buried in Yerba Buena, in the churchyard of the Mission Dolores.

Following the suicide of her husband, and allowing for the time lapse until the news reached Fort Vancouver, and for the necessary time to go by boat from the Fort to Yerba Buena, Eloisa's brother David came to take her and her three surviving children back to Fort Vancouver. Here the survivors of the McLoughlin and Rae families lived for several months until the move to a new home in Oregon City in January 1846.[23]

This beautiful and imposing home was built at Willamette Falls. Here Eloisa and the children lived comfortably in the spacious upstairs bedrooms and sitting rooms until she remarried, in 1850.

Maria Louisa, or Louisa, which she preferred to be called, seemed to be the favorite grandchild of Dr. McLoughlin. She recalled for Amos Bowman the pleasant life in his home at the Falls, the beautiful melodeon and the handsome mahogany chest of drawers her grandfather had given her. However, the former chief factor loved all three children and enjoyed the role of a proud and doting grandfather. A photograph, interesting for the intensity and solemnity of their faces, of Dr McLoughlin, Margaret, and Louisa exists in a folder in the Oregon Historical Society. He and Margaret McLoughlin seldom missed a school program in which the Rae children participated, sitting attentively and conspicuously near the front of the room[24]

In 1857 Margaret Glen, now sixteen, attended a private Catholic school, Notre Dame, in San José, California; Louisa apparently remained in Oregon City, where she attended Judge E. S. Shattuck's school.[25] She was very proud that her grandfather used her as his amanuensis from 1854 to 1857, when she was twelve to fifteen years old. His fingers were stiffened with arthritis, as he explained in a letter of January 1, 1857, to John Fraser of St. Mark, "You see, I cannot write and employ an emanuesis (*sic*), Miss Louisa Rae, my granddaughter." Four days later in another letter to the same cousin, Louisa proudly wrote the signature of the Doctor, and underneath "per Louisa M. Rae." In 1929 she recalled for Fred Lockley how "particular" the Doctor was about his letters, always having her write carefully by hand two copies of each letter, as he himself had always done, so that he would have one copy for his file. If she made a mistake or a blot, she had to copy the entire letter.[26]

Royal Family of the Columbia

At sixteen Louisa was married to Captain Josiah Myrick. The ceremony was performed May 1, 1858, by a future archbishop, Father François Norbert Blanchet. She was the mother of three children before she was twenty; a fourth child was born later. Josiah, Jr., Ida Rae, Elizabeth, and Winifred comprised the family. Josiah, Jr., had two daughters, both of whom were married, Maria to August Ferro and Elizabeth to C. L. Loomis, but there is no known record of children. Ida Rae died in 1902, presumably unmarried. Elizabeth and Winifred died in 1937 and 1947, respectively; neither was married.[27]

The father of this family, Captain Myrick, was a man of several business interests, including a skating rink, mining, and steamboats on the Willamette and Columbia, in association with Jacob Kamm and Captain J. C. Ainsworth, both prominent Portland pioneers.[28] Josiah Myrick had come from New Castle, Maine, via the Horn in the early 1850s. He died of pneumonia in 1906 while visiting the Connor Creek mines. According to the Portland *Oregonian* of December 30, 1906, services were to be held that day at the Myrick residence in northwest Portland.

The Myricks lived first in what is today the business center of Portland. According to *Samuel's Portland Directory* of 1873 (page 242) the Myrick residence was on the "N.W. corner Fifth and Pine." The Myrick business, the "Portland Skating Rink", was two blocks away on "Fourth between Ash and Pine." From here they moved to the handsome home at N.W. Johnson and Nineteenth, which they built in 1887. Typical of many of the late Victorian homes, it possessed a little less "gingerbread" than many. A number of photographs of other fine homes in the vicinity were taken from the third-floor porch of the Myrick house.[29]

A study of copies of the *Portland Directory*, successor of *Samuel's Portland Directory*, revealed that in 1936 the Myrick sisters, Elizabeth and Winifred, sole survivors, apparently, of the Myrick-McLoughlin families, lived at "1844 N.E. Johnson." The residence was razed some time after 1947, the year of Winifred's death.

In 1937 Winifred was the sole surviving child of her parents. In that year she gave to Archbishop the most Reverend Edward W. Howard a relic of her great-grandfather Dr. John McLoughlin. It was "a true piece of the cross for veneration and exposition" at the church of St. John the Apostle in Oregon City. This relic had been brought in 1847 by Father Blanchet from Rome, as a gift from Pope Gregory XVI to Dr. McLoughlin at the time he was made a Knight of St. Gregory (Civil Grade). It was considered his most prized and most precious possession.[30]

Louisa Rae Myrick was active in helping to organize the Oregon Historical Society, serving on its board of directors for several years. In 1901 she was reported present at the twenty-ninth reunion of the Oregon Pioneer Association.[31] This was the reunion at which her uncle David McLoughlin was speaker and an honored guest; he was said to have been a guest both in her home and in that of her sister, Margaret Wygant. Louisa was also a leader in helping restore her grandfather's old home to a semblance of its original appearance after it was moved up Singer Hill from the Falls to the Heights of Oregon City in 1909.[32] She and her husband were described as active in Trinity Episcopal Church. Louisa died in 1929 after a widowhood of twenty-three years.

Little is known of John Rae, the older brother of Louisa Myrick and Margaret Wygant. Born on February 3, 1839, at Fort Vancouver, it is recorded that as a very young man he visited his father's home in the Orkney Islands. He died on October 6, 1867, and was buried in Lone Fir Cemetery, in Portland.* There is no record that he was married.[33]

These meager recorded facts and a few pieces of his clothing, kilts, sporran, and hose, displayed in a glass case on the second floor of McLoughlin House, are all that remain of Eloisa and William Glen Rae's son, John.

Having discussed the descendants of Eloisa's daughter Louisa, it would seem logical at this point to discuss those of her other daughter by William Rae, Margaret Glen, but because so much more is known of Margaret's descendants, they will be reserved for later discussion. Mention should be made here of Eloisa's second family, although not a great deal has been recorded concerning them.

In 1850, after five years of widowhood, Eloisa was married to Daniel Harvey, a stable and respected man who was in charge of the McLoughlin mills and who had once been superintendent of the Hudson's Bay Company farm.

Eloisa and Daniel Harvey's family consisted of two sons, Daniel Jr. (1851-1897) and James William McLoughlin (1855-1895), and a daughter, Mary Angélique. Of Eloisa's second marriage only a few grandchildren have come to light. Daniel Jr. reportedly died a bachelor. A daughter of James W. McLoughlin Harvey, Matilda Eloisa (Lois), born in 1886, who became Mrs. George Deering of Washington, D.C., is a great-granddaughter of Dr. McLoughlin. Her aunt Mary Angélique became Mrs. Daniel Lehigh (sometimes written Leahy) and had three sons, Daniel Harvey, William Francis, and James Vincent.*

In the main hall of the first floor of the McLoughlin house is a large framed plat of Oregon City made by John McLoughlin, a gift from J. Vincent Lehigh, his great-grandson, in 1928. There is no known record of a generation or of generations beyond Mrs. Deering and her Lehigh cousins, although there are undoubtedly two or, more probably, three additional generations of descendants of Dr. John McLoughlin through Eloisa's second marriage.

*A visit to Lone Fir Cemetery, August 16, 1974, showed John Rae's tall gravestone toppled and broken by vandals, as were countless others.

*See reference note 40 at the end of the chapter.

Royal Family of the Columbia

Mrs. Deering came to light as a McLoughlin descendant in the late 1930s when she made several gifts to McLoughlin House as it was renovated. The principal gift was the large William Cogswell oil painting of her great-grandfather. Eloisa had left in her will all the daguerrotypes and other photographs to her son James William McLoughlin Harvey, who in turn passed them on to Matilda Eloisa (Lois) Harvey Deering, his daughter. Of interest is an ivory miniature portrait, said by Dr. Barker and by the Oregon Historical Society to be Dr. John, but by McLoughlin House and by other experts, including Mr. Wilmer Gardner, Oregon City jeweler and a member of the McLoughlin Memorial Association Board, identified as his brother, Dr. David McLoughlin. Regardless of whether the subject is Dr. John or Dr. David, it is believed that the miniature was made in Paris. In a McLoughlin folder in the Oregon Historical Society archives is an interesting photograph of Mrs. Deering studying the portrait of her great-grandfather or great-granduncle, whichever it may be.[34] (Other gifts of Mrs. Deering are mentioned in Chapter 19.)

In 1867 the Harvey family left the McLoughlin home at the Falls, moving to Portland. The next year Eloisa lost both her husband, Daniel Harvey, and her eldest son, John Rae. She herself died in 1884 at the age of sixty-seven.[35*]

A copy of *Samuel's Portland Directory* for 1873 listed, first, "Harvey, Daniel, res. cor. West Park and Alder" and directly under this reference, "Harvey, Mrs. E., widow" and, of course, the same address. That area today is occupied by small hotels, a jeweler's, a camera shop, a savings and loan, a cigar store and newstand, and a luggage shop. Nearby is a department store, while two or three blocks to the south is the main branch of the Multnomah County Library.

It is time now to revert to Eloisa's first marriage, and more particularly to her older daughter, Margaret Glen Rae, the child born in 1841 on the *Beaver*. It is her descendants who have been most successfully traced to the present, the 1970s, and, more specifically, to a baby girl, possibly the youngest of all McLoughlin descendants.

Louisa's older sister also was married to a man engaged in transportation, in 1858 or 1859. Like Josiah Myrick, Theodore Wygant, too, had come from the eastern United States, "walking oxen from Ulster County, New York, along the Oregon Trail," arriving finally in Oregon City, where he met Margaret Glen Rae, his future wife. For a time he was associated with Ben Holladay, the "Stagecoach King," managing part of his portage business at Celilo. He also became associated with the Oregon Railway and Navigation Company, which was later tied in with the Northern Pacific Railroad under German-born entrepreneur and financier Henry Villard.

---

*Mr. and Mrs. Harvey and their son James William McLoughlin share a gravestone in Lone Fir Cemetery. Also interred there are Eloisa's children Daniel Harvey Jr., Louisa Rae Myrick, Margaret Glen Rae Wygant, her daughter Alice McLoughlin Wygant Whidden, and Louisa's three unmarried daughters, Winifred, Elizabeth, and Ida.

All that is known of Theodore Wygant's forebears is that they "came from Kirkenwall, Scotland." Several were known to have served in the American Revolutionary War, presumably on the British side; at least one served under General Sir Henry Clinton. A picture of Mr. Wygant with several other "satellites" arranged around the great Henry Villard as the solar attraction shows a serious, full face, very hirsute, with heavy, exaggerated sideburns and large droopy mustache.[36]

The Theodore Wygants were "in the social swim" of Portland. Indeed, an elementary school and a street in northeast Portland bearing the Wygant name attest the importance of the bearers of the name.

One of the Wygant grandchildren, Mr. Thomas Marvin Whidden of Burlingame, California, remembers his grandfather as not caring to be around small children, but his grandmother Margaret as kind and affectionate and apparently enjoying the visits of her grandchildren. Mr. Whidden mentioned in passing that his grandmother and her daughter (his mother) did not see-to-eye on a number of issues.[37]

There were four Wygant children, two sons and two daughters. There is no record of the sons having children, but the two daughters, Alice McLoughlin and Nellie, produced a new generation: Nellie was married to Martin Winch. Their only child was Simeon Reed Winch, who was for a number of years business manager of the *Oregon Journal*. He, in turn, married Olivia Failing, member of a prominent Portland pioneer family, and they became the parents of two daughters, Nella Amelia, born in 1915, and Emily Failing, born in 1923.

In 1940 Nella was married to William D. McElroy. She is now living in Woods Hole, Massachusetts. Their two daughters, Mary Elizabeth and Ann Reed, both unmarried, live in Boston. Of their two sons, William Jr. and Thomas, the latter has a four-year-old daughter, Heather. The four McElroy children were born between the years 1942 and 1949.

Nella Winch's sister, Emily, wed Edward Nigel Baines early in 1955 and became the mother in 1955 and 1956 of David and Amanda Baines, who are now attending school in England. Mr. and Mrs. Baines live in Sparta, New Jersey.[38]

Following a divorce from Simeon Winch, Olivia Failing Winch died in 1942; Mrs. McElroy and Mrs. Baines have a younger half brother, Martin Tobin Winch, born in 1944 of their father's marriage to Mary Tobin, March 6, 1943. Martin, a graduate of Princeton University in 1966, and Carolyn Forbes were married in 1971 and are the parents of Paula Amelia, born July 28, 1972. The Winches live in Eugene, Oregon, where Mr. Winch is an attorney.[39]

Mrs. Simeon Reed Winch, née Mary Tobin, lives in Portland in the beautiful Northwest hills. It is she who has supplied a great deal of the preceding information.

Now reverting three generations to Alice McLoughlin Wygant, sister of Nellie, the ancestor of those just described: she and William Whidden were married

Royal Family of the Columbia

September 24, 1883. Their four children were twins, Rae Wygant and Lucy Mae, born in 1884; Austin Chamberlin, 1890; and Thomas Marvin, 1892.

Mr. Whidden, a member of the prominent New York architectural firm McKim, Meade, and White, came to Portland in 1882 to represent his firm in supervising the building of the Portland Hotel. Due to the financial collapse of Henry Villard, who was backing the hotel construction, the building stopped, and Mr. Whidden returned to New York in 1883, only to return west soon afterward to work with the new owner. This time he remained in Portland, severing his connection with McKim, Meade, and White, and in 1889 joined Ion Lewis, another eastern architect, in partnership, forming the firm Whidden and Lewis. He died in that great year of financial collapse, 1929.

Whidden and Lewis, in addition to Whidden's part in the Portland Hotel, were responsible for many of the fine homes in Portland built from 1890 to 1910, for the Portland City Hall, for several business buildings, and for college buildings on at least two campuses in the Portland vicinity. As was natural, they brought with them much of the eastern architectural style, which when combined with native northwestern architecture, resulted in a synthesis which became an entity in itself.

An example is the "Colonial Revival" of the Milton W. Smith house, in southwest Portland, reminiscent of homes of the eastern seaboard. Another, the Ayer house, on the southwest corner of northwest Nineteenth and Johnson, represents the sixteenth century English manor. Many others could be cited, several on that "elegant street of Portland", Nineteenth Street, but neither space nor the scope of this work permits. Suffice it to say, Whidden and Lewis promoted colonial and classical styles in building residences, and introduced Italian or "high" Renaissance for public and business buildings.

The first known Whidden had sailed from Portsmouth, England, to Portsmouth, New Hampshire, in 1662 with a land grant from Charles II. Among his more interesting and unusual early descendants was a grandson Samuel, who was fortunate enough to have a sturdy and redoubtable wife of six feet, four inches, who not only could, but often did, carry "hogsheads of Jamaica rum into the basement", according to present-day descendant Thomas Whidden; there were also in the early eighteenth century John and James, with heights of six feet, four and six feet, three, and weighing 265 and 255 pounds, respectively. Stephen Huse Whidden, Boston shipbuilder born in 1825 and dying in 1892, could not know that one hundred and ten years after his birth there would be a namesake who would live on the opposite side of the continent.

Mr. Whidden was, as might be expected, able to provide a more than comfortable standard of living for his family. His son Thomas Whidden has described his boyhood home as a mansion, situated near the present site of Lake Oswego High school* and near the Peter Kerr home, recently razed in building the Mountain Park development. He recalled a visit of his grandfather Theodore Wygant to his home, and that as his grandfather left he tripped over a cord which a gardener had carelessly left across the top of the concrete steps. Mr. Wygant's daughter and son-in-law (Alice and William Whidden) were greatly relieved to learn that it was principally his dignity that was damaged.

Thomas Whidden enjoyed visiting his grandparents, especially his grandmother, who could pass on to him anecdotes concerning her grandmother Margaret and her grandfather Dr. John McLoughlin. It made them seem closer to him than the far-distant great,great-grandparents they were and provided a continuity in their relationship. Mrs. Wygant could recall her grandparents clearly, for she was sixteen when Dr. McLoughlin died and nineteen when Mrs. McLoughlin died. She had lived with them for five years, one year at Fort Vancouver and four years in their beautiful Oregon City home, during the period between her father's death in 1845 and her mother's remarriage in 1850.

Tom recalls, too, his mother, Alice McLoughlin Whidden, who admitted that, yes, he did have some Indian blood, but a very small amount — only one-sixty-fourth. This infinitesimally small proportion was based on the premise that Mrs. John McLoughlin's mother was only half Indian, rather than a full Indian. Most historians hold to the latter view — that Margaret's mother was "a Chippewa woman," in which case Tom — and others of his generation descended from John and Margaret McLoughlin — must admit to a one-thirty-second proportion of Indian to white blood.

Tom Whidden, today more than eighty years old, is remarkably young; he walks briskly, climbs steep stairs without visibly huffing or puffing, and takes his teen-age grandson, Scott Whidden, on cross-country bus trips to Boston, to a Montana ranch, and on shorter excursions to his home-city, Portland, and to Seaside and other favorite spots of the scenic Oregon coast. In contrast to the staunch Presbyterianism and fervent Catholicism of his forebears, he is a faithful follower of Mary Baker Eddy and a practitioner of Christian Science, having taken it up some forty years earlier at age forty. He has described his life as being in two halves, with his embracing Christian Science as the watershed.

Tom has given the following information concerning his brothers and sister and his children and grandchildren, the "now generation" of McLoughlin descendants.

His twin brother and sister, born in 1884, followed similar life patterns, both dying in their thirties. Rae was a captain in the Reserve United States Medical Corps;

*Lake Oswego is a small town (about 18,000) built around Lake Oswego and located eight miles south of Portland. The high school was completed in 1951.

Royal Family of the Columbia

he joined the British Army Hospital unit as a volunteer before the United States entered the war, serving at a base hospital in Flanders. He was one of the first American officers to be wounded and was invalided home by way of London hospitals. He rested and recovered in the United States. He returned to service in Europe but died of pneumonia about a year later (1918). His sister, Lucy, was married twice and once divorced. She was active in supportive war work with the Red Cross and died during a pregnancy about a year after her twin brother's death.

Tom's other brother, Austin, died in 1966; he was a man of great energy and drive, in that respect resembling his famous indefatigable ancestor. Austin spent some time in Labrador with Dr. (Sir Wilfred) Grenfell, the famous medical missionary. Tom recalled Austin's bringing home as a souvenir a twenty-foot braided leather whip used in driving dog teams. He had only one child, Austin Jr., who died in 1949. Austin Jr.'s widow and three daughters, Patricia, Barbara, and Joanne, born in 1946 1947, and 1950, live in Lancaster, California.

Tom, youngest of the four children, spent his boyhood in Portland and vicinity until 1908, when he went east to attend Milton Academy, in Milton Massachusetts. He attended Harvard and has Bachelor of Science and Master of Science degrees from the University of California at Berkeley, earned in 1922 and 1923, after serving as naval ensign in the European theater during World War I.

Now a widower, he was married September 24, 1930 (his parents' forty-seventh wedding anniversary), to the former Linda B. Jockers, with whom he had two sons, Stephen Huse, born in 1935, and William Jockers, 1937, both living in Oakland, California.

Stephen is the father of two daughters, Stephanie Michelle and Shauna Marie, born in 1959 and 1962, and of a son, Gregory Scott, born in 1961. "Jock's" children are Shannon and Jocelyn, born in 1958 and 1962, respectively.

This résumé is of necessity brief, but the descendants of Dr. John and Margaret McLoughlin have been traced within unavoidable limitations to the present time, the 1970s. They are limited mainly to the children of the Chief Factor's second daughter, Eloisa, and, again, are restricted principally to the children of her first marriage, although a few descendants from the second marriage have been traced. The reason for this narrowed research is that there are no known records showing that Joseph and John Jr. had children; David's descendants have been traced, but only as far as 1951. Eliza's probably numerous descendants are unknown because she lived at so great a distance from the rest of her family, and because no known records were kept. But because Eloisa was close to her family both geographically and spiritually, almost perfect records have been kept. True, there are a few gaps, but most of the necessary statistics are accessible, and by writing, conversing, interviewing, reading, traveling, and researching, it is possible to "put it all together," or almost all of it, at least.

Alberta Brooks Fogdall

A certain diversity of pattern can be discerned in the descendants of the King of the Columbia: geographically they represent New Jersey, Massachusetts, California, Oregon, England, and, no doubt, other locales not recorded.

Professional versatility has been displayed, too, as various McLoughlin descendants have followed architecture, business, law, medicine, and journalism; some have engaged in business.

It is possible that Thomas M. Whidden at "eighty plus" is the oldest of John McLoughlin's descendants living today. At the other end of the life span, little Paula Winch of Eugene, Oregon, may be his youngest descendant. She is four times the great-granddaughter of the King of the Columbia and as such is perhaps its youngest princess.

Eloisa McLoughlin Rae Harvey, said to be her father's favorite.
Photo by Harrison Hornish, courtesy of Wayne Randolph, curator, McLoughlin House, Oregon City.

Royal Family of the Columbia

REFERENCES

CHAPTER 9

ELOISA, THE KING'S FAVORITE CHILD, HER FAMILY AND HER DESCENDANTS

1 For Example, Evelyn Sibley Lampman, *Princess of Fort Vancouver*.

2 Burt Brown Barker, *The McLoughlin Empire and its Rulers*, p. 127.

3 Richard G. Montgomery, *The White-Headed Eagle*, p. 108.

4 Barker, *op. cit.*, p. 96.

5 *Ibid.*, p. 198.

6 *Ibid.*, p. 196.

7 Eloisa McLoughlin Harvey, *Dr. John McLoughlin*, Ms., Bancroft Library, Archives, Oregon Historical Society. An interview by Amos Bowman, stenographer for H. H. Bancroft.

8 Fred Lockley, "Impressions and Observations of the *Journal* Man," *Oregon Journal*, September 19, 20, 21, 1919. (Microfilm, Central branch, Multnomah County Library, Portland, Oregon)

9 Harvey, *loc. cit.*

10 Eva Emery Dye, *McLoughlin and Old Oregon*, pp. 57-59.

11 Lampman, *op. cit.*, pp. 10-11.

12 *Ibid.*, p. 22.

13 *Ibid.*, p. 12.

14 Dye, *op. cit.*, p. 61.

15 John B. Horner, *Days and Deeds in the Oregon Country*, p. 83.

16 Montgomery calls the "leads" in this drama "Lady Calpo" and her daughter "Chowie", but more writers attribute these women to Chief Comcomly.

17 All of the material on Indian weddings and potlatches, on head-flattening, *etc.*, is taken from a combination of sources, including Montgomery, *The White-Headed Eagle;* Dye, *McLoughlin and Old Oregon; Robert Johnson, John McLoughlin;* and escpecially from Lampman, *Princess of Fort Vancouver;* T. D. Allen, *Troubled Border;* and Hermia Fraser, *Tall Brigade*.

18 Dye, *op. cit.*, p. 63.

19 H. H. Bancroft, *History of the Northwest Coast*, Vol. I, p. 36.

20 *Oregon Historical Quarterly* XLVIII p. 239.

21 T. C. Elliott, *Oregon Historical Quarterly*, 36 (1935), pp. 338-339. See notes 117 and 152. Chapter 4.

22 Mrs. Harvey, in the interview for the Bancroft Library, made no mention of the whereabouts of little John Rae during this time.

23 The materical concerning this period of Eloisa's life was recorded by Fred Lockley in a series of interviews of Eloisa's daughter Louisa Myrick, September 19, 20, 21, 1929. Mrs. Myrick was about eighty-seven at this time and her memory was probably not infallible.

24 Conversation with Nancy (Mrs. Charles) Gildea, Curator of McLoughlin House, November 16, 1972.

25 Lockley, *Columbia River Valley*, p. 64.

26 Barker, *op. cit.*, pp. 255, 257.

27 *Columbia River Vally*, *loc. cit.*

28 Joseph Gaston, Portland—its History and Builders, III, picture, p. 451.

29 Richard Marlett, *Nineteenth Street*, p. 44.

30 The *Oregon Journal*, April 15, 1938. Also, Barker, *op. cit.*, p. 320.

31 *Oregon Pioneer Association Transactions*, 1901, p. 16.

32 Oregon City *Enterprise-Courier*, April 28, 1967.

33 *Oregon Historical Quarterly*, Vol. 45, p. 86. Thomas M. Whidden's genealogical chart at the Oregon Historical Society gives his great-uncle's death date as 1879.

34 Barker, ed., "McLoughlin House." Also, author's visits to the House.

35 Barker, *loc. cit.*

36 Material and picture are found in a McLoughlin folder in the Oregon Historical Society Archives. The picture was reproduced from a copy of *West Shore* magazine of September 8, 1883, p. 199.

37 The material on Theodore Wygant and William Whidden came from letters of their grandson and son, Thomas Whidden, principally from those of March 16 and 23, 1973; and from interviews in San Francisco, December 22, 24, and 26, 1972; and in Portland, January 3, 1973.

38 Some of the material concerning Simeon Reed Winch, Martin Tobin Winch, Paula Amelia Winch, Nella Winch McElroy, and Emily Winch Baines and their children came in a letter from Mary Tobin Winch (Mrs. Simeon Reed Winch) of Portland, March 24, 1973.

39 *Ibid.*

40 A small book written by James Vincent Lehigh honoring his father, Daniel Francis Lehigh, today in McLoughlin House, is "dedicated to the memory of My Sweet Mother, Mary Angélique (Harvey) Lehigh, and My Dear Brothers, Daniel Harvey Lehigh and William Francis Lehigh." He described the wedding of his father and his mother (Eloisa's youngest daughter), which took place in Victoria, with Sir James Douglas, then Governor General of British Columbia, giving the bride in marriage. Mary Angélique Harvey Lehigh and her husband are buried beneath the altar of the Church of St. Mary the Virgin in San Francisco at Steiner and Union Streets.

The little book, entitled *Daniel Francis Lehigh,* was written in 1928-1929. Its contents were to appear in *Encyclopedia of American Biography,* published by the American Historical Society.

CHAPTER 10

WILLIAM GLEN RAE, THE PRINCESS' CONSORT

More than one historian has described Dr. John McLoughlin as an empire builder rather than as a fur trader.[1] Certainly he saw it as his responsibility to the Honourable Company to increase its influence by wise management and shrewd administration and by the extension of its power both to the north and to the south. In addition, as a patriotic British subject he saw this extension as the strengthening of Great Britain's claim to the Pacific Northwest when the boundary controversy would at last be settled.

The reaching north was accomplished principally by the addition of Fort Stikine and Fort Taku. To effect southward extension McLoughlin wanted to be innovative and establish a post in California — at Yerba Buena on San Francisco Bay. When he broached the subject to the Honourable Governor and Committee in London while on his 1838-1839 furlough, the high officials were amenable, even enthusiastic; Governor George Simpson was definitely not enthusiastic, nor even pleased, but since his London superiors seemed favorable, he agreed reluctantly with an "all right, we'll give it a try" attitude.[2]

Dr. McLoughlin had returned to Fort Vancouver from his 1838-1839 furlough in London with a sizeable increase in salary, due partly to his establishing a post in California — the first — as well as his added new responsibilities for the Puget's Sound Agricultural Company.[3]

Possibly the Chief Factor's choice of his son-in-law William Glen Rae to head the California post resembled nepotism (unless, as some historians feel, it was Governor Simpson who sent him), for he knew that Eloisa was extremely unhappy at Fort Stikine, "that miserable place," as she called it.[4]

With his innate astuteness the Doctor had no illusions as to the weaknesses of Rae's character, for he had advised Eloisa's husband — or, rather, warned him — when he had left for Fort Stikine the year before:

> You are going to a dangerous place, William; with Indians firmness and management can do anything. Avoid offense. Soothe irritation. Deal honestly. Be kind, be patient, be just, but remember Napoléon's motto, "Be Master." In a subject country always expect an attack. Look for it, prepare for it. Crush it. Trust nothing to chance.

These words of advice, born of McLoughlin's experience and wisdom, might be interpreted as encapsuling his philosophy, the creed which underlined his own policy with the natives. It also expressed his recognition of Rae's shortcomings and his resultant concern. It is only incidental that the admonition also revealed his own deep admiration for Napoléon, which he had possessed since boyhood: the insistence on instant obedience, the system of reward and punishment among the natives, and imperial vision of a vast domain (in McLoughlin's case, for England on the Pacific Coast), which also comprised his own philosophy.[5]

William Glen Rae has sometimes been labeled a mystery. His story, as it unwinds, reveals questions without answers. There is an element of mystery, too, in the absence of a picture or of a likeness of any kind extant; other than a silhouette on one of Eloisa's bracelets, displayed today at McLoughlin House, there is nothing. All it reveals is that he was "a young man of proud bearing and of clean, well-molded features."[6]

Both the Raes were probably delighted with the transfer to the South. The contrast with Fort Stikine must have been delightful beyond their fondest dreams. Eloisa recalled Yerba Buena as "a happy place". It was very small—only twelve houses, the Company store, and a sawmill. The "Spanish ladies" befriended her. Life was gay, with bull fights in the day time, dinners, suppers, and dances at night.[7]

In addition to far more pleasant surroundings, Yerba Buena provided the opportunity for Mr. Rae to prove himself, to provide proudly for his family. While Eloisa, their little son, John, and the new baby, Margaret, remained at Fort Vancouver, their husband and father established Company headquarters and prepared a home for the family at Yerba Buena.

Yerba Buena, later called San Francisco, was founded by William A. Richardson, who built the first home. The second house was built by Jacob Primer Leese, a man of influence, presumably, because his wife, Rosalie, was the sister of General M. G. Vallejo. Mrs. Leese and General Vallejo were aunt and uncle of Governor Juan B. Alvarado. Due to his prestigious connections Leese was able to acquire increasingly more of the choicest land. One piece of this fine land, 275 feet square, he sold for $4600 to Rae as Company headquarters.[8]

Eloisa recalled that her husband bought a block at the cove which contained a large house with a store on one side of the house. The building itself was described as of frame and adobe thirty feet by eighty feet on the waterfront. This was the nucleus of what later became the city San Francisco.[9]

The growth and development of the Hudson's Bay Company was significant in the growth and development of San Francisco. One writer pointed out that the history of Yerba Buena in the period of 1841-1845 was identical with the record of private transactions of the Hudson's Bay Company; the officers and servants of the Company composed nearly all of the total population of Yerba Buena during that time.[10]

Royal Family of the Columbia

Today this block bounded by Sacramento, Kearny, Clay, and Montgomery Streets, once held by the Hudson's Bay Company, 1841-1845, is occupied by several small businesses: restaurants, a laundry, a printing business, a pharmacy, import-export business, the California Human Resources Center (Chinatown-North Beach branch), and a television station, KABL, to mention just a few.[11]

At the end of 1841 the Company's bark *Cowlitz* carried a group including Governor Simpson, Eloisa, her father, and the children, John and Margaret, down the coast to Yerba Buena. The Chief Factor combined pleasure with business, enjoying his daughter's becoming settled with her family in their new home, and also taking pride in looking over the Company's new post with his son-in-law.[12]

The Governor was also looking over the post—critically; he had been completely unenthusiastic about the Yerba Bay venture from the beginning. Now he flew into a passion. Nothing was right: The location was poor; the United States was sure to win the territory south of the Columbia; Mexican red tape and unfair customs duties were economically unjust and unsound; Rae was extravagant—he had spent too much for the property; he was inefficient—his books were not kept up to date—*etc., etc.* By now the disagreement between the Chief Factor and the Governor had grown to almost feudal proportions. From California the two officials sailed on the *Cowlitz* to Honolulu to inspect Company installations there. It seems that they were hardly on speaking terms during the voyage; the White-Headed Eagle left on the bark *Vancouver* for the Pacific Northwest the very next day, February 13, 1842, after the *Cowlitz* arrived in Honolulu. From this time on, it is said that there was no further private correspondence between the two men who had developed such widely divergent viewpoints; nor did they ever meet again.[13]

For the next four years Chief Trader Rae worked under great handicaps. First, there was a drouth, resulting in general crop failures, so that he was unable to ship wheat to McLoughlin at Fort Vancouver in spite of contracts the Chief Factor had made to ship it to various consumers. In a letter to his father-in-law of October 14, 1841, Rae wrote, "This had been a most unfavourable Season for California that the Oldest inhabitants in it recollects. Since February 1840 there has been no rain."[14] (This was a period of twenty months without rain.) He had hoped, in spite of the drouth, to keep the Company in the black by dealing in tallow, hides, and furs, and had been encouraged by his success, for by the end of 1842 his operations had recovered from the 1841 deficit of 900 pounds.[15]

Second, he had difficulty in paying for casks for salting beef; he had to write to Fort Vancouver to ask for authority to draw on London for 100 pounds annually, as it is "absolutely necessary". He added, "In conclusion I have only a remark that whether my proceedings meet your approbation or not, my desire has been to promote the Company Interests and if I have failed to do so it has arisen from a mistaken view, or because I do not fully understand the ulterior intentions of the Company regarding the trade in this Country."[16] This last clause is probably the crux of Rae's whole problem and the reason for later events; the letter is typical of many which he wrote, for he needed constant reassurance and detailed instructions, which, unfortunately, he did not receive.

A third and perhaps the principal difficulty with which Rae had to contend was Simpson's intense disapproval of the Yerba Buena project, previously mentioned. Both McLoughlin and Douglas were forbidden by Governor Simpson to "waste" their time visiting Yerba Buena again, but to "make better use" of their time at their own duties in the Columbia Department![17] Going even further, in 1842, he ordered Dr. McLoughlin and Rae to close the post, to have the buildings vacated, business dealings terminated, staff and family gone by the end of 1843. McLoughlin, resentful of the ultimatum, procrastinated in following the order.[18] Unforseeably, the procrastination resulted in tragedy.

Fourth, because of the drouth, potential customers had no cash. Since the Company policy was cash or barter, but no credit, the Californians traded with ships from Boston where they were allowed to buy on credit.

On August 28, 1843, William Rae, in a letter to William Smith, Secretary of the Honourable Hudson's Bay Company, London wrote:[19]

> By a letter received from Chief Factor McLoughlin dated 29th May last I am directed to address you for the information of their Honors and to communicate my opinion regarding the California Trade.
>
> Sir George Simpson is so decidedly opposed to the Company's carrying on business in this Country that my ideas on the subject would have little effect on their Honors....

He continued that he must have a requisition for this place from Fort Vancouver. The prospects here at present are by no means good....no Grain, the Cattle are poor, the people...will not kill them and the wheat Crops have generally failed."[20] It seems that he was indicating that his opinion was worthless due to the Governor's opposition; equally, he did not wish to become involved in the controversy between Sir George and the Chief Factor, though presumably he would have had a feeling of loyalty to his father-in-law.

Nearly a year later, July 4, 1844, more than six months after the date Simpson had ordained for closure of the post, the Chief Factor was writing to the Honourable Governor and Committee in London lamenting the lack of communication which hampered Rae, due to Simpson's hostility and opposition.[21]

A combination of factors—instability, weakness, lack of direction from his superiors, lack of self-confidence, a haunting fear of failure[22]—all led to additional, contributing factors: heavy drinking, getting into debt to the rumored amount of $30,000, involvement (undocumented) with "a Spanish Senorita," and, most foolish of all, entanglement in political intrigue, in which he allegedly furnished the Californians with arms and money in November and December (1844) "to enable them to expel the Mexicans from the Country."[23]

It is understandable that a synthesis of reasons and causes could culminate in the tragedy of January 19, 1845. An official report fifteen months later, April 17, 1846, from Thomas O. Larkin, United States Consul at Monterey, to James Buchanan, Polk's Secretary of State, stated succinctly, "Mr. Rea (sic) Agent for the Hudson's Bay Company for their Establishment in San Francisco shot himself soon after the Californians rose against General (Manuel) Micheltorena."[24]

The report of his wife, or, rather, of his widow, related the tragedy in more detail. In her "Recollections" she made no mention at all of her husband's suicide, saying simply "...after my husband's death...." However, in a letter to her father, which he incorporated into a report to the London headquarters of the Company, July 19, 1845, exactly six months following the suicide, she was more graphic. Eloisa wrote her father that for two days preceding his "putting a period to his existence" her husband was "employed in writing," but later destroyed the letters he had written. He had told her repeatedly that he was in trouble and had not slept for several nights. When Eloisa, who was still weak from giving birth to a child just a few days before, asked what the troubles were, he replied there were several, but the principal one was hostility of "the Foreigners" to the Company: that they were going to attack him that same day, that they would "tie him and beat him to death." He added that all he cared about was that his wife and children not be harmed. He preferred to kill himself rather than to be beaten and abused. She had protested, asking what would happen to his family. Also, it was sin to kill oneself. He agreed, but said he couldn't help it. He gave her some business papers to keep and went into the next room. She tried, painfully and slowly, to follow him and at the door saw him put a pistol to his head. It didn't go off; she fainted and he took her back to her bed, promising her he would not kill himself, but a short time later did so.[25]

News of the suicide caused excitement up and down the coast, arousing much conjecture as to reasons that lay behind it, but the cause remained a mystery. If Eloisa knew, she did not make the reasons known. Dr. McLoughlin, too, "kept mum," taking care of the papers Rae left for him until he could turn them over to proper Company authorities.[26]

What sort of man was Chief Trader William Glen Rae, son-in-law of the prestigious Dr. John McLoughlin? His instability, weakness, feeling of insecurity, etc., have been discussed. Something of his character was revealed as he strove to uphold the character of John Jr., his unfortunate brother-in-law. One cannot help inferring that he, out of feeling of generosity and sympathy for his father-in-law, was over-complimentary to John in letters he wrote, in order to uphold the Chief Factor's defense of his son. From Yerba Buena, April 20, 1843, he wrote to Dr. McLoughlin:

> I never had and never can have a more sober, steady or better assistant than the late John McLoughlin was—he was most attentive to his duty in the Trade shop or wherever else his services were required—I saw him intoxicated only once and that was on Christmas night....I never saw the late Mr. John McLoughlin worse of liquor but once—nor did I ever see him punish the men unless they richly deserved it....[27]

In another letter to William Smith he wrote to John, "...(he) could not have been more strict afterwards (after Rae left?) at Stikine than I was whilst there and then it was necessary (to punish the men). We had some of the great Scoundrels in the Indian Country to deal with."[28]

William Heath Davis described Rae as "tall, handsome and much of a gentleman." Rae also kept a "Table always finely supplied with the best of everything."[29]

In a letter to Governor Simpson, March 18, 1838, James Douglas described both John Jr. and Rae as "stout men" and felt that both were good men at Stikine.[30] One evaluation was that John Jr. rarely drank, but that Rae drank heavily.[31]

There were numerous loose ends of Company business to be tied. Again quoting from the letter of Thomas Larkin, United States Consul, to Secretary of State Buchanan, "Mr. Mactavish replacement for Rea (sic) was to ship the furs and hides, was to sell the building for $5,000 and to sail per the next Vessel return to the Oregon with the Body of the late Agent, his Widow and children. Mrs. Rea is a daughter of Dr. McLaughing (sic) princaple Factor and Agent of the Company Establishment at Fort Vancouver...."[32]

(Taking "the Body" to the "Oregon", however, did not take place, as a later paragraph will reveal.)

The building Rae had purchased was sold to Millies and Howard, merchandisers. For one year it was rented as the United States Hotel for $36,000; it burned in the great fire of May 4, 1851.[33]

In 1854 a bizarre if not downright ghoulish discovery was made. While city laborers were digging a sewer trench along Clay Street near Montgomery they were taken aback to unearth a casket "with oval windows in its sides to see a well preserved corpse of a young man amid the tatters of a coffin lining." Pre-Gold Rush pioneers identified the body as that of William Glen Rae.

Records showed that he had been buried in a garden at the rear of his home. As the city grew and became less pastoral in character, the home and garden disappeared, resulting in this weird discovery nine years after his death.[34]

Royal Family of the Columbia

At the time of this strange event, 1854, Eloisa had been married for four years to Daniel Harvey and had begun to rear a second family. Just what happened to Mr. Rae's body has not been recorded; probably it was re-buried in a San Francisco cemetery.

Alberta Brooks Fogdall

REFERENCES

CHAPTER 10

WILLIAM GLEN RAE, THE PRINCESS' CONSORT

1 Philip H. Parrish, *Historic Oregon,* p. 86.

2 David Lavender, *Land of Giants,* p. 210.

3 E. E. Rich, *The Hudson's Bay Company,* II, p. 689.

4 Eloisa McLoughlin Rae Harvey, "Recollections," *Dr. John McLoughlin's Letter Book,* Bancroft Library, Mr., Transcript in Archives, Oregon Historical Society.

5 A. S. Marquis, *Dr. John McLoughlin* (pamphet), pp. 28, 29.

6 Robert O'Brien, "Riptides," San Francisco *Chronicle,* May 28, 1950, Archives, California Historical Society.

7 Harvey, "Recollections," *loc. cit.*

8 Anson Blake, The The History of a Montgomery Street Lot in Yerba Buena," *California Historical Society Quarterly,* II, pp. 69-71.

9 Harvey, "Recollections," *loc. cit.*

10 Alice Maloney, "The Hudson's Bay Company in California," *Oregon Historical Quarterly,* 31 (1936), p. 17.

11 Visit to and study of this block, December 24, 1972.

12 Richard G. Montgomery, *The White-Headed Eagle,* p. 284.

13 H. H. Bancroft, *History of the Northwest Coast,* II, p. 658. Lavender *op. cit.,* p. 212.
    Blake, "The Hudson's Bay Company in San Francisco," *California Historical Society Quarterly,* 28 (1929), pp. 104-105.

14 Letters of W. G. Rae to McLoughlin, October 14, 1841, Archives, California Historical Society.

15 O'Brien, *op. cit.,* June 1, 1951, Archives, California Historical Society.

16 Letters of Rae, *loc. cit.,* Archives, California Historical Society.

17 Blake, *op. cit.,* pp. 246-247.

18 Lavender, *op. cit.,* p. 214.

19 Maloney, *op. cit.,* p. 18.

20 Letters of Rae, *op. cit.,* August 28, 1843, Archives California Historical Society.

21 Blake, *op. cit.,* pp. 250-251.

22 O'Brien, *loc. cit.,* Archives, California Historical Society.

23 Letter from James Buchanan, Secretary of State, to Thomas O. Larkin, United States Consul at Monterey, October 17, 1845, *California Historical Society Quarterly,* V. p. 299.

24 Letter from Thomas Larkin to James Buchanan, April 17, 1846, p. 304.

25 John McLoughlin's report to Hudson's Bay Company, July 19, 1845, Photostat, Archives, California Historical Society.

26 *Ibid.*

27 Letter from W. G. Rae to John McLoughlin, Esquire, April 20, 1843, Archives, California Historical Society.

28 Letter from W. G. Rae to William Smith Esquire, August 27, 1843, Archives, California Historical Society.

29 William Heath Davis, *Sixty Years in California,* pp. 116, 119.

30 Letters from James Douglas to Governor George Simpson, March 18, 1838, *California Historical Society Quarterly,* 28, (1929), p. 107.

31 Jane Tipton, *John McLoughlin, Chief Factor of Hudson's Bay Company at Fort Vancouver,* Ms., p. 21.

32 Letter, Larkin to Buchanan, *op. cit.,* p. 305.

33 Blake, *op. cit.,* pp. 246-247.

34 O'Brien, *op. cit.,* December 15, 1950.

CHAPTER 11

DAVID———THE KING'S WANDERING,
FRUSTRATED SON

The youngest child of Dr. and Mrs. John McLoughlin was David, undoubtedly the namesake of his father's only brother, Dr. David McLoughlin. He was, except for his mother, the longest-lived of the immediate family, dying at eight-two in 1903. His father had died at seventy-three, his mother at eighty-five, Eloisa at sixty-seven, John was thirty, Joseph about thirty-nine, Tom McKay approximately fifty; Eliza's death date has not been recorded.

As the "baby" of the family he was reported to be a rather naughty child who misbehaved in John Ball's schoolroom at the Fort and whom Eloisa with all the superiority of her three years' seniority was called upon to curb.[1] Yet as an adult it was he who helped his sister and her children when tragedy struck.

Born at Fort William, February 11, 1821, while his father was in London in connection with the Northwest Company's merger with the Hudson's Bay Company, he may have come to the Columbia with his family in 1824, or he may have come with his mother and Eloisa (and possibly John and Joseph) a year or so later, depending upon which historian's version one prefers.

His very early education was probably at the Fort Vancouver school, for the Chief Factor saw to it that there was a school for the children of Company employees, as well as for Indian children who wished to attend. Possibly he attended a school in or near Québec, as John had, under Dr. Fraser's supervision, although none of the family letters authenticates this possibility.[2] Furthermore, he himself, when in his eighties, stated in his "Correspondence" that he stayed with his parents until 1833, when he went to Paris.[3]

In 1833 the Doctor sent David to Paris to be in the care of his Uncle David and to be with his brother John, who was studying medicine under his uncle's direction, but it was not until February 1, 1836, that there was a clue as to David's whereabouts. In an extract of a letter from Chief Factor McLoughlin to Chief Trader John McLeod on that date, David's father, after mentioning that his brother had sent young John home for "Extravagance," added, "My youngest son is, I believe, at Addiscombe College preparing to go to the East Indies."[4] Thirteen days later in a letter to his cousin John Fraser, son of Simon, Dr. McLoughlin explained, "...and My Brother writes that he proposes to Educate him (David) for the Engineer Department and send him out to India. And I have written *to desire he will do as my Brother Wishes*[5] (italics added)".

This was, of course, at a period of history when almost everyone but the young person himself decided what he was going to be and to do. In the case of John, even of

Alberta Brooks Fogdall

Dr. David, and, most surprising, of Dr. John himself, relatives were, figuratively, at least, shaking their heads and saying "he" was not "doctor material." Examples follow: Alexander Fraser, writing to his brother, Dr. Simon Fraser (before their feud), on July 20, 1808, stated, "I did not write to John McLoughlin the last spring. He will probably take the Huff and be silent. ...What and how to dispose of him you are best able to tell."[6] Among several statements doubting the wisdom of David's (Dr. John's brother) becoming a doctor, one written from Fort William, August 2, 1809, by Dr. John to Simon is this: "I am perfectly of your Opinion that my Brother David might have been employ'd to much better advantage than as a surgeon however since he is gone so far it is too late for him to retract...as for me I think that since he is about his Studies he ought to complete them...."[7] Then there was John Jr., illustration *par excellence* of troubled, maladjusted youth. Dr. Simon, writing to his nephew Dr. John, April 20, 1827, spoke of John Jr. "...I do not think he would Succeed as a Physician, he would have to go thro a long course of studies these boys (half-breeds?) are remarkable for want of steadiness and application...I would advise you purchasing an Ensigncy for him. I think he would make a good soldier he is bold and quick in his motions...."[8]

And so it was also for young David. Dr. David "decided" that his nephew should be an engineer; David spent several years in training for this work. Then, as the reader will soon learn, he was not allowed to make use of the training. The time he had spent in his special education was wasted.

According to David in his "Correspondence," written in 1900-1901, he was at a preparatory school near London "boning up" for the entrance examination to Addiscombe College, the Royal Military College for training men for East Indian service. He passed one examination, then a second, after which, on December 11, 1838, he was commissioned an ensign and was assigned to Fort William, in Calcutta.[9]

The Chief Factor left for London on furlough in the spring of 1838 and after his meetings at No. 3 Fenchurch Street, Company headquarters, he spent the winter of 1838-1839 in Paris with his brother, Dr. David. Apparently young David joined them. One writer described the situation in this way: David's father was both amazed and delighted at his son's height and at his handsome appearance in his scarlet uniform. He hardly looked like the twelve-year-old boy who had left Fort Vancouver six years earlier. David was eager to go to his assignment in Calcutta, but Dr. John had other plans for him. By now he knew that his son John Jr. had been sent home in disgrace by Dr. David. Possibly the Chief Factor felt that his youngest child should replace his older brother as "heir" to the Kingdom of the Columbia. David was not compliant. The "Indian color mounted in his cheeks (always blame it on the Indian blood!)" and he tried to explain that he felt there was no future for him in the Oregon Country—that Governor Simpson would choose his own leaders and high officials, that he, David, would have no opportunity for advancement. His father,

Royal Family of the Columbia

though displeased, kept his temper and pointed out firmly and proudly that he had been most successful at the conferences recently completed in London, had been granted a sizeable salary increase and additional responsibilities; too, he reminded David that he himself had selected most of his key subordinates and would continue to do so. David was unconvinced and the decision hung fire for a time. Then as Dr. David joined the council he agreed with his brother; he felt that his namesake had great potential and would achieve more success and prestige in the Columbia Department working with his father then in beginning a career in the army. Finally, overpowered by the two older men, whose judgment he felt was trustworthy, he agreed, and returned with his father to America early in 1839.[10]

It is not so strange that the Chief Factor wanted David with him—selfish, perhaps, but understandable; he had been tremendously disappointed in John Jr.; perhaps he could help David to become a respected and significant force in the Honourable Company.

What is difficult to comprehend, however, was Dr. David's about-face. After all, it was he who had earlier "decided" on his nephew's career. Now he was negating his own judgment. Neither of the Drs. McLoughlin could foresee the result of David's disappointment and frustration.

By May 1839 father and son were in Montréal. While the Chief Factor transacted business with Governor Simpson and other Company officials, David may have visited relatives at Rivière-du-Loup or elsewhere on the St. Lawrence. Apparently neither Dr. John nor David visited Dr. Simon Fraser at Terrebonne, near Montréal, for on February 24, 1830, from Fort Vancouver, Dr. McLoughlin wrote to his uncle apologizing for not calling when he had been in the Frasers' vicinity; "I have the pleasure to inform you that I safely arrived at my old quarters on the 17th Oct last and I much regret that my Business would not allow me in my Visit to the Civilised World to spend a longer time in the Society of my Relations...."

As they had crossed the Continent Dr. John attended a council of the Northern Department of Rupert's Land on June 6 at the Red River Settlement (near the present city of Winnipeg), and managed to secure a clerk apprenticeship for David; he also took part in making plans for taking possession the next year of Fort Stikine, a post on the 350-mile coastal strip leased from Russia.[11]

For a short time the Chief Factor had two sons working with him; John left the next April (1840) with Eloisa and William Glen Rae and others to take possession of Fort Stikine. Montgomery pictured David standing on the shore with his parents and watching his brother, sister, and brother-in-law taking off for a new adventure, while he, "not yet reconciled to his lot," was filled with envy and with regret that he was left behind.[12]

David missed John. Apparently the two young men had done well working in the Company stores at the Fort; at least their father so indicated to Dr. Fraser in an

Alberta Brooks Fogdall

October 24, 1840, letter: "...they were as attentive and smart at work as most young men...young men ought to be Kept Employed As certainly most Young Men are ruined by not being Kept Busy as Idleness is the Root of all evils...."[13]

John Minto, later a member of the Oregon Legislature, told how in 1845 he had helped bring the cattle of two members of the 1844 immigration party. He recalled reaching Fort Vancouver as the bell tolled for the "business of the day." Among the young men in "official positions at the Fort, David McLoughlin was conspicuous for his broad shoulders and suppleness combined." David began a conversation with Minto, asking his opinion of claim-jumping. Minto described him as a fine young man practicing to protect his father's rights in Oregon City. Minto saw him again in 1861-1862 when he was taking an opinion poll on "union or disunion." He reported David uninterested in political issues and that he was dressed in old work clothes of "Hudson's Bay Company days."[14]

Someone, an "old settler", described David as leading an "easy life" after his return from Europe, assisting his father in the Company store; he was quick in math, occasionally working on the accounts. He was described as "finely formed, erect, but lacking the energy and executive ability of his father."[15]

David, according to his own memory, worked ten years at Fort Vancouver as a clerk. In a letter of March 19, 1843, he wrote his cousin John Fraser that he was alone with his father and mother. (John had been murdered the year before; Eloisa was with her husband in Yerba Buena; and Joseph presumably was farming in the Willamette Valley.) In 1844-1845 he had gone on a trapping expedition in southern Oregon and California, according to another letter to John Fraser, March 15, 1845. After the closing of the Company post at Yerba Buena in 1845 he worked in the California gold fields. After resigning from the Honourable Company in 1849, he mined in Idaho and also in British Columbia for "a number of years." At one time he was appointed Constable at Wild Horse, in British Columbia. After his father's death in 1857, feeling there was really no place left for him in Oregon City, he had left, married "about 1866," rejoined the Hudson's Bay Company and operated a Company store in British Columbia and in Idaho for six years. He had also worked in a store of Francis Pettygrove, a merchant from New England.[16] More specifically, his father had bought a partnership for him in the Pettygrove store for $20,000.[17]

Apparently David did very well in the gold fields. According to another letter to John Fraser (March 18, 1849), he told of making $20,000 in gold dust in five months. He had hired "large numbers of Indians...for a year."[18]

A traditional story, called aprocryphal by more recent historians, was told by (Mrs.) Eva Emery Dye, an early (1900) biographer of John McLoughlin: David fell in love with the daughter of an English sea captain while the vessel was anchored in the river off Fort Vancouver; he wooed and won her, but both fathers were opposed and refused permission, the Chief Factor on the vague grounds of "religious scruples," the

218

Royal Family of the Columbia

Captain because David was one-fourth Indian. Discouraged, David said he would never marry a white woman, but would marry a squaw. He went to Northern Idaho, Porthill, near the Canadian border, married an Indian girl, reared a large family, and went native. On 160 acres of land given his wife by the United States government he built a large log house for his family and lived there until his death in 1903.

Most of the story was considered apocryphal because he did not marry until 1865 or 1866, sixteen or seventeen years after his supposed romance with the captain's daughter, which lapse of time could scarcely be described as "on the rebound."

At least the last part of Mrs. Dye's story was correct, for David did marry an Indian girl, Annie Grizzly, daughter of Chief Grizzley, a Kootnia (Kootenai or Kutenai) Indian. They became the parents of eight daughters, and of one son who was born in 1877 and lived until 1951. Since he died a bachelor there were no grandchildren of David's with the McLoughlin name. Only three of the daughters married, each marrying a white man; all except one of their daughters also married white men. Annie Grizzly McLoughlin died in 1897.

Putting together information provided in 1950 by both David's second-youngest daughter, Sarah McLoughlin Rogerson, born in 1885, and by her daughter Blanche Rogerson Hobbs, born in 1916, there were at that time thirty-nine of David's descendants living, ranging from three daughters and his only son, to grandchildren, and to great-grandchildren, the two youngest both born in 1949.[19] Now, in the 1970s, the likelihood of any of his children still being alive is remote, while the great-grandchildren are now undoubtedly themselves parents, providing a generation of David's great-great-grandchildren and three-times great-grandchildren of John McLoughlin.

Mrs. Hobbs claimed that her grandfather, in spite of "going native," was extremely methodical, keeping careful records in the family Bible, which unfortunately was lost in a fire.[20]

Her father, Mrs. Rogerson said, denied categorically the story of the romance with the captain's daughter. He never talked with his family of his years in Europe; they would have had no inkling of any of his past except that they overheard occasional conversations with strangers. He was the only educated man in the small town, was generous with his time, listening sympathetically to the troubles of people who came to him for help, and offering suggestions. He was highly respected as a man of peace. As the first teacher in Porthill he apparently donated his services in educating the children of the community. In addition, he kept the first weather records in Porthill. He was much missed when he died, his death leaving a gap never completely filled.[21]

A most unusual and interesting event took place in Portland in 1901. After more than forty years of absence from "civilization" David returned to Oregon and to Portland as the honored guest of the Oregon Historical Society and the Oregon

Pioneer Association. The story unfolds by means of a series of letters between David and George H. Himes, who held various offices in both organizations. David's communications are diffcult to read, written on small paper, overflowing the margins, tops and bottoms, or occupying tiny paper scraps of various shapes.

Apparently it had occurred to Mr. Himes and to others that the opportunity to collect information concerning Dr. John McLoughlin from a primary source depended mainly on David, who was his only surviving child. People were amazed that he was even still living, for he had not been heard of for many years.

However, according to Early Deane in the Sunday *Oregonian,* October 17, 1965, Mr. Himes had been assisted by David in 1898 in finding the exact location of the HBC Fort Vancouver. David was seventy-seven years old at this time.

The following material has been taken from the archives of the Oregon Historical Society:

The first letter was probably that of August 6, 1899, for it seems to be a "feeler." After mentioning a pamphlet which he enclosed, and promising to send more as they became available, he mentioned having seen David's nieces (Eloisa's daughters, Margaret Glen Rae Wygant and Maria Louisa Rae Myrick) and having walked with them to the old McLoughlin home down at the Falls. Having dispensed with the social amenities, he came to the point of the letter: The Historical Society was hoping to gather all possible information concerning John McLoughlin, "whose memory was very dear" to him (Mr Himes). Did David have any material he could send to the Society? It wanted very much to obtain material for permanent preservation.

The reply, which came from "Port Hill, Kootenai, Idaho," dated August 15, thanked Mr. Himes for the letter.

...also the Pamphlet containing kind and true references to my Father which causes overwhelming feelings to spring up within me that can't be expressed or understood...It does me honor to think that the people of Oregon do now appreciate the Kindly deeds he use (*sic*) to bestow on them and with the other hand giving them paternal care, encouraging, guiding, and guarding the early industrial life in Oregon with all his energy—in truth, and *least to say of him* he was a Christian of the highest type...receiving only abuse and detraction, his claim reserved and given to some institute were his rewards—I am glad to see good and kindly feelings to spring up among them expressed openly of my Father's good deeds.

David continued, saying that all of Dr. McLoughlin's reports to the Hudson's Bay Company in London, now in their archives, contained descriptions of the Oregon Country and of his love and admiration for it. He closed by offering "to do with pleasure anything to enhance" Mr. Himes's project.

Royal Family of the Columbia

A letter, missing, evidently invited David to come to Portland in June for Pioneer Day, June 14 (1901) to honor his father. It wasn't until March 5, 1901, that Mr. Himes sent a questionnaire for David to fill out. He asked also to write him the distance between Port Hill and Spokane and Port Hill to a railroad. The latter information was needed to raise funds for his visit.

It is not only surprising, but sad, that David from necessity left so much of the questionnaire blank, for there seems revealed in those blanks David's lack of knowledge of his own heritage, the lack of communication which must have existed between father and son, parents and child. He gave his mother's maiden name as Bruce, rather than Wadin, the latter name used by all writers except those who have based their material upon David's own writing. Left unanswered were names of both maternal and paternal grandparents, as if he knew very little either of his Fraser or of his McLoughlin relatives and ancestors. Surprisingly, he mentioned attending school in St. Cloud, a suburb of Paris, a statement no other writer has made. He described his mother as one-fourth Chippewa. The proportion of Indian to white blood in her veins still seems a subject for controversy. Most writers, however, stress her straight black hair, black eyes, and coppery skin, which seem more congruous with one-half than with one-fourth Indian blood.

Repeatedly he urged his Portland correspondents—others than Mr. Himes were writing him as June 14 drew nearer—to be sure to address his mail to Port Hill, Idaho, not Port Hope, Montana.

Two letters were written by Mr. Himes on May 16. One contained more questions, which David answered in a letter of May 25. The other asked David to be in Portland by June 12 so that he could rest before Pioneer Day, two days later. He also informed David that they were sending him a complete outfit of clothing, as well as money for fare and other expenses, and assuring him that this fact was known only to the board of directors of the Oregon Historical Society. He continued

Now I do not want you to feel that this is a matter of Charity. Poverty is inconvenient, but it is no crime. Whatever is done for you is done for the sake of honoring the name you bear, as the son of your father—a man whose kindly acts toward pioneers will be remembered through all coming time and whose name will grow brighter and brighter the more it is known.

The letter from Himes written on May 29 was more specific and detailed, informing David that a suit and a pair of shoes were ready and would be sent Saturday, June 1, or Monday, June 3, and a train ticket on the S. P. and S. (Seattle, Portland, and Spokane) railroad.

David was also requested to bring any relics whatever of Dr. McLoughlin's, or anything that had any relation to the former Chief Factor. Also, would he please bring any Indian relics of any kind, metal, bone, stone—or did he know the whereabouts of any? It sounds as if the writers were desperate; certainly they were not being exactly selective. Another request: Would he please "jot down" any reminiscences he could recall of his father—also any recollections of James Douglas, Peter Skene Ogden, and other close associates of the "King of the Columbia"?

On June 3 Mr. Himes wrote that the clothes were sent "last Saturday." Enclosed he would find a postal order for $16.00. He advised David to buy round trip tickets. "You can save a little."

Again David was reminded to bring a photo or to have one taken on his arrival in Portland; Mr. Himes reassured him that he would be met in Portland and asked him to be sure to telegraph as he left Spokane.

On June 11 a Mr. William Ryan of Port Hill (Porthill) wrote a letter on Pacific Hotel (Spokane) stationery:

By request of the friends of David McLoughlin I accompanied him from Porthill, Idaho, to Spokane and took charge of the $16.00 you sent him for expenses. Of this I expended for him the following sums:

Fare from Portland to Spokane $5.10	
Three meals 1.05	$6.15
Bed at Pacific Hotel 75 cents shirt 1.00	
Underclothes 1.00	2.75
Necktie 25 cents Handkerchief .75 cents	1.00
Telegram 55 cents	.55
Lunch to take on train 50 cents	.50
	——————
	$10.95

The balance of $5.05 I will give him with his ticket after I put him on the train for Portland. The old gentleman has lived in the woods so long that he is helpless as a child in a city.

Hoping the Historical Socity and Mr. McLoughlin may be mutually pleased with the meeting, I am..

etc. etc.

It is easily understandable under the unusual circumstances that David would be nervous. How could he not be? Aptly labeled "Oregon's Rip Van Winkle," it is remarkable that he was able to give an address, which was apparently acceptable, even if not outstanding. He told of his pleasure in being in Portland, recalled earlier days "when all this Country was a vast Forest uninhabited except by the wild and untutored redmen." He recalled the city of Portland as "nothing but a dense Forest underbrush." He became emotional. "Here today after an absence of forty-two years…I hesitated when asked to come both on account of my age and my long absence, which…unfitted me to mingle with people accustomed to the habits of civilized life." He thanked the Historical Society for honoring his father through him.

It would be unreasonable to imagine that having lived "in the wilds" for forty-two years he would have a photograph of himself. The desire of the Historical Society to have a tangible souvenir of David's visit materialized in a photograph made of him at the home of François Xavier Matthieu, who had come to Oregon nearly sixty years before with the first sizeable influx of immigrants in 1842. He had arrived penniless and had been given eighteen dollars worth of merchandise by the trusting and beneficent Chief Factor.[22] Understandably he became one of John McLoughlin's staunchest admirers. Also in the picture was Sidney Moss, a prominent pioneer and member of the Oregon Pioneer Association. The photograph, made at the Matthieu home, showed all three gentlemen, of whom David much the tallest of the three even though stooped, leaning on canes, Mr. Moss supporting himself on two canes.[23]

On July 4 the *Oregonian* carried a story that David would leave that night to return to his home: "I return to my home up there in the Panhandle of Idaho with very kindest feelings toward the people of the Willamette Valley. My old pioneer friends have entertained me right royally and I am glad to find so many of them in good health after my thirty (forty?) years' absence."[24]

On July 23 David wrote his proper "thank-you note." His words showed that he had been impressed by the entire experience; he noted especially "so many people" and the crowded condition of the cars (trains). A month later a letter dated August 13 repeated his pleasure, that he had a "beneficial time" in Portland and that he would send $10 "as soon as I can," for what reason is not known. He inquired how "Mrs. Dye's new book" was coming (probably *The Conquest,* published in 1902) and was most complimentary to "Portland City" as "showing a great deal of enterprise and courage."

There is a gap in any reference to David until 1928, when two letters concerning him and his family appeared. One was from a W. F. White of Portland on July 24, written to the same Mr. Himes as in 1900, now curator of the Oregon Historical Society. At first the letter seemed quite derogatory in tone, complaining that the mother of David's children (Annie Grizzly, a full-blood Indian) had not seemed to realize that the blood of an illustrious man flows in her (their?) veins." He asked Mr. Himes to relate the logistics of David's visit to Portland twenty-seven years earlier; he also wondered "whether it might be appropriate" to have the "presentable" members of the McLoughlin family "at an occasion like Chautauqua that is now going on at Champoeg."

In reply Mr. Himes wrote, rather cryptically, that David "made a clean breast to me of the whole situation." (Does not the colloquialism "clean breast" imply that guilt is involved?)

As for David's visit in 1901, Mr. Himes explained that David had stayed in a "good" hotel; he had also visited his nieces Louisa Myrick and Margaret Wygant, had stayed with F. X. Matthieu, at Butteville, and with Eva Emery Dye, an Oregon author, at The Dalles before he returned to Idaho. (No mention was made of furnishing a suit and shoes, along with other clothing or of paying travel expenses.) He added that David had also been honored at two receptions, one in Portland given jointly by the Oregon Historical Society and the Oregon Pioneer Association, the other by Mrs. Dye, at The Dalles.

Mr. Himes continued that Mr. White's suggestion to entertain David's children and/or grandchildren was "commendable" and that it might be done some time in the future, but that neither the Society nor the Association could afford it "at this time."

An interesting sidelight was that two of David's daughters had come to Portland several years before, seeking employment, feeling possibly that as granddaughters of Dr. McLoughlin "of such enviable fame," they would find an opening for "escape from their unenviable surroundings in the vicinity of Port Hill." The implication was that they probably had had no training and possessed no work skills; perhaps, in addition, they were not personable.

Mrs. Dye had befriended them and had tried unsuccessfully to find work for them. Finally, they had returned to Porthill. Mr. Himes added that a Mrs. French of or near Porthill had taken an interest in them and was trying to help them. Astutely Mr. Himes commented,

> David McLoughlin was a very well educated man, but throwing himself away as he did, destroyed his future. In some respects that visit to Portland in June, 1901, after an absence of 42 years, was not a kindly act. The motive, however, was to, through him, pay a tribute to his father. David appreciated that fully....it was a revelation to him...of his wasted life. "To think," he said, "of how much the Old Man did for me and of what my life might have been had I followed my father's wishes." And he wept.

This insight of George Himes leads to an attempt to evaluate David McLoughlin's life, to understand his motivation in directing his life, or perhaps in his failing to direct it, merely permitting his life—and himself—to drift with a fatalistic philosophy "What will be, will be." He expressed his philosophy in a letter of December 27, 1900, addressed to "Theodore," possibly Theodore Wygant, of Portland, husband of his niece Margaret Glen Rae, "I have spent the great part of my

Royal Family of the Columbia

life away from the advantages of civilization...among men of sound sense...everyone ought to use his own judgment and leave others alone to follow theirs." (One cannot help noticing his excellent grammar, even though "away from the advantages of civilization.") Perhaps there is an analogy here with today's dissidents. Was David an early-day "hippie"?

Mr. Thomas Whidden of Burlingame, California, a great, great-grandson of Dr. John McLoughlin, remembers his great-granduncle when David was in Portland in 1901, probably at the home of Mr. Whidden's grandparents, the Theodore Wygants. A boy of nine in 1901, Mr. Whidden recalls Dr. McLoughlin's son as tall, quiet, rather reserved, not well dressed, but rather unkempt and seedy.[25] (The reader might wonder whether he was wearing his new clothing given to him by the Oregon Historical Society and the Oregon Pioneer Association.)

A denigrating description of David McLoughlin was made by a Dr. W. W. Walkem in a newspaper, probably the *Oregonian,* November 15, 1914:

> At a point where the Great Northern Railroad intersects the international boundary line I met David McLoughlin in 1902 at a small village called Porthill—almost deserted, whose excellent English but poor associates gave good evidence that a good education had been wasted on him. He was living in a shack with a large half-breed family on land granted to his Indian wife by the United States government.[26]

A strange letter contained in David's "Correspondence," in the Oregon Historical Society is that of a Duncan MacDonald of Ravalli, Montana, April 25, 1917, written to a Margaret V. Sherlock of Seattle. Mr. MacDonald was evidently considerably disgruntled, for he wrote that he had "no desire of writing or working for notoriety for the public." He had known David McLoughlin and felt that "the loss of his girl by the Sea Capt...and knowing the feeling of the white race toward the red, is the cause of dissipation."

> The white race claims all good habits for themselves and the wicked to the red man....about our friend David, the writers are more stuck on his Prince Albert coat than in the mans character or culture. This shows how much intelligence a person knows about humanity. Don't write any more as it will do no good because it *is a race question!*

Disregarding the ambiguity caused by poor sentence structure, it would seem that Mr. MacDonald was thoroughly disenchanted with the Caucasian race and its treatment of the Red; that whites were (and are) snobbish and superficial, more concerned with a man's clothing and appearance than with the man himself. It would be of interest to know whether the writer, obviously in answer to a letter requesting information about David, was all Scottish, as his name might imply. or whether he was possibly a half-breed, which fact might affect his racial attitudes.

As witness to David's character is a letter, the sender's name illegible, asking payment of ninety-six dollars on a note drawn by a William Wright and endorsed by David. Apparently he was willing to endanger his own credit in order to help a friend or acquaintance. The letter was written April 12, 1859, the last year David was spending "in civilization", that is, forty-two years before his return in 1901.

Worth noting is not only his willingness to help another human being, but his seeming ability to do so. Granted, in 1859 he probably felt rather prosperous, for he had received one-third of his father's estate in 1857, which he had sold for $25,000 cash. Perhaps he also still had some of the $20,000 he had earned in the gold fields. Too, he was still a bachelor, having only himself to support. It was quite obviously between 1859 and 1900 that he exhausted his resources, so that he was without funds when invited to Portland in 1901. The significant fact is that when he had money he was willing to use it in helping others.

In 1901 he had the unique distinction of being the first of all "now-living" persons to see the Oregon Country, the first of the citizens of longest residence born before 1840—David was born in 1821—and he had come to Oregon (probably) in 1824.

What sort of man, then, was David McLoughlin? Was he apathetic, dissipated, shiftless, a wastrel? Or, was he simply not interested in material success, preferring to live the simple life, living away from the complexities of civilization, working among, educating, and otherwise helping the natives whose ways he had adopted? A definitive and categorical answer is obviously impossible. From a mercenary or pragmatic viewpoint, he was a total failure. From the human point of view, he was humane, a lover of his fellow man, concerned with the well-being of others.

In the Historical Society archives are several letters to David from various McLoughlin relatives, notably from Henri Auguste Miville Déchesne (Déchêne), son of Honorée McLoughlin Déchesne, a younger sister of Dr. John, and Joseph Miville Déchesne. Henri was much interested in his first cousin David, the only surviving McLoughlin. In fact, he too was surprised to find that David was still living.

Henry—it seems that he had anglicized his name—was a Doctor of Medicine, had come much earlier to Oregon (for in 1857 he had been at Dr. John McLoughlin's deathbed) and then to California; his letters were dated from Alameda.

It was a unilateral correspondence, with Henry doing all the corresponding—or so it seemed. The first letter, June 26, 1900, addressed to "Port Hole," told David that several cousins were asking for information of him and of Eloisa's eldest son, John Rae. Telling David that he hadn't seen him since 1863, Henry also reminded him that they had both been born in 1822, six months apart. (David, however, was born in 1821.) Only two Fraser cousins, he said, were still alive, both men, now eighty-three and sixty-three, both "wealthy," whereas he, Henry, was "only healthy" and had "got poor" selling real estate, having heavily mortgaged property and a nineteen-year-old son. Dr. Déchesne apparently possessed quite a sense of humor. He was certainly doing "all right" if at seventy-eight he had a nineteen-year-old son. His letters, though written in English, in their syntax revealed his French origin.

On September 21 came a letter to Henry Déchesne from "William Fraser of Fraserville" whom Dr. Déchesne referred to as "our cousin Lord of Fraserville," asking "cher Henri" for David's photograph and where Porthill was—"Dans quel État est Port Hill?"

In an October 25 letter Henry wrote that he was glad to know that David's eldest daughter "is now Mrs. Sullivan." Actually, she (Angeline, born in 1875) was his fourth daughter. Several times Henry suggested that David move to California.

On November 27 Dr. Déchesne wrote that he would have an operation for hernia in San Francisco on December 1 at 9:00 a.m. It was to be performed by "one of two of the finest European surgeons who have just come to San Francisco." A San Francisco surgeon had refused to perform surgery due to a slight chance of survival (only one in one hundred) because of his age and the danger to his heart of the anesthetic, chloroform. He promised to write if he survived the operation.

There were no further letters in the archives; apparently the "one in one hundred chances" was not enough. In this last letter Dr. Déschesne gave David the names of his (David's) grandparents and of some of his cousins, the names of David's father's birthplace, and other commonplace family facts.[27] Apparently communication among members of Henry's branch of the McLoughlins was more open than that of David's; how pitiful that David had to learn of his own immediate family from a cousin.

As mentioned above, the correspondence between David and Henry Déchesne was, or at least seemed to be, unilateral. Perhaps the latter is true; after all, David carried on a correspondence with George Himes at approximately the same period of time. It is possible, perhaps probable, that David did reply to his cousin, but that after Henry's death letters which he had received were destroyed, whereas those written to David were saved and eventually became a part of the collection today in the Oregon Historical Society's archives.

The enigma of David McLoughlin will probably not be solved. Historiographers may continue to enjoy writing of him as they see him: on the one hand, an early-day "hippie" who detested civilization and the so-called "Establishment," who enjoyed being of service to others, caring nothing for financial return; or, on the other hand, as a spendthrift who let at least two small fortunes slip through his fingers and a drifter too lazy to make use of his natural advantages and ability and too indolent to become a "success" in the world.

Then there is the perennial question: What would have been David's life if his father had not coerced him into giving up the profession for which he had been trained and had not compelled him to return to the Columbia? That too will remain an unanswered question.

Alberta Brooks Fogdall

REFERENCES

CHAPTER 11

DAVID——THE KING'S WANDERING, FRUSTRATED SON

1 Evelyn Sibley Lampman, *Princess of Fort Vancouver*, p. 280.

2 Burt Brown Barker, *The McLoughlin Empire and its Rulers*, p. 132.

3 David McLoughlin, "Correspondence," Archives, Oregon Historical Society. One must be aware that David was almost eighty when he wrote his "Correspondence." His memory could have been faulty. Pages not numbered.

4 Barker, *op. cit.*, p. 220. Addiscombe College, at Croydon, near London, served as a military college for the East India Company service. It was closed in 1862.

5 *Ibid.*, pp. 220-222.

6 *Ibid.*, pp. 150-151.

7 *Ibid.*, p. 153.

8 *Ibid.*, pp. 182-184.

9 McLoughlin, *loc. cit.* David expressed this in very simple words (at age of eighty).

10 This section has been taken in essence from Richard G. Montgomery, *The White-Headed Eagle*, pp. 248-249. He gives credit to McLoughlin, *op. cit.*, for the statement concerning the return to America early in 1839.

11 Barker, *op. cit.*, p. 244.

12 Montgomery, *op. cit.*, p. 250.

13 Barker, *op. cit.*, p. 246. The date 1840 must be incorrect, as John had left for Stikine six months previously; the letter should probably have been dated October 24, 1839.

14 *Scrap Book*, Vol. 21, p. 44, Archives, Oregon Historical Society.

15 *Oregon Native Son*, Vol. II (May, 1900-April, 1901, p. 96.

16 McLoughlin, *loc. cit.*

17 Dorothy Johansen, *Empire of the Columbia*, p. 214.

18 Barker, *op. cit.*, p. 135.

19 *Ibid.*, pp. 134-136, 139. Information given by Blanche Rogerson Hobbs, a granddaughter of David McLoughlin, April 19, 1950.

20 *Ibid.*, p. 139.

21 *Ibid.*, pp. 139-140. Information given by Sarah McLoughlin Rogerson, a daughter of David, July 26, 1956.

22 F. X. Matthieu, "Reminiscences," *Oregon Historical Society Quarterly*, Vol. II, pp. 73-104.

23 Picture between page 136 and page 139, Barker, *op. cit.*

24 Clippings of the *Oregonian, Scrap Book*, Vol. 37, p. 30, Archives, Oregon Historical Society.

25 Interview with Mr. Thomas Marvin Whidden in San Francisco, December 22, 1972.

26 *Scrap Book*, page unnumbered, Archives, Oregon Historical Society.

27 David McLoughlin's Correspondence" from which this material has been taken, unless otherwise indicated, is in the Archives of the Oregon Historical Society.

THOMAS McKAY——THE KING'S STEPSON

Thomas McKay was the oldest of Margaret McKay McLoughlin's eight children. The only son of her four children by Alexander McKay, he had accompanied his father from their home at Sault Ste. Marie to join the Astor expedition in 1810, entering the service of the Pacific Fur Company. When Fort Astoria was taken by the British in 1813, becoming Fort George, he joined the Northwest Fur Company as a clerk in the Columbia Department, after 1821 continuing with the Hudson's Bay Company, a continuous service of almost twenty-five years.[1]

Tom was born in either 1797 or 1798—the former date is more generally given. Probably the most significant event in his life—certainly it changed his entire future—was the murder of his father in August 1811 on the *Tonquin* by Indians near Nootka Sound.[2] With him died Captain Jonathan Thorn and nearly everyone on board. Fortunately Tom's father had sent him on an errand on land, or, as another story goes, Tom was ill and was left at Fort Astoria; in either case he was saved from the wholesale massacre. Tom, left alone at fourteen, did not go back to Sault Ste. Marie where his father had left, or abandoned, Tom's mother and three younger sisters. He tried to return east the next year, but due to heavy fighting (related to the War of 1812) around the Great Lakes, he was forced to return to Astoria. He sent word to his mother that he would remain west of the Rockies. Tradition has it that he swore vengeance against the Indians for his father's death.[3]

Alexander McKay, respected explorer, trader, and clerk, had accompanied Sir Alexander MacKenzie, the intrepid Arctic pathfinder for whom the great Canadian river was named, to the Pacific in 1793. Made a partner in the Northwest Company in 1799, McKay had retired from it in 1808; he then became a partner in the Pacific Fur Company in 1809. His unfortunate death on the *Tonquin* has already been chronicled.[4]

Tom, although only fourteen when his father was murdered, was a man, and a self-reliant one. It was probably thirteen to fifteen years before he again saw his mother. By that time (probably either 1824 or 1826) she had been married to Dr. John McLoughlin for more than thirteen years and was rearing a new family of four children. Tom also was now married and the father of at least one child, an infant son.[5]

During these years of his growing to adulthood, Tom had led an active outdoor life, serving as guide on numerous wilderness expeditions, and had conducted many parties into the Willamette Valley, had explored the Fraser River Valley, the

Alberta Brooks Fogdall

Umpqua and Klamath Country, and had led brigades into the Snake River Valley.[6] Many historians have described him as one of the most colorful figures of the Hudson's Bay Company régime in the Oregon Country, "a wonderful horseman and an unrivalled shot."[7] According to a historical maker in his honor in Scappoose, Oregon, "...he could drive a nail with a rifle ball." He built himself a reputation as one of the most intrepid and daring guides and trappers in the Northwest.[8] The Reverend Jason Lee left this description: "Six feet tall, intrepid, energetic, with very keen eyes and slight limp"—he was "Never scared".[9]

On the much-discussed journey of McLoughlin and Simpson to the Columbia in 1824 Tom played a significant part. The parties of the two top men of the Honourable Company on the Columbia met at Portage La Biche September 27; despite Simpson's constant pressuring of the boatmen to work harder and faster, *"Vite! Vite!"*, and their resultant resentment of him (one of them is supposed to have thrown the Governor into the water), they arrived at Jasper House, in the heart of the Rockies, October 10. Here Tom met them according to plan with two canoes for the party. Finding that there were more people than he had planned for, he supervised the building of another canoe, after which he guided the enlarged party to Fort George (Astoria), on the Columbia. (Could the "more people than...expected" indicate that the Chief Factor's family did, perhaps, accompany him after all?) A short time later Tom guided a party of forty under Chief Trader James McMillan to the mouth of the Fraser River, under Simpson's orders, to seek an alternative site for a fort, since it was felt that use of Fort George was no longer feasible.[10]

According to some historians Tom and his stepfather met for the first time on this expedition; Tom was pictured as prepared to dislike the Doctor and to resent the man who had replaced his father in his mother's affection.[11]

Other writers, however, believed that the meeting between Tom and the Chief Factor was a reunion after fourteen or fifteen years; that the Doctor had known Tom and the rest of the McKay family well at Sault Ste. Marie.[12] In either case Tom was full of questions concerning his mother and his three sisters. It was difficult for him to realize that the girls were grown up and married and would remain in Canada. Even harder for him to imagine was the existence of four half brothers and half sisters whom he had of course never seen.

What was the physical appearance of this "McLoughlin who was not a McLoughlin"? He was described by one writer as "tall, well built, and muscular, with a dark thin face, with deep-set dark eyes and heavy brows." He was a "typical Scotsman."[13] Because of a shooting accident his hip had been injured and had not healed properly; as a result he limped. He was said to be "blacker" than his half siblings, although they were also one-fourth Indian. No doubt his swarthiness was due to his being constantly outdoors.

Royal Family of the Columbia

Nathaniel Wyeth, the visionary Bostonian with the impossible aspiration of putting the Honourable Company out of business, painted Tom as "lithe and tall, with a pleasant and companionable manner, with light brown hair and vivacious eyes."[14]

Louis Labonte, that daring and industrious French Canadian who dared to challenge Governor Simpson's ruling that he must return to Canada when he completed his term with the Company, remembered Tom as "dark and tremendously powerful."[15]

Governor George Simpson considered him "one of the best Shots in the Country and very cool and resolute among Indians." However, he was a "confirmed Liar." He had "presence of mind, courage, and energy," but Simpson told McLoughlin bluntly that his stepson was "not fit to command."[16]

Just as Simpson had his opinion of Tom, so Tom had his views concerning the Governor: "...pimply-faced, pompous, nose like a ferret...low-down ornery when he wants to be...'Turk' because of his iron will and domineering disposition...every command carried an insult."[17]

Tom loved to talk—and talk—and talk—especially of his mountain exploits. He also tended to stretch the truth and had early acquired a reputation of being the greatest liar in the settlement. Yet he performed many acts of humanity and community service. One acquaintance, unidentified, described him as "a very good and amazing personage."[18] He was often seen with a long-stemmed pipe which sent out a long blue stream of smoke from the mixture of tobacco and intoxicant weed enjoyed by many Indians.[19]

This was no doubt a favorite pipe—one he enjoyed after dinner at the Fort to the accompaniment of tales of wild exploits and exciting adventures—his own or those of others, possibly of Peter Skene Ogden or of Nathaniel Wyeth or of countless others privileged to dine in the baronial-size dining hall before adjourning to the smoking room, commonly called Bachelors' Hall, since only men frequented it.[20]

Tom was the father of numerous children by two or, more probably, three wives. It is not always possible to assign them to the proper mother. One writer, however, has dared to allot three sons, William, John, and Alexander, to the first wife; one son and one daughter to the second; and two sons and one daughter to the third.[21] His best-known child was his eldest son, William Cameron, called Billy, born to Tom's first wife, Timmee ("Maiden"), in 1824.

Timmee (also called T'lkul, or "the quiet one") was the eldest daughter—apparently there were no sons—of one-eyed Chief Comcomly of the Chinooks; through her Billy was hereditary chief of the Chinooks. Comcomly's many daughters provided him with a diverse group of sons-in-law, including Casseno, Chief of the Multnomahs; Chief Traders Duncan McDougal and Archibald McDonald of the Hudson's Bay Company; and, of course, Tom, among others. Tom's princess-wife was portrayed as being extremely jealous of her husband, wanting to accompany him on all the brigades and expeditions and feeling hurt and angry when he refused to take her.[22]

Billy lived with the McLoughlin family at the Fort until 1838, attending school there under John Ball,[23] the first teacher in the Oregon Country, and his successor, Solomon Smith.[24]

Tom had at first thought of sending his eldest son abroad to study, perhaps emulating Dr. David McLoughlin or young John and young David, but Dr. Marcus Whitman persuaded Tom that since Billy would no doubt some day be an American citizen, he should have an American education. Because Billy wanted to study medicine he went east to attend Dr. Whitman's Alma Mater, Fairfield College, in Herkimer County, New York, traveling with the Reverend Jason Lee and his party. Dr. Whitman offered to help Tom defray the cost of Billy's education. Billy proved to be a brilliant student, finishing his college education and medical studies in five years. He received his medical certificate in 1843, but at nineteen was too young to receive his diploma and degree.[25]

There were McKay daughters too; two are usually indicated, although three were mentioned in Tom's will.

It is even more difficult to place the McKay daughters with their own mothers than to classify the sons. Margaret, the only daughter who has emerged as a person, was probably the daughter of Tom's second wife.* Named for her Grandmother McLoughlin, she spent the winter of 1838-1839, the winter when her father took a third wife, with Dr. and Mrs. Marcus Whitman at their Waiilaptu mission, near Fort Walla Walla. Here she helped Narcissa Whitman with her many tasks, particularly the care of little Alice Clarissa. In return she learned from Narcissa "a little book lore" and some of the household arts.[26]

Rumor was that Tom buried Timmee one day and took a second wife the next day.[27] His second wife was said to be "Umatilla Woman," or "She-who-rides-like-the-Wind." Whether Umatilla Woman died or whether she was not a legal wife is uncertain, but Tom, ready to marry a third time, swore that he would not again marry an Indian.[28]

On December 31, 1838, he married Isabelle, daughter of Nicholas and Susanne Montour, who was either "all-white" or only "slightly" Indian. She was baptized a Catholic before their marriage at St. James Catholic Church, which at that time was very near the Fort; today it is in downtown Vancouver. By this marriage there were three sons and two daughters.[29]

*See note 26 at end of chapter.

Royal Family of the Columbia

The marriage service was performed by Father François Blanchet and is said to have been witnessed by Dr. John McLoughlin, James Douglas, William Glen Rae, and Dr. William Fraser Tolmie.[30] However, Dr. McLoughlin was known to be on furlough in Europe at this time; his inclusion as a witness must be an error.

From the time his children were small Tom was most desirous that his sons have a good life. (The daughters, of course, were no problem; they would have husbands to take care of them.) He was almost painfully aware of the much greater advantages available to his half brothers, John and David McLoughlin, than to his own sons.[31]

William found "the good life" as a doctor, ministering to his fellow Redmen. Donald, a half brother, served as an interpreter to the Indian agent on a Umatilla reservation. Some became soldiers. Timmee's two younger sons, John and Alexander, were officers who accompanied Tom when he went with a small army to punish the Cayuse, following the Whitman massacre in 1847.[32] A son of Isabelle was in the army which defeated Captain Jack of the Modocs in the Modoc War 1873-1875.[33]

Tom became a prosperous farmer and entrepreneur of the Oregon Country, both in French Prairie (in the Willamette Valley) and opposite Sauvie Island, near Scappoose. He has been cited as the first pioneer in the Scappoose area, having come to the Oregon Country at fourteen; at twenty-four he stocked a ranch near Scappoose.[34]

In 1833 he retired from the Honourable Company, settling on a farm near Scappoose and becoming an American citizen.[35] On his French Prairie farm he supervised the construction of a mill. He and his wife sometimes lived on the second floor of the mill, considered "the grandest in the Valley," just as Tom was the "most wealthy man in the valley of the Wallamet." The precise location of the farm is not certain, but it was probably on the south bank of the Willamette, on Champoeg Creek, the largest stream in the vicinity. He kept the Scappoose farm, calling himself "a farmer on the Columbia."[36]

Although a man of two homes, he did not spend much time in either, for he was constantly going on journeys and brigades and conducting parties of missionaries and traders, as well as enjoying his own exploring and building projects. The term "ubiquitous Mr. McKay" is appropriately descriptive.

In 1828 as a Company employee he was sent to northern California to help retrieve the furs of American fur trader Jedediah Smith and his party, stolen by Indians who had massacred most of the party. In 1834 he was again taken away from his homes when Dr. McLoughlin sent him to build Fort Boise, on the Boise River, as a rival post to nearby Fort Hall, built by Nathaniel Wyeth. While there he served as guide for the Reverend Jason Lee and his party of missionaries from Fort Hall to Fort Walla Walla, arriving there on September 1.[37] In 1841 he helped to drive sheep and cattle from California for the Company. These are but a few of the travels which kept

Tom on the move. He found it necessary to leave his real estate in charge of an agent, tenants, or hired hands. When the flood of 1843 swept over the Champoeg plains, water ruined wheat stored in barns and granaries, for it came up as high as the second floor.[38] The next year Tom and Isabelle withdrew permanently to the Scappoose property.

His entrepreneurial activities necessarily were carried on through the cooperation and assistance of his stepfather. The Chief Factor was actually violating one of the Governor's administrative policies by allowing Tom (others too—for example, Louis Labonte and Étienne Lucier) to remain in the Oregon Country as farmers after retiring from Company service instead of returning to the point (usually Canada) where they had originally enlisted: "No officer or servant shall be permitted to remain in the Country after expiration of service." The ostensible reason for the ruling was to prevent the turning loose of undesirable whites who might foment trouble, perhaps inciting the natives to rebellion. The Chief Factor felt that this was merely a pretext and that his superior's actual motive was to prevent or at least to retard permanent settlement, particularly south of the Columbia, which would be opposed to the interests of the Hudson's Bay Company.[39]

Because Dr. McLoughlin was fond of Tom and wanted to make Margaret happy by promoting her son's interests, he had allowed Tom to continue living and farming at French Prairie; more, he countenanced Tom's selling produce from his fertile farms to travelers, supplying horses and pack animals to traders, allowing water access to visitiors, and, in general, pursuing free-lance trade with American trappers at their annual rendezvous. In addition, Tom carried on business with the Fort, selling much of his 800 bushels of wheat raised on the rich soil of French Prairie.

All of this was contrary to the policy laid down by Governor Simpson, who at last ordered McLoughlin to forbid Tom's continuing his entrepreneurial activities. Tom then resumed employment at the Fort with the Honourable Company, working once again as clerk. He spent the winter of 1838-1839 at Fort Hall, which the Company had bought from Nathaniel Wyeth, who had returned to the United States after he was finally convinced that he could not compete seriously with the powerful Hudson's Bay Company.[40] At the end of the 1838-1839 winter season Tom resigned permanently from the Company.

It was Tom's great disappointment and lifetime frustration that he was never in command of any assignment or operation on which he was sent; instead, he had to be satisfied with being second man. Gradually the Chief Factor had come to acknowledge that possibly the Governor was correct in his opinion that Tom's judgment could not always be trusted.[41]

Probably the last or one of the last excursions in which Tom participated was the punitive expedition to the Cayuse Country in 1847, as previously noted.

He died in 1849 or 1850. Wallace gives the date as 1850,[42] Barker as 1849.[43] An "Historical Marker" on North Columbia Highway in Scappoose temporizes by giving the death date as the "winter of 1849-1850." The date has been narrowed to between November 18, 1849, when Tom left written instructions for a payment from his account, and April 18, 1850, when the court appointed an administrator for his estate.[44] Apparently this five-month interval is the closest reckoning possible at this time.

The McKay will, dated February 13, 1844, is quoted from the St. Helens *Sentinel-Mist,* which in turn based its story on material in the *Oregon Historical Quarterly.*[45] In this document he "gave and bequeathed" to his wife, Isabelle, "Twenty head horn cattle, Ten Breeding Pigs, Two Plough Horses Four Breeding Mares, and all the Furniture of the house." To his daughter Mary he gave "Ten Head Cattle Two Mares and her share pigs Two Mares." Lack of punctuation tends to obscure the meaning; yet apparently the will served its purpose. Similar bequests were made to Donald, Louise, John (including one "plough Compleat"), William, Tom, Charley, and Alexander." Dr. McLoughlin, James Douglas, and several others were appointed "Executors and Sole Interpreters." Although not mentioned in this section of the will, Tom was known to possess at the time of his death a grist mill and a sawmill, together evaluated at $55,000.[46]

There were additional interesting aspects to Tom's will. It was to have been probated in Marion County in 1844 but apparently underwent several changes in 1845. Ink used in the original draft kept its color, but that used in the alterations faded, making the will extremely difficult to read. Words had been crossed out and written over, especially the amount of stock left to "Isabella" and to daughters "Mary, Maria, La Luisa, Thomas, and 'Donal'." Legatee Jason Lee was changed to Father Blanchet and Methodist Episcopal Church to Catholic Church. The assumption has been made that this change was due to the Reverend Mr. Lee's death in March 1845; no doubt, but one might also infer that Tom could have been converted to Catholicism, for his wife Isabelle had become Catholic just prior to their marriage on the last day of 1838. In addition, his mother and stepfather, as already known, had been received into the Catholic fold in 1842.[47]

Probation did not proceed smoothly. The court appointed Mr. George Groom as administrator of the estate. Apparently Mr. Groom did not keep orderly appraisals. He did not appear in court on July 21, 1851, and could not be found by the sheriff. However, his inventory of $6,781.88 was accepted on December 2, 1851. He was again cited twice in 1853 for not appearing in court and his letter of administration was revoked September 4, 1854. Apparently the eccentric and erratic Mr. Groom was also dishonest, for the inference drawn was that he had left the country and had taken a portion of the McKay estate with him.[48]

Thomas McKay was buried near Scappoose. "Near Scappoose," more than slightly vague, is apparently as definitive a location as the St. Helens newspapers[49] and the foresaid historical marker were able to indicate.[50] The grave was unmarked and neglected for over one hundred years. One hundred and twenty years after his death the Vernonia (Oregon) *Eagle* on February 22, 1968, announced a dedication service, to take place February 25, for a marker to be placed on the cleaned-up, decorated grave site, now set off with a fence enclosure. The site was not given in the news article, nor was it mentioned in the *Sentinel-Mist* or the *Chronicle,* both of St. Helens, after the ceremony, February 29. Motivating forces of the honoring of Tom McKay seem to have been Roy A. Perry of the Columbia County Historical Society and the local chapter of the Daughters of the American Revolution. Both papers carried pictures, one of which identified two young girls by name, but did not indicate any connection with Tom McKay. No mention was made of the presence of any McKay descendants. In view of the implied importance of the occasion, the information dispensed to the public was surprisingly meager.

However, at Scappoose, this writer visited Mrs. Gilbert (Rhoda) McKay, widow of a grandson of Malcolm McKay, who came to the Oregon Country in 1842 and worked in a Company store at Fort Vancouver while Dr. McLoughlin ruled the Columbia Department.[51] Mrs. McKay knew the approximate site of a marker honoring Tom, a cousin of Malcolm; whether the marker is actually on the grave or perhaps merely near it is still controversial. The marker itself does not claim that Tom's body lies beneath it; it merely "honors" him.

The location of the grave is described as "on the old Dan Freeman farm about two miles northeast of Scappoose close to the airport."[52] One "old timer," Mr. John Heglund, was kind enough to serve as guide to the exact location of the marker, though he said not to the location of the mysterious grave itself. The marker is on property of Mr. Chester J. Kumba, who owns a portion of the former Freeman farm. The grave itself, Mr. Heglund believed, may very well be about thirty feet to the east of the marker, for he has probed with a rod there over a rectangular area about six feet long and found a pronounced metallic sound not apparent in the earth around it.[53] So the mystery continues.

Some of Tom's children led interesting lives as adults. William returned from the East to give his own people the benefit of his medical education. Five-eighths Indian, since his mother was an Indian "princess" and his father one-fourth Indian, he seemed to spend the greater part of his adult life with the Umatilla Indians, rather than with his own Chinooks, of whom he was hereditary chief. In 1861 he was appointed agency physician on the Umatilla reservation by President Abraham Lincoln.[54]

The date of William's marriage, said to be the first in Wasco County, as well as the name of his bride, is in dispute: 1. He married Margaret Campbell in 1856. 2. He married Mary Campbell in 1857. Most writers support 1856 as the date and Margaret as the bride. Many believe his bride was a first cousin, daughter of one of Tom's sisters. The McKays became the parents of five children. William and Margaret McKay are buried in City Cemetery at Pendleton Oregon.* Hailed "Umatilla's First Leading Citizen," he was described as courtly, quiet, gentle, gracious and brilliant; most of all , he was "a kindly physician."[55]

In addition to his service among the Umatillas William enjoyed a life of adventure. As leader of an Indian Medicine show in which he lectured on Indian life and lore, he traveled in various parts of the United States, particularly in the East.

Earlier, in the 1850s, he had known Lieutenant Ulysses S. Grant, who had been stationed at the Fort Vancouver Army barracks.

Now, in the late 1860s or early 1870s, stranded without funds in Washington D.C., he appealed to General W. W. Belknap, Secretary of War, for transportation back to the Umatilla reservation, only to be told by the Secretary that he had "no funds to send drunken Indians around the country." William then explained his plight to President Grant, who ordered Secretary Belknap to give him rail transportation and expense money back to the Northwest. Needless to say, General Belknap was embarrassed.[56]

William's younger half brother Donald also toured with a show. Labeled as the son of Tom's third wife, Isabelle Montour, yet born in 1836,[57] his mother must have been Umatilla Woman, for Tom and Isabelle were not married until the last day of 1838. Like his father, Donald had suffered a hip injury and became a partial cripple. Also like his father and William, he knew Idaho, Oregon, Washington, and Montana "as most people know their backyards."[58]

Donald's show was similar to that of Buffalo Bill. In it he displayed his skill as a rider and his expertise with the rifle and lasso. He toured many American cities, as well as England, where His Royal Highness Albert Edward Prince of Wales, later Edward VII, was in the audience. A reprint of a "flyer" in the Historical Society archives captured the spirit of the times as it advertised the personal appearance of 'Chief of Warm Springs Indians'—from Oregon. The performance at the Broadway Theater, presumably in New York, was at 8:00 p.m. on "Sunday Eve. Mar. 11. Doors open at 7:00." Unfortunately, the year was not given. Admission was "15 cents-25 cents." Here one could see "Braves Chiefs Squaws Papooses—A Genuine Sight of a Lifetime." Donald McKay was "The Man who Captured Captain Jack and his Murderous Bands of Modocs after the Government had spent $8,000,000 and the lives of General Canby and General Gillem (Gilliam?) had been sacrificed—will Lecture on Indian Wars—their Causes and Remedies. Six different tribes of Indians on Stage."

*Dr. McKay's birth and death dates are given on the marker as March 18, 1824, and January 2, 1893. Also buried in the lot are Thomas L. McKay (1902-1965), possibly a great-grandson of William, and a daughter, unidentified.

Alberta Brooks Fogdall

More recently (date not given, although a zip code as part of the Society's address, rather than a zone, indicated a relatively recent date) a descriptive advertisement (reprint) touted "Now just $2.95 at Bookshop—Adventure book 'Daring Donald McKay or the Last War Trail of the Modocs'." The date of the book's original printing was given by the Historical Society as 1874.[59]

Donald later served as interpreter to the Indian agent on the Umatilla reservation. No mention was made of his serving at the same time that his half brother William was reservation physician. He died in poverty April 19, 1899, proud and lonely, in the stable at the feet of his horse.*[60]

The only one of Tom's daughters to be given individual notice was Margaret, mentioned earlier in the chapter. Opal S. Allen in *Narcissa Whitman* called attention to the fact that Margaret "possessed the most distinguished blood in Canada," for she was "the daughter of one of the Hudson's Bay Company's most noted leaders," the granddaughter and namesake of Mrs. John McLoughlin and granddaughter also of "famed Alexander McKay, intrepid associate of the great Sir Alexander MacKenzie." No record has been found of her adult life, of marriage or of children.[61]

Tom's granddaughter Leila, daughter of Dr. William McKay, also possessed "distinguished blood." Her mother was Margaret Campbell, whose father was Colin Campbell, a chief factor in the Northwest Company and the Hudson's Bay Company.[62]

Apparently Miss McKay preferred to keep her distinguished blood lines untainted by Indian corpuscles, for in a letter written from Cambridge, Idaho, dated August 31-September 1 (no year), she averred that of Tom McKay's three families, her father was a son of the third marriage, that his mother was a "French mother from Québec." This was highly improbable, for William was born in 1821, whereas Tom's third marriage took place nearly two decades later.

Miss McKay was most unhappy concerning a recent newspaper photograph of her father; in fact she denied that the picture was of her father, for he was "cultured and refined."[63]

The *Oregon Journal* of May 18, 1950, carried an obituary and picture. Miss McKay had died at the age of eighty-four, indicating that she was born in 1866 or 1867. Following her parents' deaths, after 1900, she had moved to Portland, where she bought a needlework and tapestry shop, which she operated as a studio. Her father, William, was described as one of Pendleton's first two physicians; the public was reminded that she was the great-granddaughter of the founder of Astoria Alexander McKay, and the step great-granddaughter of Dr. John McLoughlin.[64]

Miss McKay in the late 1930s gave to McLoughlin House a sewing case which had belonged to her mother, in fact had crossed the plains with her in 1854. A

* According to the *Dictionary of Oregon History*, p. 252, it was William who "died at the feet of his horse." It seems improbable that both half brothers died in this unusual manner.

238

beautiful memento, "made of black morocco leather, with a compartment for scissors, embossed in gold and embroidered with colored roses." At the same time she presented the House with a piece of china, a soup plate, which Dr. McLoughlin had given her parents as a wedding gift.[65]

Several descendants of Tom McKay are living today on the Warm Springs reservation, for some of the McKays preferred the Indian life-style.[66]

In 1953 Diane McKay, a descendant of Tom's son William, was chosen Queen of the Pendleton Roundup, an honor eagerly sought by young equestriennes of eastern Oregon, probably second in prestige only to the position of Portland Rose Festival Queen.[67]

In 1954 she was invited to be an honored guest at the Columbia County Fair to be held at St. Helens. Her reply "in perfect penmanship, grammar, and spelling showed her to be a person of education." She was forced to decline the invitation, as she was to attend an all-Indian beauty contest at that time.[68]

How to evaluate Tom McKay? No doubt his economic status and his financial success were due at least in part to his prestigious stepfather; however, his intrepidity, his daring, his love of adventure, his *bonhomie* with the Indians, most of whom idolized him; his sharp-shooting, his knowledge of wilderness terrain, his "tall" tales—these were an inherent part of his own character and personality: these qualities composed the man. He was the sort of man that other men—and women too—liked. One woman, long time archivist of the Hudson's Bay Company in London, Miss A. M. Johnson, felt that Tom McKay was "more than just a squaw man. He was a great man and quite well known to us."[69]

A man who admired him tremendously, yet vicariously, through the distance of time, was a Mr. Watt. Mr. Watt, whose Christian name was not revealed, was a notary public at Scappoose. For thirty years his idol had been Tom McKay. An elderly man in the 1950s, he could remember that as a young man he had known an elderly man who in his youth had known Tom McKay. This progressively distant acquaintanceship made his hero seem very close to him. He proclaimed with certainty that the tracks of the brigade of Tom McKay could still be seen in the trail he had taken to northern California to recover the prized furs of Jedediah Smith back in 1828.[70]

Alberta Brooks Fogdall

REFERENCES

CHAPTER 12

THOMAS McKAY——THE KING'S STEPSON

1 W. Stewart Wallace, *Documents Relating to the Northwest Company*, pp. 473-474.

2 Oscar Osburn Winther, *The Great Norhtwest*, pp. 91-94.

3 *Scrap Book* (38), p. 76, Oregon Historical Society.

4 Wallace, *op. cit.*, p. 473.

5 As noted earlier in discussing the journey to the Pacific Northwest of the McLoughlins.

6 John Adam Hussey, *Champoeg: A Place of Transition*, p. 93.

7 *Ibid.*

8 Richard G. Montgomery, *Young Northwest*, pp. 113-114.

9 Annie Laurie Bird, writing in *Oregon Historical Quarterly*, Vol. 40, March 1934, pp. 1-14.

10 Montgomery, *White-Headed Eagle*, pp. 64-65; 73.

11 Hermia Fraser, *Tall Brigade*, pp. 50-51.

12 Montgomery, *W.-H.E.*, *loc. cit.*

13 Hussey, *loc. cit.*

14 *Scrap Book*, *loc. cit.*

15 Montgomery, *op. cit.*, pp. 156-158; A. L. Bird, *loc. cit.*

16 Hussey, *op. cit.*, p. 93.

17 Fraser, *loc. cit.*

18 Hussey, *op. cit.*, p. 96.

19 *Scrap Book*, *loc. cit.*

20 Montgomery, *op. cit.*, pp. 161-162.

21 Reprint, the (Pendleton) *East Oregonian*, January 2, 1889, folder, Archives, Oregon Historical Society.

22 *Ibid.*

23 S. A. Clarke, *Pioneer Days of Oregon History*, Vol. I, p. 181.

24 Herbert Beaver, *Reports and Letters*, introduction, p. XIV.

25 Reprint, *East Oregonian*, *loc. cit.* William did not receive an M.D. degree until 1872, when he received the degree from Willamette University, Salem, Oregon.

26 Opal Sweazer Allen, *Narcissa Whitman*, pp. 198-199; 206.*

27 Annie Laurie Bird, *loc. cit.*

28 Evelyn Sibley Lampman, *Princess of Fort Vancouver*, p, 280.

29 Sister Mary Dominica McNamée, *Willamette Interlude*, p. 172. However, other sources, for example, the *East Oregonian*, *loc. cit.*, divide the "three sons and two daughters" between two wives: one son and one daughter for the second wife, two sons and one daughter for the third.

30 Pearl Becker, Column "Out of the Past," St. Helens *Sentinel-Mist*, May 15, 1967, McKay folder, Archives, Oregon Historical Society.

31 Fraser, *op. cit.*, p. 208.

32 Becker, *loc. cit.*

33 St. Helens *Sentinel-Mist*, November 9, 1967, Archives, Oregon Historical Society.

34 Clatskanie (Oregon) *Chief*, March 14, 1968, McKay folder, Archives, Oregon Historical Society.

35 Hussey, *loc. cit.*

36 *Ibid.*

37 Montgomery, *op. cit.*, p. 199.

*Again, an inconsistency: If Margaret were old enough to be of help in the Whitman household in 1838-39, she could not have been a result of Tom's second marriage, which reputedly took place in 1834.

38 Hussey, *op. cit.*, p. 97.

39 Montgomery, *op. cit.*, pp. 156-157.

40 Hussey, *op. cit.*, p. 94. His spending the winter of 1838-1839 at Fort Hall seems inconsistent with his marrying Isabelle Montour at Fort Vancouver December 31, 1838. Possibly he made a trip to Fort Vancouver and back to Fort Hall, but it is doubtful that a white or "nearly white" woman would make the trip back to Fort Hall.

41 *Ibid.* p. 93.

42 Burt Brown Barker, *The McLoughlin Empire and its Rulers*, p. 329n.

43 Wallace, *op. cit.*, pp. 473-474.

44 *Oregon Historical Quarterly*, Vol. 40 (1939), p. 18.

45 St. Helens *Sentinel-Mist*, May 15, 1967.

46 Hussey, *loc. cit.*

47 Becker, *loc. cit.*

48 *Ibid.*

49 The two St. Helens newspapers, the *Sentinel-Mist* and the *Chronicle* have since merged to form the *Chronicle-Sentinel-Mist*.

50 Unsuccessful visit of the author to the Scappoose-St. Helens area in search of the McKay marker and grave.

51 Letter of (Mrs.) Rhoda McKay to the author, April 23, 1973.

52 *Ibid.*

53 Visit, with Mrs. McKay, to Scappoose, St. Helens, and the McKay marker, May 2, 1973.

54 A. Pendleton *East Oregonian*, August 18, 1939, McKay, folder, Archives, Oregon Historical Society.

54 B. Scrap Book 9, p. 142, Pendleton *East Oregonian;* also *Dictionary of Oregon History*, p. 252, Oregon Historical Society.

54 C. Scrap Book 39, p. 131. The name of the newspaper was not given.

54 D. This belief is supported additionally by a folder in the McKay file in the Oregon Historical Society archives in which a letter signed "Margaret C. McKay" was written to author Eva Emery Dye, enclosing "Mr. Dye's letter to Senator Dolph." Mrs. McKay answered questions concerning the "doctor's" military service in 1866-1867, during part of the Indian wars, and enclosed official papers. No doubt, since Dr. McKay had died the previous year (1893), his widow was hoping for a pension and felt that Mrs. Dye was sufficiently well known and influential to intercede for her successfully.

As to the Mary-vs.-Margaret controversy, possibly the name was Mary Margaret or perhaps there were two sisters bearing the two names. Often she was referred to as "M. Campbell." Since on the gravestone she was "Mrs. William McKay," even that possibility of definitive identification is eliminated.

55 Walla Walla (Washington) *Union-Bulletin*, October 9, 1939, McKay folder, Archives, Oregon Historical Society. Visit of author to City Cemetery, Pendleton, October 27, 1973; additional information from Mr. Andrew Bellomo, caretaker (letter of November 1, 1973).

56 Fred Lockley, the *Oregon Journal*, interview of pioneer Dr. Charles J. Smith of Portland, September 19, 1943, McKay folder, Archives, Oregon Historical Society.

57 Judith Keyes Kinney in the *East Oregonian*, November 4, 1959, McKay folder, Archives, Oregon Historical Society.

58 *Ibid.*

59 *Ibid.*

60 Becker, *op. cit.*, February 29, 1968.

61 Allen, *op. cit.*, p. 206.

62 Wallace, *op. cit.*, pp. 431, 469-470. Actually, Leila's blood was doubly "distinguished," for if her parents were first cousins, Margaret McLoughlin and Alexander McKay were her great-grandparents in both her father's and mother's lines of descent.

63 Leila McKay, letter, McKay folder, Archives, Oregon Historical Society.

64 *Oregon Journal*, May 18, 1950, clipping in McKay folder, Archives, Oregon Historical Society.

65 *Oregon Historical Quarterly*, Vol. 36 (1935), p. 110. Also, pamphlet "McLoughlin House," printed by McLoughlin Memorial Association, 1949.

66 Becker, *loc. cit.*

67 *Ibid.*

68 *Ibid.*

69 The *Portland Reporter*, Friday p.m., October 11; Saturday a.m., October 12, 1963, McKay folder, Archives, Oregon Historical Society.

70 In the foreword of *Tall Brigade* author Hermia Fraser related her interview with the notary public, Mr. Watt. Since the book was published in 1956, the interview probably took place at about that time.

Sir George Simpson, the "Little Emperor." Copy of a daguerrotype.
Notman Archives, McGill University, Montréal

PART IV

THE KING'S LATER LIFE

Dr. John McLoughlin

Royal Family of the Columbia

CHAPTER 13

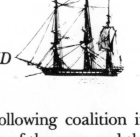

THE EMPEROR AND THE KING

GOVERNOR SIR GEORGE SIMPSON AND CHIEF FACTOR JOHN McLOUGHLIN

George Simpson, the key figure in the difficult period following coalition in 1821, has been called by some historians the perfect combination of the man and the moment, of being "in the right place at the right time."[1] However, lest his material success and professional prestige be attributed solely to chance, it should be clearly stated that he also possessed the qualities necessary for the position he held, that, by 1839, of governor of the whole HBC empire in North America. He was the first officer ever brought into the Honourable Company (or for that matter into the Northwest Company) with proper business training and background. His "orderly mind and talent for organization" had great impact. He was a "pivotal personality in the critically transitional years of the Company."[2] He was "a great executive, perhaps the greatest the fur land has ever known."[3] According to a member of the London Committee his "clear, orderly mind and a driving ambition were sustained by a physical vitality which carried him buoyantly through life." He brought to his task a combination of energy, administrative ability and capacity for reasoned judgment rare in the fur trade...he introduced order and regularity into the disturbed state of affairs he found in the Northern Department."[4]

John McLoughlin, although differing in many respects from his superior, also possessed according to historians a genuine love of responsibility, administrative ability, and strong views. In addition, he was more experienced in the fur trade than the Governor, having been with a fur company since 1803. By contrast Mr. Simpson had had only one year in the field, 1820-1821, in the Athabasca area. Many felt that the two men made an excellent team in the Oregon Country, cooperating to "infuse a new spirit of enterprise into the trade, at the same time cutting its expenses."[5]

It was perhaps in their private lives that they differed most. Dr. McLoughlin's exemplary life has been described, his "high sense of morality and his undeviating marital fidelity" stressed.

An egregious example of the Horactio Alger legend, George Simpson was born in Scotland in 1787, an illegitimate son of George Simpson. He was fortunate in that rather than being cast off and deserted, he was reared by a relative, some saying by a kinswoman, some more specifically by an aunt; others, by a grandfather, a minister. It was also fortunate that after receiving a good education he was taken as a clerk into a London mercantile house, Graham, Simpson, and Wedderburn, the Simpson partner being his uncle and future father-in-law, Geddes McKenzie Simpson. Young George's aptitude for hard work was noted by another partner, Andrew Wedderburn, later Lord Colville, a member of the HBC Honourable Committee, a Deputy Governor, and Governor from 1852 to 1856. It was he who introduced the young man to the Hudson's Bay Company. Later, Simpson acknowledged Lord Colville's significant assistance when he wrote, "To you I am solely indebted for my advancement in life."[6]

By contrast with the reputedly model life led by the Chief Factor, the Governor was the father of at least seven "bits o'brown," that is, children who were one-fourth Indian. Since his wife was Caucasion it goes without saying that the children were all illegitimate. There were two Marias, two Georges, two Jameses, and one John. The sons all had undistinguished careers in the Company; one Maria married the botanist Wallace and was drowned while young; the other Maria went to school in England and later lived in Ontario, Canada.[7]

Four of the "bits of brown," by elimination, one Maria, one George, one James, one John, were children of his mistress, Margaret Taylor (part Indian, no doubt), daughter of George Taylor, captain of York Fort schooner, and sister of Simpson's personal servant, Tom Taylor. Probably the first of these seven children was the daughter (Maria) whom Margaret bore him in the fall of 1821.[8]

The Governor had no intention of marrying Margaret, but neither did he want any other man to have her. Afraid that she might be "free of her favours" during his absences, he seriously considered having a blacksmith make a chastity belt for her, but apparently he did not follow through with the idea.

Aware of his reputation for having numerous "wives," he had a private entrance built into the governor's new residence being built at York Fort. He did not wish to be "troubled with a Lady during the busy Season" since she was "an unnecessary and expensive appendage" at a time when he could not "enjoy her charms."[9]

On February 24, 1830, George Simpson married his cousin Frances Ramsay Simpson, daughter of his uncle and benefactor. They became the parents of five children: George Geddes, who died at four months; Frances Webster, Augusta d'Este, Margaret McKenzie, and John Henry Pelly, namesake of the long-time (1822-1852) Honourable Governor.[10]

Before his marriage the Governor assumed the responsibility for Margaret's children, providing their financial support and having them baptized by the Reverend John West at the Red River settlement, thus setting an example for other "commissioned gentlemen" of the Company. In addition he "pensioned off" his "old concern" (Margaret) and arranged a marriage for her. When he was making similar arrangements for Chief Factor John McTavish's "old concern" of seventeen years' standing, he had some difficulty, for she was the niece of the Governor of Assiniboia.

Royal Family of the Columbia

Frances Simpson was only eighteen years old, twenty-six years her husband's junior. He took her from England, through Canada to La Chine and Red River, and to York Fort for the 1830 Council, then back to the Red River settlement. She was sweet, gentle, and unsophisticated; she was kind to all and well liked, but her very existence among the "commissioned gentlemen" and their Indian or half-breed wives posed a problem, for the Governor's rejection of a half-breed as wife and his marriage to an Englishwoman was considered a slight to the officers' dusky wives.[11]

Marriage and advancing middle age changed Simpson's business methods. Having already mastered his territory, he now traveled less, taking care of Company business whenever possible by correspondence. When he did travel it was more often to England, rather than to the North American wilderness. Mrs. Simpson's health was delicate. By 1832 Mr. Simpson's health was also poor; both of them were grieving over the death of their first child, a boy of four months. Both needed to go to England, to "civilization," for their health; the Governor even considered retiring. However, his health improved and he returned to North America in 1834 in "full vigour," all thought of retirement forgotten.[12] Mrs. Simpson returned to Canada later and lived with her husband at La Chine where he had acquired a large stone mansion fifty feet by sixty feet, about nine miles up the St. Lawrence from Montréal, which became the Hudson's Bay House of Canada. Here at the combined headquarters and residence officers and clerks enjoyed hospitality from 1833 until 1860, the year of the Governor's death. Delicate Lady Simpson died in 1853.[13]

But in 1835 death was still a quarter of a century away from the HBC governor. After fourteen years of experience he had mastered the technique of managing the Councils in all his departments. It was at this time that the "Little Emperor" emerged. His autocratic demeanor had the unfailing support of the Honourable Committee in London. His absolutism was based on the fact that he visited London nearly every year, returning with full information and authority.[14] While at first, early in his governorship, he had assumed a relatively democratic approach with the Councils (composed of chief factors, chief traders, and wintering partners), asking for and even listening to their counsel, after 1835 he ruled the Councils with an iron hand; even as early as 1826 he had faced few challenges, for he backed his judgement with ruthless treatment of dissenters. With vast wilderness at his disposal those who disagreed could be "promoted" to the interior of Northern British Columbia.[15]

He was limited in his autocracy only by the London Governor and by the Committee, which gave him great latitude. The relationship between them was one of mutual respect rather than of dictatorship on the one hand and obedience and tension on the other.[16]

He dominated the Hudson's Bay Company in North America for thirty-nine years, ruling a territory extending from Labrador and the St. Lawrence valley to the

Pacific Ocean, and from the mouth of the Columbia to Russian Alaska. In physical strength and endurance he could match any of his traders. His approach was a personalized one: he moved swiftly from one area to another, investigating, probing, recommending, sometimes dismissing.

Under Simpson's régime the Company prospered. After eleven years of four percent dividends the capital stock had been increased from 103,000 pounds in 1825 to 400,000 pounds and a ten percent dividend. In 1828 there were bonuses which brought dividends to twenty percent; in 1838 the stock earned twenty-five percent. The number of proprietors increased from seventy-seven in 1820, to two hundred sixty-eight in 1856, and to two hundred eighty-six in 1863.[17]

After twelve years in the fur trade he anticipated modern business methods by setting up a pocket-size notebook of *Servants' Characters,* his own personal record. In this he wrote his impressions of his subordinates. Concerning Chief Factor John McLoughlin he wrote in 1832, in part, the following apparent paradox:

> Very zealous in the discharge of his public duties and a man of strict honor and integrity but a great stickler for rights and privileges and sets himself up for a righter of wrongs. Very anxious to obtain a lead among his colleagues with whom he has not much influence owing to his ungovernable violent temper and turbulent disposition, and would be a troublesome man to the comp'y...would be a Radical in any Country under any Government under any circumstances...altogether a disagreeable man to do business with...yet a good hearted man and a pleasant companion.[18]

Names did not appear in the record, for all entries were coded by number. After the Governor's death the code on a separate sheet of paper was discovered among his documents long after the book had been read uncoded. In the perspective of more than a century, historians found that Simpson's analyses of various individuals were consistently perceptive. Of James Douglas he wrote, "Sound judgement, but furiously violent when aroused. —Has every reason to look forward to early promotion and is a likely man to fill a place at our Council board in course of time..." He was, as it turned out, correct in his understatement. James Douglas went much further than a Council board.

Throughout the years he wrote daily letters of encouragement, criticism, flattery, and news to his men. It was a significant aspect of his power of command. He was a master in the art of letter-writing. He wrote clearly, frankly, and without reservation. In a busines where colleagues rarely met, letter-writing was a cultivated art. He wrote lengthy, lucid letters to his officers full of details of the trade and of intimate, friendly news.

Royal Family of the Columbia

About 1841 his eyesight began to fail and in spite of the fact that he was forced to delegate much reading and writing of documents to assistants, the fullness and frequency of his correspondence continued.[19]

In January 1841 the Little Emperor was knighted by Queen Victoria at Buckingham Palace. In March he began a journey around the world, by horse, canoe, bateau, and ship. As part of the trip he visited various forts, including those at Vancouver, Stikine, and Yerba Buena (San Francisco); the Russian-Alaskan governor at Sitka was also visited, as were warehouses on the Sandwich Islands.

In California he saw Frank Ermatinger, who had been sent to report on the character of the country, riding in the guise of a Spanish caballero. Again visiting the northern posts, in 1842, at Stikine he found the Chief Factor's son murdered and the post in chaos. From Alaska he went to Siberia then on to Russia, visiting Moscow, St. Petersburg, and other Russian cities as part of the overland journey.

The world was changing. In England discussions with the Honourable Governor and Committee revealed concern over the place of the Company in a rapidly expanding world. There was the possibility that the "Company of Adventurers" might ultimately sell the title of the land to the Crown and assume the role of private traders without the obligation to maintain peace and good government. The necessity of periodic renewals of exclusive license to trade in lands outside the Hudson's Bay watershed (basically west of the Rockies) became of increasingly great concern. In 1857 a parliamentary committee put the Little Emperor, then seventy years old, under a cross examination so severe that he had difficulty holding his temper.

A highlight in the career of the Little Emperor was the visit to Canada in August 1860 of Queen Victoria's eldest son, the future Edward VII. After a state visit to Montréal the eighteen-year-old prince drove with his suite to a park-like island in the St. Lawrence three miles above La Chine to Sir George's country home. The prince's party as it was rowed to the island was escorted by one hundred painted, feathered Iroquois in decorated canoes. At the center of the brigade was the Little Emperor, "big as life," directing the procession in his usual commanding fashion.

George Simpson's life was drawing to a close. In the spring of 1860 he had suffered an attack of apoplexy while en route to Fort Garry and had been forced to turn back, an admission of defeat which was a great blow to his pride. He had always been proud of his active life; only three years before he had broken ice each morning for a stimulating plunge. Just three days after entertaining his future sovereign he had a second attack; after six days of intense suffering he died at Hudson's Bay House at La Chine at the age of seventy-three. The comment was made that the Little Emperor's "light had gone out" just after he had "basked in a final blaze of glory," that is, in the glory of entertaining the heir to the throne, young Prince Albert Edward.[20]

It is hardly necessary to comment that Sir George was not universally loved. He was imperious and exacting with his subordinates but always loyal to those who did not fail him.[21] He couldn't endure men who asserted themselves. For this reason, some historians say, he had assigned John McLoughlin, who was not afraid to assert himself and who had a much higher concept of service to his fellow man than had Sir George, to the Pacific Coast, a position considered to be tantamount to banishment.[22] The very quality of discipline which he imposed on his subordinates resulted in the breeding of malcontents who could not longer enjoy the special privileges that had been theirs from régimes previous to Simpson's. Cabals, formed to undermine his authority and prestige, failed because of his rapport with and backing of the London Committee.[23]

It has been said that Sir George had two loves—himself and the Honourable Company. His unswerving allegiance to the Company as an institution and to his superiors set a high standard and gave the personnel an esprit de corps which still exists in the Company today.[24]

Most emphatically not always in agreement with the Little Emperor was Chief Factor John McLoughlin. Perhaps the tall, regal King of the Columbia disliked instinctively the short, stocky Mr. Simpson whose orders he had to obey. Perhaps not. Both men shared an intense admiration for Napoléon I, with whom Simpson also shared the disadvantage, if such it was, of small stature.

From the beginning the two men had basic differences, but for several years they worked together and corresponded in a relatively pleasant working relationship, no doubt due to their consuming devotion to the Columbia Department. Dr. McLoughlin left the Department only once in twenty-one years—when he went on furlough in 1838.

The Columbia District (later Department) was in deplorably poor condition in 1824, but when the Governor returned to it for the first time, in 1828, he was most favorably impressed with the improvements made by his chief factor, who had followed the policies laid down for him by the Company and by the Resident Governor.

In one significant respect the Columbia Department differed from other HBC departments in North America—its distance, distance from York Factory, from Governor Simpson, and from the eastern councils. This anomaly made it possible for the head of the Columbia Department to enjoy a unique autonomy not possessed by other department heads.[25] Because of his extra-legal power of command he was often called governor of the Oregon Country. In fact, in *Governors of Oregon*[26] by George Turnbull, pages 1-4, the first to be listed and discussed as an *official* governor was John McLoughlin. This special status was gratifying to Dr. McLoughlin, who was an able administrator, efficient, ingenious, and innovative. A problem of the Columbia's distance from "civilization," with the Chief Factor's resultant extra-authority, presented itself whenever Mr. Simpson gave instructions or indicated policies to be followed with which Dr. McLoughlin was not in accord. Then there was conflict.

A fundamental controversy was that of posts vs. ships. Governor Simpson believed that the Company should maintain a minimum number of posts with Company vessels plying the intervening coastline. He considered this method both more efficient and less costly. Dr. McLoughlin, on the other hand, had the polarized view that four posts could be established and maintained at less cost than one vessel. In 1834 he felt so strongly "anti-vessel" that he sent the *Néreide,** back to London, only to have the London Committee retaliate by sending the *Beaver* in 1836, which was to become a symbol of differences between the two men.

The Chief Factor's antipathy toward coastal vessels came from the landman's prejudice against the unpredictability of ships, of their captains, and of their crews, and of the trouble they often caused, particularly with the natives.

In 1841 Sir George put his belief into practice when he ordered Chief Factor McLoughlin to put the coastal trade on a more economical footing. All coastal posts except Fort Simpson were to be abandoned and the *Beaver* would collect furs brought to the coast. Dr. McLoughlin stubbornly and persistently resisted the drastic change.

The Chief Factor's resentment against Simpson increased with the latter's announcement that the Company's administrative center for the Columbia Department should be moved from Vancouver to Victoria, on the southern tip of Vancouver Island, a shift which McLoughlin had long resisted, although he had reluctantly participated through James Douglas in the building of Fort Victoria. Sir George's argument, a logical one, was based on the rationale that when the British-American boundary west of the Rockies was settled Vancouver probably would be in American territory, also that in view of heavy American immigration the Fort was in an exposed position. McLoughlin's contention was based more on emotion and sentiment than on reason. Although he may not have expressed his thoughts aloud he was known to feel deeply that due to his efforts and diligence Fort Vancouver was the nucleus of a flourishing agricultural area with farms, livestock, fruit orchards, a salmon fishery, and saw and grist mills.[27] It had its own school, library, hospital, and regular Protestant and Catholic church services; it was the most important community, the educational, social, and administrative center of the Oregon Country.[28]

John McLoughlin and George Simpson had varying concepts of the role played by Fort Vancouver in the development of the Honourable Company in the West, Sir George seeing it as one of several principal forts in the HBC empire, important, but not indispensable, a stepping stone in his master plan, a means to an end. To Dr.

*The Beavers, Herbert and Jane, arrived on the *Néreide* in 1836.

McLoughlin it had permanence; he had built it; he loved it and had developed great loyalty to it through the years. It was the capital of his kingdom, of the most important department of the Hudson's Bay Company. Furthermore, he felt that the Governor's decision to close the posts was a direct slur on his management; this he could neither accept nor forgive.[29]

A miscellany of other factors was involved in the bitterness between the two HBC officials including the Company post at Yerba Buena; some historians contend that Simpson favored the establishment of a California post; others claimed that he reluctantly and against his best judgment allowed an enthusiastic McLoughlin to extend Company forts to California. Too, it was controversial whether Simpson may have been involved in Mexican political intrigues or, worse, that he arranged that weak William Glen Rae be implicated in a revolutionary plot. Also, who sent Mr. Rae to San Francisco Bay, the Governor, or the Chief Factor? Was Sir George to blame for Rae's suicide, at least indirectly? These questions have never been answered definitively.

By far the strongest factor in the final break between the Emperor and the King, the catalyst which brought the differences of the late 1830s and the early 1840s to a head, was the murder of John McLoughlin Jr.,[30] or, rather, the way in which the Little Emperor mishandled the apprehension of the murderer. There has always been uncertainty as to whether young John McLoughlin was sent to Stikine by his father, or by Governor Simpson. If by the former, the Chief Factor was guilty of nepotism and poor judgment, according to Simpson; if by the latter, Dr. McLoughlin blamed Sir George for putting John into a position for which he was temperamentally unsuited.

In any case, when Sir George stopped at Stikine April 25, 1842, and found that young McLoughlin had been murdered four days previously by some of his own men, he took evidence hastily and superficially,[31] for he was in a hurry to get to Sitka; he sent a curt and heartless verdict to the grieving father that his son's death was justifiable homicide. The Governor felt, since neither Russia nor Canada had a court of criminal jurisdiction in Stikine, a no man's land, that there was nothing to ao except to let the guilty man, or men, go free.[32] In addition, he went so far as to write John's father, asking him to say nothing.[33] Underneath this callousness one can infer that Simpson felt a man could not love or take pride in a "bit o'brown," and that consequently John's death was not really important, even to his father.

Dr. McLoughlin did not feel this way concerning his "bits o'brown." He was furious. For him it was more than a question of whether a Company employee had foolishly brought about his own death; it was the loss of a dear son, deserving or not.

He began a separate investigation at his own expense, which produced a completely different picture from that of Sir George Simpson—an isolated post garrisoned with half-savage native ne'er-do-wells who resented their officer because he insisted that they do their assigned tasks and that they observe the rule forbidding the men to bring prostitutes to the post to spend the night. Neither was he a drunkard. He had kept an orderly post in spite of great handicaps. Dr. McLoughlin was overjoyed when the London officials accepted his investigation, vindicating young John completely. The Committee Secretary, Archibald Barclay, wrote

> The crime was clearly premeditated and if ever men deserved hanging, Urbain Héroux, Pierre Kanaquassé, and the scoundrel McPherson ought to be *strung up*. It is evident that the charges of habitual intoxication and excessive severity were trumped up after the deed was committed as a screen to the villany (*sic*) of the culprits.[34]

In spite of the vindication members of the Honourable Committee would not disown or reprimand its overseas governor. They respected both men and appreciated the contributions of both to the Company. The Committee members temporized. They did not want to let either man go and hoped that they would both "cool off" after a time. If the two men could not get along with each other, one would have to be released. If a choice had to be made it would be in favor of Sir George, who had always cultivated a rapport with London. Finally the Chief Factor was told he must either get along with the Governor or leave the Company.[35]

Then came what must have been the crowning blow. On November 20, 1845, the Chief Factor quoted from a letter written by Archibald Barclay

> on the advantages...which the Governor and Committee had hoped would be derived from placing the Columbia Department under the charge of one person, have I am sorry to state not been realized...they are decidedly of the opinion that it is not advisable that the charge of so extensive a District should be confided to one individual however experience; they have therefore resolved that the Country shall be divided into two or more Districts, each to be represented by a commissioned officer....The Governor and Committee have also determined as a necessary consequence that the Allowance of 500 pounds per annum which was granted to you beyond your emolument as a Chief Factor, in consideration of the great extent and consequent responsibility of the charge committed to you, shall cease on the 31st of May 1845.[36]

What was the purpose of this unpleasant notice? Was it as punitive and vengeful as it seemed, or was it a genuine and sincere effort to increase the efficiency of the Columbia Department? Or was it perhaps a strategic device to effect Chief Factor John McLoughlin's resignation?

Alberta Brooks Fogdall

REFERENCES

CHAPTER 13

THE EMPEROR AND THE KING———GOVERNOR SIR GEORGE SIMPSON AND CHIEF FACTOR JOHN McLOUGHLIN

1 Douglas MacKay, *The Honourable Company*, p. 175.
2 E. E. Rich, *The Hudson's Bay Company*, p. 376.
3 Robert E. Pinkerton, *The Hudson's Bay Company*, p. 294.
4 Oscar O. Winther, *The Great Northwest*, p. 54.
5 *The Beaver*, house organ of the Hudson's Bay Company, Tercentennial issue, fall 1970, pp. 47, 48, 50, 51.
6 MacKay, *op. cit.*, pp. 175-176; David Lavender, *Land of Giants*, p. 117.
7 MacKay, *op. cit.*, pp. 198-199.
8 Rich, *op. cit.*, p. 383.
9 *Ibid.*, p. 453.
10 *Ibid.*, p. 463; MacKay, *op. cit.*, p. 198.
11 Rich, *op. cit.*, p. 453.
12 *Ibid.*, p. 454.
13 MacKay, *op. cit.*, p. 211.
14 Rich, *op. cit.*, p. 467.
15 MacKay, *op. cit.*, p. 203.
16 *The Beaver, op. cit.*, p. 49.
17 MacKay, *op. cit.*, p. 210.
18 *Ibid.*, p. 199.
19 *Ibid.*, pp. 200, 202, 209.
20 *Ibid.*, pp. 213-218.
21 *Ibid.*, p. 209.
22 Gordon Speck, *Northwest Explorations*, p. 365.
23 MacKay, *op. cit.*, p. 203.
24 Speck, *loc. cit.*
25 *The Beaver, op. cit.*, pp. 50, 51, 52.
26 Published in Portland, Binfords and Mort, 1959.
27 *The Beaver, op. cit.*, pp. 51, 52, 53.
28 T. C. Elliott, in an address to the Walla Walla chapter of the Washington Library Association, of which he was president, also in the *Washington Historical Quarterly*, vol. 3, part 1, October 1908, pp. 63-37.
29 Rich, *op. cit.*, pp. 716-717.
30 Walter A. Sage, "A Note on the Origin of the Strife between Sir George Simpson and Dr. John McLoughlin, *Washington Historical Quarterly*, Vol. 24, October 1933, pp. 258-263.
31 MacKay, *op. cit.*, p. 215; *The Beaver, op. cit.*, p. 54.
32 H. H. Bancroft, *History of Oregon*, Vol. I, pp. 471-472.
33 Richard G. Montgomery, *The White-Headed Eagle*, pp. 286-287.
34 *The Beaver, loc. cit.*
35 Lavender, *op. cit.*, pp. 212-215.
36 *Ibid.*, pp. 89-90.

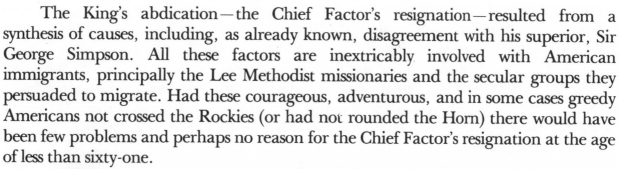

CHAPTER 14

THE KING ABDICATES—
FRIENDS, ENEMIES, AND CONTROVERSY

The King's abdication—the Chief Factor's resignation—resulted from a synthesis of causes, including, as already known, disagreement with his superior, Sir George Simpson. All these factors are inextricably involved with American immigrants, principally the Lee Methodist missionaries and the secular groups they persuaded to migrate. Had these courageous, adventurous, and in some cases greedy Americans not crossed the Rockies (or had not rounded the Horn) there would have been few problems and perhaps no reason for the Chief Factor's resignation at the age of less than sixty-one.

They came in ever-increasing numbers. The first Oregon settlers came from the great numbers of fur traders. Several numbers of American fur-trading parties and retiring employees of the Northwest Company and of the Hudson's Bay Company had settled as farmers, a large number in the Willamette Valley; a smaller number settled in the Rogue River Valley and, in Washington, in the Walla Walla Valley and in the Puget Sound area, and in numerous other places. Many of the French Canadian employees chose that part of the Willamette Valley on the east bank of the Willamette River north of present Salem; the nationality of the settlers was reflected in the name of the site, French Prairie. Among these men were Joseph Gervais, for whom the small town is named; Michel La Framboise, Louis Labonte, Étienne Lucier, and, later, François Xavier Matthieu, some of whom later participated in the formation of the Provisional Government.[1] Actually, trappers as such did little to occupy the country on any large scale, except as they blazed the way for the missionaries and farmers who migrated in the 1830s and the 1840s.[2]

Additional numbers in the 1830s came in the form of free traders, some in the ranks of such leaders as Ewing Young and Nathaniel Wyeth, spurred on by the encouragement and writings of the "Prophet of Oregon," Hall Jackson Kelley. In the custom of the times most chose Indian mates; from these unions came the "first families" of the Willamette Valley.[3]

Long after the fur trade became extinct immigrants continued to come, using the rather loosely defined "Oregon Trail," usually beginning at Independence, Missouri, making use of South Pass (an extensive gap in the Rockies), in present southwestern Wyoming, to Fort Hall (built by Nathaniel Wyeth), on the upper Snake. Some reached the Columbia by way of the Whitman Mission, which by 1840 was an important way station. Other caravans chose to reach The Dalles by way of the confluence of the Columbia with the Umatilla River, from which point the 160-mile trip to the Willamette Valley was made by canoes or bateaux.[4]

Alberta Brooks Fogdall

The earliest immigrant parties were often met at the main landings by Hudson's Bay Company employees, who escorted them on bateaux downstream to Fort Vancouver. Later, when the immigrant parties were too numerous and came too frequently to be met, they built rafts and floated persons, wagons, and other belongings precariously downstream. Frequently suffering from semi-starvation, they received comfort and aid from Chief Factor McLoughlin and his staff at Fort Vancouver, and after a rest there continued to their destination. At other times Americans in the Valley, frequently missionaries, came to the rescue.[5]

A significant factor in the increasing numbers of new arrivals was the great missionary movement to attract colonists, a principal example being the "Great Reinforcement," which arrived in 1840 from around Cape Horn with Jason Lee as the result of his pleading for "respectable" Americans to colonize the Oregon Country.

In 1843 the "Great Migration" brought 875 American settlers into the Oregon Country, resulting in an estimated total of 1500 population in the Willamette Valley. In 1844, 1400 migrated, while in 1845 the number more than doubled, with 3,000 more added to the population.[6] With each year the increase was multiplied.

The character of immigrants changed with the years; from an early conglomeration of deserters from whalers, law-breakers and fugitives from justice, former fur traders who hated the HBC, and adventurers both French Canadian and American, the immigrants changed principally to missionaries and, inevitably, to colonizers.[7]

It was of course the last group, which as it became larger and more powerful, caused the handwriting to appear figuratively on the walls of the Hudson's Bay Company and of the Chief Factor's residence.

In spite of the fact that almost invariably the HBC in the person of Dr. John McLoughlin treated these individuals who were to contribute so heavily to its—and his—downfall not only fairly, but generously and kindly, there were complaints and recriminations on the part of the settlers.

Most of the grievances were against the Honourable Company, not against Dr. McLoughlin as an individual; yet in effect they were the same. They resented especially the fact that the Chief Factor, acting on Company policy, would not sell farm animals, particularly cattle. Yes, he was kind, they said: he lent tools, seed, horses, and cows, but he refused to sell the animals, for if they were sold to the settlers, the latter might butcher the offspring; and the Company needed every available animal to develop its carefully nurtured herds.

The colonists felt, illogically or not, that the HBC was trying to keep the whole Willamette Valley for itself. Another complaint was the monopoly held by the Company; the settlers had no place either to sell furs and wheat or to buy goods except at the Company store. In fact only at the Company forge could a broken tool be repaired.[8] (In retrospect it would seem that the settlers would have been relieved and glad to have a store and a forge to provide services for them. What would they have done without these services?)

Even when in 1845 a few immigrants defied the Chief Factor's "suggestion" to settle south of the Columbia and instead went to the Puget Sound area, they carried a letter from Dr. McLoughlin to Dr. Tolmie at Fort Nisqually, asking him to let the settlers have whatever they needed that Dr. Tolmie could spare and charge the amount to Fort Vancouver.[9]

Again, word reached the Fort that some Dalles Indians were threatening trouble to Americans when they arrived at The Dalles. McLoughlin threatened punishment to the Indians if they harmed the immigrants. Many of the immigrants had been left stranded at The Dalles and at the Cascades of the Columbia, where a wagon road had to be cut around a portage. Their provisions gave out and Oregon rains inundated them. Dr. McLoughlin sent flour, sugar, tea, molasses and, best of all, boats to bring them to the Fort. The sound of the voyageurs' tune *"Roulant, ma boule, roulant"* as they approached the helpless Americans must have been figuratively as well as literally music to their ears.[10]

It was not only understandable but logical that the pioneers should have challenged the monopolistic possession the Hudson's Bay Company had claimed for nearly 175 years. They could not feel that "any King Charles" (who, after all, lived "way back," 1630-1685) had the right to "sell out" a large share of North America to a private monopoly trading company (and then, in addition, exceed even the terms of the 1670 charter by extending beyond the watershed of Hudson Bay) "to be held for all time as a game preserve to produce pelts for London profits." The Company seemed to them a "feudal relic."[11]

As the colony grew, with new settlers coming to the Valley,* the Chief Factor's kindness and generosity were often forgotten, even by those whose lives he had saved or, at least, eased; they joined his detractors, accusing him and the Company of unfairness in their dealings. Stories eventually reached potential colonists in the East.

An example was illustrated in the words of an unidentified settler: "It is true these (McLoughlin and the people of the HBC) are good folks and treat me kindly, but somehow or other I cannot like them and moreover do not like those who like them." Rather an extreme statement in retrospect, but characteristic of the times.

Another settler, who returned to the States, regretted that he had not set fire to Fort Vancouver, yet could not say why he wished to.[12]

The danger of fire to the Fort was constant. Unfriendly Indians often threatened to set fire to the stockade to avenge real or imagined grievances. Henry Williamson, a

---

*The fertile soil of the Willamette Valley attracted ever-increasing numbers of settlers, who opened retail stores in Oregon City, which took business away from Fort Vancouver stores. To meet American competition the Chief Factor opened a branch store at the Falls in Oregon City.

dissident immigrant, about whom more later, in 1844 also threatened to burn the Fort. That same year a forest fire set by Indians to facilitate their fall hunting had actually come within a few feet of the stockade before it was quenched.[13]

And yet, with all those who disliked John McLoughlin there were those who admired and some who all but worshipped him. "To many of the tatterdemalions who emerged from the trail Dr. McLoughlin must have looked like the Jehovah they read about in their dog-eared Bibles."[14] Often no bill was presented for first assistance to the colonists upon their arrival. Boats were often provided along with the loan of farm animals and supplies.[15]

One "old timer," Joseph Watt, wrote in 1886 of his recollections of the Chief Factor. He was one of a company of immigrants who arrived, their provisions exhausted. He had said to the Chief Factor, "I can't pay you", to which John McLoughlin had replied, "Tut, Tut! Never mind that; you can't suffer." He then asked the travelers to form a line as he sat at a table. The line was so long that it extended nearly around the perimeter of the large room. "Your name, if you please; how many in the family, and what do you desire?" Upon receiving an answer, the Doctor wrote an order, directed the person where to fill it, and moved on to the next.

Mr. Watt continued, recalling that when they had started to Oregon they were all prejudiced against the Hudson's Bay Company and that they had a double share of prejudice and resentment against its Chief Factor of the Columbia Department, which was dispelled by Dr. McLoughlin's hospitable and magnanimous treatment.[16]

Resentment against Chief Factor McLoughlin took numerous forms—a general resentment which resulted in malicious and petty gossip, resentment more against the Company than against the man, and might, for example, result in setting fire to the stockade. Far more pointed, more dangerous, completely personal, and with long-lasting effect was the disputing and stealing of John McLoughlin's land claims.

As early as 1829-1830 the London Committee had given a mandate to Governor Simpson, who had in turn passed it on to his Columbia Department head, namely, to acquire land at Willhamet (Willamette) Falls.[17] The Company officers had tacitly yielded as far as any expectation of England's eventually possessing territory south of the Columbia, but possession of land to the south would serve as bargaining points for Great Britain to use in the final boundary settlement.

Not only to have leverage against the United States in the boundary controversy, but also to have flour to send to Russian Alaska according to the Company's contract, was it deemed efficacious to be able to utilize water power at Willamette Falls.[18]

Therefore Dr. McLoughlin, either for himself or for the Company—which it was has never been made completely clear—took possession of a site at the Falls of the Willamette which he and Governor Simpson had chosen together at the time of Simpson's visit to the Fort in 1828. The Governor enthusiastically described the site:

Royal Family of the Columbia

"...whole Forests of Timber can be floated into a very fine Mill Seat...(and) Saws enough could be employed to load the British Navy."[19] A more prosaic description was "the side of the Falls from the upper end of the Falls across to the Clackamas River and down to where the Clackamas falls into the Wallamette (*sic*) including the whole point of land and the smaller island in the Falls on which the portage is made..."[20] To today's natives this would mean as far as the Oregon City shopping center.

Here at the site of the Falls McLoughlin built a grist mill and a saw mill and, a little later, two houses to hold his claim. Immediately upon taking possession of the site he had had timbers cut for the foundation of a house, which according to custom was a declaration of intention to build and was considered sufficient to hold a land claim.[21]

The description of the claim taken by the Chief Factor was sent to the Reverend Jason Lee ten years later because of the greed of the Reverend Alvin Waller of the Methodist Mission and of at least one faction of the Mission. The message was a "friendly" warning to Mr. Lee: Mr. Waller was given permission to build a store on the site as long as Mr. Lee realized that the land was owned by Dr. McLoughlin; he even generously helped the Mission by giving Mr. Waller some cut lumber for his building.[22] This incident was the first of numerous troublesome actions which the Methodists would take in the future.

Chief Factor McLoughin had staked a claim at Willamette Falls for business reasons and also for a home after his retirement and to bequeath to his children. He foresaw that with the fur trade disappearing, the Falls with its power would attract settlers and would in due time develop into a distributing and purchasing center for farmers. It is possible, too, that even this early (1829-1830) he had decided to become an American citizen. By 1842, in addition to three houses and the mills, Dr. McLoughlin had had all the land surveyed, had platted part of it in blocks and lots and had named the area Oregon City. He sold some lots and made gifts of others to churches and to a school.[23]

Claim-jumping became a popular pastime. Because Mr. Waller had successfully challenged the McLoughlin claim at the Falls, others followed suit. Some justified their actions by reasoning that the claim was actually held by the HBC, not by McLoughlin the man, and that a monopoly, especially a foreign monopoly, had no right to land claims, particularly at a power site in a territory which would surely soon become American.[24]

The sport of jumping claims even moved northward to Fort Vancouver. In February 1845 Henry Williamson and several companions performed a symbolic act, a warning of things to come, when they arranged logs in the shape of a hut at the gates of the Fort, posting a claim:

Alberta Brooks Fogdall

Meddle not with this house or claim
For under is the Master's name,
Henry Williamson[25]

The angry Chief Factor had the "hut" and the sign removed, but it was only by the intervention of Gustavus Hines, Elijah White, and Jesse Applegate that Williamson was dissuaded from repeating his "squatting."[26]

The Williamson incident afforded Dr. McLoughlin an opportunity to show his conviction that the right of prior claim and occupation was inviolable. It was this right which was credited with settling the boundary controversy so that today's British Columbia went to Great Britain. Without the establishment by the Hudson's Bay Company of these northern posts and their occupation of these sites, that territory would, like the Oregon Country, probably have gone to the United States; without these claims British politicians would probably not have successfully challenged the United States' claim of 54⁰, 40'.[27]

As the population of the Oregon Country, mainly of the Willamette Valley, continued to increase, a need for law and government was felt. Prior to about 1841 there was a complete lack of formal government. Article III of the Anglo-American treaty of 1818, regarding the boundary, in effect provided for joint use of the territory, but no provision was made for its government. The convention of 1827, which extended the treaty indefinitely, again ignored the subject of government. Since the disputed territory (roughly present western Washington) belonged to neither country as yet, neither nation could establish a political framework. An American in the area in the 1820s would have been limited by no other restraint than his conscience or than by fear of retribution on the part of those about him. He could have committed murder, arson, larceny, or any other crime and no white person would have had either the constitutional or the legal means of punishment.

However, some form of extra-legal government existed. Before the white man invaded the West each Indian tribe had its own laws and mores and considered them binding on others. On expeditions, one example being that of Lewis and Clark, the members were subject to rules laid down by the leaders. In the case of the Lewis and Clark Expedition the leaders were army officers; hence military rules and regulations were in force.

Members of the various fur companies—British, American, and Russian—were bound by the rules of their respective companies. Employees of the Hudson's Bay Company were obliged to obey company rules, the Company being in turn responsible to the British Government. Occasionally, of course, both Britons and Americans might take the law into their own hands.

The charter of the "new" Hudson's Bay Company, of 1821, gave the Chief Factor limited judicial rights over British subjects in the regions where British government courts had not been established; in 1835 he had acquired the right to

260

appoint justices of the peace. Obviously he could not logically or legally have control of Americans in the area, though he possessed a certain influence because of his forceful personality and his prestigious position. As already known, Chief Factor McLoughlin assumed control over the natives because of his position of authority and the fact that the Indians desired to maintain amicable trade relations with the Company.[28]

American missionary leaders such as Jason Lee, Marcus Whitman, Henry Spalding, and Catholic Fathers Blanchet, Demers, and DeSmet exercised authority both over their own workers and the neighboring Indians; the leaders in turn took their orders from a home board of missions or other high church authorities. In 1838 the aggressive Methodist missions even provided for a magistrate and a constable. These officials performed their extra-legal duties notwithstanding certain conflict with both the Indians and with Hudson's Bay Company officials.[29]

Oregon was similar to frontier areas such as Utah, Colorado, and others in which settlement preceded the establishment of civil government under the laws of the United States.

British occupants of the Oregon Country were more or less content with, or at least acquiesced in, Company rule. Not so, American settlers, who saw no reason why they should be subject to a foreign agency. More and more as antagonism between Americans and Britons increased, the need was pointed up for a temporary, or provisional, government representative of American interests which would "tide them over" until the region could achieve territorial status.[30]

The first step was taken as the result of the death of Ewing Young, who left a sizeable estate and apparently no heir.[31] After the funeral, on February 17, 1841, the Reverend Jason Lee addressed the mourners, mentioning that the need for disposing of Young's estate was the first of many such cases which would arise in the future, and urging the settlers to organize for this purpose and also for "the better preservation of peace and good order" of the settlements south of the Columbia River for the protection of those not connected with the Hudson's Bay Company. Mr. Lee was well prepared, proposing a list of offices and a slate of candidates. The list provided a hierarchy of officials: a governor, a supreme judge with probate powers, three constables, three road commissioners, an attorney-general, a clerk of the court, a public recorder, a treasurer, and two overseers of the poor. Many settlers felt that they were being forced into organization and moved to adjourn until the next day.[32]

The next day, February 18, at the Lee Mission House, the settlers, who were now joined by the French Canadians of French Prairie, made it quite clear that they were opposed to any "unnecessary" officials, electing only those necessary to handle probate cases and offenses against the peace, namely, a sheriff, three constables and a judge with probate powers. A committee was elected, headed by Father François Blanchet, to draft a civil code and to report at a June 1 meeting.

Alberta Brooks Fogdall

Father Blanchet announced on June 1 that the committee had not met. It was clear that those at the meeting did not want a hierarchy of officers; even more clearly, they drew the line at creating the office of governor, an early indication of the colonists' typical fear of a strong central government. The French Canadians (Catholics), feeling that Dr. McLoughlin would be opposed to the formation of a government, were not in favor of it, following what they believed to be his preferences.[33] Thus Father Blanchet and his followers simply let the idea of government fail by default.

Opinions of French, British, and Canadians clashed; Catholic versus Protestant elements were injected. No decisive action was taken and matters remained in abeyance until 1843 when gatherings called "wolf meetings" were held; the need to protect their farm animals from predators was an issue common to all settlers, whether American, British, or French Canadian. One meeting, on February 2, called for a second meeting on March 6 at the home of Joseph Gervais. (Wolves, bears and panthers *were* discussed, but "politicking" was the order of the day.) An important meeting at Champoeg, on the bank of the Willamette, followed on May 2. Great interest, even excitement, preceded the meeting. The deliberations that day led directly to the drawing up of the first code of laws for the Oregon Country.[34]

At the next meeting, July 5, at Champoeg, a constitution committee, which had met several times in true frontier style in an empty granary at Willamette Falls, presented its proposals.[35] Organic articles and laws modeled upon the Northwest Ordinance of 1787 and the Statutes of Iowa Territory were voted on and adopted. Three officers (*not* including a governor) composing an executive committee, again indicating a fear of absolutism, elected in May, were sworn in. A Bill of Rights was included, a testimony to the desire of the Oregon pioneers for democracy: freedom of religion, the right of habeas corpus, trial by jury, moderate fines, representative government, maintenance and encouragement of schools, knowledge and morality; fairness toward the Indians, and prohibition of slavery. Protection by a militia was also provided. An unusual and impracticable feature was that no taxes were levied; the government was to subsist on voluntary contributions.[36]

The "Great Migration" later that year changed the character of the settlers and of the government, so that in 1844 and 1845 the newer colonists, no longer of missionary leaning, insisted on changes in the organic laws. The word provisional was dropped, the Mission claim reduced, a tax schedule set up, and the three-man commission changed to a single executive. These were the more basic revisions; there were also numerous smaller changes.[37]

How did all the foregoing affect the Hudson's Bay Company and particularly Chief Factor John McLoughlin? The increased American migrations had automatically increased settler resistance to the dominance of the Honourable Company. The three distinct factions in Oregon, according to one writer, were 1. the

Royal Family of the Columbia

Company, including the Chief Factor and its French Canadian ex-employees; 2. the Methodists with their clergymen, their laymen, and their political aspirations; and 3. the independent settlers, *i.e.*, unattached missionaries, former American fur traders, and miscellaneous traders. These groups were the "common people." The last two groups, in spite of many differences, had their American nationality in common, which served to pit them against the British Company.

Dr. McLoughlin as the regional representative of both the Hudson's Bay Company and of Great Britain naturally was eager to block such a united movement against him, such as a provisional government promised to be. He reasoned that any provisional government would be predominantly American and would necessarily assume authority over all the inhabitants of the region. It would mean the loss of his power after a long period of wise, competent, and, in most cases, beneficent rule.

Once the French Canadians joined the Provisional Government, the Doctor was also inclined to join. Just at that time, however, the Methodists resumed their attack on his land claims, which caused him for a time to hold back.[38]

The Company had made a noble effort to combat the American invasion by importing Company employees from the Red River region, hoping to equal or even surpass the American population. The results, however, were abortive and unsatisfactory.[39]

In the meantime the Chief Factor and the Honourable Company were in an unenviable position. The presence of so many Americans, many of them lawless and unruly, was alarming.[40] The Doctor had written to the London officials asking for protection of Company property; the reply was ambiguous. He then asked the British consul at the Sandwich Islands for protection; there was no reply. In June 1845 he received orders to protect his and the Company's interests as best he could.[41]

The Provisional Government in the meantime was having financial troubles. The problem was solved logically by the Company's joining the Provisonal Government August 15, 1845. Both Chief Factors McLoughlin and Douglas took the oath following, in 1845, the removal of objectionable measures discriminatory against the British Company.[42] The requirement of swearing allegiance to the United States Government had been amended so that the Company officials swore to "support the Organic laws of the provisional government of Oregon as far as the said organic laws are consistent with my duties as a Citizen of the United States, or a Subject of Great Britain."[43]

When called upon to justify the step he had taken to his superiors, Dr. McLoughlin wrote,

> We have yielded to the wishes of a respectable part of the people in the country, of British and American origin, by uniting with them in the formation of a temporary and provisional government designed to prevent

disorders and maintain peace until the settlement of the boundary question....We decided on joining the association both for the security of the Company's property and the protection of its rights.[44]

The Company recognized the Provisional Government by contributing $226.65 in taxes to the Government treasury; in return it enjoyed several benefits:

1. The Company had less to fear that its territory north of the Columbia would be invaded, for the Columbia was the northern limit of the Provisional Government's domain. This limit constituted recognition of Company rights by the Americans.
2. The new government provided legal machinery to aid the Company in $30,000 in debts owed by American settlers in the Willamette Valley and in respecting Company (or McLoughlin) land claims.
3. Ruffians, lawless elements, and "desperate characters from Missouri," *et al;* could be controlled more easily when responsible to a legal authority, especially since the Americans outnumbered the British.[45]

In essence, the above was the explanation given in the Chief Factor's last letter to the Company in "McLoughlin's Last Letter," written November 20, 1845.[46]
Everyone was now awaiting the final settlement of the boundary. Both Americans and British had lived in frustration too long, uncertain of the future, unable to make long-range plans until the dividing line was determined. Settlers had been optimistic that the Webster-Ashburton treaty in 1842 settling the Maine-New Brunswick boundary on the east coast would also solve the corresponding problem on the west coast. However, it was not until four years later, on June 15, 1846, that the Buchanan-Pakenham treaty ("Oregon Treaty") set the forty-ninth parallel as the dividing line, a compromise between the 54⁰, 40' of American Manifest Destiny expansionists and the Columbia River of British hopefuls. The line was to continue from the Rockies through the Strait of Juan de Fuca, but instead of cutting through the southern part of Vancouver Island, the entire island remained British. During this troubled time British warships appeared and hovered in Puget Sound and in the Columbia, hopefully to bolster British claims. British officers appeared at Fort Vancouver, including Lieutenant Willam Peel, son of British Prime Minister Sir Robert Peel.[47]

The United States had based its claim basically upon the discovery of the Columbia River by American Captain Robert Gray; the explorations of Meriwether Lewis and William Clark; the founding of Astoria by John Jacob Astor and its restoration by the British after capturing it during the War of 1812; in addition there were the American missions and settlements north of the Columbia, *e. g.,* those of the Whitmans and Spaldings.

Royal Family of the Columbia

Great Britain based its claim to the area north of the Columbia upon the early voyages of British navigators, chiefly of Captains George Vancouver, Charles Barkley, and John Meares, and Lieutenant Peter Puget—all mostly upon the coast. British claims to the interior were based on explorations of Alexander MacKenzie, Simon Fraser, David Thompson, and others, as well as upon forts built by the Northwest Company in the headwaters of the Columbia and of the Fraser (also later forts in the North by the Hudson's Bay Company); important, too, was the ascent of the Columbia by Lieutenant William Broughton.[48]

Great Britain was plainly the loser, giving up the entire triangle in dispute in accepting the forty-ninth parallel. The treaty consisted of five articles, Article II confirming the Company's possessory rights in general, while Article III guaranteed its rights specifically in regard to the Cowlitz farms and the Puget's Sound Agricultural Company.[49] Dr. John McLoughlin was given credit for the Company's retention of possessory rights, due to the firm stand which he took against American interlopers on Company property north of the Columbia during that confusing, troubled year, 1845. His staunch belief in "possession by right of prior occupation" was of the highest practical and financial advantage to the Honourable Company in terms of the Oregon Treaty settlement.[50]

E. E. Rich in his *The Hudson's Bay Company* wrote that the Company lost heavily as a result of the boundary decision, for the average annual profit from Fort Vancouver alone was more than 30,000 pounds, while other posts in the surrendered area yielded more than 10,000 pounds in profits.[51]

Payment was not made until between 1869 and 1871. The United States paid the Company a total of $650,000, $200,000 of which was for Puget's Sound Agricultural holdings. The first payment was made in September 1869. It took twenty-five years to settle this problem resulting from the treaty, with assessments of properties, offers, rejections, surveys, the United States Senate's rejecting of offers, and commissions studying the question for five years. The Civil War with all its problems intervened; the possibility of England's recognizing the South as a belligerent retarded settlement of the claims. The settlement was made amicably by the British and American commissioners with no necessity to call in an umpire.[52]

Many, both British and Americans, had felt before 1846 that war was inevitable. The climate of opinion was set for it momentarily. James K. Polk was set for it, or so it seemed, with his "54°, 40' or fight" campaign slogan. Temporarily the British were annoyed by the campaign propaganda, but soon dismissed it as for local political consumption; however, President Polk's inaugural address, in which he claimed that the United States had "clear and unquestionable" title to "the country of Oregon" aroused the British public sufficiently that for a short time war talk swept the country. Then both nations became involved with other problems; for the United

States, Texas and California posed questions to be solved, as did the abolition issue and the coming slavery problem. In Great Britain Her Majesty's Government, with Sir Robert Peel as prime minister, was at the moment in a rather undecided frame of mind; to fight or not to fight—that was the question. The government did not want Great Britain to be involved in war, yet not to fight might imply a loss of national pride. Both English-speaking nations were much relieved when the controversy was settled peaceably.[53]

By the time the boundary controversy was decided the King of the Columbia had abdicated, relinquishing his royal duties to his heir, Chief Factor James Douglas. It was in Oregon City in November 1846, now living in his new home, that the former chief factor learned of the long-delayed boundary settlement, which had taken place five months previously, June 15. The news had come to Fort Vancouver via the British *Toulon* and had been relayed by James Douglas to Oregon City, which had replaced Champoeg as capital of the Provisional Government.[54]

Why had His Majesty King John moved from a position of authority and prestige with the Hudson's Bay Company to one of obscurity as just another (American) citizen of Oregon City?

Dr. McLoughlin's problems were all of necessity bound up with the settlers, for had there been no settlers or had there been fewer settlers there would have been no, or, at least, far fewer, problems. This, in spite of the fact that E. E. Rich stated that the Oregon frontier was settled by the climate of American politics rather than by the number of immigrants.[55] However, to be specific, McLoughlin blamed the Little Emperor for all or most of his troubles, whether justifiably depends upon the historian.

The Governor's storming at his subordinate for kindnesses to the settlers, his callous and brutal mishandling of the murder of John Jr., and his possible indirect culpability both in John Jr.'s death and in the suicide of Eloisa's husband William Rae, their differences relevant to forts and vessels, to the Puget's Sound Agricultural Company, to expansion into California, to his (and the Company's) joining the Provisional Government—all these and more have been recorded. Perhaps the "dirtiest trick" played upon John McLoughlin was the order (referred to earlier) given by Mr. Simpson in a letter March 15, 1829, to hold grist and saw mills and other property and to move enough servants to the Falls to care for them. This command was completely ambiguous as to whether he was to hold the property for himself or for the Company, but, obediently, he acted as instructed. So indefinite and unclear were the directions that even James Douglas, who tried always to avoid involvement in his superiors' differences, stated they were "as vague and mysterious as the oracle of Delphi."[56] In 1844 it was obvious that he had been trapped. Sir George insisted that the Chief Factor had acquired the property for himself, not for the Company. The

Company then forced him to pay for the property, which he did most reluctantly, with the strongest possible protests.[57] Even then he was unable to retain the property. For years, ever since the Reverend Mr. Waller's first infringement, there had been continuous litigation between the Chief Factor and the Mission. Finally, on April 4, 1844, Dr. McLoughlin entered into a settlement with Mr. Waller, paying him $500 and, in addition, eight lots and three blocks in Oregon City; also he gave the Mission six lots and a full block. Optimistically he hoped that this would end the affair. Unfortunately, his troubles had just begun; they would continue to pursue him even in Oregon City.[58]

No doubt John McLoughlin had hoped to continue his work for a few more years, probably until his sixty-fifth birthday. However, the combination of troubles with Sir George Simpson and the Company and the harassment he endured from the Methodist Mission caused him to resign from the Hudson's Bay Company in 1845.[59] He began building a spacious home at the Falls, to which he moved during the spring of 1846. He undoubtedly hoped for a happier life among Americans because of his many kindnesses to them and because he intended to join them as an American citizen. Here, too, he was doomed to disappointment.

Douglas MacKay, historian of the Honourable Company, paid a compliment to John McLoughlin when he wrote, "The strongest man to break with Simpson was Chief Factor John McLoughlin, the "Big Doctor" who for twenty years ruled like a benevolent feudal baron an empire reaching from Honolulu and California to Alaska."[60]

Less complimentary was his statement in the Company's house organ, *The Beaver:*

McLoughlin himself attributed his decline to Simpson's malevolence...but in a sense he was his own worst enemy. At a time when the Hudson's Bay Company was increasingly aware of the implications of its continental responsibilities and involvements, 'the Doctor' with his swash-buckling ways and *cavalier treatment of instructions* (italics added) had already become an anachronism.[61]

The "anachronism" was to live on for eleven years more in Oregon City.

REFERENCES

CHAPTER 14

THE KING ABDICATES—
FRIENDS, ENEMIES AND CONTROVERSY

1 Oscar O. Winther, *The Great Northwest*, p. 109.

2 Earl Pomeroy, *The Pacific Slope, A History*, p. 19.

3 Winther, *op. cit.*, p. 108.

4 *Ibid.*, p. 109.

5 *Ibid.*, p. 110.

6 *Ibid.*, pp. 123-124.

7 Katharine B. Judson, *Early Days in Old Oregon*, p. 250.

8 David Lavender, *Land of Giants*, p. 184.

9 Jalmar Johnson, *Builders of the Northwest*, pp. 73-74.

10 Opal Sweazer Allen, *Narcissa Whitman*, pp. 282-283.

11 *City of Portland*, I, p. 67.

12 Jane Tipton, *John McLoughlin, Chief Factor of Hudson's Bay Company at Fort Vancouver*, p. 84.

13 Lavender, *op. cit.*, p. 246.

14 Johnson, *op. cit.*, p. 64.

15 George W. Fuller, *A History of the Pacific Northwest*, pp. 210-211.

16 Joseph Watt, "Recollections of Dr. John McLoughlin," *Oregon Pioneer Association Transactions*, 1886, pp. 23-26.

17 Richard G. Montgomery, *The White-Headed Eagle*, p. 143.

18 Horace S. Lyman, *History of Oregon*, Vol. III p. 423.

19 Dorothy O. Johansen, *Empire of the Columbia*, p. 133.

20 Montgomery, *op. cit.*, pp. 264-265.

21 Lyman, *loc. cit.*

22 Montgomery, *loc. cit.*

23 Frederick V. Holman, *Dr. John McLoughlin, The Father of Oregon*, pp. 102-159 (general description).

24 Sister Mary Dominica McNamee, *Willamette Interlude*, p. 112.

25 Johansen, *op. cit.*, p. 191; E. E. Rich, The Hudson's Bay Company 1670-1870, Vol. II, pp. 732-733.

26 Johansen, *op. cit.*, pp. 191-192.

27 Rich, *loc. cit.*

28 Winther, *op. cit.*, pp. 127-128.

29 *Ibid.*

30 *Ibid.*, p. 129.

31 Several years later a son, Joaquin, was discovered. The value of the estate (held by the state) was paid to him (Winther, p. 130n.).

32 Johansen, *op. cit.*, pp. 184-185.

33 *Ibid.*

34 Winther, *op. cit.*, pp. 131-132.

35 Joseph McLoughlin, the Chief Factor's eldest child, was on the committee which drew up a code of laws and on July 5, 1843, voted the adoption of the first article (Burt Brown Barker, p. 329n.).

36 Winther, *op. cit.*, pp. 133-134.

37 Johansen, *op. cit.*, p. 192; Winther, *op. cit.*, p. 135.

38 Montgomery, *op. cit.*, pp. 295-297.

39 *Ibid.*, pp. 278-279.

40 *Ibid.*, p. 306.

41 Fuller, *op. cit.*, pp. 201-202.

42 Montgomery, *loc. cit.*

43 Mary A. Avery, *History and Government of the State of Washington*, pp. 154-155.

44 Fuller, *loc. cit.*

45 Winther, *op. cit.*, pp. 136-7.

46 Reprint in *Oregon Historical Quarterly*, October 1915. Also in E. E. Rich, ed., *McLoughlins* Fort Vancouver Letters, specifically pp. 97-105.

47 T. C. Elliott, "McLoughlin and His Guests," *Washington Historical Quarterly*, Vol. 3, Part 1, p. 76.

48 John Garraty, *The American Nation: A History of the United States*, pp. 316-317; Johansen, *op. cit.*, pp. 207-210; Winther, *op. cit.*, pp. 146-148.

49 Winther, *op. cit.*, p. 150.

50 Johansen, *op. cit.*, p. 208.

51 Rich, *op. cit.*, Vol. III, p. 731.

52 Johansen, *op. cit.*, p. 209.

53 Winther, *op. cit.*, pp. 46-48.

54 Lyman, *op. cit.*, Vol. III, pp. 436-437.

55 Rich, *op. cit.*, Vol. III, p. 717.

56 Tipton, *op. cit.*, p. 116.

57 Burt Brown Barker, *The McLoughlin Empire and its Rulers*, p. 49.

58 Montgomery, *op. cit.*, pp. 302-303.

59 Lavender, *op. cit.*, pp. 213-215; also, Edwin V. O'Hara, *Pioneer Catholic History*, p. 90.

60 Douglas MacKay, *The Honourable Company*, p. 208.

61 Glyndwr Williams, "Simpson and McLoughlin," *The Beaver*, p. 55.

One of the best-known likenesses of John McLoughlin, believed to have belonged to his granddaughter Margaret Glen Rae Wygant.
Photo from Oregon Historical Society Archives, Portland.

Royal Family of the Columbia
CHAPTER 15

THE KING IN EXILE
DR. McLOUGHLIN IN OREGON CITY

The later life of Dr. John McLoughlin might be said arbitrarily to begin in 1845-1846, when he resigned from his position as a chief factor in the Hudson's Bay Company and moved in January 1846 to his new and at-that-time pretentious home at the Falls of the Willamette in Oregon City.[1] However, more than one historian, including E. E. Rich, placed the beginning of this period of his life earlier, in 1841-1842, identifying the last visit of Sir George Simpson to Fort Vancouver as the crucial point in the Chief Factor's life. Dr. Rich also stated that Dr. McLoughlin himself in his letters attributed the sorrow and tragedy of his later years to Governor Simpson in general and to his 1841-1842 visit in particular: "Sir George Simpson's Visit here in 1841 has cost me Dear," he wrote in 1846 in his last letter to Sir John Pelly, the Honourable Governor, in London.[2]

As he went to Oregon City his family consisted of his wife, Margaret, his son David, his widowed daughter Eloisa, and her three children, John, Maria Louisa, and Margaret Glen Rae.[3] They moved into their beautiful new home completed in 1846. The Doctor has been described variously as disillusioned, bitter, and discouraged when he moved at sixty-one.[4] He has been equally described as "still energetic"[5] and as having brought with him the same zealous spirit in retirement which had actuated him in managing the huge Columbia Department.[6] He and Margaret had moved to Oregon City with high hopes, planning to claim and use the land, on some of which had been built gristmill, sawmill, stores, their home, and other property.[7]

Too, he was pictured as having difficulty in curbing his anger if he met one of the numerous settlers who had borrowed money and goods from him in past years and who consistently refused to repay him, even though able to do so. He would begin instinctively to bring up his famous gold-headed cane, then catching himself, would stop and mutter "God forgive me," and hurry on. His granddaughter Louisa Rae told how he would sit for hours sorting his numerous papers into categories according to probability of payment, entering them in his books of different colors, and, finally, wearily fall asleep over them.[8]

The former Chief Factor felt that he had left Company business in excellent hands. James Douglas, his long-time assistant and protégé, had been groomed by his benefactor as his successor—and so he became. He had "filled in" for Dr. John on numerous occasions and was now thoroughly experienced and highly capable of continuing the work of his long-time friend.[9]

In Oregon City Dr. McLoughlin was not universally well treated. He was the object of dislike and of suspicion by many Americans.

Alberta Brooks Fogdall

Several reasons existed for this hostility:

1) He was a Catholic in a strongly Protestant community.

2) He had an Indian or rather, half-breed, wife.

3) He was British; Great Britain and America were on opposite sides of the boundary controversy.

4) He represented a powerful monopoly.

5) His acts of kindness were not known to a majority of the settlers, as many were late immigrants.

6) He was an "aristocrat," was a wealthy man in a position of authority. To most Americans he *was* the Hudson's Bay Company.[10]

Charges against the Hudson's Bay Company included their seizing valuable land sites and occupying strategic points with forts, their preempting twelve sections of land at Fort Vancouver for farming and pasturing; also, the Company employees, Indian wives and half-breed children comprised most of the population of the settlement of seven or eight hundred persons.[11]

Once settled in Oregon City, the Doctor began to take the steps necessary for acquiring American citizenship. Probably he had both emotional and pragmatic reasons for so doing. Certainly as an American, he felt, he would have a better opportunity of holding the land which both groups and individuals were attempting to take from him. However, he was represented as wishing American citizenship as a matter of principle as well as of expediency, for he admired the republican form of government and had in 1838 while in Canada enroute to London shown tangible sympathy for rebellious Canadians who were asking relief from repression.[12]

He counseled with Jesse Applegate, indefatigable immigrant of 1843, and with Chief Justice Peter H. Burnett of the Provisional Government. The former urged him to take the oath of allegiance to the United States immediately, but Justice Burnett claimed that as a justice in the Provisional Government he did not have the authority to administer the oath under the Territorial Government; that Dr. McLoughlin should wait until a Territorial justice arrived who would be qualified to give the oath. As a result the former Chief Factor remained in limbo until after William P. Bryant was appointed chief justice of the new Oregon Territory on April 9, 1849. On May 30 the Doctor made that oath of allegiance and took out his first papers; he cast his first vote in the Territorial election in June, as a Democrat. On September 5, 1851, he finally achieved his goal, becoming a full citizen after nearly two and one-half years of waiting.[13]

Reams could be written on the negligence and venality of Justice Bryant, who served only five months of a nearly two-year term, but it suffices here to say that he and Samuel Royal Thurston engaged in a conspiracy to force Dr. McLoughlin to give up his land and in other ways humiliated and degraded him.[14]

Royal Family of the Columbia

Using the flashback technique and reverting to 1841, it is recorded that a number of members of the Methodist Mission had formed the Oregon Milling Company and had concentrated their activities on an island at Willamette Falls which John McLoughlin had claimed as early as 1829. He had made improvements on it and in 1842 had erected a sawmill and a gristmill; in 1843 he had had the claim surveyed by Jesse Applegate. Moreover, he had built his home there and had lived on part of the claim since 1845.

In 1846 George Abernethy, Oregon's only Provisional Governor (1845-1849), and financial manager of the Mission, claimed the Milling Company and the island, later called Abernethy's, or Governor's Island. In 1849 Judge Bryant purchased the Abernethy (Mission) interest, thus beginning the controversy over ownership rights.[15]

Thurston, a Sammy-come-lately, having arrived as recently as 1847, was young, intelligent, brilliant and, so far as John McLoughlin was concerned, a demagogue. He has been described as having "both eyes and both ears open for the main chance," the "main chance," of course, being McLoughlin's Oregon City property.[16]

He had seen the entrenched power of Abernethy and the Mission. He had also heard the rumble resulting from Henry H. Spalding's ridiculously false accusation that the Hudson's Bay Company and the Catholic Missionaries, working together, were responsible for the Whitman massacre, i. e., that they turned savage Indians loose on the mission, and that they had warred on the United States government for many years. Thurston, having managed to be elected as Territorial delegate to Congress, bruited the false stories about Washington in order to create the Congressional atmosphere he needed for his purpose. He managed to get a rider included in the Donation Land Law of 1850 which, in effect, defrauded McLoughlin of most of his land, "Abernethy Island" going to the "Wallamet milling and trading companies" (Abernethy), and the rest of his claim to be at the disposal of the legislature for a university.[17]

Among the methods Thurston had pursued in influencing Congress was the issuing of a circular letter full of exaggeration and lies. Also, he had asked several who, he knew, disliked McLoughlin to write letters to Congress. Hall Kelley was understandably among them; he complied only too gladly, writing a diatribe of contempt and vindictiveness. Nathaniel Wyeth, too, was asked, but he, in spite of his financial defeat at the Doctor's hands, wrote that Dr. McLoughlin's treatment of him had always been just, fair, and friendly.[18]

Lieutenant Charles Wilkes had been sent by sea in 1836 by the United States government (but did not arrive until 1841) to explore "the territory of the United States on the seaboard" and "the coast of California with special reference to the Bay of St. Francisco..." Also sent, but by land in 1843, was Captain John C. Frémont, to complement Wilkes's explorations. The Chief Factor had been sufficiently perceptive to realize that the real purpose of the expeditions, hidden under the ostensible explanation of scientific information about a "navigable river",[19] was all a part of the American concept soon to be labeled "Manifest Destiny." Both these Americans wrote favorably of the former Chief Factor; Frémont, in particular, wrote to Dr. McLoughlin, assuring him that he (Frémont) would repeat what he had "already said publicly and to thank you for the kind and hospitable treatment...in 1843." He it was, probably, who first made the suggestion, to be followed later, that the "Good Doctor" should be recognized not only as the founder of Oregon City, but also as the "Father of Oregon." In the Oregon Historical Society archives are copies and excerpts of other letters complimentary to Dr. McLoughlin. Among noted letter-writers were Samuel K. Barlow of Barlow Trail fame, Father François Blanchet, a bishop, later an archbishop, of Oregon City; and General M. M. McCarver, a well-known early citizen of Oregon City and Commissary-General of the Oregon Volunteers during the Rogue River Indian Wars of 1855-1856. All of these—and many more—expressed their gratitude for kindly treatment and hospitality on the part of the former Company official.[20]

Justice Bryant in his legal capacity was bribed to assert that the Mission-Abernethy claim antedated McLoughlin's, and that in any case the Doctor as a foreigner was not eligible to own land, purposely ignoring the fact that Dr. McLoughin had applied in good faith for American citizenship.[21]

The *coup de grâce,* however, was the rider (previously noted), clause eleven, of the Donation Land Law, which was Thurston's vindictive method of dealing with the man he so irrationally disliked. The rider provided that no private individual could hold a claim to

> extensive water privileges or other situation necessary for transaction of mercantile or manufacturing operations...Provided that nothing...should be so construed as to affect any claim of any mission of a religious character made previous to this time....

This bit of legislation thus blatantly and effectively froze out McLoughlin and confirmed the Mission's and Abernethy's claims to 23,040 acres.[22]

Even Oregon Citians, antagonistic as many of them were to the Doctor, couldn't accede to this wrong. Friends of his had attempted earlier to send a memorial to Congress, hoping that it would tend to counteract Thurston's efforts. Unfortunately, due to the slowness of communication, their attempt was too late. A public meeting had been called September 19, 1850, by friends who were angered at Thurston's persecution of McLoughlin. Resolutions were passed declaring that the selection of Dr. McLoughlin's Oregon City claim for a university site was "uncalled for by any considerable portion of citizens of the Territory" and was "invidious and unjust" to Dr. McLoughlin. It added that he "merited the gratitude of multitudes of persons in Oregon."

Royal Family of the Columbia

Relevant to the persecution of McLoughlin is an original clipping of the *Oregonian* printed during this period, dated December 17, 1852. Framed and hanging in the upstairs hall of McLoughlin House, the article speaks against petitions sent asking the Oregon Legislature to use McLoughlin's lands for a university and asks that "justice be done to an old, tired, and faithful friend to this country..."[23]

As a concession to justice the McLoughlins were allowed to continue living in their "forfeited" home at the Falls. Their life there was as happy as possible under the circumstances. They have been described as often sitting on the porch of their home, greeting and visiting with the passers-by. "By his side sat his faithful and loving wife—she who had stood beside him through all these troubled years of unswerving loyalty. She realized the Great White Eagle's spirit was taking its last flight, and, although her own heart was bursting, she brought him solace and comfort to the end."[24] Their home was always open; two large couches in the Doctor's reception room were often occupied by those who had no other place to go.[25]

Dr. McLoughlin served as mayor of Oregon City in 1851, winning forty-four of sixty-six votes; the small number of votes cast was due to the narrow electoral base of adult male property owners.[26] (Presumably the ballot was also limited to Caucasians, or at least to half-whites; since half-breeds were allowed to hold property according to the Donation Land Law, it is feasible that they also had the ballot.)

In 1850 the Doctor participated for the first time in celebrating the Fourth of July, though he was not yet a full citizen. He is recorded as giving a toast, "To Oregon—from the fertility of its soil, the salubrity and mildness of its climate, the finest place in North America for the residence of civilized man."[27]

During the first part of his life in Oregon City, between 1846 and 1850, he built houses, sawmills, and gristmills, providing employment for needy immigrants. He was denied permission to run a ferry across the Willamette at Oregon City as it would "give him too much power," but was allowed to construct a canal around the falls because he was willing to do it at his own expense and because it constituted a public improvement. He also had a millrace built, but when ready to construct locks, was forbidden to do so, for, as with the ferry, he would have controlled too much water power.[28]

The former King of the Columbia gave away three hundred lots for private and for public use, his beneficiaries including the Catholic school and the Methodist, Baptist, Presbyterian, Catholic, and Congregational churches, an egregious example of ecumenical and unbigoted philanthropy. Oregon City High School today is located on land donated by Dr. McLoughlin for a Protestant seminary. Another gift was land for a jail. Interestingly, some of the townspeople objected to the "luxury" of a log jail.[29]

He was always happy to have people around him who would accept his leadership. He possessed great executive ability, seeing what needed to be done and knowing how to do it, a carry-over, of course, from his days as a "top executive" with the Honourable Company. He was sociable, ready to talk, perceptive, quick to note every detail and incident.[30]

As one might expect, historians have conflicting interpretations concerning Dr. McLoughlin's financial status following his severance from the Company. The traditional view has been that he had been drastically mistreated both financially and emotionally by the Honourable Company. Some authorities, to the contrary, believed that the Hudson's Bay Company had treated him with consideration, not closing his books when he resigned in 1845. After a one-year furlough he was given a leave of absence for two years, with his final retirement to be dated from June 1, 1849. For one year following that he received a full chief factor's share of profits and for the next five years one-half share each year. In addition he was not charged the cost of trying to bring the murderer of John Jr. to justice.[31] Beginning with 1847 he was carried on the books as "Ret'd" (retired) and after September 1857 as "Dec'd" (deceased), and continued to be carried by his son-in-law, Daniel Harvey, executor of his estate, until it was finally closed November 23, 1868, after Mr. Harvey's death. The Company paid interest on his account up to May 1, 1863, six years after his death.[32]

Again, in defense of the Honourable Company, and flashing back to 1834, Governor Simpson had asked the Honourable Governor and Committee in London for a special grant of 600 pounds for Dr. McLoughlin for his professional services as a physician during the epidemic fever of the Columbia Valley during the period 1830-1833, and another special grant of 500 pounds in special recognition of the extraordinary responsibilities and difficulties he had faced. In 1839 the Governor and Committee voted the Chief Factor 500 pounds per annum over and above the two-eighty-fifths of the profit to which he was already entitled as a chief factor; this was continued until June 1, 1846, although he had retired six months before. The Honourable Company lived up faithfully to its contract.[33] In addition, it did *not* make him responsible for the debts of the Oregon pioneers to the Company.[34] All of these Company actions are difficult to reconcile with the opposing, traditional viewpoint.

For example, according to the long-accepted view: (1) His salary was reduced by 500 pounds. (2) He was an anachronism,[35] and most unsatisfactory to the Company; therefore, he would share the command with Chief Factors Douglas and Ogden.[36] In addition he had to bear all the expense of the trial of the murderer of John Jr. and pay the debts of the settlers to the Hudson's Bay Company.

Which polarized view to accept? The reader is free to interpret. Many will no doubt find the solution in a synthesis or a compromise of the two opposite interpretations.

Royal Family of the Columbia

Regardless of his treatment by the Company—favorable or not—Dr. McLoughlin was a wealthy man even after losing much of his Oregon City property, as shown later when his estate was probated.

During his life in Oregon City he felt unhappily caught between two antagonistic forces. On the one hand the Americans resented his English nationality. On the other hand the English felt that he had in a sense betrayed them by his generosity and many kindnesses to the Americans, making it easier for them to colonize the territory in dispute. To the latter charges he had replied repeatedly that he had merely acted as a Christian,

> "saving American citizens...from the Indian tomahawk...as I felt convinced that any disturbance between us here might lead to a war between Great Britain and the States, I felt it my bounden duty...to act as I did...which I think averted the evil (war)."[37]

The eleven years which he spent in Oregon City were frequently humiliating and disillusioning. Once King of the Columbia, ruling his domain with an iron but just hand, he was now just another Oregon Citian, well known and prestigious up to a point, but without actual power.

Margaret's support and affection were all-important to his morale, as to a lesser degree were the presence of Eloisa and her three children. David was often absent—in the gold fields or in other places of interest to one of his restless, wandering nature.

In addition to the comfort of having his family near him was the honor which came to him in 1847, the Knighthood of St. Gregory, bestowed upon him by Pope Gregory XVI. The document and medal, on display at McLoughlin House, are tangible evidence of this high honor, one of the extremely few bestowed. In part His Holiness had written:

> We have been informed on the highest authority that you are esteemed by all for your upright life, correct morals and zeal for religion and that you are conspicuous for your allegiance to ourselves and to the Chair of Peter.[38]

Background for this signal honor was the Pope's creation of Oregon as an apostolic vicariate with Father François Norbert Blanchet, a friend and associate of Dr. McLoughlin, as archbishop. The insignia received from Pope Gregory at the hands of Father Blanchet on his return from Rome were highly cherished by the Doctor.[39]

Also in 1847 was the Whitman massacre at Waiilatpu, near Fort Walla Walla, Dr. McLoughlin, who kept abreast of events outside his Oregon City microcosm, recalled his repeated warnings to Dr. Marcus Whitman concerning the Cayuse and

277

Alberta Brooks Fogdall

the danger of settling north of the Columbia. Chief Factor James Douglas, at Fort Vancouver, was cautious in regard to sending a punitive expedition against the wily and guilty Cayuse, saying there were no funds for the purpose. Meanwhile many adventurous Oregon settlers fought on their own authority. Too, Peter Skene Ogden hastened to the scene with an armed party to rescue the survivors of the mission. The Chief Factor, impatient with inaction, persuaded Tom McKay to lead a contingent of French Canadians and half-breeds against the Cayuse. He gave Tom not only moral support, but also necessary financial support.[40]

Admirers of John McLoughlin have not hesitated to point out that it is no mere coincidence that during his reign at Fort Vancouver there were no Indian wars, while less than two years after his rule ended the Cayuse War erupted, to be followed by almost continuous Indian wars for the next thirty years.[41]

Knowing the Doctor's character, it is safe to assume that he supported his church, St. John the Apostle Catholic Church, not only with his money but with his physical presence; he also maintained a high interest in education and in political affairs, both local and national.

The proclamation of Oregon as a Territory in 1849 was as exciting to John McLoughlin as it was to the Americans he was soon to join as a fellow citizen. The culmination of great effort by many interested settlers who had frequently been frustrated by the apathy of the federal government to organize the territory, the bill was passed by Congress by a narrow margin and was signed by President James K. Polk on August 14, 1848; the following March (1849) Joseph Lane, first Territorial governor, declared the Territory of Oregon officially in operation.[42] Also in 1849 came the final removal of the HBC Western headquarters from Fort Vancouver to Fort Victoria on Vancouver Island.[43]

Early in 1850 the United States established a military reservation at Fort Vancouver, building a post on the bluff behind the old fort.* For a time the old trading post continued to operate within the Fort's boundaries.[44] If the former "Hudson's Bay Man" felt lonely, isolated and desolate, it is not difficult to understand. He had built the Fort; he had chosen its site; it was his "baby"; he was proud of it and had hotly defended it, its location, its importance to the Company; he had fought as long as possible to prevent a change in its status.[45] Now it was gone. So, too, were his son and namesake and his son-in-law. Marcus Whitman and Jedediah Smith had been murdered by Indians. The Reverend Jason Lee had died in the East. Nathaniel Wyeth, who had remained his friend in spite of business rivalry, was in Boston. James Douglas was of course at Fort Victoria; other former associates, such as Dr. William Tolmie, John Work, Peter Skene Ogden, had scattered to other posts. Only his friend

*The last of the skeleton HBC staff left the Fort in 1860. In either 1865 or 1866 the Fort was burned completely, whether by the Army, accidentally, by Indians, or others is not known.

278

Royal Family of the Columbia

Dr. Forbes Barclay had moved to Oregon City, where he set up a practice and was McLoughlin's personal physician. Today the Barclay House, now a private museum of Northwest memorabilia, sits next door to McLoughlin House.*[46]

In the early 1850s the former Chief Factor supervised a sawmill, a gristmill, and his store, formerly a Company branch which he had set up in 1844; later, due to Oregon City's antagonism toward the Hudson's Bay Company, the store was operated under the name of its manager, Chief Trader Archibald McKinlay.[47]

Supervising these relatively small businesses kept him pleasantly occupied. The most unpleasant and arduous aspect of his life, affecting him both physically and mentally, was the struggle to collect the more than $30,000 owed him by settlers who either completely repudiated their debts, or "skipped" to live outside the Territory, feeling they would then be safe from prosecution.[48]

He began to lose weight, so much that he appeared gaunt and emaciated. He forced himself to keep going with almost his usual energy and vitality; his church, his charities, the schools, and what remained of his business did not suffer.

By August 1857 he was forced to admit he could not continue on his feet. During this time L. F. Grover, who was to become governor of Oregon from 1870-1877 and a United States Senator, stopped to visit the Doctor on his way from Portland to Salem. Dr. McLoughlin pleaded with his guest,

> I shall live but a little while...I am an old man and just dying, and you are a young man and will live many years in this country, and will have something to do with affairs here...I became a citizen of the United States in good faith. I planted all I had here, and the government confiscated my property. Now what I want to ask of you is that you will give your influence after I am dead to have this property to go to my children. I have earned it as other settlers have earned theirs, and it ought to be mine and my heirs'.[49]

He was greatly pleased during this time when Senator Henry B. Foote of Mississippi stopped in Oregon City to pay him a courtesy call. After talking for a few moments, the Senator commented to Dr. Henri A. M. Déchesne, McLoughlin's nephew, how much his uncle resembled Andrew Jackson. The Doctor, who was a great admirer of Jackson's, answered smilingly, "I thank you for the compliment."[50]

With him as he died were his family, Dr. Déchesne, and Dr. Forbes Barclay, his long-time friend and associate. As Dr. Déchesne entered his room the morning of September 3, 1857, he greeted his uncle in French, the family's more-often used language, *Comment allez-vous?*" "*A Dieu*" was the response. ("How are you?" "To (With) God.")

*On May 1, 1976, Barclay House was reorganized and began serving luncheons and teas.

Alberta Brooks Fogdall

REFERENCES

CHAPTER 15

THE KING IN EXILE
DR. McLOUGHLIN IN OREGON CITY

1 Dr. McLoughlin had laid out and platted the area then known as Willamette Falls and had renamed it Oregon City. It has been pointed out by Mrs. Charles (Nancy) Gildea, hostess at McLoughlin House, that the Doctor showed his (future American) patriotism by naming Oregon City streets for American presidents, in chronological order.

2 E. E. Rich, ed., *The Letters of Dr. John McLoughlin from Fort Vancouver to the Governor and Committee*, Vol. III, 1844-1846. The quotation is from the introduction, written by W. Kaye Lamb, p. XI, also from p. 171 in letter dated July 12, 1846, to Sir John Pelly, and also from *The Beaver*, fall 1970, p. 55.

3 Richard G. Montgomery, *The White-Headed Eagle*, p. 310.

4 *Ibid.*, pp. 308-309.

5 Eugene Snyder, *Early Portland: Stumptown Triumphant*, p. 58.

6 Ada Losh Rose, in the Gresham (Oregon) *Outlook*, October 18, 1935.

7 Helen Krebs Smith, *With Her Own Wings*, pp. 23-24.

8 Maria Louisa Rae Myrick, interview by Fred Lockley in the *Oregon Journal*, September 19, 20, 21, 1929.

9 Rich, ed., *McLoughlin Letters, op. cit.*, p. 313.

10 Jane Tipton, *John McLoughlin, Chief Factor of the Hudson's Bay Company at Fort Vancouver*, p. 131.

11 Melvin Clay Jacobs, *Winning Oregon*, p. 240.

12 Montgomery, *op. cit.*, pp. 242-243. Canadian Louis Joseph Papineau attempted a coup, inspired by the American Revolution (The attempt was abortive.)

13 *Ibid.*, p. 316.

14 H. H. Bancroft, *History of Oregon*, Vol. I, pp. 505-506.

15 Montgomery, *loc. cit.*

16 David Lavender, *Land of Giants*, p. 274.

17 Dorothy O. Johansen, *Empire of the Columbia*, p. 231.

18 Frederick V. Holman, *Dr. John McLoughlin*, pp. 148-153.

19 Johansen, *op. cit.*, pp. 199-200.

20 Letter of Frémont to McLoughlin, 1851, quoted by George H. Himes, assistant secretary of the Oregon Historical Society in 1905, in *Scrap Book*, Vol. 72, p. 35.

21 *Ibid.*

22 *Ibid.*

23 *Scrap Book*, Vol. 76, p. 69. This action is probably responsible for the clipping in the upstairs of McLoughlin House described in a following paragraph.

24 A. S. Marquis, *Dr. John McLoughlin*, p. 1.

25 Montgomery, *op. cit.*, p. 322.

26 Snyder, *op. cit.*, p. 25.

27 *Ibid.*, pp. 45-46.

28 Ada Losh Rose, *loc. cit.*

29 Fred Lockley, *Columbia River Valley*, pp. 759-760.

30 Rose, *loc. cit.*

31 Tipton, *op. cit.*, p. 128.

32 Burt Brown Barker, *Financial Papers of Dr. John McLoughlin*, p. 16.

33 *Ibid.*, p. 17.

34 Tipton, *Loc. cit.*

35 *The Beaver*, p. 55. House organ of the Hudson's Bay Company: tercentennial issue of the Company's founding, fall 1970.

36 Lavender, *op. cit.*, p. 215.

37 Montgomery, *op. cit.*, p. 320.

38 E. V. O'Hara, *Catholic History of Oregon*, p. 90.

39 *Ibid.*

40 Charles H. Carey, *History of Oregon*, p. 547.

41 Montgomery, *op. cit.*, p. 313.

42 Johansen, *op. cit.*, p. 319.

43 Montgomery, *op. cit.*, p. 319.

44 Johansen, *op. cit.*, p. 209.

45 *The Beaver, op. cit.*, p. 53. The remnants of the Fort were destroyed by a fire of unknown origin c. 1866.

46 Bancroft, *op. cit.*, Vol. I, pp. 39-40. Today may be seen in Mountain View Cemetery, Oregon City, the graves of Dr. Barclay, his wife, Maria; two sons, and two grandsons.

47 Johansen, *op. cit.*, p. 214.

48 The State of Oregon Archives (Salem) contain details of numerous cases in which Dr. McLoughlin was plaintiff against various debtors.

49 Holman, *op. cit.*, p. 159.

50 Correspondence of Dr. Henri A. M. Déchesne, son of Dr. McLoughlin's sister, Angélique Honorée, included with David McLoughlin's "Correspondence", Archives, Oregon Historical Society.

51 Montgomery, *op. cit.*, p. 324.

First reburial of John and Margaret McLoughlin, July 6, 1948. A second reburial took place in 1970. Dr. Burt Brown Barber is in the center foreground.

Photo from Oregon Historical Society Archives, Portland.

PART V

EPILOGUE——AFTERMATH

Courtesy Oregon Historical Society.

When St. John the Apostle Church was enlarged it covered the McLoughlins' graves; the tombstones were embedded in the foundation.

CHAPTER 16

THE KING IS DEAD
HIS MEMORY LIVES ON

The White-Headed Eagle lay in state in his home, a silver crucifix on his breast, in a "great kite-shaped oaken casket," massive candelabra at head and feet. The light illuminated his "snow-white hair, his strong, dignified, sorrow-lined features."[1]

Relays of men who had loved him carried the coffin through the streets to St. John the Apostle Catholic Church, situated on land he had donated overlooking the Willamette River. Here the service was held.

Crowds of men, women, and children lined the streets to watch the funeral procession with mixed emotions, "conscience, remorse, sorrow," on the part of some who had wronged him, cheating him of his property; of friends who grieved for his loss; of Indians, too, whom he had treated fairly and justly.[2]

This description appeared in the Oregon City *Enterprise-Courier* on September 10, 1957, exactly one hundred years after the funeral obsequies for Dr. John McLoughlin.

When a great individual or a controversial figure has been wronged during his lifetime, it is often true that a reaction sets in following his death. A desire to make reparation may take one of several forms, a memorial in the form of a monument, a statue, or a portrait; a new "title," a "special day," or other variations.

John McLoughlin was honored by at least one of each of the above types of restitution, no doubt also by others not recorded.

Quite possibly the reparation which the White-Headed Eagle would have most appreciated if he had known, the most tangible, and the one he had hoped for, was a legislative act on October 11, 1862. This was the fulfillment of the request, almost from the Doctor's deathbed, made of a future Oregon governor, L. F. Grover. On the last day of its session the Oregon Legislature "did try a righteous act by restoring to the heirs of the late Dr. McLaughlin (*sic*) the Oregon City land claim." There followed fulsome praise of the Doctor, citing his generosity and kindness to the Americans. "...now that the title is settled, the curse removed and justice done we may expect that the natural advantages will be developed and the historic old town contend for the palm with her younger rivals (Portland? Milwaukie?)."[3]

The semantics are rather grandiose. What happened in plain language is, simply, that Eloisa and Daniel Harvey, now the Doctor's sole heirs, had to pay $1,000 for that "state university" many of McLoughlin's antagonists had insisted on; they then received all lands not previously given or sold with the exception of "Abernethy's Island."[4] In other words, the restitution made was only a partial one. It was, of course, better than no restitution at all.

Alberta Brooks Fogdall

On February 5, 1889, an oil painting of the Doctor was presented to the Oregon House of Representatives. The Honourable John Minto, mentioned earlier, a member of the House, delivered the presentation address; his Excellency Sylvester Pennoyer, Governor of Oregon, gave the acceptance speech. Mr. Minto also presented to the Honorable (Judge) Matthew P. Deady a copy of the pamphlet "Speeches of the President and Acceptance of the Oil Painting of Dr. John McLoughlin."[5] Many illustrious Oregonians were present for the ceremony.

Sixteen years later, October 6, 1905, under the auspices of the Oregon Historical Society, "McLoughlin Day" was celebrated during the Exposition in Portland commemorating the centennial of the Lewis and Clark Expedition. The principal oration was delivered by author Frederick V. Holman, president of the Oregon Historical Society, and "McLoughlinophile" *extraordinaire*. Mrs. Josiah Myrick (Louisa Rae) was present at the ceremony honoring her grandfather.[6]

Two years later, again on October 6, an elementary school in Oregon City was named for him. At the dedication ceremony it was again Frederick V. Holman who eulogized the former Chief Factor, concluding his address, "To this Noble Man, to this Great White Chief, to this Grand Old Doctor, to this savior of the Oregon Pioneer, to this great Humanitarian, the Father of Oregon, be honor and praise for all time."[7]

It was also in 1907 that the Oregon Legislature designated him officially as "Father of Oregon" in recognition of his contribution to the development of Oregon.[8]

In 1921 Dr. McLoughlin was named one of two Oregon candidates for the National Hall of Fame. Thirty-one years later, February 14, 1952, an address by Leslie M. Scott, son of Harvey W. Scott, pioneer editor of the Portland *Oregonian*, dedicated the statue of Dr. John McLoughlin in Statuary Hall in the Capitol in Washington, D. C.[9]

Another out-of-the-ordinary honor is the fact that in the Portland metropolitan area three arterial streets bear his name; there are McLoughlin Boulevards in Oregon City, in southeast Portland, and in Vancouver, Washington.

That he was considered worthy of being honored has been shown too by the naming of one of three new buildings of Clackamas Community College, southeast of Oregon City, for him.

Not only in Oregon, but also in distant Rivière-du-Loup, the Doctor's birthplace, there was interest in doing him honor. Here in 1946 on the St. Lawrence River, in Lower Canada, citizens of the Provinces of Ontario and Québec, led by J. P. Bertrand, head of the Thunder Head Historical Society of Port Arthur, Ontario, by the Reverend John W. Beard, pastor of the Mt. Tabor Presbyterian Church in Portland, and by Dr. Burt Brown Barker of Portland, planned the setting up of a monument in his honor.[10]

Royal Family of the Columbia

The Aberdeen (Washington) *Post* on September 12, 1925, marking the one hundreth anniversary of the building of Fort Vancouver, reported a new honor for the King of the Columbia. The Pacific Coast Lumber Industry had just named him "Father of the Pacific Coast Lumber Industry" and cited him for having built the first sawmill in the Northwest, in 1827, at Fort Vancouver.[11]

Of special interest, because children were involved, was the unveiling, on June 8, 1941, of a bronze bust of the Father of Oregon at Willamette Falls, near the original site of his home. Paid for by the Parent-Teachers Association of Oregon and by the nickels and dimes of Oregon school children, the statue was presented by Mrs. F. W. Blum, president of the Oregon Congress of Parents and Teachers, and accepted by Leslie M. Scott, representing Governor Charles A. Sprague. Also on the program was Dr. Burt Brown Barker, who told of the great constructive work done by Dr. McLoughlin.[12]

In addition to ceremonies, memorials, "special days", etc; eulogies *per se* have followed him through the years, at first almost continuously, then sporadically. Due to limitation of space, only a few examples can be cited.

According to Horace S. Lyman the Honorable J. Quinn Thornton, who had served several years as McLoughlin's personal attorney, described him at a meeting in 1874 of the Oregon Pioneers Association as "...a man of great goodness of heart, too wise to do a foolish thing, too noble and magnanimous to condescend to meanness, and too forgiving to cherish resentment."[13]

Historian Hubert Howe Bancroft was emphatic on the subject of John McLoughlin's individuality, even uniqueness:

> ...he was an altogether different order of humanity from any who had hitherto appeared upon these shores. Once seen, he was never forgotten Before or after him his like was unknown; for he was far above the mercenary fur trader, or the coarse illiterate immigrant. As he appeared among his pygmy associates, white or red, there was an almost unearthly grandeur in his presence. Body, mind, and heart were all carved in gigantic proportions...[14]

Bancroft was obviously a McLoughlinophile and of course wrote in the rhetoric of his day—1888.

Lyman revealed in much of his writing that he shared with noted literary historian Thomas Carlyle the "hero" or "great man" concept of history, the theory that "The course of history has always been modified by the appearance of great men." During the "Age of McLoughlin", 1824-1825, "almost every event and action in the whole territory was referred to the Chief Factor and waited for final disposition on his decision...He ruled for twenty years a country as large as Charlemagne's, as absolutely and worthily as Charlemagne." Lyman felt that the occupation of Oregon (by Americans) was inevitable, but not its *peaceful* occupation; that without McLoughlin Oregon would have had to pass through the same ordeal that Texas had been forced to do; he "gave to America all she could have gained by war and saved England all that she could have gained by war." Like many others, he felt that McLoughlin was instrumental in preventing war between the United States and Great Britain concerning the boundary. "He wrote his life in deeds" could well serve as a résumé of the life of the Father of Oregon, or, perhaps, as his epitaph.[15]

T. C. Elliott, frequent writer for the quarterlies of both the Washington and Oregon Historical Societies at the turn of the century, in answering the charge against McLoughlin that he was an autocrat of the Oregon Country, maintained that an autocrat was both a despot and an aristocrat, whereas, the former Chief Factor "loved to be on common ground with the common people. Nothing revealed this more than his treatment of the common immigrant."[16]

An interesting thought was expressed in *History of the Willamette Valley* in the 1920s regarding McLoughlin's character: "In his place (position as Chief Factor of the Columbia Department) an ignorant or an evil man could have worked vast mischief or trouble."[17]

Frederick V. Holman wrote subjectively in 1907, "He was god-like in his great fatherhood, in his great strength, in his great power; he was Christ-like in his gentleness, in his tenderness, in his humanity."[18]

In the *Oregon Journal* of October 17, 1931, two days before the one hundred-forty-seventh anniversary of John McLoughlin's birth, an unnamed writer admitted that "Neither Great Britain nor America can be proud of the treatment accorded him."

On Christmas Day, 1962, an article in the *Oregonian* told the story of the former Hudson's Bay man, "A doctor who disliked medicine, but who contributed a great deal to Oregon's history in other ways has been honored by the Oregon State Medical Society." It continues, "Dr. John McLoughlin's portrait hangs in distinction at the society's office in Portland. It was painted by artist H. Elmer House and presented to the society recently by Haack Laboratories."

Ralph Friedman, writing in the *Oregonian* in 1966, said in part,

No figure had as great impact on the region as John McLoughlin whom the Indians called "White-Headed Eagle." There was no Indian trouble until Americans came in great numbers. Some of the greatest trailbrazers of the Northwest served under Chief Factor John McLoughlin. Every important figure in the annuals of Northwest history was associated in some way with the Fort.[19]

Royal Family of the Columbia

Among these were Nathaniel Wyeth, Hall J. Kelley, Peter Skene Ogden, Ewing Young, Jason and Daniel Lee, Jedediah Smith, the Whitmans, the Spaldings, and countless others.

Typical of many dramatic events of the year 1949, centennial year of Oregon's achieving territorial status, was the "spectacular" (pageant) honoring the White-Headed Eagle held in Eugene that summer, in which literally everyone was urged to participate, "the more, the better." Whole families were cast as "pioners of Old Oregon" and the climax was a gigantic representation of Dr. John McLoughlin with "Willamette Falls" in the background. Miss Doris Smith, revered veteran actress-director, was brought from Portland to direct the huge outdoor historical drama.

Interest in the McLoughlin saga has continued to the present day also in the form of plays. One illustration is a two-act play, "Hudson's Bay Man," presented March 30 and 31, 1968, in the ballroom of Portland State College (now Portland State University). For this benefit for the scholarship fund of Phi Beta, an honorary fraternity of drama and music, a notice in the *Oregonian* of March 24, (1968) promised a new interpretation of Mrs. McLoughlin who "used Spode china every day and real silver." Even in the Christmas season of 1973, Dr. John McLoughlin is remembered. In a prominent Portland department store a large Christmas tree is dedicated to him and to "McLoughlin House, a reminder of our yesterdays."[20]

As the White-Headed Eagle's legend grew, there increased also appreciation of his life and of his acts. One of the most meaningful and tangible marks of appreciation, along with a desire to educate the public, is today's Fort Vancouver. Declared a National Historic Site on July 9, 1954, its eighty-nine acres are administered by the National Park Bureau of the United States Department of the Interior. In 1966 the National Park Service reconstructed the north stockade, the north gate, and a portion of the east stockade of the Fort.[21] Measurements of the original building were marked off and labeled as part of the continuing reconstruction.

During exhaustive (and most interesting-to-watch) excavations bones were found, including the skeleton of a French voyageur, which had been transferred from two previous gravesites, the last one in the path of Interstate 5. Artifacts and bits of dishes were among the "finds," as were bottles, some still containing medicine and liquor. Countless pieces of fine Spode china formed an eye-catching display, interesting to sight-seers who came to the Visitors Center at the Fort and who enjoyed trying their luck at finding "just the right" oddly-shaped piece to fit into a plate or bowl.[22]

Recently the Spode exhibit was moved and was replaced with a large painting mounted in a glass display case of the Fort as it probably was in 1845-1846. Also in the lobby, maps, an HBC flag, and a banner with the company motto, *Pro pelle cutem,* are among many interesting memorabilia of the fur-trading era. A full-length painting of Dr. John McLoughlin with his famous gold-headed cane is hung near the main door.[23]

A spacious adjoining room contains large mock-ups of the Fort of the 1840s which extend entirely around the perimeter of the room. A diorama of the Whitman-Spalding party's arrival at the Fort in 1836 is of interest to visitors too. Also adjoining the lobby is a small auditorium in which relevant slides are shown.[24]

A short distance from the Visitors Center is the Fort Site itself, a mecca for lovers of Pacific Northwest history. Much progress has been made in the reconstruction of the Fort: In addition to the stockade (1966), the bastion in the northwest corner (1974), and bakery (1975), a temporary "Indian-trading" store has been finished (1976). Most of all, the "palace" of the chief factor of the Columbia Department, the King of the Columbia, has now been completed (1976). This residence is the most important part of an ongoing project of the National Park Service estimated to cost from $750,000 to $1,000,000. Built carefully and authentically on the foundations of the original, this unusual historic edifice is much appreciated by the public.[25]

In an attempt to achieve a balanced, unbiased evaluation of John McLoughlin, it is difficult to find unfavorable viewpoints, since they are in the minority. However, there were the Hall Kelleys, the William Slacums, the Samuel Thurstons, and the Ewing Youngs who thoroughly detested him for what they felt were justifiable reasons. Kelley and Young had not been hospitably received earlier at the Fort by the Chief Factor because he had been led to believe that they were involved in horse theft. Thurston, as explained above, wanted the McLoughlin land claims. William A. Slacum, American Naval purser, pretended, as McLoughlin said, to be a "private gentleman" when he came in December 1836. A year later Slacum, influenced by Hall Kelley's diatribes, presented a memorial to the Senate formulating American claims. He also put before American legislators and electorate propaganda statements damaging to the Honourable Company, which on the Columbia was the same as John McLoughlin, stating that the Company and the Chief Factor had incited Indians to attack American trappers and settlers.[26]

Hall Kelley had probably been the most vociferous of all the McLoughlinophobes. The so-called "Prophet or Oregon," he had been a victim of "Oregon Fever" in its most virulent form; a persistent colonizer, he believed firmly and fanatically that the Company and especially the Chief Factor had stood between him and the achievement of his goal. "The persecuting monster anticipated my coming...(and) was ready with sword in hand to cut me down...I was treated with every demonstration of inhumanity, "Ewing Young, influenced by Kelley, joined in the latter's verbal chastisement of McLoughlin; when visiting Kelley, whom the Chief Factor was caring for at the Fort, he spoke of "personal abuse just received."[27]

Royal Family of the Columbia

In sum, these four men and others like them were able to influence countless others, usually unjustifiably, against Dr. McLoughlin.

Perhaps a balance of the two diametrically opposed views of the Doctor, *i.e.,* saint or devil, has been accomplished by David Lavender, writing in the 1960s, and by Douglas MacKay, late editor of the Hudson's Bay Company's house organ, *The Beaver,* who wrote his *The Honourable Company* in 1935-1936.

Lavender in his *Land of Giants* seems to write with objectivity in his evaluation of John McLoughlin:

> Legend in Oregon had inclined to hallow John McLoughlin almost beyond humanity. The portrait needs adjusting. An autocrat of violent prejudices and flaring temper, he was considerably less than a saint, yet at the same time (had) an impulsive generosity that lifted him far above the level of just another able fur trader. Though he was *by no means a great man* (italics added), destiny made him, even more than it did Simpson, the central figure in the twenty-year drama to control one of the richest sections of our continent.[28]

MacKay, too, analyzed the Honourable Company's Great White Eagle:

> McLoughlin had the Rhodes touch of imperial vision...His slice of empire, unlike many of his colleagues' (was) not cramped into deep valleys or exposed on the plains to extremes of wind and temperature. He was a veritable lotus leaf...The sea, the forest, and the rivers...were all his. Small wonder that he broke with his superiors and threw in his lot with Americans who were coming by land and sea...His is the tragic story of a man who had power, intelligence, and human kindness, but who collapsed from shattered illusion—a big man *who just escaped greatness* (italics added).[29]

It is interesting to note that Lavender and MacKay agreed that although Dr. John McLoughlin possessed many fine qualities, he was not a "great" man, whatever the definition of that word may be. However, the two writers would no doubt agree that he embodied many of the synonyms for "great" listed in the most recent edition of *Random House Dictionary of the English Language:* unusual, notable, remarkable, of high official position, distinguished, famous, outstanding, gigantic, enormous, immense, grand, vast, and, of course, numerous other adjectives (page 577). Just which quality or qualities he lacked in their evaluations is not clear. Quite possibly they felt that his "great" temper and his illusions were his "greatest" weaknesses—that they prevented his attaining that synthesis of intangible, abstract qualities which constitute true greatness.

Alberta Brooks Fogdall

REFERENCES

CHAPTER 16

THE KING IS DEAD
HIS MEMORY LIVES ON

1 The Oregon City *Enterprise-Courier*, September 10, 1957.

2 *Ibid.*

3 *Scrap Book*, Vol. 112, p. 17.

4 Burt Brown Barker, *Financial Papers of Dr. McLoughlin*, p. 15.

5 Printed by Fred C. Baker, State Printer, Salem, 1889.

6 *Quarterly of the Oregon Historical Society*, October 6, 1905, p. 54.

7 *Ibid.*, Vol. 8 (1907), pp. 312-313.

8 Burt Brown Barker, "McLoughlin House, National Historic Site, 1949.

9 *Ibid.*, Reprint, 1961.

10 News clipping of the Portland *Oregonian*, Microfilm, Oregon Historical Society. Also in *Oregon Historical Quarterly*, March, 1946, p. 107.

11 Folder, Archives, Oregon Historical Society.

12 *Oregon Historical Quarterly*, Vol. 42. (1941), p. 273.

13 Horace S. Lyman, *History of Oregon*, Vol. IV, reporting Oregon Pioneers Association meeting at Aurora, June 16, 1874, Appendix B., p. 375.

14 H. H. Bancroft, *Works*, Vol. 38, *History of Oregon*, Vol. II, p. 433.

15 Lyman, *op. cit.*, Vol. II, pp. 353-355.

16 T. C. Elliott, "McLoughlin and His Guests," *Washington Historical Quarterly*, October 1908, p. 73.

17 Robert C. Clark, *History of the Willamette Valley*, p. 594.

18 A. S. Marquis, *Dr. John McLoughlin*, p. 31, quoted from Frederick V. Holman, *Dr. John McLoughlin*, page not cited.

19 Ralph Friedman, Portland *Oregonian*, 1968. Exact date not available.

20 The Portland *Oregonian*, March 24, 1968.

21 Brochure "Fort Vancouver, National Historic Site" available at Tourist Facility at Fort Vancouver. Also, the *Oregon Journal*, September 21, 1962.

22 Visit to Fort Vancouver.

23 The Portland *Oregonian*, October 12, 1971; Kathleen Piper, "bones and Bottles shoveled into view at old fort site." Also, visit. Also, the Portland *Oregonian*, May 12, 1973.

24 Visits to the Fort.

25 The *Oregonian*, October 12, 1971; May 12, 1973, and visit to the Fort.

26 Montgomery, *op. cit.*, The White-Headed Eagle, pp. 76-77.

27 Fred W. Powell, ed., *Hall J. Kelley on Oregon*, p. 16.

28 David Lavender, *Land of Giants*, pp. 118-119.

29 Douglas MacKay, *The Honourable Company*, pp. 153-154.

CHAPTER 17

THE KING AND THE COURTS
CLAIMS AND COUNTER-CLAIMS

Financial complications of the exiled King of the Columbia did not end with his death. To the contrary, they seemed to increase. Of great interest is the account book so meticulously kept by Dr. McLoughlin and, later, by his son-in-law and executor, Daniel Harvey. The first inventory, made September 10, 1857, just a week after his death, and the second inventory, on November 10, reveal names of prominent pioneer Portlanders. Eight long pages contain records of promissory notes written by citizens whose names survive today in Portland streets, building, fountains, and small metropolitan areas: Couch, Flanders, Lovejoy, Durham, and many others in amounts varying from $20.37 to $215. In addition, the Doctor's attorney, J. Quinn Thornton, owed $278, George Abernethy and Co., $3,141.95*; Amory Holbrook, $173.18; Bishop Blanchette (*sic*) $20.75. There are infinitesimally small accounts too: *e.g.*, a "Mr. Dusenbery" appeared on the account books for years for the debt of $1.95; Dr. Forbes Barclay, $3.75; G. W. Atkinson, $4.40. Nor were close relatives exempt from indebtedness: The Doctor's son David at first owed $3,600, then, later $9,294.78; his grandchildren John and Margaret Rae owed combined amounts of nearly $2,000. Mrs. McLoughlin's grandchildren William, Margaret, and John McKay together owed almost $1,000. The McLoughlins' older daughter, Eliza Eppes, was posted as owing nearly $12,000, no doubt in connection with her unauthorized sale of her father's property in Rivière-du-Loup. Étienne Grégoire, whose widow, Victoria, married the Doctor's eldest son, Joseph, owed $150—and so it went.[1]

In his meticulousness, Mr. Harvey was careful to note his own financial relationship with his father-in-law's estate, showing that on November 10, 1857, the estate owed him $19,423.95, while he owed the estate $1,879.08.[2]

Had these relatively small debts been all that were owed to John McLoughlin, or to his estate, all the litigation which ensued would have been unnecessary. As noted elsewhere, numerous Americans were in debt to the former Chief Factor, due either to loans of supplies or of money. Some, but all too few, were honest and repaid him. Others, for various reasons, usually resentment against the Hudson's Bay Company, of which to many Dr. McLoughin was the living symbol, purposely refused to reimburse him even though they were able to do so. Some, only a few, were unable to make repayment. Many had moved out of the Oregon Territory, in order to be outside the jurisdiction of the courts.

---

*This amount is probably that involved in the controversy over ownership of "Abernethy's Island."

In many cases Dr. McLoughlin was reimbursed in the form of writs of attachment. One example was his winning an attachment suit on February 20, 1852, from William Card for $798, receiving property in lieu of the money owed him, since Card, the defendant, had refused to honor his promissory note. Just the day before, the court had authorized Joseph L. Meek, deputy sheriff of the Territory, to serve a writ of attachment against J. G. Grey for the same reason. On March 25, just a few weeks later, the Doctor won a judgment of $466.66 against Tomas Purvis. Frequently the Honorable J. Quinn Thornton was his attorney, although at various times he used also the legal services of Amory Holbrook and Milton Elliott.[3]

In sum, the year 1852 saw a "whole slew" of cases on the circuit court docket in which John McLoughlin was the plaintiff against both resident and non-resident debtors, either to collect on promissory notes or to regain land or other property. In nearly all cases judgment was in favor of the plaintiff, many through default, *i. e.*, non-appearance of the defendants. In most of this litigation, writs of attachment and notices of sheriff's sales preceded the satisfaction of McLoughlin's claims.[4]

There were also suits on file in the 1850s which were the reverse of those described, *i. e.*, suits in which Dr. McLoughlin, or the McLoughlin estate, was the defendant. On February 18, 1858, five months following John McLoughlin's death, Judge Robert Caufield summoned Daniel Harvey, as his father-in-law's executor, to appear in court to answer the complaint of attorney Milton Elliott against the estate; Mr. Elliott claimed that there was a balance of $190.45 owed him for services rendered by him "as attorney and counselor" to Dr. McLoughin. On March 2 Mr. Harvey answered, asking for proof: 1. Mr. Elliott had not made specific charges clear. 2. It was not clear that the service had actually been performed. 3. Even if performed, the fee seemed excessive. Mr. Elliott answered (no date cited): 1. The service had been performed. 2. He submitted an itemized statement. 3. The charges were fair. 4. If Dr. McLoughlin were living, he would pay the fee for services without hesitation. Mr. Elliott won this lawsuit. The estate paid the fee and received a paid-in-full receipt dated September 14, 1858.[5]

An unusual, weird, even ghoulish charge was filed September 6, 1859, two years and three days after the death of Dr. John McLoughlin, charging him with assault and attempt to rape. No date was given for the alleged offense.[6] How a man dead for two years could possibly have committed a repugnant crime such as assault and attempted rape, or any crime, has gone unexplained. Even if alive such a crime was impossible for a man of Dr. McLoughlin's strict morality to commit.

Persistent microfilm research in Portland and Oregon City newspapers dating for several months following September 6, 1859, has failed to solve the mystery. Hopefully, continued perseverance will eventually effect a solution.

Dr. McLoughlin's will was an intricate and a seemingly difficult one to administer. As a wealthy man and potentially an extremely wealthy man, he had rather far-flung properties, from eastern Canada to Oregon City, Portland,

Canemah, Linn City, Champoeg, and other points in the Willamette Valley. Moreover, so much of his wealth was on paper, much of it to be collected by his heirs and executor, much of it in uncollectible promissory notes. Other aspects of the will were also unusual, as will be seen.

A rather cryptic article appeared as comparatively recently as February 6, 1934, in the Oregon City *Banner-Courier* (later, the *Enterprise-Courier*), story of the McLoughlin will was in the vaults of the Clackamas County clerk, among hundreds of valuable documents stored there. Fifteen years later Dr. Burt Brown Barker stated that the Doctor's will and estate papers had been found recently in "an old unused safe" in the office of the clerk of the probate court of Clackamas County, in Oregon City.[7]

According to these newly discovered records the McLoughlin real estate holdings, most of them in Oregon City, amounted to more than $85,000, consisting of one hundred scattered lots, the equivalent of twenty-four full blocks. Of the hundred lots, thirty-three were located in the present business district of Oregon City. His residence was appraised at $5,000. In addition, there were various out-buildings near the main house, and three stores, as well as an old building across the street from the home. Two lots were located in Canemah, two in Linn City (West Linn).[8]

Interesting documents, many of them original, some copies of facsimiles, some "true copies,"[9] include the paper dated September 7, 1857, four days after Dr. McLoughlin's death, binding Daniel Harvey, Forbes Barclay, François Xavier Matthieu, and Thomas Lowe as executors; each, except Matthieu, was found to forfeit $100,000 is he failed to carry out his obligation.[10]

Another document, tied in ribbon, worn and frayed like the others, but green rather than red, and dated September 30, 1857, was signed by Judge Robert Caufield, who appointed Amory Holbrook and two others to appraise the entire estate. The total, which included many promissory notes not honored, amounted to $171,999.28, which was broken down into valuable assets of $142,505.02 and worthless (uncollectible) assets of $29,414.26, which included debts of his grandchildren and of his daughter, totaling $11,688.32.[11]

On September 25, John H. Couch, A. L. Davis, and Amory Holbrook pledged legally to appraise the McLoughlin property in Multnomah County, lot number one in block number three, in what is known as Couch's addition, in Northwest Portland. They did so at $1,000.

Next, on November 7, further property appraisals were made: 293 acres in Marion County, one block in Champoeg, and lots bordering the Willamette River, containing two granaries, the total being approximately $3,600.[12]

On October 5, 1858, Mr. Harvey petitioned "Honble the Probate Court of Clackamas County Oregon Territory" for a grant of additional time to write up a final settlement of the estate "since so much of the estate consists of individual debts which cannot or will not be paid at present."[13]

Alberta Brooks Fogdall

A document of February 21, 1858 (1859?) stated "The will has been today exhibited to the Probate Court" by executor Daniel Harvey with Dr. Forbes Barclay as witness."

The will itself began "In the name of God Amen" (as all wills apparently began a hundred or more years ago). He bequeathed "all his lands and real estate situate(d) and lying in the Parish of Rivière-du-Loup in Canada East...to my daughter Eliza Epps, widow of the late deputy commissary General Epps of the British Army...to be enjoyed by her during her natural life...after her decease to her children to be divided equally."

To his wife, Margaret, he bequeathed "all my china, linens, glass, household goods and furniture (except my plate)...to hold as her own absolute property...the use and enjoyment of my plate during her lifetime and afterward to my daughter Eloisa Harvey." (Today's readers, especially, females, will probably note with interest and also with ironic amusement the singular pronoun "my". Typical "male chauvinism", the "libbers" would claim. It was, of course, characteristic of the period.)

The rest of the real and personal estate was to be divided equally among his only surviving son, David, his daughter Eloisa, and her husband, Daniel Harvey.

In lieu of dower rights Margaret McLoughlin was to have $1,000 annually, "free of all taxes and deductions, to be paid quarterly on the first of January, of April, of July, and of October." She was also to have "use of the house where I now dwell...with the garden and its privileges thereunto...."

If any dispute or controversy should arise, no suit should be brought and the chief executor should decide the outcome; his decision would be final.

There is a concluding statement to the effect that the copy was compared with the original and was a correct transcript; it was signed by James Frazer, Clackamas County clerk.[14]

On May 20, 1859, David signed two documents; in the first he sold his one-third share of his father's estate to Daniel and Eloisa Harvey for $25,000 cash. In the second document he stated that he was satisfied with the settlement and released his brother-in-law from further liability from his bond as executor of his (David's) share. Both documents were carefully witnessed and signed.[15]

Documents pertaining to the will are in a large folder in the state archives on the outside of which is a notation from London (the official's signature illegible), "Please have this altered from John McLaughlin to John McLoughlin and all cases of misspelling. The alterations must be done by proper officials, 24 Bridge Row, Cannon St. Lon." (Part of the address was also illegible.)[16]

To cast ahead, first twenty years, and, again, a generation later, in connection with the will, the controversy or dispute which the doctor had feared and perhaps foreseen occurred.

The entire estate, valued at $142,585.02 had passed into the hands of Mr. and Mrs. Harvey because, as stated, David, apparently needing cash and wishing to leave Oregon City, had "sold his birthright for a mess of pottage," the "birthright" being one-third of the total estate, the "pottage" being the $25,000, slightly more than one-half of the amount he would have inherited.[17]

The Harveys moved to Portland in 1867. Mr. Harvey died at The Dalles December 5, 1868. His will named Eloisa as executrix and two men as executors. Because Eloisa was unfamiliar with legal matters, one of two men, Aaron E. Watt, served as the actual executor. At this time the estate totaled $89,005.25, of which $50,900.75 was personal property, and $38,104.50 real property. The latter amount was less than when inventoried soon after Dr. McLoughlin's death because Mr. Harvey had disposed of much of the real estate to Eloisa, to their three children, and to his three stepchildren, Eloisa's son and daughters by her marriage to William Glen Rae.

As executor Mr. Watt filed reports at intervals until September 4, 1878. The estate had become sufficiently involved that the heirs and legatees filed objections, and on January 6, 1879, three persons were appointed to act as referees to determine the status of the estate. April 30, 1880, the referees filed their report after several long controversial hearings. This report evaluated the personal property at $73,252.05 and real estate at $38,020.00, making a total of $111,272.05, about $30,000 less than the original estate, but $22,000 more than the inventory made after Mr. Harvey's death in 1868.[18]

Eloisa died October 24, 1884, leaving a will dated June 22, 1883, which was filed for probate in Multnomah County November 11, 1883. In this will provisions were made for her six children. Her son James William McLoughlin Harvey was appointed sole executor, and he was given charge of the remainder and residue of her estate, including provision for his brother and sister and for his two half sisters and half brother. Evidently James Harvey was careless in handling the estate, for his sister Angélique (Mrs. Daniel Lehigh) filed a petition December 28, 1885, to have her brother removed as executor. After a heated controversy he was removed. His successor closed the estate with a final accounting (amounts not stated) February 9, 1887.[19]

To summarize, the estate of Dr. John McLoughlin had in less than thirty years passed through three wills to his children and to his grandchildren with the arguments and disputes he had feared, litigation or controversy every ten years and the resulting internecine hostility.

If there is any inference to be draw from the whole sequence of Oregon City land claims, the jumping of those claims, the non-payment of many debts owed to John McLoughlin, the court litigation, the various wills, all the controversy which followed, and intra-family hostility, it might be the remarkable fact that in spite of all his financial setbacks he was able to leave his family a very sizeable estate. An estate of approximately $15,000[*] in 1857 would be worth many times that amount today, nearly 120 years later. Had he not been deprived of much of his property, if many just debts owed him had been paid, he would perhaps have died a near-millionaire, especially by late twentieth-century standards.

[*] $150,000.00

Alberta Brooks Fogdall

REFERENCES

CHAPTER 17

THE KING AND THE COURTS
CLAIMS AND COUNTER-CLAIMS

1 McLoughlin (folder) file, State of Oregon Archives, Salem.

2 *Ibid.*

3 *Ibid.*

4 *Ibid.*

5 *Ibid.*

6 *Ibid.*

7 Microfilm, Oregon Historical Society.

8 Burt Brown Barker, ed., *Financial Papers of Dr. John McLoughlin,* Reprint, 1944, 1949.

9 Transcript made at the same time as the original.

10 State of Oregon Archives.

11 *Ibid.*

12 *Ibid.*

13 *Ibid.*

14 All the preceding material concerning the McLoughlin will is taken from the State of Oregon Archives.

15 Barker, ed., *loc. cit.*

16 State of Oregon Archives.

17 Baker, ed., *loc. cit.*

18 *Ibid.*

19 *Ibid.*

CHAPTER 18

A CASE FOR SHERLOCK HOLMES
McLOUGHLIN AND THE MYSTERY WOMAN

In addition to the implausible mystery cited in a recent chapter, another puzzle has interested historians, that of the "mystery woman" Catherine O'Gorman. Her story is narrated briefly in a pamphlet "John McLoughlin House" edited by Burt Brown Barker in 1949, but is completely ignored by the same author in any letters or appendices in his *The McLoughlin Empire and its Rulers,* published in 1959.

The story goes that for nearly nineteen years, fom 1838 until 1857, the year of the Doctor's death, he paid Mrs. O'Gorman amounts each quarter varying from ten pounds to forty pounds. During part of this time he was also paying his older daughter, Eliza Eppes, amounts varying from 100 pounds to 300 pounds yearly. The payments to Mrs. O'Gorman were made through the London office of the Honourable Company, the clerk always writing of "Dr. McLoughlin" or "your friend," with no relationship indicated. A letter written by Mrs. O'Gorman in 1843 mentioned "Dr. McLoughlin (whose daughter I am)..." and in a letter of 1857 "...the death of my kind stepfather, Dr. John Maclaughlin...a good and substantial friend as well as a relative...my late father." Thus she was a friend, a daughter, a stepdaughter, a relative, and, again, a daughter, of John McLoughlin. Yet the Doctor made no provision for her in his will, his surviving children, Eloisa and David, and also Eloisa's husband, Daniel Harvey, receiving all of his property. (Eliza had sold his farms and apparently had retained the amount of the sales; her father bequeathed this Rivière-du-Loup property to her in his will.)

Who was this mysterious Catherine O'Gorman? Also—a minor mystery—why did she misspell his name one time, but not the other, and why the Scottish "Mac" rather than the Irish "Mc" of his paternal ancestors?

McLoughlin detractors tried to find an illicit relationship: perhaps Mrs. O'Gorman was an "old concern"? Perhaps she was an illegitimate daughter? Perhaps she was blackmailing him due to some dark secret in his past? How intriguing!

Admirers of the Hudson's Bay man denied the accusation—to anyone knowing the high moral character of the man, any shameful backstreet connection was unthinkable.

Dr. Barker made the assumption that the lady of mystery was probably Dr. McLoughlin's stepdaughter, one of the three daughters of Mrs. McLoughlin and Alexander McKay. All three girls had remained in Canada, marrying early. According to "Correspondence" of their half brother David McLoughlin, today in the Oregon Historical Society archives, two of the girls married a Lieutenant McCormack, of the British Army, and a Captain McCargo, who ran a merchant freighter on Lake Superior. The third, Mary, married James Sinclair, an HBC chief trader and chief factor. It is known that one of the three daughters married a Campbell (for a daughter of theirs, Margaret, married her cousin William McKay, as described earlier). Considering other errors and the lack of knowledge David possessed (at eighty) of his family, could he perhaps have converted "Campbell" into "McCormack" or "McCargo"?

It is nearly impossible to convert Sinclair into "O'Gorman", slightly less difficult to change either "McCormack" or "McCargo" into O'Gorman, but during a period when McLoughlin could be "Machlan", Bethune, "Bathein"; or Wadin, "Wodden"; anything might happen. McCormack has also been written as "McConnick." Mrs. McConnick's husband died in India; his widow was said by Dr. Barker to have lived in England on a pension of one-half her late husband's salary. It was possible that Dr. McLoughlin helped her financially.

Perhaps, then, again taking into consideration the casual and inconsistent orthography of the day, McConnick somehow became corrupted to O'Gorman, though the possibility does seem rather remote. It is also possible that Mrs. McConnick (or McCormack) remarried, becoming Mrs. O'Gorman. Regardless of the recipient's identity, the mystery itself is still another illustration of Dr. John McLoughlin's humane benevolence and generosity, of his consideration for others.

The assumption discussed here is just that, an assumption, not a definitive solution, but knowing the fidelity of John McLoughlin to his marriage vows, it seems unlikely that he was involved in a sinister or illicit "affair." Since neither this writer nor Dr. Burt Brown Barker is a sleuth, the solution will no doubt have to await the brilliant mental gymnastics of Perry Mason, since the services of A. Conan Doyle's brilliant detective are not available in this, the twentieth century.

CHAPTER 18

A CASE FOR SHERLOCK HOLMES
McLOUGHLIN AND THE MYSTERY WOMAN

All documentation is from Burt Brown Barker's "John McLoughlin House except the notes on the marriages of David McLoughlin's half sisters, taken from his "Correspondence," written when he was eighty, in the archives of the Oregon Historical Society.

Seal of the Hudson's Bay Company

THE KING'S LAST HOME
McLOUGHLIN HOUSE

Of all the property belonging to the former King of the Columbia, undoubtedly the most precious to him, if not the most valuable, was his home, built in 1845-1846 on the east bank of the Willamette, facing the Falls. Although in the early 1850s he lost the land on which it was built, as mentioned earlier, he and Mrs. McLoughlin were allowed to continue living there.

Appraised in 1857, following his death, at $5,000, a magnificent sum in the mid-nineteenth century, the house was built entirely of lumber from the McLoughlin sawmills, with the exception of the window frames and doors, which were brought around the Horn from Boston. After the family no longer lived there the once-beautiful home became a boarding house; at one time it was the "Phoenix Hotel."[1] Some additions, more or less "tacked on," and the passage of time resulted in deterioration and a sadly dilapidated appearance; basically, however, as later developments revealed, the house was still structurally sound.

After 1900 the Hawley Pulp and Paper Mills, which gradually evolved into today's Publishers Paper Mills, bought the property and some nearby adjacent land. In 1905 the Oregon City electorate voted on the creation of a special tax to purchase the house, claiming that a double purpose would be served: to preserve a beautiful structure and to put it to practical use as offices for city officials. Apparently the tax failed, for there was no further record of it.[2] (Incidentally, George H. Himes of "David McLoughlin-Pioneer Day" fame wrote [newspaper clipping undated and not labeled as to origin] praising the action of Oregon City citizens in buying [attempting to buy?] the house.)[3]

In 1909 the owners of the Hawley Mills, wishing to enlarge their plant and needing the site of the house, offered the building free to those Oregon Citians who wanted to preserve it. The McLoughlin Memorial Association was formed for legal purposes, and with the Oregon Historical Society, the Oregon City Historical Society, and many interested individuals raised $1,000.[4]

In June 1909 with extreme difficulty the house was moved from Third and Main Streets up steep Singer Hill to McLoughlin Park on the bluff. Located on land donated to Oregon City by Dr. McLoughlin in 1850 when he platted the city, the house, now called McLoughlin House, is between Seventh and Eighth Streets on Center. The location is described legally as lot six, block twenty-nine. The entire block was owned by the Doctor with the exception of lot seven, held by J. Quinn Thornton, attorney and judge.[5]

Alberta Brooks Fogdall

The story goes that the house was much wider than a certain section of the hill, with the result that the house hung perilously over the edge. In order to prevent it from tipping, the side of the house away from the bluff was sandbagged, thus balancing it; it was then carefully and laboriously moved on up the hill into position, where today it looks haughtily down upon the city, a curving street, a freeway, and the Willamette River.[6]

Interestingly, even surprisingly, there was strong opposition to moving the house up the hill, some fearing that its presence would lower real estate values, others not wishing to see Dr. McLoughlin so honored. Court action was brought to obtain an injunction forbidding the establishment of the house in the park; the McLoughlin Memorial Association, however, successfully opposed issuance of the injunction.[7]

It was natural that the house required repair after its long neglect and its shaky journey from the depths to the heights. It was given fresh white paint and a new roof; soon it regained its original exterior appearance. The interior, too, was refurbished; Eloisa's daughter Louisa Myrick took an especial pleasure in overseeing the restoration of the interior, which acquired a reasonable semblance of its appearance during her grandparents' residence there. Donated materials and labor, in addition to a grant of $1,250 from the Oregon Legislature, and other gifts "pieced out" an integrated reconstruction which endured until 1934.[8]

The newly-restored McLoughlin House, called the symbol of the opening and development of the Pacific Northwest, was officially dedicated September 15, 1909, at 2:30, with an address by Frederick V. Holman, president of the Oregon Historical Society. Several hundred participated in the ceremony, including a few "old timers" who as "young timers" had known Dr. McLoughlin in his later years. Oldest pioneer present was François Xavier Matthieu, identified in an earlier chapter.[9]

Through the succeeding years articles and stories of the House appeared sporadically in Portland and Oregon City newspapers. On November 16, 1925, its history was narrated in the *Oregonian*.[10]

In 1935 the House was in need of repairs and refurbishment. Under the Civil Works Administration program of President Franklin D. Roosevelt funds were available. Architects who planned the work were careful to adhere to the 1845-1846 architectural style. The porches were removed and replaced by flagstone terraces. Copies of the original locks were made by hand in England. Fireplaces and flues were repaired; new wallpaper similar to the original was hung. A bathroom installed earlier on the second floor for the caretaker's use was removed. These changes added up to restoring Dr. McLoughlin's home once again as nearly as possible to its mid-nineteenth century appearance.[11]

When Supreme Court action ended many of the "alphabet" agencies of the New Deal régime, funding stopped. A McLoughlin Memorial Association petition to

Congress resulted in a grant of $12,000, so that in 1939 the House was once more renovated. Another dedication took place on August 18, when a new plaque was unveiled.[12]

The House achieved a new honor in 1941 when the federal government named it a National Historic Site, the first to be so named in Oregon and the eleventh in the United States. As a result McLoughlin House is administered jointly by the National Park Service of the Department of the Interior, the Municipality of Oregon City, and the McLoughlin Memorial Association.[13]

In 1950 Tom Lawson McCall, later to be a governor of Oregon, represented Governor Douglas McKay at a new dedication of the House. Previous to this time there had been an apartment upstairs for the caretaker. Now the entire house was made open to the public following necessary interior changes.[14]

An article in the *Oregonian* of December 23, 1956, told of landscaping the lawns and moving a cannon dated 1789, which had formerly been at Fort Vancouver, near the House.

In common with countless other structures, the House was damaged by the "Big Blow," nickname for the Columbus Day storm of 1962. Greatest damage was sustained by the roof.[15]

On August 16, 1967, a tea was held for the public at McLoughlin House, with a "silver offering" to help defray maintenance costs. As part of the program, the skirl of bagpipes reminded the visitors of the Doctor's part-Scottish ancestry, of the Frasers, and of the bagpiper who traditionally stood behind the Chief Factor's chair at the "gentlemen's" dinners in the Fort dining hall. The *Oregonian*, describing the event a week later, August 23, described the House as the "Mount Vernon of the West," one of the few remaining pioneer buildings of the Oregon Country. It was said to represent "the romantic epoch of the state's history in transition from the fur-trading to the settlement eras." A ceremonial tea honoring Dr. McLoughlin was held most recently in August 1973, with tours of the House and appropriate music by bagpipers.[16]

Obviously no modern plumbing was built originally into the house, nor is there any there today. The casual visitor may not be conscious of the absence of a kitchen; as in many homes of the early-and mid-nineteenth century, particularly in the South, the kitchen was situated in a separate building, located to the rear of the house. In this way the heat of the kitchen did not overheat the rest of the house in summer; also, the danger of fire to the main house was reduced. The kitchen of McLoughlin House was not moved from its original location at the Falls, but was "lost," along with the woodshed and the other outbuildings which had deteriorated during the years.[17]

Miss Vara Caufield, one-time secretary-treasurer of the McLoughlin Memorial Association and a former curator of the House-Museum, writing in the 1930s (exact date not given), described the interior: "A large gold-framed mirror made in France" graced the entrance hall, which runs full-length from the front entrance to the back door. A velvet carpet also made in France and the grand piano in the drawing room, brought around Cape Horn, were much admired. Mrs. McLoughlin's desk and her beautiful lacquered Chinese cabinet, along with the famous Cogswell oil portrait of Dr. McLoughlin, also enhance the drawing room.[18]

The massive buffet in the dining room was once the property of the Hudson's Bay Company and was at Fort Victoria, finally being purchased for the House to accompany the huge mahogany dining-room table which had once accommodated at least twenty-four "gentlemen" in the Fort's baronial dining room. The Georgian-period table and the twenty-four chairs, also former Company property, had been moved to Fort Nisqually when Dr. William F. Tolmie went to be in charge there in 1840. Later Dr. Tolmie had them in his Victoria home. The chairs became scattered, but gradually nineteen of them were collected and either purchased or received as donations by the House, and today are in their proper places at the outsize table.[19]

Adjoining both the drawing room and dining room are two very small rooms. These four rooms may have been a child's room, a den, a study, or a sewing room. One small room adjacent to the drawing room is thought to have been the Doctor's medical office, for a side entrance which existed at that time would have been a convenient semi-private access. A mortar and a pestle, presumably Dr. McLoughlin's, sit today on a desk in another of the four small rooms and on the desk's shelves are a number of valuable books from the Columbia Library. Today the two small rooms off the drawing room are furnished as bedrooms.[20]

In one of the small rooms off the dining room is a large display case containing a number of McLoughlin memorabilia, including the ivory miniature portrait, said to be either Dr. John or Dr. David McLoughlin; the Apostolic brief with the decoration of the Order of the Knight of St. Gregory; a silver medal, a mother of pearl cross, the Doctor's snuff box, a gold "mourning" ring, two gold pencils of the Doctor's and the McLoughlin coat of arms, consisting of a lion rampant between two erect swords, and with the motto *"Vinces Virtute."*[21]

Dr. McLoughlin used the motto on his personal seal and the lion rampant on his family silver. The sterling silver, a few pieces of which are displayed in the case, was appraised about forty-five years ago at $554. Most of the silver came into the possession of Matilda Eloisa Harvey (Mrs. George) Deering, a granddaughter of Eloisa, who had it appraised by the director of the Metropolitan Museum of New York. Some was from the late seventeenth century and extremely valuable. Mrs. Deering found that it sold readily. Among the remaining pieces are a teapot, a sugar bowl and tongs, and some occasional spoons and knives. The flat silver is marked "J. Mc" and was made in Edinburgh between 1829 and 1837; probably it was purchased while Dr. McLoughlin was in London on furlough 1838-1839. The Doctor's watch, described previously, is also displayed.[22]

A seeming oddity in the downstairs of the House is the reversal of front and back entrances. The present "front" entrance, opening on Central Street, is the original "back" door. The present back entrance, opening on the surrounding McLoughlin Park, was once the front entrance. Glass on the sides of the present main entrance includes some of that installed originally, now more than 125 years old.[23]

The upstairs consists of a large hall and four bedrooms (or, as in the time of the McLoughins' residence, three bedrooms and a sitting room). From the hall there is an unimpeded view of Willamette Falls. Each bedroom contains a large bear rug of Canadian or Alaskan origin. In one is an interesting trundle bed, in another, an antique cradle. In the sitting room, above the rosewood melodeon given to Louisa Rae (Myrick) by her grandfather on her eighth birthday are pictures of Eloisa and of her youngest daughter, Angélique Harvey. Mrs. McLoughlin's magnificent mahogany chest of drawers and an applewood table imported from England are also part of the second floor furnishings. The large glass display cupboard in the hall containing the Scottish Highlander clothing of Eloisa's eldest child, John Rae, has been described earlier.[24]

Because of their affection for and pride in their Oregon City home, it is particularly appropriate that today John and Margaret McLoughlin rest nearby. Quite a story precedes their being there, however.

Their first resting place, following their deaths in 1857 and 1860, was the churchyard in front of St. John the Apostle Catholic Church. When the church was widened and lengthened about 1900 the graves were covered, and the headstones moved to form part of the foundation. July 4, 1948, the bodies were moved to Fifth and Washington Streets, the site planned for the new church, as the present church building was soon to be razed. Archbishop Edward Howard officiated at the reburial and a memorial service was held. Dr. Burt Brown Barker gave an address and quoted from a letter of ninety-one years before describing the funeral service and sermon of 1857.[25]

A change was made concerning the site of the new church building, causing the graves to be left in their isolated location a few blocks from the House. Here they remained for twenty-two years. Finally, on August 31, 1970, the bodies were placed in new bronze caskets and buried between McLouglin House and Barclay House. The Most Reverend Robert J. Dwyer, Archbishop of Portland, was principal celebrant of the Requiem Mass held at St. John the Apostle Church. The Archbishop had given permission earlier to move the bodies, according to the *Oregonian* of June 24, 1970. As part of the burial ceremony, witnessed by a number of official guests, the Archbishop consecrated the new graves.[26]

Dr. John McLoughlin and his wife of forty-six years were home at last.

Alberta Brooks Fogdall
REFERENCES

CHAPTER 19

THE KING'S LAST HOME
McLOUGHLIN HOUSE

1 McLoughlin folder, Archives, Oregon Historical Society.

2 Oregon City *Enterprise-Courier*, November 8, 1905, Archives, Oregon Historical Society.

3 McLoughlin folder, Archives, Oregon Historical Society.

4 *Ibid.*

5 *Enterprise-Courier, op. cit.*, April 28, 1967.

6 *Ibid.*

7 *Oregon Historical Quarterly*, Vol. 10, 1909, p. 385.

8 *Enterprise-Courier, loc. cit.*

9 *Oregon Historical Quarterly, loc. cit.*

10 McLoughlin folder.

11 Burt Brown Barker, ed., "McLoughlin House," pamphlet.

12 *Enterprise-Courier, loc. cit.*

13 *Ibid.*

14 McLoughlin folder.

15 *Ibid.*

16 *Ibid.* The author attended the 1973 Memorial Tea.

17 Burt Brown Barker, ed., *Financial Papers of John McLoughlin*, pp. 15-16.

18 McLoughlin folder.

19 Microfilm, Oregon Historical Society (October 16, 1972).

20 Visits to McLoughlin House.

21 *Ibid. "Vinces Virtute"*—"You Will Win With Courage."

22 Visits to McLoughlin House.

23 Visits. Also Mrs. Charles (Nancy) Gildena and Miss Isabel VanLaningham, curator and assistant curator of McLoughlin House.

24 Visits.

25 "News Notes", *Oregon Historical Quarterly*, Vol. 49, 1948, p. 257.

26 Various news clipping from the *Oregon Journal* and the Portland *Oregonian*, McLoughlin folder.

Made a Knight of St. Gregory in 1847 by Pope Gregory XVI, this signal honor was a source of great pride to Dr. John McLoughlin. It partially compensated for the disappointment and unhappiness caused by his treatment at the hands of Sir George Simpson and of hostile Americans in Oregon City.

For a number of years the stained glass window was a part of St. John the Apostle Catholic Church in Oregon City. Later, the window was given to the Clackamas County Historical Society, where it is now on display in the annex.

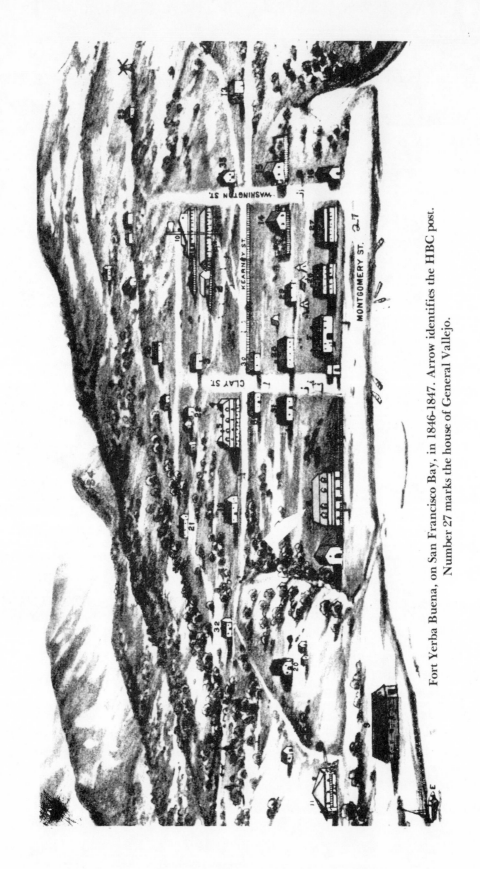

Fort Yerba Buena, on San Francisco Bay, in 1846-1847. Arrow identifies the HBC post. Number 27 marks the house of General Vallejo.

Abbott, Maude E., *History of Medicine in the Province of Quebec,* Ottawa, McGill University, 1931.

Allen, Opal Sweager, *Narcissa Whitman,* Portland, Binfords and Mort, 1959.

Allen, T. D., *Troubled Border,* New York, Harper and Brothers, 1954.

Avery, Mary A., *History and Government of the State of Washington,* Seattle, University of Washington Press, 1961.

Ball, John, *The Autobiography of John Ball,* Grand Rapids, the Dean-Hicks Company, 1925.

Bancroft, Hubert Howe, Works, Vol. 38, *History of Oregon,* Vols. I, II, San Francisco, The History Company, 1884, 1886, 1888.

Barker, Burt Brown, ed., *Letters of Dr. John McLoughlin from Fort Vancouver 1829-1832.* Portland, Binfords and Mort, 1948.

——————; *The McLoughlin Empire and its Rulers.* Glendale, Calif., Arthur H. Clark Co., 1959.

Beaver, Herbert, *Reports and Letters of Herbert Beaver 1836-1838,* Portland, Champoeg Press, 1959, (Thomas E. Jessett, ed.).

Bryce, George, *The Remarkable History of the Hudson's Bay Company,* Vols. 22, 27, 28, 29, 30, London, 1900 (No publisher listed).

Carey, Charles H., *A General History of Oregon,* Portland, Metropolitan Press, 1935.

Case, Robert Ormond, *Empire Builders,* New York, Country Life Press, 1947.

Caughey, John Walton, *History of the Pacific Coast,* Los Angeles (published privately by author), 1933.

Clark, Robert C., *History of the Willamette Valley,* Portland, Chicago, S. J. Clarke Publishing Co., 1927.

Clarke, S. A., *Pioneer Days of Oregon History,* Vol. I, Portland, J. K. Gill, 1905.

Davis, William Heath, *Sixty Years in California.* San Francisco, 1889, (Publisher not given.)

Dye, Eva Emery, *McLoughlin and Old Oregon,* Chicago, A. S. McClurg Co., 1900, 1906.

Franchère, Gabriel, *Voyage to the Northwest Coast of America,* Chicago, Lakeside Press, 1954 (Milo M. Quaife, ed.)

Fraser, Hermia, *Tall Brigade,* Portland, Binfords and Mort, 1956.

Fuller, George W., *A History of the Pacific Northwest,* New York, Alfred A. Knopf, 1941.

————, *The Inland Empire,* Spokane, Shaw and Borden Company, 1928.

Gaston, Joseph, *Centennial History of Oregon,* Vol. I, 1811-1912, Chicago, S. J. Clarke Publishing Co., 1912.

Gay, Theressa, *Life and Letters of Mrs. Jason Lee,* Portland, Metropolitan Press, 1935.

Hawthorne, Julian, *Story of Oregon,* Vol. I, New York, American History Publishing Co.

Holbrook, Stewart, *The Columbia* (Rivers of America Series), New York, Rinehart and Co., 1956.

Holman, Frederick V., *Dr. John McLoughlin, The Father of Oregon,* Oregon Historical Society, 1907.

Horner, John B., *Days and Deeds in the Oregon Country,* Portland, J. K. Gill, 1927.

Hussey, John Adam, *Champoeg: A Place of Transition,* Portland, Oregon Historical Society, 1967.

————, *The History of Fort Vancouver and its Physical Structure,* Tacoma, Washington Historical Society, 1957.

Jacobs, Melvin Clay, *Winning Oregon,* Caldwell, Idaho, Caxton Press Ltd., 1938.

Johansen, Dorothy O., *Empire of the Columbia,* second edition, New York, Harper and Row, 1967.

Johnson, Jalmar, *Builders of the Northwest,* New York, Dodd, Mead, and Co.

Johnson, Robert C. *John McLoughlin, Patriarch of the Northwest,* Portland, Metropolitan Press, 1935.

Jones, Nard, *Marcus Whitman: The Great Command,* Portland, Binfords and Mort, 1968.

Judson, Katharine B., *Early Days in Old Oregon,* Chicago, A. S. McClurg Co., 1916.

Lampman, Evelyn Sibley, *Princess of Fort Vancouver,* Garden City, Doubleday and Doran, Inc., 1962.

Lang, H. O., ed., *History of the Willamette Valley,* Portland, Himes and Lang. 1885.

Laut, Agnes C., *The Conquest of the Pacific Northwest,* New York, Moffat, Yard, and Co., 1914.

Lavender, David, *Land of Giants,* New York, Doubleday and Doran, 1958.

Lockley, Fred, *Columbia River Valley from The Dalles to the Sea,* Chicago, S. J. Clarke Publishing Co., 1928.

————, *Oregon Folks,* Oregon Journal edition, New York, The Knickerbocker Press, 1927.

Lyman, Horace S., *History of Oregon,* Vols. II, III, IV, New York, North Pacific Publishing Society, 1903.

MacKay, Douglas, *The Honourable Company,* New York, Bobbs-Merrill, Co., n. d.

McNamee, Sister Mary Dominica, *Willamette Interlude,* Palo Alto, Pacific Books, 1959.

Meinig, D. W., *The Great Columbia Plain , A Historical Geography, 1805-1910,* Seattle, University of Washingtoln Press, 1968.

Merk, Frederick, ed., *George Simpson's Journal; Fur Trade and Empire,* XXXI, Cambridge, Harvard University Press, 1931.

————, *The Oregon Question*, Cambridge, Harvard University Press, 1967.

Montgomery, Richard G., *The White-Headed Eagle*, New York, The MacMillan Company, 1934.

————, *Young Northwest*, Portland, Binfords and Mort, 1941.

O'Hara, Edwin V., *Pioneer Catholic History*, Portland, Glass and Prudhomme Co., 1911.

Parrish, Philip H., *Historic Oregon*, New York, The MacMillan Company, 1937.

Pinkerton, Robert E., *The Hudson's Bay Company*, New York, Henry Holt and Co., 1931.

Pollard, Lancaster, *Oregon and the Pacific Northwest*, Portland, Binfords and Mort, 1954.

Pomeroy, Earl, *The Pacific Slope: A History*, New York, Alfred A. Knopf, 1965.

Powell, Fred Wilbur, ed., *Hall J. Kelley on Oregon*, Princeton, Princeton University Press, 1932.

Rich, E. E., *The Hudson's Bay Company, 1670-1870*, Vols.. II, III (introduction by The Right Honourable Sir Winston S. Churchill), New York, The Macmillan Company, 1960.

————, ed., *McLoughlin's Fort Vancouver Letters*, Second Series, 1839-1844; Third Series 1844-1846, London, Hudson's Bay Record Society, 1943, 1944.

Robertson, Frank C., *Fort Hall: Gateway to the Oregon Country*, New York, Hastings House, 1963.

Scott, Harvey W., *History of the Oregon Country*, Cambridge, Riverside Press, 1924 (Leslie M. Scott, ed.)

Scott, Helen Huggins, *The Hudson's Bay Company*, Seattle, University of Washington Press, n. d.

Snyder, Eugene, *Early Portland: Stumptown Triumphant,* Portland, Binfords and Mort, 1970.

Speck, Gordon, *Northwest Explorations,* Portland, Binfords and Mort, 1954.

Vaughan, Thomas, and George A. McMath, *A Century of Portland Architecture,* Portland, Oregon Historical Society, 1967.

Vestal, Stanley, *Joe Meek, Merry Mountain Man,* Lincoln, University of Nebraska Press, 1967.

Victor, Frances Fuller, *The River of the West,* Hartford, 1870 (No publisher given).

Wallace, W. Stewart, *Documents Relating to the Northwest Company,* Toronto, Champlain Society, 1934.

Winther, Oscar Osburn, *The Great Northwest: A History,* second edition, New York, Alfred A. Knopf, 1952.

Diorama, in the museum of the Fort Vancouver Visitors Center, is of the arrival of the Whitman-Spalding party at the Fort on September 12, 1836.

Courtesy of National Park Service, Harper's Ferry, West Virginia

PERIODICALS, PAMPHLETS, ARTICLES, QUARTERLIES

The Beaver, Hudson's Bay Company Tercentennial Issue, Autumn 1970, Spring 1963, Winter 1972, and Autumn 1973.

Barker, Burt Brown, ed., *Financial Papers of Dr. McLoughlin,* Oregon Historical Society, 1949.

——————, ed., "McLoughlin House," for McLoughlin Memorial Association, 1949.

——————, ed., *Oregon, Prize of Discovery, Exploration, and Settlement,* Oregon Statuary Committee, 1952.

Dryden, Cecil P., *Give All to Oregon,* New York, Hastings House, 1968.

Elliott, T.C., Numerous articles in historical quarterlies, principally in the *Oregon Historical Quarterly* and the *Washington Historical Society Quarterly* (since 1936 entitled *Pacific Northwest Quarterly.*

Lampman, Ben Hur, "There was a King in Oregon," *Elks' Magazine,* April 1925.

Marlett, Richard, *Nineteenth Street,* printed for the Oregon Historical Society, 1968.

Marquis, A. S., *Dr. John McLoughlin* (pamphlet).

Smith, Helen Krebs, ed., *With her Own Wings* (Collected biographies), Portland, Beattie and Company, 1948.

HISTORICAL QUARTERLIES

British Columbia Historical Society Quarterly, Vol. VI, No. 1, January 1949.
California Historical Society Quarterly, Vols. 5, 11, 28, 45, 46.
Oregon Historical Quarterly, Vols. 2, 10, 17, 27, 31, 36, 45, 40.
Washington Historical Quarterly, Vols. I, III, IV, V, XV, XXIV.
History Today, September 1971, Vol. XXI, No. 9, London.

Alberta Brooks Fogdall
ENCYCLOPEDIAS, DIRECTORIES, MISCELLANEOUS

Catholic Church, Volume I.

City of Portland (No information given concerning publisher).

New Catholic Encyclopedia, Volume IX, 1966.

Oregon Native Son

Oregon Pioneer Association Transactions

Portland Directory

Samuels' *Portland Directory*

Scrap Book, Volumes 21, 35, 36, 38, 40, 57, 66, 72, 76, 112.

ESSAYS, THESES

Bowers, Helen, "Trade and Administrative Policies and Practices of John McLoughlin," winning essay, Reed College, 1942.

Pike, Clarence J., "Petitions of Oregon Settlers," University of Oregon, 1933.

Sampson, William Rea, *John McLoughlin's Business Correspondence, 1847-1848,* M. A. Thesis, University of Wisconsin, 1964.

Throckmorton, Arthur L., *Oregon Boundary Question,* M. A. Thesis, University of North Carolina, 1946.

Tipton, Jane, *John McLoughlin, Chief Factor of Hudson's Bay Company at Fort Vancouver,* M. A. Thesis, University of Washington, 1955.

ORIGINAL SOURCES

Diary of (Sir) James Douglas of the Hudson's Bay Company, "Continuation of the Voyage to Sitka (1841-1843)". Read in the original at the Provincial Archives, Victoria, British Columbia, Canada.

NEWSPAPERS

Aberdeen (Washington) *Post,* September 12, 1925

Clatskanie (Oregon) *Chief*

Gresham (Oregon) *Outlook,* October 18, 1935

Oregon City *Enterprise-Courier,* September 10, 1957

Pendleton (Oregon) *East Oregonian,* August 18, 1939; November 4, 1959; January 2, 1889 (reprint)

Portland *Oregon Journal,* March 21, 1962; September 19, 1943; May 18, 1950

Portland *Oregonian,* October 23, 1966; August 31, 1970; February 3, 1935

Portland *Reporter,* October 11, 12, 1963

St. Helens (Oregon) *Chronicle,* May 30, 1968

St. Helens *Sentinel-Mist,* March 14, 1968; May 15, 1967; November 9, 1967; February 29, 1968

Vancouver (Washington) *Columbian,* December 13, 1966

Vernonia (Oregon) *Eagle,* February 22, 1968

Walla Walla (Washington) *Union-Bulletin,* October 9, 1949

MANUSCRIPTS— TRANSCRIPTS

Harvey, Eloisa McLoughlin, "Dr. John McLoughlin, Recollections," the Bancroft Collection, Archives, Oregon Historical Society.

Jacob P. Leese Papers (August 7, 1843) the Bancroft Collection, Archives, California Historical Society.

McLoughlin, David, Correspondence," from "John McLoughlin's Book," Archives, Oregon Historical Society.

ORIGINAL SOURCES [CONTINUED]

William Glen Rae Papers (April 18, 1843), the Bancroft Collection, Archives, California Historical Society.

Original manuscripts and transcripts of will of Dr. John McLoughlin, handling of the estate, litigation concerning debts of American settlers, *etc.,* Oregon State Archives, Salem.

MICROFILM

The Alice Fraser Prevost letters: Letters of the Fraser-McLoughlin families sent to Dr. Burt Brown Barker by Alice Prevost, a descendant of Colonel Malcolm Fraser, founder of the North American branch of the Fraser family; Oregon Historical Society.

Oregon Journal — September 19, 20, 21, 1929: Interviews by Fred Lockley of Maria Louisa Rae Myrick, daughter of Eloisa McLoughlin Rae Harvey, in which she relates her recollections of her earlier life, some of it, no doubt hearsay.

Miscellaneous other material relating to the Fraser-McLoughlin families and their various branches, principally from the Oregon Historical Society.

Index

Columbia Library, 94, 306,

Columbia River and Valley, 19, 50, 59, 60, 61, 66, 70, 78, 79, 81, 91, 92, 95, 98, 105, 107, 110, 115, 119, 122, 124, 193, 215, 216, 230, 255, 257, 261, 264, 266

Comcomly, chief of the Chinooks, 193, 194, 231

Couch, John H., 293, 295

D

Deady, Judge Matthew P., 286

Déchesne (Déchêne) Dr. Henri Auguste Miville, 226-227, 279

Deering, Matilda Eloisa Harvey (Mrs. George), 27, 198, 199, 306

Demers, Father Modeste, 74, 261

DeSmet, Father Peter John, 261

Dickson (Dixon), "General" James, 149, 154, 158

Donation Land Law, 273, 274

Douglas, Amelia, 73, 81, 83, 86, 88, 90, 97, 101, 123

Douglas, David, 94, 105-106

Douglas, James, 45, 54, 72, 74, 76, 77, 80, 81-86, 89, 90, 91, 94, 97, 151, 152, 156, 222, 233, 234, 248, 251, 263, 266, 271, 276, 278

Dwyer, The Most Reverend Robert J. Archbishop of Portland, 307

Dye, Eva Emery, 192, 218, 219, 223, 224

E

Edinburgh, University of, 22, 34, 35, 36

Elliott, T.C., 77, 88

Eppes, William Randolph, 26, 143, 145-6, 147, 187, 296

Ermatinger, François (Frank), 90, 91, 68, 100, 192, 195, 249

F

February Revolution, 19

"Filly", 193, 194

Finlayson, Roderick, 179-180

Fisher, Dr. Sir James, 33, 34, 35

Forts (Posts), (Excluding Vancouver), Adelaide (later, Victoria), 70, 84, 85, 278, 306; Boise (Fort Snake), 91, 233; Colville (Spokane House), 68, 79, 105, 106, et al.; Cowlitz, 74, 80, 81, 195; Frances, 55; George (Astoria), 60, 61, 83, 100, 105, 109, 117, 127, 186, 193, 278; Hall, 81, 91, 108, 114, 121, 233, 234, 235, et al.; Langley, 61, 79, 137, 193, 195; McLoughlin, 79, 150, Nisqually, 70, 79, 80, 81, 84, 114, 257, 306, et al.; Simpson, 79, 152, Stikine, 13, 79, 81, 83, 151, 152, 153, 155, 156, 207, 217; Taku, 79, 81, 83, 207; Walla Walla (Nez Percé), 92, 97, 121, 122, 125, 233, 277; William, 18, 50, 53, 55, 82, 185, 191, 215, 216 et al.

Fraser, Alexander, 12, 16, 21-24, 26, 29, 31, 35, 36, 37, 145, 147, 148, 194

Fraser, Elisabeth (Betsy), 24, 26, 154

Fraser, John (son of Simon), 22, 24, 26, 29, 142, 143, 146, 147, 150, 154, 191, 215, 218

Fraser, John Malcolm (half brother of Simon), 22, 29, 139, 145, 187, 188

Fraser, Colonel Malcolm, 19-22, 23, 26, 29, 35, 36, 74

Fraser River and Valley, 24, 59, 85, 137, 229, 230, 265

Fraser, Simon (explorer), 24, 265

Fraser, Simon, Lord Lovat, 19

Fraser, Colonel Simon, son of Lord Lovat, cousin of Malcolm, 19, 35

Fraser, Dr. Simon (son of Malcolm), 21, 22, 23, 24, 26, 29, 31, 35, 36, 37, 49, 52, 139, 140, 141, 142, 145, 146, 187, 191, 215, 216

Fraser, William, brother of John Malcolm, 21, 22, 24, 227

Fraser, William, cousin of Malcolm, 29, 30

Frederick, Duke of York, second son of George III, 40

French Canadians, 65, 83, 74, 77, 100, 104, 137, 153, 156, 192, 231, 255, 256, 261, 262, 263, 278

French and Indian (Seven Years') War, 19

French Prairie, 74, 233, 234, 255, 261

garet, 53-54, employed by Northwest Company, 49-50, goes to London for merger, 50-51, to Paris, 52, ordered to Columbia District, 55-56, journey to Pacific, meeting with Simpson, 58-59, builds Fort Vancouver, 59-61, description of, 65-66, relation with Indians, 69-70, intermarriage, 69-73, education, 73-74, lack of bigotry, and return to Catholicism, 77-78, work at Fort, 66-67, business competition with Americans, 78-79, builds other forts, 68, 79, trading vessels, 79-80, Puget's Sound Agricultural Company, 80, only furlough, 80-81, Cattle brought in, 80, "luxury" at Fort—dining, 93-94, 110, 121, Problems with Beavers, 86-90, clothing, 95-96, brigades, special days, 97-100, treatment of visitors, 105-111, 118-119, 120, 122-124, 125, problems with John Jr., 139-152, his murder, 153, Simpson's attitude, 153, 155-157, antipathy between Mc Loughlin and Simpson, 250-253, Rae to Yerba Buena 207-212 his suicide, 211, brings David back to Vancouver, 216-217, compared with Simpson, Chapter 13, *passim*; resigns from HBC, 253, 255, land claims at Willamette Falls, 258ff, claim jumpers 259-60, Provisional Government, 261-264, boundary settlement, 264, moves to Oregon City, 275, treatment by Americans, 271-276, Mayor of Oregon City, 275, ecumenicalism in land-gifts, 275, Knighthood of St. Gregory, 277, death, 279, funeral, 285, honors and memorials, 285-289, reconstruction of Fort Vancouver, 289-290, inventory of estate, 293-295, will, 296-297, probated, 297, litigation, 297, McLoughlin home moved, 303-304, description, 304-307, three sites of McLoughlin graves, 307, Stained glass window, 309

McLoughlin, John Jr., 22, 29, 31, 38, 57, Chapter 7, 139-158; 179-181, *passim;* to Paris, 142; 181, 191, 215, 217, 218, 232, 233, 252, 266
McLoughlin, Joseph, 14, 22, 26, 53, 58, 67, Chapter 6, 135-138, *passim;* 179, 185, 215, 218, 293
McLoughlin, Margaret Wadin McKay, 22, 53, 54, 55, 57, 68, 71, 76, 77, 82, 86, 88, 96, 98, 123, 135, 157, 158, 179, 185, 194, 202, 203, 204, 215, 229, 232, 238, 271, 277, 289, 296
McLoughlin, Maria Elisabeth (Eliza), 22, 31, 53, 58, 72, 73, 81, 143, Chapter 8, 185-190, *passim;* 190, 191, 215, 293, 296
McLoughlin, Maria-Eloisa, 31, 53, 57, 67, 72, 83, 91, 95, 96, 98, 136, 145, 146, 147, 185, Chapter 9, 191-204, *passim;* 207, 213, 215, 217, 266, 271, 277, 285, 295, 304
McLoughlin, Marie-Louise (Sister St. Henry), 19, 22, 29, 30-32, 54, 74, 81, 140, 145, 146, 179, 186, 191
McLoughlin, Mary Short, 29
McLoughlin Memorial Association, and Board, 199, 304, 305
McLoughlin Park, 303, 307
McLoughlin, Victoria McMillan Grégoire, 137, 293
McMillan, James, 59, 137, 230
"Manifest Destiny", 264, 274
Marie Amélie (Queen, wife of Louis-Philippe), 39
Matthieu, François Xavier, 223, 224, 255, 295, 304
Meek, Helen Mar, 125, 127, 128
Meek, Joseph, 121, 125, 127, 128, 294
Methodist Missions, Missionaries and Lee Mission House, 100, 108, 111, 116, 118, 125, 255, 261, 262, 267, 273, 274
Minto, John, 218, 286
Montgomery, Richard, 13, 23, 29, 30, 33, 34, 56, 57, 83, 135
Montréal, 22, 34, 47, 48, 52, 54, 81, 89, 90, 93, 139, 143, 146, 186, 216

This melodeon was a gift from Dr. McLoughlin to his granddaughter Maria Louisa Rae on her 8th. birthday.

Photo by Harrison Hornish

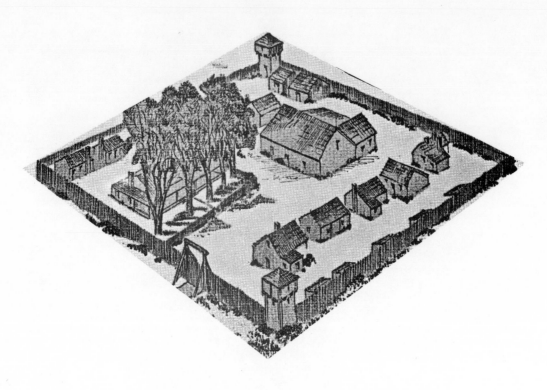

Old Fort Nisqually
Built by Dr. McLaughlin in 1833

Restored blockhouse

The early view of Oregon City on the reverse of this sheet could be dated ca 1850. A drawing of Dr. Mc-Loughlin's home appears in the border on the left side.

CHAS. TAYLOR.

G. ABERNETHY.

EXPRESS, JAS. STRANG, MASTER.

ELK, C. L. SWITZER, MASTER.

DR McLOUGHLIN, FOUNDER OF OREGON CITY.

E. LA FOREST.   JOHN A. POST.

B. A. HUGHES.

CATHOLIC CHURCH.

W. F. HIGHFIELD.

E. MILWAIN.

W. B. PARTLOW.

AINSWORTH & DIERDORFF.